THE DOLLAR BILL KNOWS NO SEX

THE DOLLAR BILL KNOWS NO SEX

LESSONS IN LIFE AND MONEY

WENDY RUE

The Founder of the
National Association for
Female Executives

KARIN ABARBANEL

McGraw-Hill
New York   San Francisco   Washington, D.C.   Auckland   Bogotá
Caracas   Lisbon   London   Madrid   Mexico City   Milan
Montreal   New Delhi   San Juan   Singapore
Sydney   Tokyo   Toronto

Library of Congress Cataloging-in-Publication Data

Rue, Wendy.
    The dollar bill knows no sex : lessons in life and money / Wendy
Rue, Karin Abarbanel.
       p.   cm.
    Includes index.
    ISBN 0-07-057787-0 (hc : acid-free paper)
    1. Self-employed women. 2. Women in business. 3. Women-owned
business enterprises. 4. New business enterprises—Management.
5. Entrepreneurship. 6. Success in business. I. Abarbanel, Karin.
II. Title.
HD6072.5.R84   1997
658.4'21'082—dc20   9651761
                                               CIP

McGraw-Hill

A Division of The McGraw-Hill Companies

1 2 3 4 5 6 7 8 9 0 DOC/DOC 9 0 2 1 0 9 8 7

0-07-057787-0

*The sponsoring editor for this book was Susan Barry, the editing supervisor
was Patricia V. Amoroso, and the production supervisor was Claire B.
Stanley. It was set in Fairfield by Terry Leaden of McGraw-Hill's
Professional Book Group composition unit.*

Printed and bound by R. R. Donnelley & Sons Company.

In loving remembrance
of my father, Harry,
and mother, Sally,
Stanley, and Dr. Rosenberg,
who continue to inspire me
to move on.

                    W.R.

To my family, whose loving
support and encouragement
have always meant so
much to me:
Dorothy and Albert,
David and Alex,
Stephanie, Judy, Peter,
Joan, and Luis.

                    K.A.

CONTENTS

FOREWORD

I first met Wendy Rue back in my "salad days," when I was young and green. I had finished college and graduate school and been knocking around the work world for a while. By some stroke of luck, a wonderful opportunity came my way: the chance to write a job-finding guide called *The Woman's Work Book*. Was I excited! I had a book contract! No matter that it paid about 50 cents—I was going to be a writer! After about two weeks, my excitement turned to panic. I was in way over my head and I knew it.

In desperation, I turned to a list someone had given me of women's groups. Scanning it, I came across the name the National Association for Female Executives. It sounded huge and important. A little nervous, I dialed its number and instantly heard a throaty voice at the other end say, "This is NAFE! Wendy Rue speaking." I explained my project and Wendy told me about NAFE and that she was its president and founder. She invited me over to her "office" to talk about my book. "What luck!" I thought as I hung up. "My first try and I actually got the president of this big organization on the phone!" Little did I know that NAFE's office was Wendy's hot-pink-and-white apartment way over on York Avenue, her desk was a coffee table, and NAFE wasn't huge, but so tiny that the names of all its members fit into a shoe box!

Somehow, I found York Avenue and met with Wendy. She was, as always, dressed in California white. She chain smoked and worked the phone the way most of us breathe oxygen. Altogether, she was jazzy and fun. "Hey," I remember thinking in the middle of our meeting, "maybe the business world isn't so boring after all!" We talked about NAFE and what Wendy was trying to do. And we talked about my book. Wendy was very helpful. She gave me some good ideas and the names of several women to interview.

But most of all, she was encouraging. She didn't make me feel crazy or too inexperienced. Or that I had bitten off more than I could chew. Far from it! Instead, her attitude seemed to be, "Sounds like a great idea! Someone should really be doing it. Why not you?" She seemed to admire the audacity, the chutzpah, I showed in taking on such a grandiose venture. In fact, she made me feel downright proud of myself! Her enthusiasm really gave me a boost.

Well, I did go on to finish *The Woman's Work Book* (with the help of a coauthor who, thankfully, knew what she was doing!). It was the first of several books for me and the beginning of a long association with NAFE. Somehow, it only seems right that I should be helping Wendy write her first book, just as she helped me write mine.

Karin Abarbanel

INTRODUCTION

Picture this:

An entrepreneur who's a cross between Private Benjamin and Auntie Mame, with a big dream. She has a high school diploma, two kids, three divorces, no money, and no business training.

The words *no* and *you can't do that* aren't in her vocabulary. She's insecure but driven. Oblivious to corporate rules and business taboos, she uses her naïveté, intuition, and marketing experience to negotiate high-powered deals with companies like AT&T, Hertz, and American Express.

By doing it her way, she turns her dreams into dollars—founding the leading and most prestigious association of businesswomen in America and becoming a millionaire.

That entrepreneur is me, Wendy Rue. In many ways, my story isn't all that unusual. Most people who dream of starting their own business have more in common with me than they do with Donald Trump.

Yet most people—especially women—who dream big dreams never make it to first base. They never get their ideas out into the world or their products on the shelves. And they never win the recognition, financial freedom, and emotional independence that could be theirs.

What stops them from putting their dreams to work? Mostly it's fear. Most would-be entrepreneurs lack the courage to be different—to step out of their comfort zone—and take the plunge. They dare to dream but are afraid to *do*.

And so, instead of shaping the life they want, they sabotage themselves. They say they need a degree, high-powered contacts, or a fat bankroll. They create excuses and barriers to keep success out instead of letting it in. So they sell themselves short. They let what they don't have and think they need stop them from getting what they want.

But *you're* different. I believe you have the courage to dream and the drive to bring your dream alive. And I want to help you do just that. How? By showing you how to beat the odds. In *The Dollar Bill Knows No Sex*, I'll teach you how to rewrite the rules of business, sell persuasively, market yourself, and build a support system for success. If I can make it, you can, too!

Believe me, I did it the hard way. My rise from road bum for a fly-by-night franchiser to the founder of the leading businesswomen's organization in America doesn't exactly play like *How to Succeed in Business Without Really Trying*. I didn't have a degree, a fat Rolodex, a Julia Roberts smile, a Pollyanna childhood, or a Brady Bunch family. My path to success and financial freedom was strewn with frustration, mishaps and mayhem, unemployment, bouncing checks, and near bankruptcy.

As the mother of two young boys, I *had* to work. None of my three husbands—not even the rich one!—was inclined to support me. Divorced and alone, I faced the anxiety and fear of being on my own that so many women know all too well. Yet, despite all the obstacles I encountered, my mix of naïveté, intuition, and passion drove me to:

- Launch a highly profitable string of teen boutiques in L.A. at age 18—a retailing first.
- Create a top-rated executive search firm—the first ever owned and run by a woman.
- Found the National Association for Female Executives (NAFE) and build it into the largest for-profit association of businesswomen in America.
- Promote innovative marketing ventures to AT&T, American Express, Ford, and other Fortune 500 companies.

- Help hundreds of thousands of women establish financial credit and achieve success.
- Negotiate an acquisition deal that made me independently wealthy.

In *The Dollar Bill Knows No Sex*, I'll share with you the secrets of my unique and highly successful selling style. I'll show you how to make your fears and anxieties work for you instead of against you. I'll show you how to persuade other people to buy into your dream. And how to:

- Find the courage to be yourself—a one-of-a-kind winner.
- Tap your emotions for exciting, marketable ideas.
- Make your own rules and use them to achieve success.
- Start small but look big through creative co-ventures.
- Bounce back when disaster strikes.
- Build a support system for success.
- Gain the confidence—and dollars—of key decision makers.

After years of listening to "that will never work," "you'll never make it," and "you can't do it that way," nobody knows better than I do how to help you harness your strengths, bend the rules, beat the odds, and win financial freedom.

Like many women, you may be just a heartbeat away from success. You have everything you need right now, *today*, to achieve your dreams. You just need an extra dose of support and marketing savvy. If so, then *The Dollar Bill Knows No Sex* can help you take the leap. Happy flying!

ACKNOWLEDGMENTS

There are so many people I'd like to thank for helping to make this book possible:

My sons, Dennis and Harlan, for surviving so many ups and downs and turning out to be fine human beings and successful entrepreneurs. Max, for holding me together when I thought I was falling apart. Myrna, for reminding me of stories I should tell and for always keeping me laughing. Roufa, for his support and sense of fun. The NAFE staff, who always came through and gave so much in those early years: Susan Strecker, for making everything happen and everyone happy, Leslie Smith, Venice Bartholomew, Michael Korman, and Paul Lippman. Special thanks to the members of my ever-changing support team, especially Dr. Herbert Thomas, for his constant encouragement, Julia Walsh, Sister Colette Mahoney, John Bennet, Fran Gare, Judy Briles, Fayne Erickson, Evelyn Russell, Michael Hanssen, Jay Stuart, and Grace Tuason, my personal assistant, for her daily support and encouragement. And Doris Michaels, for her inspiring pep talks and her faith in this book. Most of all, my thanks to my coauthor, Karin Abarbanel, for her wonderful writing and her creativity in capturing on paper what NAFE—and dreams—are all about.

Wendy Rue

THE DOLLAR
BILL KNOWS
NO SEX

DREAMER ON SUNSET BOULEVARD

A fable:

Once upon a time in the City of Angels (also known as Los Angeles), there lived a little girl. As fate would have it (and fate, as we all know, runs a very tricky business!) she was born into a family where the women were judged only by their beauty and their ability to win wealthy husbands.

Unfortunately, the little girl was not a beautiful child. Surrounded by a bevy of blue-eyed blondes with peaches-and-cream skin, she had jet-black hair and a dark complexion. She had eight aunts, each more beautiful than the next, a sister and a cousin, also beautiful, whom she grew up with. They were the swans, she was the ugly duckling.

By the time she was nine, her only ally, her father, fell upon hard times, lost the little wealth he had, and no longer had any place in the family. The two of them were looked down upon and drew comfort from one another. Naturally, this made them very close.

The little girl just didn't seem to have a place in the world. She became a matter of great concern to her mother and the rest of her family. Worried about her future, they put their heads together and decided that something had to be done. Somehow, they had to find a way to help her attract a husband. After all, wasn't that a woman's reason for being, her sole purpose in life? In those faraway days, it was.

With her father no longer living at home, and her family fretting over her prospects, the little girl was lonely. She hardly ever played with other children and spent most of her time by herself. So she became a dreamer and dreamed of better things to come. And though times were hard, she struggled to stay true to herself and never let go of her dream. Her path was not an easy one. Along the way, she learned about courage and pain, fear and anxiety, laughter and tears. But through it all, she kept her dream alive. And one day, lo and behold, her dream came true!

That little girl, that ugly duckling, was me, Wendy Rue. I've been a misfit all my life. One of my earliest memories is of listening in at the kitchen door of our old, ramshackle house in Los Angeles while the women in the family held their all-important "summit meeting." This weekly kaffeeklatsch—my grandmother's brainstorm—had only one item on its agenda: a review of the romantic prospects of unmarried family females, at home or across the country. Half the meeting was spent trading dating stories and the other half plotting serious strategies for attracting and snaring any and all eligible males who wandered into the family web. I used to love eavesdropping on these meetings, hiding and giggling with my cousin, Fran. That is, until one night when the summit turned out to be all about me. As I sat behind the kitchen door, breathless with anticipation, my mother asked the inevitable question: "So…what do we do about Wendy?"

I wasn't more than nine at the time, but already, in my mother's beautiful hazel-brown eyes, my prospects seemed dim. For her, there was only one measure of success, one American dream: marriage. And not just any marriage, but a substantial one. Forty years ago, this was by no means a new idea, but for my mother, it was the one, the only path to success for a woman. Her mother, Rose (the queen of the roost, whom we all called Bubbah), had arrived in America from Romania 30 years before with eight daughters in tow, three of them unwed. My mother, married for 10 years, considered herself an absolute authority on the subject. In her opinion, Wendele, as she called me, had precious little marriage potential.

Unfortunately, I could see her point. If ever there was an ugly duckling, I was it. I was short and dark like my grandfather. While my mother had the exotic good looks of her Gypsy ancestors, I was fat, awkward, and pigeon-toed. My Buster Brown haircut didn't help. My younger sister Myrna, with her blue eyes and Shirley Temple curls of strawberry blond, was the obvious beauty. While everyone gushed over her glorious future, they groaned over mine. No matter what language I heard it in—English, Romanian, Yiddish, or German—the message was always the same: "Poor Wendy."

Listening to the summit meeting at which my fate was debated, I began to feel the first stirrings of resentment at being labeled "different." Even at the tender age of nine or ten, I knew enough to realize that what was happening was unfair. People around me, who hadn't a clue about what I was thinking or feeling, had found me lacking in some way. They had no idea who I was, yet thought they knew everything about who I should be. As I grew older, my sense of the unfairness of this kind of treatment became more and more intense. Eventually it grew into anger, which fueled my as yet unformed dreams about equality and independence. In later years, this anger drove me forward, often recklessly.

If the women in my life found me wanting, my father thought I was wonderful. To say my parents were poles apart in both personality and outlook is putting it mildly. While my mother seemed frustrated by life and driven in her pursuit of status, my father, Harry Fox, was sociable, gentle, witty, and a joy to be with. His idea of happiness and emotional fulfillment was economic independence: having enough money to do what he wanted. Most of the time he did. He had the easy sex appeal of Jack Klugman, whom he resembled, and the bemused approach to life of a Walter Matthau. Women adored him and he adored them back. He knew my low status among the family's females and always tried to make me feel good about myself and somehow special. I was his *Schwundelkopf* (mixed-up head), his companion, his confidante, his student in the art of life, as well as his daughter. He was my mentor, my cheering squad, my emotional anchor. I didn't just love my father, I idolized him.

He emigrated to the United States in the 1920s and became a clothing merchant. Settling in Detroit, he learned retailing from one of his brothers and then went off on his own. At some point soon after, Harry met Sally—Sally Gilbert, my mother. She was a young, pretty salesclerk almost 20 years younger than he. They fell in love and married. From what I've been told, the first years of the marriage were happy, if not blissful. That is, until I contracted double pneumonia when I was 18 months old. So serious was my illness, that the doctor actually pronounced me dead. Difficult, even from birth, I refused to give up the ghost. While my nurse frantically poured sour milk down my throat, my grandmother, Bubbah, stood in a corner mumbling an ancient Gypsy incantation over red beads. I've never been sure which one of these techniques revived me, but I roared back to life, astounding my doctor. Even then, I guess I had a mission and wasn't meant to leave this earth until I fulfilled it.

After assorted relocations, my family settled in Los Angeles on Alfred Street in the heart of the city's Borscht Belt. To make this move, my dad was forced to close down his business in Detroit, where some members of our family still lived. As in so many immigrant households, as word of California's sunshine trickled back to chilly Detroit, there was a constant ebb and flow of aunts, cousins, friends, and suitors. Holding court in the midst of all this family chaos was Bubbah: a matriarchal tyrant, all of 4 feet 8 inches tall.

It was because of Bubbah that I received no religious training. Although she was an Orthodox Jew, Bubbah never let Myrna and me go to temple on Saturday. She believed the practice of separating men from women in synagogue was discriminatory, and although she and all her daughters attended, she was determined that my generation should escape this kind of bias. So Myrna and I would walk her to temple and meet her afterward, but we did not enter. Bubbah's stand on this issue was my first taste of feminine independence and it made a huge impression on me. So much so, that years later when I encountered resistance, the image of Bubbah's stubborn rejection of the status quo never failed to inspire and spur me on.

When I was about nine, my father's retail business in L.A.

went bankrupt. It took him several years to recoup his losses, and my parents' marriage didn't survive this blow. Although my father was no longer living with us, things didn't change much. He was at the house constantly ("Children need to see their father," Bubbah would say). He was part of all our family decisions; and most important to me, since I was at the height of my ugly-duckling phase, he was still my constant companion. He took me everywhere, especially as I grew older: to his new store, to the fights on Friday nights, or to the racetrack, where he treated me more like a date than a daughter. He taught me how to pick winners in the ring, how to handicap horses, and how to sell things. "Never be afraid to do something different," he would tell me. "Give people a reason to buy something. They may not always know what it is, but give them a reason." It was through his stories and by watching him sell that, slowly but surely, the seeds of entrepreneurship were planted within me.

While my father taught me lessons in life, my mother was ruthlessly practical. Since I lacked beauty, she felt talent might do the trick. At the summit meeting called to discuss my prospects, it was decided I should have piano lessons so I would have something to fall back on in the very likely event that I wouldn't find a husband. Ever anxious to please, I went along with this plan. Twice a week for three years, Mr. Frobisher, my piano teacher, came to our house in beard and threadbare coat to teach me notes, chords, and sight reading. With lots of practice, by age 12, I was banging out Beethoven and Brahms. My mother was impressed; my cultural achievements gave her something new and different to talk about with her friends. Her pride knew no bounds when I was accepted on a scholarship at the Philadelphia Conservatory of Music.

To tell the truth, music brought me no fulfillment. I was a good technician, but my heart was never really in it. Slowly, I realized that I wasn't playing for myself, I was playing for my mother's idea of what I should be. That never works. For the first of many times in my life, I came to understand that trying to be someone or something you're not, just to satisfy someone else's need, always creates hunger instead of happiness. Real joy comes from the ideas and actions *you* believe in and carry out, no matter how large or small.

When I turned 13, something wonderful happened: I grew up and slimmed down. The wrong lumpy parts became the right lumpy parts. My features, hidden for 12 years by baby fat, emerged. I became attractively appealing. I discovered makeup and tight sweaters, and boys discovered me. One evening, my mother returned from work to find about two dozen boys on the small lawn in front of our house on Alfred Street. They hadn't come to listen to the strains of the waltz music that wafted out my window, they were there to see the pianist. I had painstakingly dolled myself up for the benefit of my would-be beaus, with a sexy blouse, red lipstick, and more makeup than the Rockettes' entire chorus line.

My mother was absolutely furious! After giving up on wedding bells for me, she had come to accept and even relish the idea that I would bring an aura of culture and refinement to the family. To my dismay and amazement, boys and marriage no longer had any place in her plans for me. She pulled me off my piano stool and marched me to the bathroom, where she scrubbed off all the makeup it had taken me hours to apply. "Three years of lessons," she fumed, rubbing my face until it smarted. "Three years and now this!" She gestured out the window where all but a few of the boys still stood, hoping for a repeat performance. "What's it going to be, Wendy? Music or boys?" my mother demanded. The word *boys* dripped with disdain. I looked at the motley crowd of teenagers hanging around outside, some of whom I didn't even know. Then I looked at the piano. This was a "Life Moment" and I knew it. Independence Day had arrived. "Take it away!" I said, dismissing my musical career with a wave of my hand.

The day after this scene, I applied for my work permit after school. I was only 13 at the time, but through the magic of makeup I made myself look 16. As so often happens, my increasing need to become self-sufficient put me beyond my mother's control and made her angry. She was heartbroken about my rejection of a musical career and jealous of my popularity and dates. I was out all the time. Having chosen boys over Beethoven, I felt obliged to be serious about my decision. I was willful almost to the point of being wild. I felt I didn't belong anywhere. Part of this outlook was teenage angst and part of it was reality. What with marriages, divorces, and relocations, my family life wasn't exactly the Brady Bunch. Things became so bad that my little sister Myrna began living with Bubbah in one location while I lived with my mother in another—hardly an ideal situation. No wonder I felt lost!

My work permit in hand, I quickly found a job selling in a retail store. I also harbored a secret dream: Like every other Hollywood kid, I wanted to be an actress. This dream gave me my first taste of bartering: A theatrical agent agreed to give me acting lessons in return for my services as his receptionist. This agent's major claim to fame was a Shirley Temple lookalike; his wife guarded this child protégé 24 hours a day. He attracted other students through acting classes and showcases, to which he invited friends in the business. I studied the lines he gave me day and night, but he never let me perform. When I asked him why, he answered, "I'm sorry, Wendy, but you'll never make it in show business. You're not pretty enough."

Once again, the ugly duckling emerged to haunt me. Angry and upset, I left the acting studio forever. In my mind, the agent had led me on. I felt used and discriminated against because of my appearance. I became more determined than ever to make a success of myself in my own way and on my own terms. In a long moment of honest analytical thought, rare for one so young, I realized that my appearance wasn't going to bring me success. I had to develop other assets. After accepting this reality, I began to gravitate toward other people, usually older adults, who could teach me something. This expanded my intellect and my experience. But more important, it taught me a lesson that has helped me immeasurably throughout my life: Never be afraid of people who know more than you do. Don't let your ego get in the way of seeking these people out. The more you ask of them, the more they can teach you.

This unorthodox approach to learning was not something I learned at home. Unlike many immigrants, my family didn't place a high value on education. My mother viewed it merely as a means toward social betterment. My father, largely self-taught, looked upon formal learning with suspicion and even a little scorn. In spite of my parents' views, they both realized that a high school diploma was essential. So I shuttled back and forth to various schools, doing little work and reveling in my growing sex appeal and popularity. In many ways, my high school years were like a stop-and-go film. Every time we moved, my new school would test me, add a few points to my IQ, and nudge me up a grade. Fortunately, I was a bright kid and could handle the pressure. (In succession, I attended Los Angeles High, Hollywood High, and Fairfax High, graduating from Fairfax at age 15.)

At the time, earning my own way and being independent were more important to me than academic success. To achieve this, I took two jobs after school: as a salesclerk in a sportswear store and as an usherette at a movie theater on La Brea. Most of my earnings were spent on clothes and makeup. On my shopping excursions, I became aware of how badly teenagers were treated in stores. Without an adult beside them, kids were either ignored or made to feel so unwelcome that they were intimidated into leaving. I was infuriated when my friends and I were treated this way. No one seemed to realize, although it was clear to me, that teenagers were emerging as an economic force. (Years later, I saw the same phenomenon taking place in the women's market.) Teens had enormous buying power and a need to express themselves, yet they were made to feel unimportant. This was something I vowed to change someday.

In the last half of my senior year, I asked my parents for permission to take time off from working and concentrate on my studies. My heavy schedule was exhausting me and I wanted to see just how well I could do academically with the freedom to study full time. Reluctantly, my parents agreed. Over the next six months, I really buckled down and graduated near the top of my high school class. I was proud, but unclear about my future. What I did know was that my formal education was over.

Even during my nose-to-the-grindstone days at school, I still managed a very active social life. Plenty of guys my age called me, but I felt little in common with them and preferred dating older boys. After graduation I met a real heartbreaker named Frank Shafer at a USO party. He was about 22, in the service, handsome and dashing. He came from a wealthy family and had all the credentials I knew would please my mother and reassure my father. I lied about my age, and we started dating. Things were getting pretty serious with Frank when my dad stepped in. Relieved that I'd made it through high school, my father decided to give me a graduation present: a visit to New York on one of his buying trips. I expected resistance from my mother, but there was none. Secretly, I think she was pleased, knowing through long experience how hard it would be for my father to ride herd on me.

We took the Super Chief, and the minute we left L.A., I was ready to party. What my father thought would be a leisurely, perhaps even educational, cross-country tour was for me a kind of rolling Roman carnival. There were boys chasing me down the aisles and temptations everywhere: in the dining car, the bar car, the baggage car. After spending a day trying to keep track of me, my dad was exhausted. He caught up with me one afternoon and said, "Look, I've never bought you a present. If you promise to stay where I can see you, when we get to New York, I'll buy you anything you want." I laughed and said, "OK, but you can't get me what I really want." "So what is it?" my dad asked. "A big brother," I replied, choosing something outrageous and impossible for him to deliver. My father looked at me for a long moment and then began to laugh. "When we get to New York," he told me, "you'll meet him."

Once ensconced in our New York hotel, my dad made dozens of calls to business contacts while I saw the sights. I asked a couple of times about seeing my brother, but he kept putting me off. "Maybe tomorrow or the next day," he said casually. I began to think the whole brother story was just a ruse to keep me in line. My father had told me that he'd been married a couple of times before he married my mother. But what I didn't know was that he and his first wife had a son named Max. Or that she and Max had relocated to Canada after she divorced my dad and remarried. A day or so later, there was a knock on the door. My father answered it and came back followed by a large, serious-looking guy with dark hair and sharp, smiling blue eyes. He reminded me of Raymond Burr. They were both grinning.

"Wendele," my father said, "I'd like you to meet your brother Max."

"So this is my little sister!" Max said, picking me up in a giant bear hug. It was love at first sight, and I was crazy with excitement. From the moment we met, it was as if we had known each other all our lives. Max was about 28 at the time and a successful, self-made tycoon. He was so thrilled to finally meet me that he took me on a two-day trip to Toronto. Everyone thought I was his girlfriend, and Max didn't discourage their ideas—he'd just laugh slyly. We had a ball!

Over the years, Max became everything one could ask for in an older brother, offering helpful advice on my business ventures and supporting me throughout my ups and downs. The solid citizen, suit-and-tie type, a hard-driving, pragmatic businessman, and a college graduate, Max was the perfect complement to my off-the-wall flamboyance. He was the greatest gift my father could have given me. After all the excitement in New York, returning to California and my old routine was a major anticlimax. So what's a nice Jewish girl going to do? Get married.

As soon as I walked through the door, Frank rushed back into my life. About six years older than I, Frank seemed impossibly romantic and sophisticated. What did I know? At 16, my favorite food was French fries and my idea of foreign travel was dinner in Chinatown. The day after my dad brought me back from New York, Frank gave me an engagement ring. We decided to wait a year, which made me feel grown up and safe. Then Frank shortened our engagement to 6 months. I started getting nervous. A week later, he said we had to get married in 10 days; his father owned a Beverly Hills apartment house, and we were going to have to take over its management. When I told my parents about Frank's explanation, they were skeptical. They later admitted agreeing to this whirlwind wedding only because they both thought I was pregnant, which hurt me tremendously. They were wrong, but our son, Dennis, was born exactly 9 months and 9 days after Frank and I tied the knot.

The Beverly Hills property we were to manage turned out to be a broken-down building in downtown L.A., where Frank and I did not live happily ever after. It soon became clear that my husband was not a world-beater. He was the spoiled son of a wealthy father and thought the world owed him a living. My father quickly sized up our situation. In an effort to help, he set up a small custom furniture business for Frank. When that failed, he supplied Frank with several lines of clothing to sell. But the only one who did any selling was my dad.

Meanwhile, Frank's father and mine assisted us with matching infusions of cash, most of which Frank used to pursue his true passion: buying cars. Naive and innocent, I had no idea where the money we were living on was coming from, but it never occurred to me that Frank wasn't supporting us. At about this time, we moved out of our rental apartment into a small condo, a wedding gift from both our parents. I kept my job at the sportswear shop until the day before Dennis was born. I loved working. Once Dennis arrived, I spent a few weeks at home, but I couldn't take being without a job to keep me busy and on my toes. By noon, the baby was fed and bathed and I was bored. I soon found myself taking him downtown in a taxi every day to my mother's or my father's store. This routine went on for some months.

Then one day my dad sat me down and said, "Schwundel, do you realize that between Frank's father and me, we've put up more than $50,000 for your living expenses?" I was horrified and embarrassed to learn how irresponsible Frank had been. "Daddy, I had no idea this was going on. Please help me get back on my feet," I pleaded. "What are you going to do?" he asked. My anger at the way teenage shoppers were treated gave me the answer. "I want to open a retail store for teenagers so I can start taking care of myself and Dennis," I told my dad. Despite the fact that I was 18 years old and had no management experience in retail, my father thought my plan was sound. Opening a store was something he knew about and could help me with. Secretly, I think he was hoping that Frank and I could run the store together and build our own life. But like most dreams built on someone else's fantasy, things didn't work out that way.

At his store in downtown Los Angeles, my father geared his merchandise to the large Mexican population that lived there. The Mexican women who bought his clothing and stockings were small, and one of his best-selling items was a short skirt. My idea was to sell the same skirt but in a completely different part of town and to a completely different market: teenage girls. My father helped me find a rental space on Sunset Boulevard and gave me some of his merchandise on credit. I opened for business, excited and proud. But the store failed because of its location. I opened a second store in the San Fernando Valley, which didn't do much better. However, my third store, located just across the street, quickly took off.

One of the unexpected and unwelcome results of my plunge into business was the criticism I received. My mother and father were supportive. My brother Max offered advice and encouragement. But the carping of friends and other members of my family was almost unbearable. The women were especially annoying. Safely ensconced in their traditional roles as wives and mothers, they looked upon me with disapproval. By working, I was acknowledging that my husband couldn't support us, something a wife just didn't do. I don't know how many times I heard, "Why start a store for teenagers? No one does that, especially not a woman."

The profitability and success of my store, Wendy's Teenscene, should have been a source of happiness. Instead, I almost lost everything because my mother became terminally ill. I nursed her through the last painful months of her life and totally neglected the store. When I couldn't be with Dennis, he was well cared for by a wonderful nanny and by Frank's grandmother, who lived nearby. After my mother died at the age of 39, I fell into a deep depression; it was two more months before I felt strong enough to go back to work. I had left the store's day-to-day operation to Frank. Too late, I discovered that his idea of management was to build a set of model trains in the back room and spend all day playing with them. When I returned to Wendy's, I found everything—the stock, the books, the shelves—in chaos.

Once I took charge again and followed through on some of my ideas, the store's sales increased. At the time, my vision of creating a shop catering strictly to teenagers was revolutionary. Although no one realized it—least of all me—I was one of the first proponents of "niche marketing." The concept was equal parts fantasy, inspiration, and necessity—an excellent mix of qualities for any entrepreneur. Still a teenager myself, I knew what my friends wanted without market studies, surveys, or a consulting firm. I even established a layaway plan, giving my young customers their first exposure to credit and the responsibility of making regular payments. Not once during the time my Wendy's Teenscene stores were in business (there were eight of them over the years) was I ever burned. Kids wanted to be trusted, and they responded by being trustworthy.

Strangely, the money Teenscene brought in did nothing to improve things on the home front. The store was doing well and our bank account was growing, but Frank couldn't handle my success or independence. His initial support soon gave way to the realization that I was outearning him, causing him public embarrassment. We didn't fight, but it was clear we were heading downhill. Divorce was the only answer. My dad, though he never said so, shared my view that my marriage wasn't working. So I thought he'd be pleased when I met him for lunch one day in early November.

He was sitting at the table with a longtime female companion named Stella. After some small talk, I finally said, "Dad, I'm going to divorce Frank," expecting him to be relieved and supportive. Instead, he shook his head and said, "Bad timing." I was hurt and astounded. "I thought you'd be proud of me for making a tough decision like this. You know it's not working." He sighed. "Schwundel," he said coolly, "it's the Christmas season. You need Frank to help in the store. It's the wrong time for this." Apparently, I wasn't the only one with man problems, because Stella suddenly jumped to her feet and screamed at him, "There's never a right time for you! You're trying to ruin Wendy's life just like you've ruined mine!" But Stella didn't just steal my moment for sympathy, she committed grand larceny by picking up a pitcher of water and pouring it over my dad's head. As she fumed, I stomped out of the restaurant.

When I arrived home, my father had somehow gotten there before me and was deep in conversation with Frank. My tears and rage boiled over. "Right time? There is no right time," I wailed. "And no matter what the two of you think, you're not going to change my mind," I yelled, slamming the door and flinging myself, Scarlett O'Hara style, down on my bed for a nice, long cry. The heart-to-heart talk Frank and my father had that night seemed to make a difference. Frank became very sweet and helpful.

We were so busy during Christmas that I stopped thinking about divorce. Frank helped me out at the store through January. But by then our old problems had surfaced again and reality set in. I knew our marriage would never work and so did my father. "Before you end things with Frank," my dad told me, "you have to promise me one thing, Wendele: You'll never take child support from him. You'll always be able to take care of yourself and your baby. Don't burden Frank by forcing him to give you money. Let him start over." I wholeheartedly agreed and was divorced by February at the age of 19. Dennis was 2. Compassionate as he was, my dad took Frank home to console him and sent me to my brother Max, who offered comfort and made me laugh again. For a long time, I'd felt lonely and trapped. But the world was mine if I had the courage to reach for it. As always, my dad was waiting for me, ready to help.

A MILLION-DOLLAR MARKETING LESSON FOR $1.49!

Harry Fox, owner of the Hosiery Box. That was my dad—my very first entrepreneurial role model. But how can I capture the complexity, the contradictions, the compassion of the man who was my father—my mentor, my coach, my cheerleader, my support system of one?

The son of a rabbi, he was trained to become a rabbi himself, yet became a retailer instead. He was highly educated, yet felt that most formal training was impractical and even useless in day-to-day life. He taught me the value of emotional independence, yet constantly worried about my future and survival as a single mother. He took enormous pride in me and my business success, yet wanted me to have the security he felt only marriage and a husband could provide. In a sense, I was his son in business and his daughter in life. I could never win with my dad, but I could never lose either. He was always there for me—teaching me, guiding me, nurturing my business drive and my young dreams.

Perhaps it was the emotional ups and downs he faced in his own life that made my father more concerned about my safety and security than my success. He grew up in a small Polish village at the turn of the century. The eldest son of a rabbi, he was deeply enmeshed in religious training through his early twenties. Engaged to marry the youngest daughter of a well-to-do family, his life seemed secure and his path clear.

He would study, raise children, share his growing wisdom, and prosper, as his father and his father's father had done. That's what should have happened.

Instead, his engagement was suddenly destroyed by a scandal involving his intended's older sister. Heartbroken and disillusioned, he turned his back on everything he had known and thought he wanted. He set sail for America and landed in Detroit, where he began his long career as a merchant.

Starting with nothing, he began building a new life for himself selling hosiery and lingerie. His first store did well and he married and had a son, my half-brother, Max. He was a wealthy businessman with several stores by the time he had divorced his second wife and fallen in love with my mother. Twenty years younger than he was, my mother was working for him as a salesclerk. I was born soon after my parents married.

Unfortunately, I did not bring the joy expected. I was a sickly baby, plagued with health problems. My hospital bills quickly drained my father's resources. Doctors told my family I wouldn't survive infanthood. When I refused to comply and give up the ghost, someone suggested that a warmer climate might help. My mother began chasing the sun, carting me from place to place until she finally ended up in Los Angeles. My father followed. Four years later, Myrna, my baby sister, was born. Forced to give up the business he'd spent years building in Detroit, my dad had to start all over in a strange, unfamiliar city. Shortly after he opened his first retail store in L.A., he went broke. Surviving wasn't easy, and my mother couldn't hide her disappointment in the decline of my father's earning power. Neither could my two aunts, cousin, and grandmother, all of whom had moved in with us once we settled in California. My father's situation was a constant topic of conversation and discontent. He finally left home when I was about nine and was forced to peddle hosiery door to door in order to support himself and my family.

Eventually, with money he'd saved and help from his fourth wife, he was able to open a new store, the Hosiery Box. On the corner of Third and Broadway, it was located at a busy intersection in downtown L.A., right in the heart of the retailing district. The Hosiery Box was an instant success. It was my father's refuge, his domain, and his anchor. It was a tiny hole in the wall that probably measured 9 by 12 feet at the most. It was filled from floor to ceiling with boxes of hosiery, in hundreds of different sizes, colors, and styles. When I stepped into the store, as I did most afternoons after school, I found myself in another world.

It was a world of bright, shiny packages, soft silky stockings, dreams on display. It was a busy, exciting world where something new was always happening. It was a world where I wasn't just a kid, I was a contributor. I could be helpful and useful, unpacking boxes, setting up window displays, serving customers. It was a world of choice, where people could pick out what they wanted or put in a request for something special. Above all, it was a world where equality and fairness reigned—where a dollar bill gave everyone exactly the same buying power, whether it was clutched in the hand of a little Mexican teen dressing up for Saturday night or fished from the purse of a young secretary rushing in to buy a pair of stockings on her lunch hour.

Trim, short, with blue eyes and a twinkle in his smile, my father had a restless energy and drive. Saint Harry, he definitely wasn't! He had four wives in all; he couldn't stay married and he couldn't stay unmarried. With dad as a role model, it was little wonder my own domestic life was never a smashing success! With all the turmoil he experienced on the personal front, work was my dad's salvation and he tackled any business problems that came his way with guts, gusto, and ingenuity. He never let his ego get in the way of making a deal.

Like most business owners, he was always on the move—meeting with vendors, talking with manufacturers, lining up new sources of supply. He had a big network of friends and business associates and was constantly asked for his advice and ideas. I was fascinated by the way my father handled people, how comfortable and special he made them feel. He was a superb salesman, and like most successful salesmen, he was a keen observer and a great listener—he always listened with compassion and without judging anyone who came to him for help.

My dad really loved sales—it was his calling and his mission. He believed that sales was more than just an honorable profession, it was an art. He felt that selling was the greatest job in the world and that nothing would happen in business if no one sold. He had a very straightforward, sincere style, which people found refreshing and reassuring. Respect, trust, and honesty were the three qualities he demanded in all his business relationships.

Above all, my father was a leader and an innovator. He had a true talent for seeking out voids in the marketplace and then figuring out how to fill them profitably. That was what made him a successful entrepreneur. He created a niche for himself that no one else understood how to fill. He also had enormous respect for and a deep understanding of his customers—who they were; what they wanted; how, where, and when they liked to buy. His sales philosophy was really very simple. He believed that it was his job to prove to people that he was giving them a good value and his responsibility was to deliver on that promise.

My dad never had any formal business training, but he was a born teacher. From the time I was old enough to be on my own, every day after school, I'd head over to my dad's store, not just to help out, but to hang out, to listen to my dad talk about business and selling. The lessons he taught me aren't the kind you'll find in a Harvard Business School case study, but they're just as valuable and probably a lot more relevant to you as a budding entrepreneur. Of all the things I learned from my dad, there are six pieces of advice that have worked for me time and again and that I want to share with you now:

LESSON 1   NEVER CHASE THE COMPETITION

The first—and probably most valuable—lesson my dad taught me was the fruit (as most really helpful lessons are) of a crisis. It was the early fifties and the American economy was humming—pushed into high gear by the Baby Boom and consumers' insatiable desire to buy anything and everything. Businesses thrived and sprang up overnight. Competition soared. And, unfortunately for hosiery merchants, hosiery prices fell though the basement. Back during the war, when raw materials were scarce, nylons were more precious than gold. A pair of stockings as a gift from a guy was guaranteed to win just about any woman's heart. Prices were high and it was a great time to be in business.

The fabulous fifties were another story. Nylons were plentiful and getting cheaper by the day it seemed. One afternoon, when I was about 12, my dad took me up and down the busy street where his shop was located. Store after store was plastered with signs advertising bargain-basement hosiery prices: "$1.49 a pair," "$1.18 a pair," "2 pairs for $2.50." Retailers seemed to be desperate—they were practically giving their merchandise away. I knew that hosiery was my father's lifeline, and I was worried. What would happen to him? My dad took me back to his store and with a very serious face asked me, "Well, Schwundel, you've seen how things are. What should I do?" "Gee, Daddy, I don't know," I answered. "The cheapest price I saw was $1.18 a pair. Could you sell yours for $1.15?"

"You're not my daughter!" he replied in a voice half serious, half teasing. I knew right away that he had something up his sleeve and I couldn't wait to find out what it was! It wasn't long before I did. He took me to the back room of his store where he kept a tremendous inventory—he always invested heavily in whatever he believed in—and pulled down a huge cardboard box from one of the top shelves. "Open it, Schwundel," he said. Grabbing a pair of scissors, I quickly pried the flaps loose. What a surprise! What a treasure! Inside were the most amazing stockings! Stockings with golden clocks appliquéd on them. Stockings with fancy seams. Stockings aglow with colored sequins and rhinestones. They were gorgeous! I'd never seen anything like them! And neither had anyone else in L.A., that was for sure. Why? Because my dad had discovered his hidden treasure on one of his buying trips to New York. And while storekeepers up and down the street were fighting with each other over nickels and dimes, my dad was planning to sell his fancy new stockings for more than double the price of his competitor's hosiery: $2.95.

He looked at me, shook his finger gently, and said, "Schwundel, don't ever look in a store window again! If you do, you're not my daughter! Always, remember: Find something different and you'll be a success." And that's exactly what his pricey, $2.95-a-pair stockings were—an instant success! No sooner did we put them in the window, than they went flying out the door.

To this day, I've followed my dad's advice. I've never looked to see what other people were doing in any business I've been in. I've always come up with my own ideas and followed my own intuition about what people want and what they're willing to pay for it. I look for a void in the market, just as my dad did, and then find a way to fill it. "I don't ride to beat the boys, just to win!" That's how one of the first female jockeys described her racing style—and it sums up my approach to marketing exactly. Never chase the competition. Why not? Mainly because you'll spend half your energy and time trying to play catch-up with someone else and the other half looking over your shoulder to see who's trying to catch up with *you*. Pour that same energy into winning, and you'll have a shot at the gold. Always run your own race—and never look in a shop window again!

LESSON 2   NEVER LET A FEW MISTAKES STAND IN THE WAY OF YOUR DREAMS

I once heard someone say that an entrepreneur is someone who'll go over, up, under, around, and through any obstacle that blocks the path to his or her dream. To me, that's a pretty good description of what it takes to bring an idea to the marketplace.

My dad learned how hard it is to hang on to a dream early in his career. After his big success in Detroit as the prosperous owner of a chain of hosiery stores, he bombed out when he tried to make it in L.A. The first store he opened was a disaster. He managed to keep body and soul—and his estranged family of seven females—together by doing something that most people, especially people with his background, would have considered incredibly demeaning: peddling hosiery door to door.

But my father didn't see it that way. He was a survivor. If he had to peddle stockings to retain his independence and fulfill his obligations, then he was prepared to do it, not begrudgingly or bitterly but with grace and flair. Slowly, he built up his cash reserves once more until he was finally able to open up the Hosiery Box. When that store succeeded, he rented another. And just three years after he was driven to sell door to door, he went back and rented the same store he'd gone bankrupt in—just to prove to himself and his vendors that he could make a go of it.

As a survivor myself and someone who once worked as a road bum for Edie Adams' "Cut n' Curl" franchises during a low point in my checkered career, I've always found my dad's business ups and downs comforting and inspiring. If someone as sharp and streetwise as he was could take a dive and climb back out, well then, so could I. Beyond his resilience and stick-to-it-iveness, my dad taught me another, even more important lesson: a mistake is just that, a mistake! It's not the end of the world, or a life sentence, or a scarlet letter. It's just a detour, a blip on the radar screen. It's something you have to laugh at and then move beyond. It's not an albatross you have to wear around your neck for the rest of your life. That is, unless you make it one.

I'll never forget the rocky road I started on when I began my teen shops—the first of its kind in L.A. and in all of America for that matter. My first store was a bust. It was the old story: location, location, location. There weren't enough teens in the neighborhood where I was to support my business. I decided to try again. I moved to the San Fernando Valley, where the demographics seemed tailor-made for my merchandise. I opened my new store with great expectations, only to watch, day after day, as it remained almost empty and my bills piled up.

As usual, my dad was there to help—and to observe the passing scene. "You know, Schwundel," he said to me one day; as we sat together waiting for customers who never arrived, "I've been watching the other side of the street. There's plenty of traffic over there. For some reason, people don't want to cross over to where you are. Maybe it's too shady over here. Maybe people don't know this part of the neighborhood well enough to buy in. Who knows? I think you should move your store across the street."

Needless to say, this solution was too simple, too sensible, for me to accept. For me, the problem had to be much deeper and tougher to solve. "That can't be it!" I wailed. "Maybe this whole idea is just bad, no good, a big fat disaster."

"Listen, Schwundel," my dad said patiently. "You've always wanted to have a teen shop all your own where kids can come to relax and shop. Are you going to let a few mistakes stand in the way of your dream? Why make something simple so complicated? Pick up the phone and pack your boxes!" And, after a few more days of sitting around biting my fingernails, that's exactly what I did. As usual my dad turned out to be right, and the new store thrived.

Rest assured, if you have a dream for sale, you're going to take a beating in the marketplace sooner or later. You're going to make mistakes. Probably some big ones. And how you handle these mistakes, or disasters, or crises, or challenges, or obstacles—or whatever else you want to call them—will be one of the keys to your success or failure. Are you willing to pick yourself up and start over if you have to? Are you willing to swallow your pride and take on anything and everything that comes your way just to keep your dream alive so you can fight and, hopefully, win, another day? Are you willing to put your ego aside and admit that you were wrong, misguided, caught off guard, blindsided, unaware, or just plain pigheaded? Are you more afraid to appear naive, foolish, or even stupid than you are determined to be a success?

LESSON 3   USE THE FAMILIAR
TO SELL THE NEW

Whole books have been written about the psychology of consumers—just check the business or marketing section of any
bookstore. But when all is said and done, as my father knew
so well, there's one unshakable truth you need to know about
your customers' buying patterns, whether you're selling a
Mercedes or mascara. Consumers, young or old, wealthy or
surviving on a shoestring, are creatures of habit.

Consumer products firms have spent millions in research
to ferret out this fact—one that my father learned on his own
through observation and long experience. What's more, buying
habits take root surprisingly early. Some experts say brand loy-
alties are formed at the tender age of four or five. No wonder
advertisers spend billions on children's TV!

And no wonder that it's a lot easier to convince consumers
to try a "New, improved" version of an old product than it is to
persuade them to make a permanent switch to a new brand.
Think about it for a minute. What does that "New, improved"
label really mean? Isn't it just a way of fine-tuning an existing
product and then attaching the word *new* to it to make people
feel as if they're making a whole new buying decision, when in
fact they're just settling for the same old shampoo or tooth-
paste they've bought for years?

No one knew better than my dad that customers are creatures of habit and that trying to disrupt their buying patterns
is a recipe for disaster. In his view, when introducing a new
line, the key to success wasn't trying to *change* a customer's
buying habits but to *confirm* them. Whenever he had something new and different to sell, he always set out to make his
customers feel comfortable about the buying decision he was
asking them to make. He did this mainly by stretching their
imaginations and making them feel that what he was selling
was more or less a "souped up" version of what they were
already buying—the same model car, but with a faster engine.

Take those fabulous, glitzy New York stockings, for example. When my dad put them up for sale, he didn't just stick them in the window with a sign saying, "2.95 a pair." Nor did he place his red-hot new product next to the plain-vanilla stockings everyone else was selling up and down the street. Contrasting the old with the new in that way would have been too shocking. It would have been asking his customers to take too big a leap out of their work-a-day lives and into a world of total fantasy.

So exactly what *did* he do? How did he get those stockings to leap up and dance out of his store at the then-outrageous price of $2.95? He did it by creating a bridge from the old and familiar to the new and unfamiliar—by filling his windows, not just with beige nylons, but with more expensive stockings in different colors as well. He lined up his old, plain-vanilla nylons next to the colored stockings, and then placed his fancy new line next to those. By taking this approach, he allowed his customers' eyes—and their minds—to travel an uninterrupted journey from their old, familiar choice to something a little more exciting and out of the ordinary, to a product that really stretched, but didn't snap, their imaginations.

I've used this same technique time and again in my own businesses. When I first opened my teen shops, for example, I stocked my stores with some of my dad's merchandise, namely short skirts. Colorwise, they didn't offer much selection: The skirts were brown, gray, and navy. The most exciting shades were royal blue and hunter green. I had other ideas, however. I had the same style skirt made up in soft pastel colors—pink, cream, and mint green. The perfect shades for the sunny L.A. market, or so I thought. I couldn't wait to hang those skirts on the rack in all their pastel glory and watch the young teens I was selling to scramble for them. I just knew they'd love them!

Whoops! Day after day, those snappy little skirts sat there, unloved—and unsold. Then one morning, for some reason, my father's stocking strategy floated into my mind. I pulled out some old gray, brown, and navy skirts and lined them up on a rack, then added the royal blues and hunter greens, and completed the row with my soft pastels. I watched the girls finger the familiar old brown, navy, and gray skirts, move down the rack to the royal blues, and then focus on a pink or mint green skirt and pull it off the hanger to try on.

Bingo! My new colors were a not-so-instant hit! By pairing my new line with familiar shades, I returned the teens I was selling to back to their comfort zone—giving them the confidence they needed to choose a fresh new shade instead of the old ones they were used to buying. Instead of asking them to make a whole new purchasing decision, I helped them extend their original buying pattern a little farther down the line—or the rack, to be exact.

As I'll explain later, I used basically the same technique with great success. I teamed up with American Express and "borrowed" its brand recognition and well-established credibility to help market the National Association for Female Executives (NAFE). By associating NAFE with a familiar, well-respected company, I created a comfort level and acceptance for an entirely new concept: membership in a woman's association that no one had ever heard of.

LESSON 4   FOCUS ON VALUE, NOT PRICE

My dad believed that any customer who walked through the door of one of his stores had the right to three things: respect, courteous service, and value. He would never try to fool or pressure or cajole anyone into buying something. As a salesman, his approach was not to sell based solely on price or product benefits but to demonstrate to his customers why his product offered them a good value for their money. He felt his role wasn't to direct or dictate his customer's taste or ideas but to offer them persuasive reasons reinforcing and supporting their decision-making power as buyers.

For my father, value was like a three-legged stool: It was determined by price, performance, and quality. Selling based on value was also a tricky business because, in his experience, people often confused a good value with a bargain price. In my dad's view, one of his key responsibilities as a salesman was to help people understand the difference between the two. He generally did this by showing, rather than telling, them what he wanted them to know.

He took the same approach with me. As he so often did, my dad used a story to teach me how important it was to prove to customers that they were receiving a good value for their money. When he was starting out in Detroit, he said, he carried flannel nightgowns in his hosiery store. As the winter season wound to a close one year, he decided to put them on sale. The next morning, he put up a big sign in the window that read, "Regular $5.99, on sale for $2.89." He had the nightgowns neatly folded on a table in front of the store and expected to do a brisk business because he was offering such a great bargain. But nothing happened.

All morning and into the early afternoon, he watched people look at the sign and then pass the table by. Something was wrong. He was offering people a good buy, but no one was biting. Finally, he couldn't take it anymore. He gathered up the nightgowns, took them outside where a light rain was falling and stood with them in his arms until they were just slightly damp and wrinkled. Then he brought them back in and returned them to the table in a disorderly pile. According to my dad, they were gone in 10 minutes. "What happened?" I asked. "What changed people's minds?"

When the gowns were neatly folded on the table in perfect condition, my dad explained, people figured the sale was a ploy and that there was something wrong with them. Why else would they be marked down from $5.99 to $2.89—less than half price? So people weren't buying. Once they could see that the gowns were wrinkled and therefore no longer in "perfect" condition, they felt that the sale price was justified and that they were still getting a good buy for their $2.89. At that point, the basis for their decision shifted from price to value, my dad explained, because he had proven to them that they were getting a fair return on their dollar. That's when they started buying.

My father's strong belief in value as the basis of sales was ingrained in me early in my business career. In fact, as soon as my first teen shop began doing well, I borrowed a leaf from his book in a way that surprised and pleased him no end. When I opened my store, as I said earlier, one of the lines I carried was the short skirts my father also stocked. One day, I had a real brainstorm. Since we were both buying the skirts in such large quantities, why couldn't we manufacture them ourselves? That way, we could get exactly the colors and materials we wanted. "What, you don't have enough problems?" my dad responded. "Now you want to go into manufacturing?" Even though he dismissed it, I could tell that the idea intrigued him. And about a week later, he said, "You know, Schwundel, I think we should manufacture our own skirts!" "That's a great idea, Dad!" I answered. And that's what we did.

Once we had our manufacturing arrangement set up, I wanted to take things a step further. I told my dad I wanted to take out an ad in the local paper saying:

Factory to You:

$5.87

The ad would go on to say that we were able to offer skirts normally priced at $7.99 for $5.87 because we had cut out the middleman. To attract attention, I used what in the industry is called a bastard price, $5.87, instead of $5.95 or $5.99. My dad was opposed to the idea, but I decided to do it anyway. I bought the ad on my own and was absolutely thrilled when it came out. At the end of the day the ad had run, my dad called me and said, "Well, Schwundel, how'd you do today?" "Daddy," I told him excitedly, "we tripled our business! I sold 150 skirts!" "Isn't that nice," my dad answered. "Let's see? Just imagine if you'd sold them for $6.99—you would have tripled your business, given your customers a bargain, and actually made some profit!"

While my dad thought my price was too low, secretly, he was very proud of me. He told all his friends about my ad and how well it had worked. And while I may have lost some money on my merchandise my first time around, he realized that my ad reflected what he'd been trying to teach me. By using the headline, "Factory to You" followed by the "$5.87," I was placing value ahead of price—both in my own mind and in the minds of my customers. Ever since that ad, I've continued to sell based on value and its always proved to be a profitable strategy for me.

LESSON 5   ENJOY THE REWARDS OF YOUR WORK

My father was a great believer in pleasure and fun as the just rewards for had work. He used to call me every morning when I had my teen shops, just to see how things were going. If I was up early, he'd tell me, "You're a businesslady! You're working too hard. I think you'd better take off the afternoon and go with me to the races. You need to relax." If I was still sleeping when he called, he'd say, "What, you're a businesslady and you're still asleep at eight? You should be working harder! I have a buyer you should meet. Let's have lunch. After, we'll go to the races." And whichever way the day went, we worked hard and had fun at the same time.

My dad also believed in treating yourself well while still living within your means. As I quickly found out, there's a real art to doing this—one that I learned the hard way. I had just gotten a divorce and was a newly single mother with a small baby. I had no money. And on top of all my other problems, I needed to buy a car. Driving from Coldwater Canyon, where I lived at the time, into L.A., where my teen boutique was located, wasn't exactly a picnic. The mountains around my house were treacherous and I was terrified of having a breakdown somewhere along the way.

Faced with all these problems, I decided, as usual, to consult my dad. I told him I wanted to buy a new car, something reasonably priced, like a Ford or a Pontiac. My dad looked at me and said, "So you want to be a big shot! Your business is just getting on its feet and you don't have any money. What do you need a new car for? Your ex-husband's a used-car salesman, let him find you something."

No matter how I protested, my father kept insisting that I should buy only what I could afford. "That's great!" I told him finally. "I'll send you all the repair bills." Taking his advice, I bought an old Ford convertible for next to nothing. And most of the time, it did exactly that—nothing! Every time I opened the door, the car broke down. After 20 trips to the repair shop, I'd had enough. I decided to bite the bullet and get another car. A friend in the car business promised to find me a one-year-old Buick convertible for $1500 less than a new car. I was thrilled! I couldn't wait to tell my dad how smart and sensible I was being.

My friend Gene had just driven the car in front of my store when my father called. "Dad," I said excitedly, "I listened to everything you told me and I'm just about to buy a one-year-old Buick convertible. Isn't that great?"

Silence greeted me. "So what's the matter?" my father said, his voice booming through the phone. "You didn't learn your lesson yet? You haven't had enough with used cars? If you buy this car, you're not my daughter!"

I was devastated. I couldn't bear to offend my father, so I had to return the nearly new Buick to the showroom. "Now what should I do?" I asked myself in frustration.

That night, my dad came over for a visit. He sat down beside me, patted me on the back, and said, "Well, Schwundel, you've survived your first year. Your business is doing much better than before. Now you can afford a new car, instead of a used one. So what kind of a car do you *really* want?"

"What I really want is a big, beautiful, brand-new, shiny red Buick convertible," I answered instantly.

"Well if that's what you want, then go buy it! You've worked hard, you can afford it now, and you deserve it! Here's $500 to help you out."

One day, not long after, as I was shopping around for my

new Buick, I happened to see a red Pontiac for about $1800 less. I called my dad to ask his advice again.

"But you don't want a Pontiac, you want a Buick," he said. "Why settle for less than what you really want? If you buy that car, you're not my daughter!"

I couldn't take it anymore! So a week later, I bought a magnificent new red Buick convertible. I climbed into it and drove away from the showroom feeling like a millionaire—not like the scared kid with a few extra bucks in her pocket that I really was. I called my dad right away and invited him over to admire my new wheels.

"It's beautiful!" he beamed. And before I had time to bask in his approval, he quickly added, "My daughter! A Pontiac wasn't good enough for her!"

My dad taught me to work hard, but he also showed me how to take pleasure in my success and to reap the benefits it offered me. While he knew it was important to live within your means, he also felt you had an obligation to treat yourself well and to go for what you really wanted once you had earned the opportunity to improve your lifestyle and circumstances. Work for the sake of work, without the capacity to enjoy the things that money could buy, didn't make sense to my father. I've always felt the same way.

LESSON 6   BELIEVE IN YOURSELF

Only after a long career as a business owner and after watching countless women struggle to find a home for their dreams have I come to realize how fortunate I was in having a father who encouraged my aspirations. My idea to start the first teen shop in the country wasn't just ambitious; some people thought it was crazy. Teens don't have any money to spend, they told me time and time again. But my father never laughed at me or told me I didn't know what I was doing. He knew I was angry about the way teens were treated. And while he may have had his doubts about the whole teen shop idea, that didn't really matter. He may not have understood or shared my dream, but he believed in me and my energy and ability. That's what was important. He knew that if I wanted to make something happen badly enough, I had the drive to pull it off.

My dad was always generous with his advice, but he never made my decisions for me. He constantly tried to bolster my confidence, but he never hesitated to tell me when he thought I was wrong. The message that came through to me in all this was simple, but powerful: Dad believed in me. And because of his encouragement and the interest he took in my ideas, I believed in myself. This belief was really his legacy to me.

Believing in yourself isn't just *important* for you as an entrepreneur, it's absolutely essential. With that belief, you can move mountains if you have to. And if your ideas are big enough—and risky enough—you'll need to. Without that inner sense of strength, you'll crumble at the first big obstacle that comes your way or you'll make it over the first hurdle, only to stumble the next time someone throws a major roadblock in your path.

What does believing in yourself really mean? When you strip everything else away, it means that you know, in your heart and soul, that your idea or product is worthy of the life you're trying to give it. That it's worth fighting for and that you are strong enough and sure enough of the rightness of what you're doing to make it happen, whatever the cost. Yes, you'll make mistakes and do dumb things along the way, but so what? If you really believe in yourself and what you're doing, then you'll be flexible enough to know when to push harder and when to hold back. Sometimes your ego will be center stage and sometimes you'll operate quietly behind the scenes. You'll trust your instincts and learn to listen to your intuition instead of the people around you, who'll often be all too eager to tell you what to do and how to do it.

Believing in your dream isn't just essential, it's also irresistible. It draws to you the people and resources you need to bring your dream to life. Belief in yourself is the foundation for your support system for success, which we'll be talking about throughout this book. As your dream takes shape, it's vital that you find one person you trust and admire—someone who has both wisdom and common sense—and make that person the core of your support system. Be sure the person you choose really believes in you and can nurture your emotional growth and spirit, as well as your business ideas and success. As a woman, I think this is especially important. Our support system should never be just one-dimensional.

Finally, look for someone who will challenge you to be more and do more than even you think you're capable of. It's not enough to have someone say to you, "Hey, you're doing a great job. Keep up the good work!" You need someone who can help you think bigger and stretch yourself in surprising new directions. Someone who'll say, "Now that you've accomplished X, why not expand your horizons and go for Y?"

The person you turn to for this kind of guidance can be a family member, a close friend, or even just an acquaintance you admire. He or she doesn't even have to be in the line of business or industry you want to enter. What's important is that the person you ask to play this role in your life really respects your ability and drive and that he or she is willing to take a stand when it comes to giving you an opinion. If you find more than one person like this, count yourself lucky—and cherish their friendship and counsel.

DOING IT YOUR WAY

My dad was proud of my growing business; he really believed in me and in my sales talent. He felt I had a natural flair for retailing and the drive to succeed. Yet he secretly worried about my future. Although I was good at handling sales, managing my life was another story. My first marriage to Frank had been a disaster, yet my dad still felt I needed a husband to give me emotional support and provide for me and little Dennis. Of course, my dad had been married four times so he should have known better, but he decided to add matchmaking to his repertoire of sales skills.

He singled out a business acquaintance named Alvin as prime husband material. I was 22 at the time and Alvin was in his thirties. He was a successful manufacturer and a lawyer as well. To my father, he seemed to have a good head on his shoulders and to be as solid as the Rock of Gibraltar. In short, he was exactly the kind of man my dad thought could take care of his Schwundelkopf. Alvin was also short and squat, with thick horn-rimmed glasses, a monotone voice, and a perverse sense of humor. Why Dad settled on this frog instead of finding me a prince, I'll never know. Lonely, preoccupied with my business, anxious about raising Dennis on my own, I wasn't exactly the belle of the ball anymore. In fact, I hardly went out. All I did was work, spend time with my son, sleep, and work some more. Dating just wasn't on my to-do list.

Yet my dad persisted. He kept throwing Alvin and me together. Alvin was no Rock Hudson, but he did have a few things going for him. He was smart, very attentive, and seemingly successful. My dad was ill and I was worried sick about him, while he was sick with worry about me. After about 12 months, my desire to ease his mind about my future overcame my better judgment and I married Alvin. We were en route to Hawaii for our honeymoon when I received a phone call telling me to come home; my father had suddenly passed away. We returned to L.A. on the next plane. I was absolutely grief-stricken. My emotional anchor was gone. Suddenly, I was adrift. My cozy world was shattered and empty. I was inconsolable. I couldn't go to work. I didn't even want to leave the house.

After about a month, Alvin insisted that I begin to pull myself together. He suggested that we go away. It was on this trip to Las Vegas that a couple of buyers came over to us one night at dinner and congratulated Alvin. I thought they were talking about our wedding, but it turned out they were referring to the sale of his business. When I asked him why he hadn't told me about something so important, he said he didn't want to burden me when I was so upset. Then he added, "The truth of the matter is, I didn't sell my business; it went bankrupt." I felt betrayed. I thought of my dad and how he had entrusted my future to my second husband in the hopes I'd be taken care of. Given this news, there was only one thing for me to do. "Let's go home," I told Alvin. "I've got to get back to work."

During this difficult time in my life, Alvin offered cold comfort. My marriage to him quickly proved to be worse than my marriage to Frank. Once again, I found myself with another husband to support. In addition to everything my dad meant to me emotionally, he had also handled the contract manufacturing end of my business, which was really beginning to take off. Having been in manufacturing himself, Alvin assured me that he could take this over. Foolishly, I believed him.

Eventually, Alvin went into partnership with his father and began doing well. But as his building business prospered, our personal life soured. The end came when he started asking me to sign real estate contracts. I asked him what they were, but he insisted they were nothing important. Naively, I did as he requested. Then one evening when we were out to dinner, I jokingly said to him, "Alvin, why haven't you brought home anything for me to sign lately?" to which he coolly replied, "In that last contract, you signed away your rights to our community property." When I asked him why he'd been so underhanded, he simply answered in his humorless voice, "I don't trust you." "If you don't trust me, how can you live with me?" I responded. "You're beautiful and you make me laugh," he answered. About a week later, I had some papers drawn up for *him* to sign—divorce papers. Marriage number two had lasted all of 18 months. Max flew out to L.A. to console me. He had become a substitute father, and I needed his support more than ever.

Despite my personal problems, my business was thriving. My Wendy's Teenscene boutiques were a smashing success. The kids loved them and so did I. The decor of each store was designed as a teen fantasy. It was a cross between a disco, a stage set, and a clubhouse. When it came to creating an atmosphere of fun and "funk," I pulled out all the stops. The stores featured high-tech neon tubing, huge movie screens, and colorful jukeboxes that glowed and vibrated with the latest rock hits, drawing kids like a magnet. Each shop was built on levels, and clothes hung from brightly colored pipes. Mint green, adobe pink, and a wild fluorescent yellow were the colors I chose for the short skirts that had become my trademark. There were also scarves, bags, patterned stockings, jewelry, and racks and racks of coordinated outfits. Wendy's Teenscene was a girl's shopping heaven—and haven.

As late afternoon rolled around, girls from 13 to 18 literally swarmed into my stores. Some of the kids would watch movie clips flashing across huge screens as they tried on oversized shirts and scarves. Another bunch of girls spent most of their time trying on makeup. Still others gathered around a counter, drinking Coke and discussing their boyfriends. The energy level was always high, and everyone, including me, had a great time. At the height of my Wendy's Teenscene success, I was barely in my twenties, with bleached blond hair, false eyelashes, and fingernails so long they could tap dance. In true

California style, I always dressed completely in white. My standard outfit was a white leather miniskirt, white blouse, white patterned stockings, and enough jewelry to finance a round-trip ticket to China. Every penny I owned was tied up in my boutiques. In all, I started eight stores, although I never operated more than two at the same time. Teenscene was my home away from home.

My second successful store was presided over by Sal Harris, my male assistant buyer/accountant/confidant. Sal always dressed as if he worked in a bank instead of a boutique. He wore pinstriped suits, vests, and a red carnation. Graying and gorgeous, Sal was one of my store's biggest attractions and he knew it. In his early forties, he looked like he'd be more at home in a Bloomingdale's catalog than behind a counter ringing up sales for a covey of crazy teenagers. Sal was a unique mixture of "dreamboat" sexiness and the hip, with-it dad that every adolescent girl secretly dreams about. A male chauvinist and proud of it, his not-so-secret ambition was to become the mayor of Los Angeles. To fuel his fantasy, he studied acting and public relations in his spare time.

Life was really good for a while. The cash register was always full, I always had a new (or almost new!) car, Dennis and I lived in a nice apartment or rented house. I not only had my own little retailing empire, but the chief buyer for a huge department store encouraged me to create a line for sophisticated teens. It was the first private brand label in the fashion industry. I began making the same arrangement with stores in other cities.

While my operations weren't exactly models of efficient retailing, I was making a lot of money. I paid my bills on time, never bounced checks, and always knew, to the penny, how much I was taking in. However substantial my retail ventures seemed to be, though, my stores were succeeding despite my lack of business training, not because of it.

One day, as I walked into my bank to deposit the day's receipts, Mr. Lloyd, one of the bank managers, beckoned me over to his desk. Since conversations with a banker are generally not about good news, I became a little nervous. "Wendy," he said to me, "I want you to take out a loan." I went into a panic. "Why?" I responded anxiously. "My business is doing well. I don't owe anyone any money. Is anything wrong with my account?" "No, there's nothing wrong," he assured me. "You're the kind of person whose business is going to grow. At some point you'll want to expand, so you're going to need credit. I want you to take out a $10,000 loan and then repay it." To me, this amount of money seemed overwhelming. But I sat down and took out the loan that very afternoon.

The next day, I went back to Mr. Lloyd's office and said, "OK, now I want to pay my loan back!" "No, Wendy, you can't do that," he said patiently. "You have to pay it back over a year. That's the way you establish credit." And that's exactly what happened. Later, when I expanded into contract manufacturing, Mr. Lloyd put me in touch with Bud Blue and Frank Morgan of Federated Bank of Boston, who arranged a $50,000 credit line for me.

In spite of being a successful businesswoman—or perhaps because of it—I yearned desperately for a normal family life. I wanted to fit in, to belong. Being an outsider was lonely. And so I turned for solace to a friend; Clifford Rue, an old high-school beau, reentered my life. Voted most likely to succeed in our class, he always had lots of money, dressed well, and looked after himself. Handsome, dapper, and young, Clifford wooed me as no one had before. You'd think I would have learned my lesson by now, but no. After a whirlwind courtship, we were married in what I later found out was the famous mafia gangster Bugsy Siegel's suite in Las Vegas. This fact alone should have tipped me off about my newest helpmate, but it didn't. I didn't know Bugsy from Bugs Bunny. And I wouldn't have cared anyway. I was crazy about Cliff and deliriously happy for a while.

Prior to our marriage, Clifford had been a heavy gambler. I refused to tie the knot until he started a legitimate business. To satisfy my demand, he opened a night spot called the Club Seville. His partner was a famous Latin dancer, and the club featured Latin music. Gaily decorated in cabana-type stripes and lush tropical colors, Club Seville quickly became a hot spot for the Hollywood crowd and a gathering place for all the "in" movie stars. I finally thought I was on easy street.

After working nonstop during the day, I'd go home, relax for a while, then once or twice a week head over to the club. My kid sister, Myrna, had her own TV show at the time, and loved being an insider at "the" club in town. She and I enjoyed dressing up like movie starlets, and the staff treated us like celebrities. About a year after Cliff and I married, our son, Harlan, was born. I was on cloud nine. At last, all the parts of my life seemed to be in harmony instead of at odds with each other. I had a great little business, a handsome husband, two wonderful children, a nice home, money to burn. What more could I ask for?

It was all too good to be true. One crisp fall day just after school had started, I was in my main store chatting with two girls I knew when we heard a commotion at the front door. Before I even turned around, I knew it was Aunt Bea, one of my mother's sisters. Aunt Bea had been a real beauty in her day, but she was close to 50 and time had taken its toll. She was as wide as Sal was tall—and the two of them couldn't stand each other. Bea was an incurable gossip. She was also the self-appointed watchdog of my San Fernando Valley store. Aunt Bea was working for me because she used to work for my dad and I felt a strong family responsibility to her. To be honest, I often wished she was in Timbuktu instead of at Teenscene!

As soon as I saw Aunt Bea clutching her handbag to her heart, I knew something big was up. Before I could blink, she'd slipped into her favorite Sarah Bernhardt pose. "We're ruined," she wailed. "How could you do this to me? What would your mother, God rest her soul, say if she were here? What would your father say? Better they're not here to see it. Better I should bear this burden alone. What else is an old woman good for, but to suffer? But to suffer is not enough; I should also be embarrassed? Wait, I'm going to faint, I can feel it. It's coming, just like in the movies. Only in the movies, when Rita Hayworth faints and then wakes up, it's all just a dream. She's not married to a schmo, she's married to Cary

Grant. But you, Wendy, you had to do it your way. You had to marry not just one deadbeat, but three!"

I had no idea what she was talking about, but Aunt Bea was milking her moment of stardom for all it was worth. "Husband number one, Frank, was a lazy bum who sat around waiting for his father to keel over. Who brings home the bacon and takes care of the baby? Wendy. Husband number two: Alvin. He goes broke just a few weeks after Wendy marries him and sticks her with the bill for the honeymoon. And now, we come to number three, Clifford. Not enough he spends all his time at the racetrack and dresses like an Arab oil sheik. No! He has to go and get himself arrested."

With this grand statement, she pulled out a crumpled newspaper from her bag and flashed the headline at me: "Clifford Rue Arrested on Murder Rap." I rescued the paper, read the first paragraph, and nearly fainted myself. I couldn't believe it. Clifford, of all people, sitting in jail! I had absolutely no idea what was going on. In my naïveté, I thought that, for love of me, Cliff had given up his old ways. I later found out that he had been mixed up with the mob long before he met me and still was. He'd gambled his nightclub away and was desperate for money. He'd either murdered a local bookie or taken the blame for someone else. To this day, I don't know which.

Suddenly, the phone rang and Sal picked it up. "If it's a reporter," I moaned, "tell him I can't talk, I'm too busy having a coronary."

"It's Bud Blue, the guy at Federated Bank of Boston," Sal replied, "and *he's* having the coronary!" I grabbed the phone and tried to calm Bud down. He had just arranged for my all-but-finally approved line of credit and was having a fit because he'd just seen the six o'clock news. If his boss, Ed Carroway, heard about Cliff's arrest, Bud was afraid he'd lose his job. I was more scared than he was. I'd just purchased a ton of inventory based on my credit line. If Carroway withdrew my credit, I was finished. Of course, all this had to happen in November, just as we were heading into Christmas, the biggest retailing season of the year.

As I was reassuring Bud, the other phone line rang. It was Frank Morgan. He had heard the news and was furious. He insisted that I call Ed Carroway to find out which way the wind was blowing. My hand was shaking as I dialed Ed's number in Boston. Finally, I got through. Ed, a blustery, conservative banker with a thick Irish brogue, couldn't have been sweeter. Jovial and patronizing, he told me not to worry my pretty little head about my credit line. Just take care of the kids and get a good lawyer, he advised. I could see the conversation was going nowhere and ended it as politely as possible. I was so angry, my ears were smoking! I called Frank, assured him that everything was under control, and arranged to meet him at Carroway's office in exactly a week.

It was crisis time. I called a summit meeting of family and friends at my apartment. What a cast of characters! First, there was Max, who flew in from Toronto in response to my SOS call at two in the morning. Then there was Sal, who carefully checked all the closets to be sure there were no reporters around who could ruin his future as a politico. Aunt Bea was there, of course. In keeping with the occasion, she sailed in the door dressed in black crepe. Myrna arrived last, late as usual. In true Hollywood fashion, she was dressed in Greta Garbo shades and a trench coat. She was on her way to Vegas for her first nightclub engagement. There was no way my no-good jailbird of a husband was going to rain on her parade!

I explained my credit situation as calmly as I could and asked for advice. Needless to say, everyone had a strategy for handling Carroway. Aunt Bea suggested that I dress in black, play Scarlett O'Hara, flash pictures of my two kids, and beg for mercy. She pulled out a hat and a black cape she'd just bought at a thrift shop and offered them to me. "Are you kidding?" I told her. "This is 'Wendy Goes to the Bank,' not 'Phantom of the Opera'!" Next came Sal. Subscribing to the "behind every successful woman there's a man" theory, Sal offered to fly to Boston, do all the talking, and salvage my business. He was willing to help me out by providing the image of stability he felt sure Carroway wanted. But he'd do this for me if and only if I promised to shape up, dress like a bank president, and let him do all the talking.

Like Aunt Bea, Myrna suggested that I play the damsel in distress. She advised me to bring my baby Harlan to Carroway's office and play on his fatherly instincts. Myrna then took Harlan on her lap and told him he had to be a big boy and help his mommy. Apparently, Harlan wasn't listening. He started to wail and wet his diaper.

"Baloney!" was Max's response to all this well-meaning advice. "Just be yourself, Wendy!" he bellowed. "Be straight-forward and honest. Let the man know you've got some guts, and you'll be a winner." Suddenly, all the tension I'd felt building up inside me was released. When Max spoke, it was as if I was hearing my father. "Be yourself, Wendele! That's good enough for anyone, the president included!" That's what dad would have said. I thanked everyone for their help, marched to the closet, put on my heart-shaped sunglasses, pulled out a bottle of suntan lotion, and announced, "I'm going to see Carroway myself! But first, I'm flying to Palm Springs to get the best suntan in California!"

A week later, my plane landed in Boston in the middle of a full-scale blizzard. The doors opened and out tumbled a long line of weary business travelers, briefcased and winter-coated. Then it was my turn. Dressed in a full-length hot-pink bunny-fur coat, I floated down the stairway into a huge white stretch limo. After a quick ride, I breezed through the revolving door of the granite-faced Federated Bank of Boston building and caught the elevator to Carroway's executive suite on the 30th floor.

There I met Bud and Frank, the two straight-arrow bank managers who'd approved my credit line. As soon as they heard the clickety clack of my high heels on the polished marble floor, they knew they were in trouble. And when they saw me in person, they knew they were in *big* trouble.

Looking back on it all I can understand their sense of impending doom. My outfit must have seemed absolutely outrageous! Under my pink bunny-fur coat, I wore a chic, up-to-date California white silk mini dress. I looked like anything but the typical female executive—and certainly not like one on the verge of disaster. My high heels were three inches tall and as sharp as lasers. My five pounds of jewelry clanked like a loose car muffler. "Oh my God," moaned Frank. "I knew it. I knew I should have jumped out the window this morning before I caught the 7:02!" Bud just shook his head and said, "Just two more years and I'd have been golfing in Florida!"

I marched into Carroway's office, threw my coat on the floor, and curled myself up in the corner of his couch. For probably the first time in his life, Carroway, a big, blustering Irishman with steel gray hair and steel gray eyes, was at a loss for words. After a few seconds, he found his voice. "Who the hell are you?" he fumed. "And what the hell are you doing in my office? The Pussycat Club is three blocks down the street!"

"Now, now, Ed," I laughed, "is that any way to talk to one of your clients? Hi, I'm Wendy, the owner of Wendy's Teenscene boutiques. What's your problem with my credit line?"

"My problem," fumed Ed, "is that Federated Bank of Boston is one of America's oldest and most conservative banks. We do business with the Fortune 500 and our reputation is as good as gold. Now I sympathize with your situation, my dear," Carroway continued in a smooth, ingratiating voice, "and I know we agreed to open a credit line for you. But how can you manage it all? You have two small babies and a husband in jail. Don't you have enough on your hands without worrying about money?"

"Well, Ed," I quickly replied, "let me set your mind at ease. First of all, we're not talking about my first husband, we're talking about my third. As for the kids and my business, I've been taking care of them on my own for a number of years now. Teenscene is the hottest store in L.A. This murder trial doesn't change a thing."

Suddenly, the skeptical look on his face disappeared. Ed threw back his head and laughed heartily. "Wendy," he said, "I like your style! You remind me of my Aunt Jen, bless her soul.

She raised six kids, worked hard, and lived to be 102 because she drank a pint of Guinness every day! If she could make it, by God, so can you!" With that, he pressed a button on his phone and said, "Ms. Reynolds, a lunch reservation for two, please." He helped me into my coat, we walked out arm in arm, and bumped into Bud and Frank, who had been hanging around outside Carroway's office. "See you later, boys!" Carroway called out as we waltzed into the elevator.

After giving me an earful over lunch about his long-lost aunt, Carroway picked up the phone and spent two hours calling every one of my suppliers, and personally guaranteeing my credit. I know this whole story sounds as if I made it up, but it's absolutely true. If I hadn't been there, I never would have believed it myself. I was all but paralyzed by anxiety when I went to see Ed Carroway. I was angry at having to put on such a bizarre performance but relieved I was able to pull it off. After leaving his office, I went back to my hotel room and had a good long cry.

The next day, I climbed on the plane back to L.A., feeling spent but victorious. Once home, I sent Dennis to Chicago so he wouldn't be taunted by his friends during Clifford's trial. Cliff was set free on bail, and I got him the best criminal lawyer available. Despite my heartbreak and confusion, my determination to justify Ed Carroway's faith in me was so strong that it kept both me and my business from falling apart. Max and Myrna were very supportive throughout this terrible experience. Clifford was sentenced to five years in jail. To this day, I have no idea what actually happened. All I know is he left jail a millionaire.

I've recounted this tale of woe and redemption at such great length because it showed me just how important it is to be yourself in business. Whatever crisis or challenge you face, you'll be presented with two choices: doing it your way or doing it someone else's way. But to my mind, there's really only one choice: doing it your way, whatever that way is. Let me tell you why and how:

KNOW WHAT YOU WANT

Creativity isn't just the product of your own ideas; it's also sparked by what you see and hear when you listen with intent. Whenever I'm facing a tough decision, I always try to remember my dad's views on giving advice. He never told other people what to do; once they decided for themselves what they wanted, he helped them figure out how to get it. Doing it your way doesn't mean ignoring the advice other people give you. It means using that advice to help you decide not *what* you want to achieve but *how* you can reach the goal you've set for yourself.

Many people listen to outside advice for the wrong reason: because they want someone else to tell them what to do or to make a decision for them. In my view, that's a big mistake. Listening is important for three reasons: to gather information and learn something of value, to hear confirmation of what you know is right, or to find out what *won't* work for you so you can figure out what will. Never look for the right answer to a problem or the right decision outside yourself. Look for the echo that resonates with your own heart's desire and intuition.

When my banker, Mr. Lloyd, advised me to take out a $10,000 loan, for example, I was absolutely petrified, but I followed my instincts. At the time, $10,000 seemed like $1 million to me. But I trusted Mr. Lloyd's judgment. And although I knew nothing about credit or how a loan worked, I did know two things: First, I wanted to build my business, and second, it takes money to make money. So when Mr. Lloyd talked, I listened. And what he said made sense to me. Yes, I was afraid. I had nightmares for weeks after I took out my loan. But I went ahead anyway, because I realized that he was telling me what I already knew myself: I wanted to grow.

The most important thing Mr. Lloyd taught me was that the best time to get credit is when you don't need it. You never know what ups and downs the future has in store for you. The sooner you lay the foundation for growth, the better your chances of success. Establishing credit is much more than just a smart business decision; emotionally, it's an affirmation of your intent to build your venture into something bigger and better.

To this day, Mr. Lloyd is one of my heroes. Tall, with a no-nonsense style cloaked in a pinstriped suit, he looked beyond my dangling earrings and miniskirt. He saw me not as a flighty female but as an experienced businessperson with a sound idea and the skills to carry it through. At a time when it was extremely rare for a woman to obtain a loan, Mr. Lloyd was willing to bank on my talent. Now there was a man who understood that the dollar bill knows no sex!

The Carroway crisis offers an example of how listening can help you screen out bad advice and clarify your own feelings and strategy. When I called my family summit meeting after Clifford was arrested, I had already decided what I had to do: convince Ed Carroway to keep my credit line open. What I was looking for were ideas on how to accomplish this goal. My sister Myrna and my aunt Bea suggested I turn on the tears and play on Carroway's sympathy. Sal suggested I make myself invisible and let him talk to Carroway, man to man. None of their schemes felt right or honest to me. When Max finally spoke up, he confirmed what I already knew: Whatever the risk, I had to be myself and tough out the situation. There was no way I could hide behind my tears or let a man do my talking for me. Listening to ideas I felt compelled to reject just strengthened my resolve. It also helped me crystallize my own strategy.

MAKE FRIENDS WITH YOUR ANXIETIES

Fight your anxiety and you'll fuel it. When you find yourself in a business crisis, don't ever let anyone comfort you by telling you it could be worse. Face the fact that you're in a mess and examine every aspect of that mess—and I mean every angle!—no matter how anxious this process makes you. Trying to gloss things over won't solve your problems, it will only make them worse. Fool yourself and you'll end up playing the fool—every time.

Don't turn your back to the wall, turn your face to the wind. You can let your anxieties overcome you by refusing to confront them head on, or you can use them to help you mobilize all your resources and chart a path to success. Face your insecurities as honestly as you can. Let them out instead of trying to hold them in. Let them rise to the surface where you can see them for what they are. Accept the fact that your anxieties are trying to tell you something.

But while you're in this vulnerable state, try not to make any major decisions. Stay out of traffic. Divert yourself until you calm down, feel in control, and can identify the real reason you're feeling anxious. If you go through a laundry list of things you have in the works, usually you'll pinpoint the source of your distress. When you find out what's fueling your apprehension and insecurity, you'll feel your mood lift. You'll be able to think more clearly and calmly and decide on the best course of action. Once you've taken these steps privately, you can find the courage to face the music in public.

DON'T BE AFRAID TO BE AFRAID

I think fear is the number one business killer. People are so afraid to be afraid that they never get beyond their fear. Because they refuse to acknowledge their fears to themselves in private, they can't find the strength to put those fears aside in public. And so fear immobilizes them and they never take the risks they need to take to get where they want to go. Don't let fear stop you! See it for what it is. Fear is no more than a signal that you're about to grow. Growth means sailing into uncharted waters. Growth and fear go together.

Up until the time disaster hit me—and believe me, my husband's murder trial *was* a disaster, emotionally, financially, and personally—my business life had been relatively sheltered. I ran my little boutique, took my rent money directly from the till every Friday, paid all my bills on time, and patted myself on the back for being a smart little businesswoman. My family and friends (except for my dad!) shook their heads over my marriages and "indulged" my business drive while they waited for me to catch or be caught by a real husband who knew how to provide for a wife and kids. My life was more or less under control.

Then the roof caved in. Comfort turned to crisis, and for the first of many times, I was fighting for my business life. Without the credit Carroway had the power to deny me, I stood to lose *everything*. Absolutely everything I had. It was sink or swim—and Ed Carroway was my life jacket. Walking into his office and selling myself was the toughest, scariest thing I had done up until that point in my life. Some time later, Bud and Frank told me that they'd been frantic with worry about their jobs, but that my show of strength had been a real learning experience for them. *Show* was exactly the right word. I hid my fear from Carroway, not from myself. By acknowledging my fear and anxiety, I was able to manage them long enough to allow Ed Carroway to see beyond them.

USE YOUR FEMININITY, BUT PLAY FROM STRENGTH, NOT FROM WEAKNESS

I've always celebrated the fact that I'm a woman. Just about everything I say and do flows from my sense of my own femininity. But I feel that I've used that femininity to radiate strength, not helplessness. When I walked into Ed Carroway's office, I could have taken my aunt's advice. I could have played the damsel in distress and cried and told Carroway about my two kids and my three rotten husbands. But he would have thrown me right out on my ear—and he would have been justified! Instead, I was both openly feminine and crisply businesslike. I used my femininity to demonstrate my sales skills, not to win sympathy for my personal problems.

If you were to ask me to tell you one of the most important

ideas I have been able to convey to members through NAFE, it is this: As a woman, you can compete successfully with a man without making him feel rejected or diminished. How? By treating him as an equal—and by acting as his equal in word and deed. You can do this only by using your femininity as a source of strength. This holds true for both employees and entrepreneurs. Feminine wiles are for the bedroom—and often they don't even work there. Forget about bringing them into the boardroom or to the bargaining table.

BE YOURSELF—BOLDLY

Ed Carroway represented the "big" world of business to me. He was the head of one of the largest banks in the country. I was really just a California kid with a nickel-and-dime business so small he could have put it in his pocket. But I knew who I was and what I wanted. What's more, I was willing to stand up and fight for it. It was my feistiness, above all, that caught Ed Carroway's attention and won his support. Life is too short to pretend you're someone you're not, unless you're in Hollywood getting paid big bucks to do it.

Once you decide to go into business and run your own show, you've made a decision to put yourself on the line. That means *being* yourself all the way. If you aren't totally convinced about your ability to succeed (even in the face of your deepest fears), then you should probably forget about being an entrepreneur—because you aren't one anyway. If you are committed, then turn on the heat full blast. Be yourself 150 percent! Don't hide your light under a bushel! Being yourself means speaking the truth as you see it and letting the chips fall where they may. If you're too ambitious, too enthusiastic, too intense, so what? What have you got to lose?

Don't be afraid to be different in a business setting. Call people by their first names. Treat everyone equally, from secretary to CEO. A little joke and a big smile go a long way in creating a relaxed atmosphere, one that will make it easier for you to achieve your goals. I've been told that my style is unforgettable, not just because of my unconventional business attire, but because of the way I make people feel comfortable and free to express themselves. People I've done business with see my open and direct way of working as refreshing and reliable.

DON'T LET RULES OVERRULE YOU

Don't set out to break the rules you encounter just to be different. There are no guarantees, no matter what you do. So why not make your own rules? You'll keep everyone around you guessing and have a lot more fun! Most corporate people are afraid of being judged negatively if they say the wrong thing at the wrong time. They tend to be noncommittal and concerned about rocking the boat. As an entrepreneur, you don't have to play those games. You have the opportunity to enjoy the freedom to be yourself and do things differently. In fact, it's expected of you. This means saying what you think, admitting your mistakes, doing things according to your own light, and asking for help. In the long run, being true to yourself isn't just emotionally satisfying, it's good business. People will always know where they stand with you. This gives them confidence in their own judgment and in you.

Having sent two husbands to psychiatrists because I felt their personal problems were ruining our marriages, it was time for me to see how I'd contributed, so after Clifford's trial, I started seeing a psychiatrist. Lying on his couch one afternoon, out of the blue, I found myself telling him tearfully, "I'd like to teach women about equality and being financially independent, but who'd send their daughter to a school whose founder has been married three times and involved in a murder trial?" My shrink just laughed gently and said, "Well, Wendy, if anyone can bring money, sex, and equality for women together, it's you!" With his words, my dream overcame my depression, and I said, "You know, some day I will!"

Who would have believed that less than 10 years later, I would do exactly that!

DON'T BUY INTO A SUPPORT SYSTEM FOR FAILURE

My marriage to Alvin, my second husband, was short and anything but sweet. But in his own negative way, he was probably more responsible for my growth than any other man in my life except for my father. My business was thriving. I was scared to death of opening a second Wendy's Teenscene, but Alvin challenged me to do it. And I did.

When I needed merchandise from New York but couldn't get delivery, Alvin brought home an airplane ticket one evening and dared me to fly to the East Coast, hoping, I suppose, that I would either refuse or fall flat on my face. I did neither. Instead, I took the ticket, flew to New York on the red eye, and returned the next day with exactly what I needed. Alvin may have wanted me to fail and even abused me verbally, but his constant challenges pushed me beyond what I thought my limits were. To this day, I'm grateful to him for helping me grow. He offered a support system for failure, but in defiance, I channeled my anger at him into positive, decisive action.

Not every entrepreneur has as emotionally chaotic a personal life as mine was at this point in time. And as you'll see later, things became worse, before they got better! But whatever hand life deals you, if you're an entrepreneur, you'll find a way, just as I did, to turn things around and make them work for you.

DO YOU HAVE WHAT IT TAKES TO BE AN ENTREPRENEUR?

A re you insecure, naive, and a misfit? How about anxious, approval-seeking, and relentless? And don't tell me you're also a demanding perfectionist? Welcome to the club! Let's face it: Being an entrepreneur is no picnic. Sure, once you "make it" and the money and orders start rolling in, you'll be hailed as a "genius," a bold innovator, a pioneer. Getting there is the problem. I know. It took more than seven years until NAFE, my biggest entrepreneurial success, made a dime—and three more years before it became profitable and I was able to take more than cab fare and my rent out of the business. During those lean years, believe me, no one was calling me a genius. Neurotic, obsessed, crazy, and driven are a few of the nicer labels that spring to mind. I've also been referred to as a kvetch, a nut, and of course, that old standby, a royal pain in the ass.

There's really no way around this simple truth: Entrepreneurs think differently, see things differently, and act differently than most other people do. If you're going to follow your entrepreneurial instincts, then you've got to learn to live with the way other people will view you. Some of the very traits you'll need to succeed—dissatisfaction, perfectionism, relentlessness, to name a few—aren't going to win you any popularity contests. Of course, you know all this already. And if these personality traits drive your friends and family crazy, imagine what it's like having to live with yourself 24 hours a day. The anxiety! The insecurity! The desperate search for approval!

Entrepreneurs are movers and shakers. They help make the world go 'round by triggering change—and that can be pretty threatening to most people. The irony of all this is that our very dissatisfaction and nonconformity are actually the main sources of our power and creativity. No wonder we entrepreneurs so often feel like lonely misfits out of step with the rest of the world. We are!

Entrepreneurs stake their claim to success by energizing ideas, pushing ahead relentlessly, and motivating people around them to see things differently and move in new directions. In my experience, most entrepreneurs capture the world's attention and accomplish their goals in one of two ways: as visionaries or as business owners. A handful of entrepreneurs—maybe 5 percent—are visionaries. These are the true mavericks of business, the dreamers who also possess the drive to create something entirely new, a "first." They conceive unique ventures, build new industries, invent new products, discover new frontiers, and lead new social movements. By any measure, visionary entrepreneurs are a rare breed. In the best of all possible worlds, they would be cherished and encouraged. But there's a little problem: Most people simply can't grasp what the visionary is aiming at and find her personality hard to deal with. My teen boutiques and NAFE were both "firsts," and as a maverick myself, I encountered my share of resistance to these ventures.

Creative business owners, on the other hand, demonstrate their entrepreneurial drive in a different way. They fulfill their dreams by expressing their flair and originality within the framework of a traditional business they've bought, launched, or built. They enrich or improve upon the way a business is normally operated or a product or service already out in the world is produced and marketed. In short, they build better widgets. Entrepreneurs who function in this way aren't really bucking the system or going beyond it, they're working within it, although they may push its limits pretty aggressively. Intrapreneurs operate in somewhat the same mode: They express the entrepreneurial aspect of their personalities by bringing new insights and ideas to their companies—and stretching the boundaries of the corporate world.

My dad was a creative business owner. As I described in Chap. 2, he was tremendously innovative in the way he marketed his merchandise and ambitious to the point of owning several hosiery stores. But he never really advanced beyond the mentality of a storekeeper. Even getting him to think about helping me move into the manufacturing end of my teen business was really a major step for him and one he never felt totally comfortable with. Expanding an existing enterprise is often the chief ambition of a business owner. I once knew a women's shop owner, for example, who came up with the idea of offering "For Men Only" nights once a month. She had a list of all her customers' sizes and color preferences, and she invited the men in their lives to spend an evening in her store shopping for just the right gift. This was a highly successful and very entrepreneurial promotion.

The advice and ideas in this book are of value to anyone from the visionary entrepreneur to the intrapreneur. Each brand of entrepreneur has her own dreams and goals, but as comrades-in-commerce, entrepreneurs share many of the same personality traits. Do you share them, too? Are you an entrepreneur in your own mind and heart? Do you have the will, the determination, the chutzpah to say yes to your dream? To help you decide, I've developed a checklist for you—the kind our readers found helpful in NAFE's magazine, *Executive Female*. You can work through the list by yourself at your convenience. There's no need to feel any pressure, so try to be as honest as you can. Which of these qualities do you identify with? Remember, some of them aren't exactly flattering. They're also not offered in any order of importance.

As an entrepreneur, you'll need to be:

_____ a doer	_____ committed
_____ a survivor	_____ enthusiastic/inspiring

_____ naive	_____ honest
_____ insecure/anxious	_____ optimistic
_____ a visionary	_____ instinctive
_____ a nonconformist/misfit	_____ spontaneous
_____ restless/difficult	_____ approval-seeking
_____ relentless	_____ a leader
_____ a perfectionist	_____ courageous

Now that I've made you nervous, hopeful, and perhaps even a little relieved, let's explore some of these characteristics more closely:

A Doer. Nothing ever just happens, not in this world, anyway. No one places your dream in front of you, whole and in perfect working order. Making that dream come true takes hard work, incredible persistence—often in the face of overwhelming odds—and sometimes even heartbreak. That's why entrepreneurs are doers and drivers. They are willing to step up to the plate and strike out over and over until they finally hit that home run. They also have a sense of urgency about their mission. Once they've committed to a course of action, entrepreneurs rarely stop to think about whether it's worth it or not. They don't stop to evaluate it from all sides, and they don't exactly know what the results are going to be; all they really know is that something is going to happen. Launching a new venture is a little like going to a surprise party. It creates a sense of excitement, anticipation, and intellectual curiosity.

But whatever their mission and however they express their drive, one thing is clear: Entrepreneurs may march to the beat of a different drummer, but to be successful, they can't march alone. They need help from the planners and managers of the world. These are the talented employees and corporate decision makers who understand and value the entrepreneur's dream. They can recognize a good idea, appreciate its worth, and use their experience and skills to help bring it to life. The wise entrepreneur values and nurtures these allies. Without their commitment, she can't bring her dream to fruition (see Chap. 5 on support systems for success).

A Survivor.   Talk to any entrepreneur for about five minutes and you may not learn much about her, but you'll know one thing for sure: You've met a survivor. No entrepreneur I've ever known has been unscarred or lived without fear. Our dreams have been knocked around and our egos bruised and battered. But once a survivor, always a survivor. And more often than not, that's what being an entrepreneur is about: surviving. Staying in the game. Refusing to give up, give out, or give in.

The word *failure* just isn't in the entrepreneur's vocabulary. She won't take no for an answer, because she doesn't know how to. She keeps moving. Every rejection becomes an opportunity, because she simply can't *not* put her idea out into the world. Strangely, she even finds comfort in the fact that she's had problems before because she knows she was able to surmount them. If she's done it before, she figures she can do it again. And again, if she has to!

Many people find this kind of drive very disturbing. The entrepreneur's almost compulsive need to keep doing something, anything, even in the face of defeat, just doesn't make sense to those around her.

Naive.   One of an entrepreneur's secret weapons is naïveté. In one of his less charitable moments, a friend of mine described my unconventional business style this way: "Wendy, you're the only person I know who can be standing in quicksand up to your ass and not even know it!" I think it's safe to say that most people view naïveté as a negative quality and a liability in business. They see someone who's naive as lacking in experience or judgment, as unworldly and perhaps even ignorant.

But to me, the word *naive* summons up a completely different image: a naturalness, freshness, and inquisitiveness that's totally free from the kind of posturing, cover-your-butt attitude and one-upmanship that you find so often in the business world. Frankly, if they didn't have an extra large dose of naïveté, most innovators wouldn't have the guts to do the things they have to in order to succeed. They'd simply be too scared, or embarrassed, or repressed, or competitive. In short, they'd be more concerned with their image than with results.

Naïveté is a rare and precious asset. It allows you to be yourself, take a fresh look at how things are done, admit your mistakes, and ask the questions you need to have answered in a way that conveys your curiosity and drive to master the task at hand. You approach everything with a can-do, energetic attitude that even the most jaded businesspeople find immensely appealing and winsome. When you're naive, you don't know enough to be impressed with power brokers, flashy projections, or sticky problems. And if you've got it, flaunt it! Let me show you what I mean.

Once I decided, after much floundering around, to create NAFE, an association for women, one of our more conservative board members said to me as tactfully as he could, "Wendy, you really don't know anything about what an association is or does. Why don't you talk to someone who runs one?" I didn't really see the point of doing this, but just to please him, I agreed. I ended up calling Jim Hayden, president of the American Management Association, a powerful and prestigious business group. By some quirk of fate, Jim answered the phone himself and for some unknown reason, he agreed to meet with me at my recruiting office.

When Jim walked in at precisely 4 P.M., he was every inch the high-level corporate dynamo with places to go and things to do. He was about 6 ft 2 in tall, with steel gray hair and sharp, twinkling blue eyes. I proceeded to grill him about what the AMA did, what his function was, and how many members he had. With each answer, I grew more and more excited. "You know, Mr. Hayden," I said, "you're a very experienced executive and my association, NAFE, is all about equality. So I'd like you to consider becoming our first president!"

Ever the perfect gentleman, Jim thanked me for the kind offer, looked at his watch, and said, "I'm very flattered, but at present, my commitments are overwhelming. As a matter of fact, in about 15 minutes I have to catch my private jet for our annual conference. It's been a pleasure meeting you, Ms. Rue!" Though I never persuaded him to join NAFE, Jim gave me some very valuable advice and contacts. We also became good friends. One of the reasons Jim and I hit it off so well was that I didn't know enough about him to be impressed or intimidated. I just naturally expected him to want to help me and he responded in kind. This attitude has always worked wonders for me.

INSECURE/ANXIOUS. You have to accept a high degree of uncertainty and insecurity to pursue the path of an entrepreneur. When people talk about someone being insecure, they generally describe the person as being indecisive, frightened, or withdrawn. But in an entrepreneur, insecurity means something different. An entrepreneur is insecure because she's always treading new waters. Anyone doing this is bound to feel out of her depth, and you have to give an entrepreneur credit for finding the courage to stay afloat. Her only resources are her experience and her instincts; to succeed, she has to learn to trust them.

Insecurity means being on the edge, at the frontier, in the vanguard. So by definition, it's not a comfortable place to be. As an entrepreneur, you're an explorer, an innovator. You're entering uncharted territory; what lies behind you is of no help to you. You have to find the strength to push forward and figure things out as you go. There is no textbook that says, "This is the way you do it." And there's no one who can tell you, "These are the five steps you should take to make your idea work."

Imagine landing in an unfamiliar country unexpectedly, not knowing the language or the customs. That's the best way to describe the kind of insecurity I'm talking about. In the business world, as an entrepreneur, a dreamer, and perhaps even a visionary, you have to accept the fact that you're in a foreign country. No one really understands what you're doing until a product or service takes shape and attaches itself to your dream. Then you have something people can see and touch and try out for themselves. But as insecure as you may be inside, you can never reveal your self-doubt to the outside world. You always have to carry yourself in a self-assured fashion, because you're so vulnerable.

By the way, the insecurity you feel as an entrepreneur never goes away, no matter how seasoned and successful you are. For example, in writing this book, I've entered a whole new world once again. Even though people have told me, "Wendy, you have a history of doing anything you set your mind to, no matter how frightened you are," I still feel anxious. I'm putting myself on paper for all the world to see. This isn't like making phone calls, giving speeches, or running a meeting. The written word is permanent. It has a life of its own. Is my message important? Will I be of help to my readers? Will I be able to reach them and give them what they need? All these questions make me very nervous.

How do you deal with this insecurity? You accept it. But the best advice I can give you is to cultivate your support system—people who believe in you—and rely on their encouragement (see Chap. 5). In the early days of NAFE, for example, I had two good friends, Stanley Haltman and Dr. Alan Rosenberg, along with my family and a few other believers. They used to kid me out of my fears and remind me of all the other times I said I was frightened and of the things I had accomplished in spite of my anxieties.

A VISIONARY. To me, a visionary isn't someone who's flaky or impractical. Yes, she may have her head in the clouds, but if she's an entrepreneur, she also has her feet on the ground and her hand in her pocketbook. She understands that we live in an economic world and that her dream will be accepted and brought to life if and only if people are willing to pay for it. To her, money says, "I believe in you." A visionary entrepreneur isn't someone with four horns or mystical gifts no one else can understand or relate to, but she does see an extra dimension.

I've known many business owners who were highly successful, but lacked vision. I can still remember an afternoon I spent with Howard, the president of a major textile firm. Elegant and successful, he had built a giant business. Soon after I moved to New York, Howard invited me to lunch. Afterwards, he took me to the very top of the Empire State Building to his fancy suite of offices, where he pointed out the tiny cars and buses below. Then he looked at me and said, "Wendy, we're all just a bunch of fleas on the face of the earth." What a depressing thought! Even though I was flat broke and jobless at the time, I decided I couldn't—and wouldn't—think the way Howard did. I didn't want to see myself—or anyone else, for that matter—as one of those little fleas, helpless and meaningless. I wanted to be something more. I wanted to make a real contribution.

A visionary entrepreneur could never look at life the way Howard did. Where most people see a picture of a street with a car parked in front of a house, somehow, this rarest of entrepreneurs sees something more. She sees the trees shading the street and children playing by the house. While others see only the bare bones of the scene, she breathes life into it by dreaming of what it might become. In her best moments she possesses a kind of magic. She has the power to say, "Yes I can!" and make the world believe it right along with her.

A Nonconformist/Misfit.   An entrepreneur doesn't practice being different; it's just her nature. She doesn't wake up every morning and say to herself, "Okay, if I'm different, then I'm an entrepreneur. So how can I be different today?" She just goes about her business and finds that she's out of step. She's a misfit. I never started out trying to set myself apart. Just the opposite! I was always looking for a place where I could be accepted and still be myself.

For example, people have always viewed the way I dress as a kind of statement, a way of standing out. I didn't see it that way at all. I didn't even think about my appearance. Wearing California white had been a trademark for me ever since I was a teenager. It made me feel comfortable. If I was uncomfortable, I couldn't function. So the way I dressed was necessary for me. The fact that it attracted attention when people first met me didn't really matter, because I could have worn black and still attracted a lot of attention. What *did* matter was accomplishing my goal, whatever it was.

What's the price you pay for being a nonconformist? Without a doubt, you'll find that many people feel threatened by your unconventional style. For example, I can remember a meeting I once had with a life insurance company. I walked into the company offices and found myself, as always, the only woman. All the men at the meeting had their "business as usual" yellow pads in front of them. As we discussed an upcoming promotion, I noticed that there was very little give-and-take and not a single helpful idea—just an awful lot of writing, which really bothered me.

At the end of the meeting, I announced that I wanted to gather up all the yellow pads. They were peppered with plenty of doodles, but absolutely nothing of any value. The men marched out of the meeting furious and indignant. To me, the whole session had been a complete waste of time, although it helped me indirectly. I called the vice president of production and told him I was the head of my company and only wanted to work with top executives like himself, not with junior employees who had no ideas. From then on, that's exactly what we did and the program ran smoothly. Being unconventional may not always win you fans, but it usually gets results!

RESTLESS/DIFFICULT.   Dissatisfied. Neurotic. Impossible to please. Doesn't know how to relax. Easily agitated. High-strung. These are some of the ways most people describe this demanding aspect of entrepreneurship. And it's all true. There's no comfort zone for an entrepreneur. As soon as you get comfortable, you become restless. You're not satisfied with where you are and what you've done. Once you've accomplished a goal, whatever it is, you have to find something new to tackle. You may not know what or why. You just know that you have to keep going, until something inside of you clicks and a little voice says, "Hey, this is it. Pursue it!"

Once I closed my teen shops in L.A., I moved to New York. After years of bouncing around, I started an executive recruiting business, which became very successful. But as soon as I entered the comfort zone, I became very restless. I wanted to move on. My recruiting business wasn't a dream, it was a necessity. It was a stopgap. I was doing well financially, paying my bills, and sending my five-year-old son to private school. But I was doing the same thing, day in and day out. I'd built a great business, but all it could do was go up or down, it couldn't change. It couldn't become anything different. This was very confining. I knew there was something more I was meant to do. No one around me could understand my problem and I really couldn't explain it to them. Everyone just thought I was being difficult.

The restlessness you experience as an entrepreneur doesn't just make *you* antsy; it can drive the people around you nuts! But there's an upside to all this angst. When you're restless, you're also in a state of anticipation. You're highly sensitive and exceptionally intuitive. You have your antennae up. You can use your restlessness to help you clarify the next move you should make. The best way to do this is to make some changes in your life. Start by dumping your routine; don't be so predictable. Do things you don't want to do or have been afraid to try. Venture out to places you haven't been before. Call people you've heard about or wanted to learn more about, but haven't had a chance to meet. Do whatever you can to shake things up. In short, don't fight your restlessness and dissatisfaction, use them!

RELENTLESS. When an entrepreneur commits to a course of action, she is absolutely driven to follow the path she's set for herself. There's something almost manic about her single-minded devotion to her goal, and once again, it often mystifies and annoys the people around her. Just when they think she's ready to give up, she finds a whole new angle! I started NAFE in my recruiting office in 1972. It was 1979 before we were able to pay our bills and show any kind of profit. I had to give up the beautiful office I'd worked so hard for and run NAFE out of my apartment. During its start-up, I was broke most of the time and constantly on the edge of financial disaster.

I can't tell you how many times people said to me, "Wendy, why don't you quit? Go back to the recruiting business; you were making a good living there. Nobody even understands what you're talking about. You're just knocking your head against the wall." There were any number of negative views about NAFE as it struggled to stay alive. But I knew NAFE was the thing I'd been working toward and the answer to my life-long dream of equality. What people said upset me, and some-times I even thought about taking their advice. But only for about half a second, because I also knew that somehow, some way, I was going to figure out how to get NAFE off the ground. People kept asking, "*How* do you know?" My only answer was, "My gut tells me I can do it." People got very tired of hearing about my gut, but there was no way they could stop me.

A PERFECTIONIST.   The entrepreneur is a perfectionist, which is often very frustrating to people. She's determined that everything that happens must be absolutely perfect, that it sat-isfy the vision she has in her mind. She will not settle for any-thing less. Realistic expectations aren't in her vocabulary. What does perfectionism mean? To the entrepreneur, it means that, in her mind's eye, the product or service she's created cannot possibly be any better. Sometimes this requires throw-ing a whole program off schedule and going back to the draw-ing board while she finds exactly the right spot to put some-thing she visualizes as being extraordinarily vital to the mix. Responding to these kinds of demands and meeting the stan-dards an entrepreneur sets can be a real challenge for the peo-ple she works with. That's why it's so important that she share her vision and keep her supporters and staff excited about it.

COMMITTED.   Being committed is like having good credit. You make a promise to yourself and to others involved with your venture that you're going to do something—and come hell or high water, you are obligated to make it happen. When you are committed to something, it means you have a deep, unshakable knowledge about its value and rightness. You don't just believe, you *know*. It is this commitment that fuels the relentless pursuit of your dream beyond the boundaries of logic and circumstance.

ENTHUSIASTIC/INSPIRING.   When I think of enthusiasm, I think of a great performer, someone who makes you want to sing and dance right along with them. Enthusiasm is the greatest motivator going and an absolute must for a successful entrepreneur. Have you ever heard one of those inspiring "yes you can!" speakers and found yourself saying, "Boy, I feel great! Now I know I can make that dream of mine come true!" That's the transforming power of enthusiasm: It enlarges and energizes. What inspires someone to want to become part of *your* dream? The enthusiasm you project.

A very successful textile executive I met during my recruiting days comes to mind here. Joe's ability to show enthusiasm was his greatest talent. It gave him a magnetism that drew in everyone around him; his team couldn't do enough for him. One day, a junior-level manager called me to tell me that Joe had just had to fire him. I expected him to be angry, but instead he was full of concern for Joe. He felt absolutely terrible that budget cuts had put Joe in the position of having to fire him when his department really needed his help. Instead of feeling bitter, he left saying, "If there's ever anything I can do for you, Joe, please don't hesitate to call." This is a true story and it shows just how powerful enthusiasm can be.

Enthusiasm makes people feel more alive. It makes them want to be part of something bigger than themselves and step off their own paths for a while. An enthusiastic person who's also an entrepreneur knows what she wants and has the courage to make decisions. This makes other people feel very safe and comfortable. They also feel directed instead of lost.

Another important aspect of enthusiasm is keeping employees and supporters motivated. Often, this means being extra careful not to put other people's ideas down. If you have to, put someone on hold for a while, but never knock people when they come to you with ideas you might not think are right. They're just showing you that they want to help and be a part of things. Don't ever say, "Oh, that will never work!" As any entrepreneur knows all too well, this kind of response really discourages openness and creativity.

HONEST. Honesty is the backbone of success for an entrepreneur. Especially when you're just starting out, your integrity is your most precious asset. Often, it's your *only* asset—that was certainly my situation when I first started NAFE. The value of your ability to be honest, both with yourself and the people you work with, can't be measured. All you really have going for you are your word, your good intentions, and your ability to deliver. If you misrepresent yourself or what you have to offer, you can quickly find yourself in hot water. The old saying "Honesty is the best policy" is doubly true for an entrepreneur—even if being honest means saying, "I'm sorry, I've made a mistake."

In NAFE's early days, after I'd managed to get the support of four corporate sponsors for our first mailing, I found out that I had given them some completely wrong information. I'd been told that a list of working women existed and could be purchased. I was misinformed on both counts. There was no list of working women and any other lists that were available could only be rented. What a disaster! After finding this out, I immediately called each of my sponsors, told them my mistake, and offered to refund their money. That honesty paid off a hundred times over. If I hadn't told the truth, NAFE might never have come into being. Why? Because these companies realized that they could trust me to operate ethically. I wasn't just out to make a buck. So my sponsors stuck with me during our rocky start-up.

Another time, I found myself in a tremendously embarrassing position. My brother Max invited me to go on a short cruise around Cape Cod with his family. I loved being with Max and we had a great time—until the cruise ended. As we landed at the dock, Max handed a personal check for several thousand dollars to the captain and told him boastfully, "You'll have no problem cashing this. My sister will take care of it. She's very well connected with American Express." I cringed. Little did Max know that my credit card was overextended. All during the trip, I had been bragging about landing American Express as NAFE's first client. But despite this big success, NAFE was still broke and to pay our bills, I'd pushed my credit card to the limit. Of course, I was too embarrassed to admit this to Max.

I took the captain to the nearest bank on Martha's Vineyard, which had all of two tellers. My only chance was to call John Bennet, my contact at Amex. I got him on the phone and told him my problem. In a very critical tone, he agreed to guarantee the check but asked to see me in his office as soon as I returned. Sighing with relief, I sent the captain on his way, cash in hand.

A very chastened Wendy Rue showed up at John's office the next morning. "Wendy," he said sternly, "you're traveling around the country, representing Amex. You have to have a valid American Express card!" I replied, "I know that, John. But quite frankly, one of the major reasons I'm behind in my payments is that your billing department has made me wait over 60 days for a payment that's due NAFE." To my immense relief, John began to laugh. "Wendy, you're something else!" he said. Then he called someone at payroll and said, "I want a check for NAFE immediately and all future NAFE bills to be handled in 30 days." There's no doubt about it: Honesty pays!

OPTIMISTIC.   A successful entrepreneur always lives on the sunny side of the street. She has to convey an upbeat, confident, can-do attitude, no matter how big the obstacles and problems she faces. I learned from the time I was very young that optimism is a must for an entrepreneur. As my dad taught me, from the moment you set foot in your place of business until you walk out the door, you have to have a smile on your face.

I know one entrepreneur who was going through a tough divorce. She came into work one day, but was feeling so low that she invented an excuse for herself and left her office. Why? As she put it, "I didn't want my staff to see me in such bad shape. I knew they'd be worried, not just about me, but about my business and their jobs." In my view, she made exactly the right decision. If she couldn't appear confident to her staff, the best thing for her to do was to disappear until she could pull herself together.

When someone comes to you with a problem, no matter how big, you have to say, "Hey, don't get all upset over this;

we'll work it out!" Keeping your staff buoyed up and excited on a daily basis is the best way to get the job done, whatever it is. And always share good news. If a big deal comes through, throw a big party. Celebrate! Give out bonuses. Show people you appreciate them.

Instinctive.   When we were running a NAFE convention in 1984, enrollments weren't coming in as quickly as I expected them to. One day, I walked into the office and announced at an editorial meeting that we were going to have to put out an extra issue of NAFE's magazine. The entire staff was up in arms. This meant interrupting their schedule and taking on an enormous, almost impossible, task. Everyone tried their damnedest to talk me out of it, but there was no way they could do it. I knew I was right. I told them, "My gut tells me this is what we have to do. The last issue of the magazine went out too early. We need something to reach members closer to the convention date."

Once again, my staff tried every argument they could think of: Instincts aren't always right. I should give it more time. People always wait till the last minute to register. And so on. "No," I responded. "People need to see something in front of them closer to the meeting date." Of course, being the boss, I got my way, although everyone was furious with me for weeks. But I was right. The magazine was produced, it hit our members' homes three weeks before the convention date, and the enrollments came flying in. It turned out to be the biggest women's convention the New York Hilton ever hosted. We had 1784 NAFE members there—and almost 200 of them were men! It was the most exciting moment of my career. But without that extra magazine, we wouldn't have come anywhere near the attendance we achieved.

Gut, instinct, and intuition are three words that will appear throughout this book, and for good reason. I think that one of the hardest things for women to do is to have faith in their instincts. Women are still questioned more than men about everything. They're expected to have concrete answers—solutions that are rational and understandable in the business sense. Men, on the other hand, aren't usually grilled about how or why they've made a decision. They simply assume a position of authority. Men may follow their gut, but they don't talk about it. "Woman's intuition" gets plenty of press, but whoever heard of a "man's intuition"?

SPONTANEOUS. The entrepreneur is always ready for something new. She sees or hears something she likes, and (eureka!) she knows she's found it. All of a sudden the timing is right and everything clicks. It feels good. There's no anxiety involved. The decision to go forward is made, just like that! To be spontaneous means to be free, unhampered by a preconceived plan, and open to new experiences. I've always walked into meetings with an open mind, prepared to listen and learn, and ready to run with any good ideas that surfaced. This ability to operate flexibly and "in the moment" conveys a bold, fresh, innovative attitude that people find very appealing. It helps you radiate confidence, creativity, and a sense of enjoyment that will draw people to you.

APPROVAL-SEEKING. Outwardly, the entrepreneur is a nonconformist who conveys the message, "I don't give a damn what the world thinks." In secret, however, she's very sensitive and yearns for approval. The entrepreneur is always seeking recognition and acceptance. Success is approval. So the entrepreneur is driven to achieve success, not as an end but as a means. The only way to know if a venture is worthy of respect and of value to people is by its acceptance in the marketplace. Entrepreneurs also crave another kind of approval: They want to win the admiration of their peers and the people who work with them. They want others to accept and share their perfectionism.

A LEADER. What makes a leader? What makes other people want to help an entrepreneur realize her dream? It starts with enthusiasm; people are entranced and motivated by passionate belief and action. Then, by virtue of her enthusiasm, an entrepreneur becomes a leader. She makes people want to be around her and help her dream take wing. She knows what she wants even though she may not know exactly how to get there. This certainty and drive toward a goal is very appealing. It's the responsibility of a leader to convey energy and forward motion—to project an upbeat attitude all the time. So no matter what problems beset you, as an entrepreneur you have to appear confident and in control. That's what people expect of leaders—and you have to deliver.

COURAGEOUS.   To survive the ups and downs you'll face takes real courage. You have to be a fighter. Time and again, you'll feel tempted to give up, to chuck your whole venture. "What am I doing?" you'll ask yourself. What keeps you going when you feel this way? Mostly, a sense of self-pride. *Failure* is a word that doesn't exist in the entrepreneur's dictionary. But being courageous doesn't mean that you're completely fearless or that you're not hurt by rejection and setbacks. It means that you don't let your fear or rejection or problems stop you. You push through them, past them, around them, under them, over them.

I learned about courage when I had to confront Ed Carroway, the Boston banker, and convince him to keep my credit line open so I could salvage my manufacturing business. I was scared stiff when I went to see him. Afterwards I went back to my hotel room and cried like a little girl. But this experience taught me two important lessons: the importance of putting up a brave front and the tremendous respect that people have for courage. This was the beginning of a determination to be myself, regardless of the loneliness and criticism I would have to face. It was then I knew I was a winner.

As this long list of qualities suggest, being an entrepreneur isn't the easiest calling in the world. It takes tremendous drive and energy. And then, of course, there's that all-important gift of the gods: a sense of humor. Believe me, there's no way I could have lived to offer you this advice without one. If I could, I'd emblazon the words, "And don't forget to laugh!" at the top of every page in this book.

Now that I've taken you this far, it's time to stop and take stock. To be honest, despite all its demands, there's a lot of mystique associated with entrepreneurship. Entrepreneurs are seen by the business world as God's chosen people. Crazy, but chosen. And as we all know, people often aspire to things that aren't really right for them. Maybe you're an entrepreneur. And maybe you're not. If you're not, so what? Get busy and dream another dream! If you are, then go for it! You'll have the chance to reap some wonderful rewards. When your dream takes flight, there's nothing like it!

BUILDING A SUPPORT SYSTEM FOR SUCCESS

As an entrepreneur, you are a bundle of contradictions. On the one hand, you're a lone wolf, an outsider, someone who doesn't just march to the beat of a different drummer but dances to it! On the other, you crave acceptance, approval, and recognition. You need the support of other people to make your dream a reality and their approval to feel that your dream is worth struggling for. No one can make it alone. You need help—and lots of it. You also need encouragement—and lots of it. In short, you need a support system for success. But finding one isn't always easy. Here's what I mean.

One day I received a call from Beth Hanson, a student at Cincinnati University. She told me excitedly that she was a NAFE member and wanted to start NAFE networks on campuses all across the country. I encouraged her enthusiasm and offered to help by sending her magazines and creating a special $19.00 membership fee for college students. Beth was thrilled! I hung up the phone bemused at her ambitious plan. To be honest, I never expected to hear from her again. But I did. About a month later I found myself on a conference call with Beth and the dean of students at Cincinnati U. Beth proudly announced that she had recruited 100 NAFE members, and her dean invited me to make a presentation to them. Needless to say, I was overwhelmed. Not only had I never attended college, I had never been on a campus in my life. I was so excited, I even ordered a suit with a skirt for the occasion. White, of course!

I arrived at the university in my blue jeans and spent the night in a sorority house, feeling like a student myself and chatting till 4 A.M. with a bright and lively crew of young women. My first stop the next morning was a woman's business seminar. I couldn't have been more eager to see what happened in a college classroom and to hear the advice offered to the sharp, energetic young women who'd spent most of the night before sharing their hopes and dreams with me. It was nearing June and so Professor Hingeldorfer (or whatever his name was!) was lecturing on a subject close to my heart: "Planning Your Future." I fully expected him to wax eloquent on the wonderful opportunities open to his talented female students. Was I in for a surprise!

The good professor's 40 minutes of hot air all boiled down to one incredibly depressing message: "Don't get your hopes up. Don't shoot too high. Don't expect too much." I couldn't believe my ears! The more I listened, the angrier I became. Finally, I stood up and said, "Am I hearing you correctly, Professor? Are you preparing these women for failure? Are you preparing them for rejection? I didn't think that's what college was all about! You should be showing them how to succeed and compete on an equal basis." With that, I left my seat and walked out of the classroom. The students applauded and proceeded to follow me from class to class all day. I felt like the Pied Piper!

Why was I so angry? After thinking about it, it suddenly dawned on me that all my life I'd been battling the kind of support system for failure that I heard described that morning. And of all places, to find it at a college, where young people should have been schooled for success! The whole idea made me absolutely furious! I realized then as never before that it takes a lot of courage to be successful—to buck the system and swim against the tide. Often, it means leaving friends behind and giving up ways of working and living that are secure and familiar. Success demands change. And change is very hard to embrace. It's a lot easier to stay comfortable and not rock the boat. So without consciously realizing it, people are more prone to fall into the trap of a support system for failure than they are to seek out a support system for success. But if there's one message I want you to take away from this book, it's this: *Reject support systems for failure—whatever form they may take in your life—and build yourself a support system for success.* Here's why:

A support system for failure holds you back. It encompasses all those people in your life who are afraid of taking risks and want you to be afraid too. When you complain about how hard things are, these are the people who seem to sympathize with you, but are really undercutting you and fueling your negative energy. They're dissatisfied but unable to find the strength to risk anything major to change their situation. Since misery loves company, they want to recruit you as a member of their club. So they try to make you feel contented with doing less, having less, and being less than you have the potential to be. They want you to stay in your comfort zone where things may be a little dull, but where they're safe and predictable.

A support system for failure thrives on excuses, obstacles, and labels. Excuses like women don't get a fair shake or they can't compete because they don't have the high-powered contacts that men do. Obstacles like lack of money or lack of an MBA or lack of market research. Labels like you're too unconventional (or too corporate), too inexperienced (or too demanding), too old (or too young). A support system for failure has only one reason for being: to legitimize its members' lack of success by adopting a safety-in-numbers approach. "You can't beat us, so why not join us?" That's their motto. That's why they want to recruit you. To do that, they're prepared to constrain and diminish you so that you won't overreach yourself—or them.

Building a support system for success takes work, but a support system for failure is easy to find—especially for women. When Dennis was a baby, for example, and I began building my retailing business, people would constantly try to make me feel embarrassed about my ambition. They would say, "What do you want to expand for? Your first store is making enough money, why do you need another one? You're married. You have a child. Why aren't you satisfied? What more do you want?" Fueling guilt and negative energy are two of the major ways in which support systems for failure try to undermine confidence. As women, even today, we're very vulnerable to people who try to assault our business success by questioning our commitment to family. This rarely happens to men.

How do you avoid this trap and create a support system for success? Who should belong to it? What can you ask of its members? What will they want from you in return? In a nutshell, a support system for success is an informal, loosely connected web of people who are willing to become emotional—and sometimes financial—stakeholders in your success. The members of this special team are believers and generally successful in their own right. They are willing to invest their time and energy in you—and share their experience and ideas with you—because they believe you have what it takes to deliver on your dream. They won't always tell you what you want to hear or approve of everything you do, but they *will* encourage and uplift you. They will also tell you the truth as they see it. When you're feeling low, they'll say, "Keep going! You can do it!" When you ask for their feedback, they'll reply, "I think your idea is great! How about adding this to it?" If they think you're off course, they'll tell you.

A support system for success doesn't hold meetings, it holds your hand. It's not about formal structure or one-size-fits-all strategies. It's not about dollars and cents. It's about belief in your ability and drive. It's about nurturing and empowering you emotionally to enable you to achieve your mission: transforming your dream into a reality. It's about stretching you and pushing you toward your dream. If your dream is like a flower struggling to blossom, then the members of your support system for success are the roots that nourish that dream and sustain both you and your vision through sun and storm.

As I said earlier, my first and most important supporter was my dad. When he died, I felt totally alone. But he must have been watching out for me from above, because soon after he passed on, my first support system for success began taking shape. Let me give you the flavor of this first team of believers from my retailing days:

MAX.   I admired my brother Max tremendously and it meant the world to me when he began taking an active role in my business life. Max was strong, confident, warm, witty, and a self-made millionaire by the age of 29. As my closest business confidant, he bolstered my spirits, defused my fears, and let me know that he was behind me all the way. Even though he was a solid family man, he never criticized me for my personal failures or let them dampen his admiration for my accomplishments. He loved to brag about me to his friends. He considered me to be not only creative but also very resourceful. In general, he made me feel damned good about myself.

MYRNA.   Beautiful, bright, and talented, my sister Myrna always gave me a shoulder to cry on and made me laugh, even when things were at their worst. In spite of the fact that she would have preferred to see me solidly married, Myrna never let her views on my personal life stop her from giving me practical advice. When I was down and out in New York, Myrna (who had also moved east) and her husband were very helpful in caring for Harlan. Our careers were worlds apart: I was in business and Myrna was a gifted singer, writer, and song producer. She was also an entrepreneur in her own right as the founder of March on Music, Inc. Myrna and her husband, Dr. Roufa, both had an intuitive sense about people that I really valued and relied on. Their advice saved me from lots of pitfalls. People used to ask what I did and they would answer, "We don't know, but she makes a lot of money at it!"

BESS COOPER.   There I was minding my own business and not looking in anyone else's store window just as I promised my dad, when, lo and behold, one day someone looked in *my* store window and liked what she saw! That someone was Bess Cooper, one of the biggest buyers of junior sportswear in the country. Almost overnight, she changed my life. She sat down, introduced herself, and said, "I want to buy your merchandise for the May Company. I'd also like you to travel with me to New York on buying trips, because your color sense is the best I've ever seen." Bess's confidence gave me the courage to expand into contract manufacturing. She also opened up the New York fashion world to me. We became good friends. I used to love it when she'd call and say, "Wendele, can you make it to New York next week?" You bet I did!

ARNOLD KINSEY. Arnold was the head of the biggest fashion buying office in Los Angeles. After getting wind of the work I was doing for Bess Cooper, he encouraged me to branch out and began promoting me to the industry as the "hottest fashion find of California." Arnold opened up lots of doors for me and I really respected his advice and experience. His support encouraged me to sell my last store and start manufacturing "The Wendy Look." Arnold was fun, very attractive and worldly, and had a great eye for fashion. I learned a lot from him.

ED CARROWAY. I've already talked a lot about Ed's importance to me as the head of the Federated Bank of Boston. But let me say just a few words about the part he played early in my career as part of my first support system. When his bank extended credit to me, Ed didn't know anything about me except my name. But when my credit line was threatened and I met Ed face to face to persuade him to help me, he saw something worth investing in. Ed Carroway—the big-time financier—believed in *me*, little Wendy Rue, in her pink bunny-fur coat. Amazing, but true! My meeting with Ed was a real eye-opener for me. For the first time, a total stranger and successful businessman showed confidence in my sales talent and ability to build a business. Ed did far more than extend me credit; he taught me how important it was to surround myself with people who believed in me.

When I went to New York and started over, my support system changed. As always, Max and Myrna offered encouragement. But I also began making new contacts. Two of the people I became closest to were Stanley Haltman and Dr. Alan Rosenberg. Together, they formed the core of my support system for NAFE:

STANLEY.   My boyfriend Stanley was a big man with a big heart and the personality of a world-beater. He was totally unconventional in his dress and presentation. He was also highly principled and a perfect example of someone who believed in himself. He never let money or corporate politics get in the way of doing what he felt was the right thing. That's why he was extremely well thought of and loved within the fashion industry. He was a kind and wise person, with a relaxed and bemused attitude toward the world. No matter how bad things were, he could always make me laugh. He used to love to go to meetings with his tie undone and bang his fist on the table to make a point. And yet, all the stuffy corporate people I was doing business with adored him. He was a breath of fresh air and a straight shooter. He was totally up front about everything. With Stanley, what you saw was what you got. He was not only my boyfriend, he was my adviser and helpmate. Even though I didn't always like the advice he gave me, I knew that he spoke out of a sense of caring, as well as experience. I've never met his equal.

DR. ALAN ROSENBERG.   Another one of a kind. The psychiatrist I began seeing, Dr. Alan, was shocking in his style and approach. He sat in his office for sessions naked from the waist up, with his little Japanese house girl, Kami, waiting on him hand and foot. Due to a serious auto accident, he had trouble with his balance and lumbered as he walked. He wore thick horn-rimmed glasses and had the forbidding appearance of a Frankenstein stalking the streets of New York. But beyond this gruff facade was a sweet and kindly man. Brilliant and insightful, he would have run a close second to Einstein. Well educated in the school of life, his key purpose in treating me was to preserve my free spirit. He and Stanley became instant friends. When I was down, I could always count on Dr. Alan for words of wisdom and total support. "Who the hell is he?

What's he ever done?" he'd bellow when I'd tell him about someone who was giving me a hard time. Dr. Alan loved the whole idea of NAFE and did everything he could to support my crazy dream. He constantly reminded me that if you lose yourself, you lose everything.

These are just a handful of the many wonderful people who helped and encouraged me over the years. There are so many others I could talk about! My first banker, Mr. Lloyd, for instance; John Bennet of American Express; Ed King, a first-rate accountant; Jean Schoonover, who gave NAFE the benefit of her P.R. talent; Fran Gare, the coauthor of Dr. Atkins' diet books and one of my closest confidantes; Dr. Herb Thomas, a psychiatrist. The list goes on and on. These people not only believed in me; many of them backed me with hard dollars. This is the kind of solid reinforcement *you* need as well. So here's some advice on how to build a support system for success to help make *your* dream a reality:

THE FIRST MEMBER OF YOUR SUPPORT SYSTEM FOR SUCCESS IS *YOU*

The foundation for any support system for success is your belief in yourself and in your right to be who and what you want to be. If that's an entrepreneur, great! If it's a wife and mother or a member of someone else's support team, then more power to you! Just be sure it's what *you* want—and not what someone else thinks you want or need. Whatever your dream, if you believe in yourself, then you'll attract people who'll support you. If you're wishy-washy and look for people who'll always agree with you or tell you what to do, then your lack of self-confidence will be apparent. Your support team will realize very quickly if you're phony or insecure, and they'll drift away from you like smoke in a breeze. Seeking support is not the same as looking for approval. If you don't believe in yourself, how can you ask anyone else to believe in you?

If the members of your support system for success are like

the roots of a plant, then your belief in yourself and your dream is the soil in which those roots take hold. If your belief is shallow, then the roots will wither; if it's deep and strong, then your dreams will be nourished by your team of believers. Their support is critical for many reasons. First, because it encourages and energizes you, especially during down periods when it's easy to fall into a fearful, dejected way of thinking. Second, because it forces you to do more and be more in order to justify their faith in you; it pushes you out of your comfort zone. Third, because it acts as a sounding board, offering counsel and fresh ideas. Fourth, because it gives you inspiration by offering you role models whose success and style you admire and want to emulate. And finally, because it holds you to a standard of excellence and a level of performance that can inspire you to reach beyond your self-imposed limits.

TRUST IS THE FOUNDATION OF YOUR SUPPORT SYSTEM

Without trust, you can't build a support system for success. Your supporters must believe in your absolute integrity and honesty, and you must be able to trust their judgment and advice. That's why Stanley was such a great supporter. He was totally honest and fearless. He never let his personal feelings about me get in the way of what he felt was right and never hesitated to criticize me if he thought I was wrong. I trusted him completely.

When NAFE was just starting out, I was broke all the time. I was constantly bouncing checks for my rent, my food, and my electricity bill. But somehow, my neighborhood creditors trusted me. They knew that I was honest and would pay them when I could. And so, the little guy on the corner would say to me, "Well, OK. I'll let you have another month to get it together." This faith really kept me going when I was down. The trust these local tradespeople had in me made them as much a part of my support system for success as the top executives I worked with.

CHOOSE SUCCESSFUL PEOPLE AS MEMBERS OF YOUR TEAM

People who lack the drive to succeed generally want to pull you down to their level. In contrast, people who've made it to the top are secure enough to share their success. They tend to pull people up to their level, if they believe in them. Since they've already achieved their major goals, they're not afraid of compromising their position or status. These people also have a need to grow. They need fresh ideas and are willing to buy them. They're constantly searching for new angles, new ventures, new challenges.

People who are successful also enjoy finding someone they can spur along the road to success. Why? Mainly because it gives their egos a boost and makes them feel good about themselves. Most successful people are generous givers not just of money but of time, experience, and ideas. These people have arrived. So one of their biggest psychological payoffs is helping someone else whom they believe has the talents and guts to make it too. They enjoy championing someone who shares their drive and intensity. They like the idea of picking and backing a winner; it helps validate the choices that they've made in their own lives. They also get a charge out of coaching an eager new entrant to the winner's circle. And believe me, these people have a lot to teach you!

Where do you find these dynamic, demanding supporters? The answer is anywhere and everywhere. They can be recruited from your family, friends, business acquaintances, partners, clients, customers, and even your staff. How do you persuade someone outside your immediate circle to help you? By asking. You can't railroad anyone into becoming part of your support system. You have to pique their interest and win their admiration. Remember, most people are flattered when you call them up and ask for their advice. So don't be afraid to do it, but always in a sensitive and savvy style.

As your venture takes shape, start reaching out to the kind of people you feel you can work with. Whenever possible, try to get them out of their office for lunch or a drink, so you can create a friendly, relaxed atmosphere. Of course, you're not going to call anyone and announce, "Hey, I'd like you to be part of my support system!" You're going to contact them as you would any other businessperson to tell them that you're starting a new venture, you've heard about what they've done, and would like to get together to see if your project would be of interest to them. If they find your proposition intriguing and viable, you'll know soon enough. They'll express genuine interest and invite you to keep in touch. With time and luck, their interest may even convert to active involvement. There's nothing fancy or formal in this approach. You're not asking for anything that demands too much energy or commitment.

But remember, when looking for winners to enlist in your dream-building, never go to them with hat in hand. You must have something of value to offer them. If you have something they want, then they have a reason to help you, to build you up. What you offer them can be intangible: It can simply be the chance to share in your enthusiasm or the fun and sense of adventure that flow from being part of a start-up venture with lots of potential. Or it may be the chance to relive their own early success through you. Or what you have to offer may be more concrete: a business opportunity that seems viable and appealing.

Take John Bennet at American Express, for instance. When I sat down with John shortly after launching NAFE, he asked me, "What does Amex need NAFE for, Wendy?" And I answered, "Credibility." John laughed, but after thinking about my answer for a minute or two, he said, "You know something, Wendy? You're right." Amex became NAFE's first corporate sponsor, and John became part of my support system for success. John knew nothing about me, but he sensed that I could deliver. He also had the courage to follow his convictions and give me a start—and he became not just a member of my support team, but my corporate mentor. Whenever I was unsure about how to handle a corporate situation, I always called on John for advice. He was generous with his time and experience because he wanted our joint venture to succeed. And he wanted to see *me* succeed. It never bothered him that I was naive. What fascinated him even more was that I was never too embarrassed to ask a question—even about something very basic. He really had fun educating me!

BE PREPARED TO PAY A PRICE FOR THE SUPPORT YOU RECEIVE

Access to all the wonderful resources your support team can offer you comes with a price tag: It obligates you to deliver on your dream. The members of your support team expect success from you. That's their return on their investment in you. They demand that you don't disappoint them—that you make good on the time and effort they've expended on your behalf. While they may give generously, the members of your team need to be nurtured, too. They need to feel that they've done something of value in helping you and that they showed keen judgment in recognizing your talent and drive. They want to point with pride to the role they played in your success. The pressure these expectations exert on you can be tremendous. With all these people betting on you, how can you fail?

It's also important that you respect your support team's time and never abuse the privilege of associating with its members. Only contact them and ask for help or ideas when it's absolutely necessary. Like most successful people, the members of your team are going to be extremely busy and lead intense, sometimes stressful, lives. Of course, there are some people on your team—family members, for example—whom you can call on freely for encouragement and ideas or just to connect. But other members of your team must be treated more gingerly. You must value their time. Never call members of your support team or organize a get-together with them if you don't have something very important and specific to discuss.

LET YOUR SUPPORT SYSTEM CHANGE AS YOU CHANGE

A support system is very fluid. It changes as your needs evolve. While family members or very close friends will form its core, a good support system releases some people and brings others on board as circumstances and your growing maturity and success dictate. Neither you nor the people you rely on should feel guilty about this process. It's an inevitable fact of life. People change and their needs change.

A support system can also take different forms, depending on your situation. A business partner can be part of your support system. A brainstorming session where you bring together talented people to kick around an intriguing idea can serve as a kind of ad hoc support system: The feedback you receive can recharge you emotionally. The people who work for you—who are pulling for you day in and day out—can be important members of your support system. A networking group can also offer a formalized kind of support system, although its key goal isn't so much emotional support as it is professional growth through the exchange of information and contacts.

Diversity is one of the keys to a strong support system for success. In building your support team, you want to be able to draw upon a wide range of experience, talents, industry backgrounds, and personal histories. Being able to tap into this breadth and depth of support enriches you tremendously. That's why it's very important to choose people outside your field as members of your support system. They offer a fresh perspective and prevent you from becoming insulated and isolated. This nurtures your business as well as your emotional well-being.

FIND ROLE MODELS TO INSPIRE AND MOTIVATE YOU

As you begin to build your support system, it's vital that you seek out role models whose accomplishments and style you want to emulate. Look for people who have a level of confidence and ease in their business dealings that you admire and want to develop in yourself. You'll learn so much from their success! While many people have inspired me over the years, two very different women instantly spring to mind as my personal role models: Julia Walsh and Sister Colette Mahoney.

Julia is everything Irish. She's a big woman, with a big heart, a big soul, and a big, hearty laugh to match. She has snow-white hair and piercing blue eyes that cut to the core of things. She's funny and witty and as loyal as the day is long. I first connected with Julia back when NAFE was just getting started. She'd heard about what I was trying to do and liked the idea. We met for lunch one afternoon and after talking to her for five minutes, I became a fan of hers and she became a member of my support team. What a life Julia's lived! What incredible things she's accomplished!

Her list of firsts is as long as my arm: The first woman to graduate from Harvard Business School's Advanced Management Program. The first woman member of the American Stock Exchange. The first woman to serve on the Amex Board of Governors. The first woman broker to work for Ferris & Co. The first woman to start her own investment firm, Julia M. Walsh & Sons, in Washington, D.C. Now re ,tired, Julia served on numerous business boards during her career and was always active in community affairs. And she did all this while raising 12 children!

Left as a widow in her thirties with four small boys, Julia knew she needed help at home if she was to successfully pursue a career as a stockbroker. Being a creative business-woman, she made her mother-in-law, Helen, an offer too good to refuse: Julia agreed to pay her 20 percent of everything she earned after taxes if Helen would care for her children and run her household. She also offered her a pension, health benefits, profit sharing, and even vacation with pay! Eventually Julia married Thomas Walsh, a real estate executive, also widowed. He had seven children. Together, they had a daughter.

Hearing Julia talk about the career obstacles she faced while raising a dozen kids was always incredibly inspiring. She had accomplished so much, yet she was completely down to earth, full of fun, and endlessly curious. Julia had a gift for making everyone around her feel good about themselves. She could hold an audience spellbound with her story, and I never tired of hearing her tell it. She gave a number of talks for NAFE, and our members just loved her. After she spoke, they would flock up to the podium to talk with her. She was the kind of person you wanted to spend time with and learn from. Her zest for life was absolutely contagious!

I admired Julia tremendously, and I'm proud to say we became good friends. Her self-confidence, ease with people, generosity, joy in life, and consummate business skills were all qualities I wanted to develop more fully in myself. Whenever I had the opportunity, I observed Julia's style and delivery. She taught me a great deal and helped NAFE in many ways. In turn, as NAFE grew, I was able to help her by offering her firm's investment services to our members. Being able to return the support she gave NAFE was a big thrill for me.

Sister Colette Mahoney couldn't have lived a more different life from Julia Walsh's. The former president of Marymount Manhattan College, Sister Colette spent many years encouraging women, both young and old, to pursue challenging careers. She transformed Marymount Manhattan from a sleepy little college into a well-respected, innovative institution. A nun with a worldly mission, she certainly didn't live in an ivory tower! Like Julia Walsh, Sister Colette's drive and energy have won admiration in many circles. Over the years, she's helped guide a host of educational, social, and business institutions, from the Girl Scouts of America and the United Way to the Dollar Savings Bank and the Manhattan Life Insurance Corporation. Sister Colette holds many honorary degrees and has always been a popular speaker. Feisty, independent, and unafraid to buck the system, she's the model of a true leader. Her devotion to service has inspired me and countless other women.

I hope you're lucky enough to have people as dynamic as Julia Walsh and Sister Colette in your life. But you don't have to know role models personally to "enlist" them in your support team. You can pick celebrities or leaders whose style and gifts you admire and want to emulate. Find out as much about them as you can through books, articles, tapes, and so on. Learn their backgrounds and personal histories. Analyze what it is about them that appeals to you. Is it what they've done or how they've done it, or both? Is it the way they've overcome obstacles in their lives and turned them into opportunities? Is it their single-minded drive or the many detours they experienced on the road to success? Is it their ability to learn from their failures? Is it their quiet, behind-the-scenes impact or their willingness to speak out and be counted? What do they have to teach you about making your own dream come true?

KEEP YOUR SUPPORTERS POSTED ON YOUR PROGRESS

As your support team takes shape, it's important to keep its members involved and committed to your success. Without burdening them, you want to make them feel that they have an important role to play in making your venture a reality. The best way to do this is to call or arrange a lunch date to let them know how things are going and how their ideas and suggestions have helped you. You can also send them press releases and press clips about projects you have under way so they'll be up to date on your venture's progress. And, of course, if you hear or read about some exciting new development in their business or personal life, be sure to acknowledge it. Let them know that you care about them as people—not just as mentors and/or clients. Keep the lines of communication open and

you'll develop some very rewarding and long-lasting friendships as well as business relationships.

SHARE THE WEALTH: JOIN SOMEONE ELSE'S SUPPORT SYSTEM

As your own venture takes wing, you touch the lives of more
and more people. I know this happened to me. As NAFE grew
more successful, not only did its membership increase, but a
whole array of talented people came into its orbit as vendors,
seminar speakers, and program planners. It was very exciting
for me to see this happen. I especially enjoyed being able to
give NAFE's business to small, growing companies. Even more
satisfying, people began turning to me for help and advice.
Like my dad, I tried never to send anyone away empty-handed
or empty-hearted.

After a career as a stockbroker, for example, a friend of
mine named Judy Briles decided to pursue her dream of
becoming a writer and motivational speaker. She knew a lot
about the financial needs of women and wanted to write how-
to books on the subject. Eventually, she went on to write several popular guides, including *The Women's Guide to Financial
Savvy* and *Money Phases*. Judy's bubbly personality and enthusiasm coupled with her solid background in finance seemed
like a winning combination to me, and we hit it off instantly.
My friends and I call her "Sparkle Plenty" because of her
upbeat approach to life.

After finding out more about the direction Judy was moving in, I started thinking about how to help. First, I gave her
the names of some business contacts in financial services who
were likely to find her approach to women and money refreshing. Then, when her first money book came out, we reviewed
it in NAFE's magazine, *Executive Female*. When NAFE started
organizing networking seminars and held its annual conference, Judy was a featured speaker. She also became the editor
of NAFE's newsletter, *More Money*. Judy's association with

NAFE helped her build the credentials she needed to launch her speaking career. Today, Judy is the author of more than a dozen books and constantly in demand as a speaker. Seeing her living out her dream has been great fun.

Through my relationship with Sister Colette, I found another very satisfying way to offer support to someone else: NAFE provided a full scholarship to Marymount Manhattan College to a talented student named RoseAnne Paccione. A single mother, RoseAnne had already spent many years in the work force when she won a NAFE-sponsored essay contest on lifelong learning.

Reaching out in this way is so satisfying. Being part of someone else's support system gives you a tremendous sense of accomplishment. It affirms choices you've made and successes you've achieved. It's also easy and enjoyable. Giving advice and ideas, getting together for an occasional lunch or meeting, sending someone a card or flowers when they're feeling low or when they've made a big sale—that's all it takes to be a part of someone else's support system for success. With so much negativity clogging the airwaves, finding "can do" people to encourage you—and playing this role yourself—is absolutely essential.

In founding NAFE I met so many wonderful people who encouraged and helped me along the way. And I wound up with an incredible support system for success: over 200,000 talented, dynamic NAFE members. Who could have asked for more?

BOUNCING BACK FROM ROCK BOTTOM

Show me an entrepreneur, and I'll show you someone who's been bumped and bruised, felt down and out, and hit rock bottom more than once. I know, because I've been there myself. In fact, I've hit rock bottom so many times, I have skid marks on my rear end! If there's one thing I've learned from being down and out, it's this: There's a lot to be learned from being down and out.

My trips to rock bottom have provided me with more ideas, insights, and wisdom, than my successes. Most entrepreneurs I know feel the same way. Why? Because once you hit rock bottom and manage to climb out of the hole you've found yourself in—or dug yourself into—there's nothing you can't do. You're a survivor, and that's one of the key traits of an entrepreneur (see Chap. 4). Being able to laugh at yourself and the crazy predicaments you'll find yourself in also helps.

During my checkered career, I had to struggle time and again, not just to keep my dream of equality alive, but to survive and hold my family together. The wolf was always at the door; I was always running just to stay in place; and despite my best efforts, I often found myself robbing Peter to pay Paul. My first trip to the bottom was taken compliments of my third husband, Clifford. After I recovered from the shock of Cliff's arrest for murder, I realized the danger my family and I were in: His situation threatened to destroy my business and our livelihood.

At the time of Clifford's arrest, I still had two boutiques, but I was moving away from retail sales and into contract manufacturing. Bess Cooper at the May Company had discovered my flair for designing teen clothes and encouraged me to branch out into private brand labeling under the name "The Wendy Look for Campus Shops." As a result of Bess's support and my own drive to expand, I decided to give my last retail store to my cousin and focus on fashion design and manufacturing. My older half-brother, Max, began to cast an eager eye at my business potential and decided to help finance my expansion into manufacturing, as did a bank in California.

This was an exciting time for me. I was gaining recognition for my original designs and even had my own showroom at 1407 Broadway—New York's fashion mecca. High-powered fashion executives were jumping on my bandwagon, giving me "open to buy" budgets of $10,000 or more. I was setting up Wendy Look boutiques in department stores across the country. This new business proved to be far more profitable than my retail stores had ever been. I was in demand and in the money, and my support system was humming along. I was really swinging!

A year later, I was broke. This time around, my trip to rock bottom was paved with good intentions—and bad business decisions. To market my Wendy Look in-store boutiques, I was spending most of my time on the road. I was busy day and night, buying fabrics, selling, putting on designer shows—and loving every minute of it. As my business adviser, Max decided I needed an expert to manage my finances and production. Max also thought he'd found the perfect guy to help me, a "numbers" man named Milt. So what if Milt's main job qualification turned out to be that he was bigger than my portly brother? So what if Max and Milt exchanged blazers in the middle of Milt's job interview and Max decided that a guy with Milt's impeccable taste had just the kind of back-office experience his little sister needed? What did I know? I adored Max and trusted his judgment.

While Milt was back in my showroom in L.A. taking orders and handling production—or so I thought—I was selling my heart out. Unfortunately, Milt had sticky fingers. Instead of doing his job, he spent his time writing up phony orders and siphoning cash out of what I thought was my exploding bank account. I began to suspect something was wrong. Every day, I called my brother and said, "Max, there's something going on with Milt." And every day, Max answered, "What are you worried about? Stay out there selling. Let Milt do his job." I should have followed my instincts: My gut didn't fail me—I failed my gut. I returned to L.A. one day only to find that Milt had totally mismanaged production and shipped huge amounts of merchandise to the wrong stores. Big orders were being returned, and my credit line was frozen.

My business quickly went from boom to bust. In the face of the mess Milt had created, there was only one thing for me to do: close my manufacturing company. My brother and lawyer wanted me to declare bankruptcy, but I stubbornly refused to take this step. I felt it would damage my name and business reputation beyond repair. My instincts said no, and this time I listened. On my own, I contacted my most loyal customers, and they agreed to buy the balance of my merchandise. After settling with my creditors for 10 cents on the dollar, I shut my business down. To this day, it's clear to me that avoiding bankruptcy was absolutely the right decision.

Knee-deep in disaster, I needed a lifeline. While negotiating with my creditors, I frantically began designing a couple of new lines. In fact, the day a padlock was put on my door and the last of my stock was being packed up, I was being interviewed in the front office by *Women's Wear Daily* about my latest creations. But my reputation had suffered a major blow, and the outlook in L.A. was anything but sunny. Hoping to return to retailing, I sent Johnny, one of my former store managers, to Texas while I went to Chicago in search of a fresh start. This plan quickly went nowhere because my credit was shot. I tried borrowing money from friends, but they weren't able to help me. While all this was going on, Clifford was released from jail and began making my life miserable.

Knowing that I was vulnerable because my business had gone bust, he wanted our son Harlan. But however tough things were, reconciling with Cliff wasn't a choice I was prepared to make.

Putting as much distance as possible between myself and L.A. seemed more and more appealing. Leaving wasn't easy, however. Dennis, my son from my first marriage, was about to go off to college. Even though he was thrilled to be on his own, Dennis was angry about my decision to leave home. It was a tough time for both of us. One thing was clear: I couldn't stay where I was. And so, within weeks, Dennis was settled at school and five-year-old Harlan and I were New York bound.

New York was much, much faster paced than L.A., and that suited me just fine. I also found New Yorkers more open. They were demanding, but they knew how to listen and make decisions. What you'd done in the past didn't matter, just where you were going. Ever the optimist, I was excited and energized by this move. Life was just beginning and I was ready to cast my hat in the ring! My sister, Myrna, had already done exactly that. A budding cabaret singer whose stage name was Myrna March, she loved New York and felt it was the right place for us both. Not to mention the fact that having me around the corner would cut her phone bill; now we'd be able to talk day or night and drive each other crazy locally instead of long distance!

Once I was settled, one of the first people I called was my old friend, Ed Carroway. Ed didn't sympathize with me about my problems—that wasn't his style. What he did do was call several manufacturers he knew and set up appointments for me. But it was his advice, rather than his contacts, that I valued most. "Wendy," he told me one day over lunch, "always remember that you have four things going for you: your talent, your guts, your tenacity, and your sense of humor. Hang on to them and you'll come out on top."

Little did I know then how wise a man Ed really was. And little did I know that my whole New York job search was doomed to failure from the start: None of the jobs I took panned out. Working for someone else just wasn't for me. But while my efforts to scare up a paycheck proved to be both frustrating and funny, they were also invaluable. My sojourn on Seventh Avenue taught me some priceless lessons about myself and business. Most of all, it showed me that learning how to manage disappointment and failure is one of the keys to successful entrepreneurship. Seeing adversity as an adventure, cherishing friends and a sense of humor, and refusing to surrender your dream are a big part of what success is all about—not grabbing some mythical brass ring. Based on what I've learned the hard way, here's a survival strategy for bouncing back when disaster hits:

LIGHTEN UP!

"Down and Out in New York" would have been a good title for this chapter, because that's exactly what I was when I arrived in New York with some suitcases full of clothes, a few phone numbers, a fashion line, and five-year-old Harlan in tow. Just how broke was I? Well, let's put it this way: When I first arrived, I moved into a hotel on West Fifty-eighth Street, because all I could hope to do was pay my way from week to week. At one point, I found myself sneaking out of the hotel in the dead of night, with a drowsy Harlan under my arm, because I owed a few weeks' back rent and couldn't pay it. I checked into another hotel and found it equally depressing. New York living wasn't exactly a dream come true. The Park Avenue penthouse I'd fantasized about seemed farther away than the moon.

My cashflow soon slowed to a trickle, and I was forced to borrow money from my brother, Max, which didn't please him at all. He couldn't understand anyone not being able to make a living. Still, I had Dennis to support and Harlan to take care of. Ever since our plane had touched down in New York, I worried about Cliff coming after Harlan. As a working mother, I felt he'd be better cared for and safer in a private school, so I used my small cash reserve to enroll him in one. Paying his tuition was a constant struggle. Every Friday, my darling little son would arrive home with a note pinned to his jacket: "Don't send this boy back to school without money!"

Things were tight, so tight, in fact, that I actually turned to my kid sister, Myrna, for job help. A big mistake! Myrna was younger, but felt she understood the ways of the world better than I did. Soon after I moved to New York, she introduced me to a woman named Irene. Irene had once worked as a buyer for some of the lower-priced chain stores and was now a recruiter for the fashion industry. But her kind of "recruiting" wasn't exactly what I had in mind!

Everyone I met through Irene seemed to be a middle-aged male executive who offered to discuss my career plans over dinner. Knowing that New Yorkers worked 24 hours a day, I went along with this somewhat unusual interviewing style. But every dinner ended exactly the same way—not with a much-needed job offer, but with an invitation to climb in the sack! Talk about naive—I didn't have a clue about what was going on. But even *I* knew something wasn't quite kosher!

One of the guys who wined and dined me turned out to be pretty nice, so I told him my tale of woe and then said, "Do me a favor and level with me. I've been offered money, pent-houses, tickets to Broadway—everything but a job. What's going on?" The fellow looked at me and laughed. "Wendy, don't you know who Irene is? Her job is to provide fresh young talent to the fashion industry's male executives looking for some fun. That's why they call her the 'Moonlighting Madam'!"

One thing the misadventure with Irene and her merry men taught me was that I needed to lighten up. Ed Carroway told me to hang on to my sense of humor and he was absolutely right. My midnight flit from the hotel, the Moonlighting Madam, my sister Myrna's well-meaning but zany attempts to help me were all pretty funny. My life in New York was like something out of a soap opera or a B movie. Just thinking about the overblown egos I'd deflated and left for the Moonlighting Madam to massage made me laugh. Justice was served! As soon as I remembered not to take myself or my problems too seriously, I was able to adopt a "This too shall pass" attitude—especially about my lack of money. Nothing lasts forever I reminded myself, not even being broke. Once I stopped being so hard on myself, I was free to start looking ahead and making plans to better my situation.

So when disaster hits and you're feeling low, give yourself a break! Go ahead and feel sorry for yourself for a day or two if you need to. Then do whatever you have to to snap yourself out of it. Watch one of those old, feel-good movies or persuade a friend with a good sense of humor to treat you to dinner. Call an old roommate and trade funny stories about the way things were. Be good to yourself instead of being down on yourself. You've been in some tight spots before and you've managed to survive. And you'll survive whatever life's handed you right now, too. Lighten up and your mood will lift. Once that happens, you'll feel better about yourself and begin to see the way out of whatever mess you're in.

And remember, "This too shall pass." Knowing that whatever you're doing to survive is temporary makes it easier to accept. Just don't fool yourself. Don't start settling for second best. If you've been downsized and really want to start your own business, for example, accept the fact that you may have to consult for a while to make ends meet. Or, you may have to moonlight and hold down a regular job while you plan your business start-up. Measures like these are means to an end: achieving financial freedom as an entrepreneur. You may be in a survival mode right now, but that's not where you want to be down the road. "My dream may be on hold for a while, but I'm still going for it!" *That's how an entrepreneur thinks.*

P.S.   A few months after I set up my own fashion consulting business, I got a call from one of Irene's "boys" asking me to do some work for him. I quoted him a figure that was twice my usual fee. He knew it too, but he was so desperate to have me bring some L.A. sunshine into his dismal line that he had no choice but to pay me exactly what I asked for. Was cashing that check ever sweet!

DECIDE HOW LOW YOU'LL GO

During this time in my life, I had to take on work I felt was demeaning, just as my father had to do when he was forced to peddle stockings door to door. At first, I tried to salvage something from L.A. by arranging to sell junior fashions for a small company dealing in junior petites. It was a broken-down line that was actually ripped off from my own patterns. Not only did the guy who ran the business steal my ideas, he added insult to injury by doing an absolutely lousy job of knocking them off! There I was at 1407 Broadway—the place where I'd once been queen, with my own showroom and orders flowing like honey—sitting at a broken-down desk selling a line nobody wanted to buy. This had to be one of my lowest moments.

Everyone who walked in wanted to hear the gory details. "Your line was so fabulous! Everything you did was so beautiful! What happened?" Day after day, people who used to envy my skyrocketing (but short-lived) success would stop by to schmooze and sympathize—and secretly revel in my downfall and comeuppance! This nightmare lasted about six months. Finally, I couldn't take it any more. I left my desk for lunch one day and never came back.

Though a resounding flop financially, this experience gave me some real food for thought. First, I realized that I had to leave the past behind me. I'd reached the end of the line in terms of exploiting my L.A. fashion look. I either had to breathe new life into it for the New York market or let it go. That part of my life was finished. I had to go forward. But the petites fiasco showed me something still more important: I was an entrepreneur, not a handmaiden to a hack!

Even though I was broke and struggling to survive, I had to draw the line somewhere. I was willing to swallow my pride, but I wasn't willing to sell my soul. Just as I refused to go back to Clifford or let Irene turn me into one of the best-kept mistresses in New York, I wasn't going to let myself sink to the level of the sleazy guy who ran the petites line. That was lower than rock bottom in my mind. Once I knew there were some things that I absolutely, positively couldn't and wouldn't do no matter how tough my situation was, I began to feel better about myself. I began to focus my energies and make some choices, instead of desperately grabbing at anything that came my way. This was a real turning point for me.

How low can you go? There's a simple answer: As low as you're willing to let yourself fall. That's one of the things I've learned about hitting rock bottom. When you're going through those really lean times in your life, it's very important that you—and you alone—decide just how far down the bottom is going to be for you. Don't let circumstances or the people around you decide this for you, because if you do, you'll find it even harder to bounce back. Once you know exactly where rock bottom is, you can find your footing and figure out a way to climb back up again. Otherwise you'll find yourself falling down a bottomless pit.

SEE ADVERSITY AS AN ADVENTURE

One morning I opened up *Woman's Wear Daily* and saw an ad that really intrigued me. I can still remember its exact words:

ARE YOU A MAN WHO WANTS TO CONQUER THE
WORLD?
ARE YOU A MAN WHO WANTS TO BECOME A
MILLIONAIRE?
ARE YOU A MAN WHO HAS NO END TO HIS
AMBITIONS?
IF THE ANSWER IS YES, CALL
FRANCHISES UNLIMITED!

I didn't call, but I did sit down and write a simple letter saying, "Have you ever thought about a woman?" Well, that got Franchises Unlimited's attention! A fly-by-night operation, the company sold turnkey businesses like "Big Beefy Burger" franchises. A sales manager called me down for an interview and gave me a job. I became a road bum for Edie Adams' "Cut 'n Curl" hair salons.

As a hair-salon rep, I traveled seven days a week and lived out of my suitcase. My retail sales background was a big asset: I brought in more people as potential buyers than any of Franchise Unlimited's other salespeople, all of whom were men, of course. I was able to romance the product, explain the advantages of being a franchiser—everything except deal with the numbers. I'd told my sales manager up front what my talents were, and he had agreed to give me support on the back end of the sale: I'd bring in the prospects and someone else would handle the paperwork. That was our deal. I delivered, and then after four months I was fired for failing to close the sale on any of my leads. The company used me and then got rid of me when I'd served their purpose. I was devastated. Once again, I didn't fit.

My career as a franchise rep proved short but very enlightening. First, it reinforced what I'd discovered earlier: I didn't want to work with people who were less than honest. But most important, my days and nights on the road taught me to treat adversity as an adventure. Being on my own in this way, without all the pressures and ego attached to running a business, was exciting. Sometimes, it was even fun. It was a challenge to drive into a new city or town, meet people who were complete strangers to me, and learn about their hopes and dreams. I began to see that I really was my father's daughter— I loved sales just as much as he had. I also really enjoyed outselling the sales*men* I competed against.

Knowing that I could feel adventurous and challenged by selling—something that most people found difficult and even frightening—really gave me a boost. I was also willing to try just about anything. At one point, I found myself in Haiti on a wacky project for the African-American singer Miriam Makeeba. Imagine Lucille Ball trying to explain how to sew a fashion line in less than seven days to a bunch of women who didn't speak a word of English and you'll have some idea of what this was like! I produced the line. At the end of a week of everything but fun in the sun, I was $1700 richer, but ready to blow every penny recuperating at a health spa!

Being able to view a business misfortune or detour as an

adventure is vital to your success as an entrepreneur. The root of the word *adventure* means "something about to happen." Having an adventure means you're in a state of anticipation, of unknowing. Something, anything can happen at any moment. You're moving forward, but you don't know where. The old rules and tools that worked for you in the past may not work for you now. Old beliefs may have to be abandoned. At the same time, something new and exciting—and even better—may lie just around the corner. Who knows? If you can be open enough to see the setbacks you face as opportunities and let go of the past, then you can free yourself to envision a bigger, brighter future. You never know what the unknown has to offer. You never know where you're going to find your dream. Optimism, a sense of adventure, and taking a flyer now and then are what being an entrepreneur is all about.

REMEMBER, WHEN YOU HIT ROCK BOTTOM, YOU'LL FIND YOURSELF WAITING THERE

When I came to New York I made up my mind to create a whole new life for myself and Harlan. My biggest fantasy was about being part of a major corporation. I'd met lots of top fashion designers who all seemed to enjoy a great deal of prestige and power. They were respected for their talent and ideas. They led what seemed like very glamorous lives. I wanted to be one of them and belong. Being a fashion designer for a major company seemed like a dream job. And it was for someone. It just wasn't me. Or so I found out.

Mattel Toys had run an ad for a fashion coordinator who understood contract manufacturing. That job seemed to have my name on it. I went over to interview and immediately panicked when they called me in for a psychiatric evaluation. I went through their tests, went home, and had a stiff drink. A few weeks later, a letter arrived in the mail. It said something like this, "Dear Mrs. Rue: We passed your resume through our entire company, but we just don't feel that someone of your talent would be happy at Mattel. We wish you the best of luck." If I'd received a letter like that at a time when nothing was happening, it would have devastated me. Fortunately, that same day brought me a job offer, so I took this turndown as a compliment. The position I landed was with a firm called Classic Fabrics. I interviewed with the president, Arthur Gutman, and spent an hour telling him how I could improve his sales by taking his one fabric and expanding it with coordinated fabrics I'd design for him. Arthur was polite, but discouraging: "I don't think this is the right place for you. I don't think you'd fit in as a fashion coordinator."

The very next morning at 8:30, I called Arthur and told him I needed to see him. When I arrived at his office, I said, "I don't want to be your fashion coordinator. I want to be your consultant. And I don't want to get paid. I'm going to turn your fabric line into multiple sales, and when I do, you can pay me retroactively." In short, I gave Art an offer he couldn't refuse—always a wise sales move (see Chap. 11). By making it easy for him to say yes, I gave myself an opportunity. Arthur called in his top salesman, Arnie Savoy. "Hey, Arnie," he laughed, "show this lady around. She wants to be a consultant and she's not getting paid till she makes us lots of money!"

Seventh Avenue back then was everything you've heard about: It was a real rat race. Everyone was stealing from everyone else. Fashion was a tough, low-margin business with a crazy, creative energy. It was the time of pink Cadillacs, beautiful women in gold lamé jumpsuits, and all-expense-paid junkets. Guys who spent their lives hustling for a buck—that was Seventh Avenue. It was also a man's world. The only women with any status were designers.

Arnie Savoy, Arthur's best producer, did whatever he had to do to make a sale. A tall, skinny guy with red hair, he always carried a pair of scissors in his pocket so he could snip off a piece of fabric from a competitor's rack as he passed it on the street. In fact, years after leaving the fashion industry, I met Arnie at the races. We chatted for about 15 minutes and went our separate ways. After I came home and took off my coat, wouldn't you know it? I found a big hole in my blouse!

Not long after leaving Classic Fabrics, I met Arnie for lunch at his favorite haunt on Thirty-sixth Street. He turned to me over a drink and said, "Tell me the truth, Wendy. You're not really 36, are you?" "You're right, Arnie," I admitted. "I lied about my age to give myself more credibility with Art. I'm really only 26." Arnie laughed and said, "You know something, Wendy? For 36, you're sensational—a real knockout. But for 26, you're definitely over the hill!" That's Seventh Avenue!

In spite of the rough-and-tumble atmosphere, I was thrilled to be working with Art and Arnie. At last, I had a chance! Classic only had one simple knit fabric. I called some eyelet embroidery people I knew and had them embroider it with three or four different colors to create coordinated jackets, slacks, and skirts. In three weeks, I tripled the company's sales. True to his word, Art gave me a substantial retroactive salary. My four months at Classic were productive, but I quickly became frustrated. Secretly, I wanted to create entirely new fabrics. Arthur wisely guessed my ambitions and saw I'd outlived my usefulness. He had found his little niche and was perfectly happy to work within it. He wasn't prepared to change his company in order to satisfy my desire to move beyond his current line. Art and I parted but remained good friends.

At this point, I'd lost just about everything: my business, my success, my income, my identity as a "hot" fashion designer. And if I didn't make a change, I was in danger of losing something far more precious: myself. I was trying to twist and turn myself into something I wasn't, to make myself fit where I didn't belong. But it wasn't working.

I realized, once and for all, that I was a dyed-in-the-wool entrepreneur. Anything less wasn't going to satisfy me. No amount of trying would allow me to succeed within the framework of a corporation. I had always had my own ideas, brought them to life, and then made them work. I didn't have to get anyone else's okay to make a decision. I didn't have to fit into anyone else's pattern. The whole concept of trying to fix things, add some creativity, and then fine-tune someone else's work was totally foreign to my personality and business style. I was doomed to failure in any kind of structured environment.

Facing up to this led me to start my own fashion consulting business. I was doing fairly well until Cliff reentered the picture. I was forced to close down shop and start over yet again. I went to work as an independent contractor with an executive recruiting firm. I began running a textile desk and it was an instant success. The firm's owner, Mel, paid 25 percent on commission until a recruiter reached $5500; after that the recruiter kept everything he or she made. I reached the $5500 after only four months, which didn't make Mel too happy, since he was paying my overhead, but not seeing any more profit. One day I told him, "You know, Mel, this textile desk is very lucrative. Why don't we advertise and build this business as partners?" He smiled a sardonic smile and said, "I'll think it over, Wendy." The next day I arrived at work to find my files gone and a note on my desk saying, "You are no longer employed here."

Once again, I was devastated. This job had been about as close to being on my own as I could come without hanging up a shingle, but I still got fired. Being successful at my work seemed to make me even more vulnerable than failure. But the very next day, Lady Luck hit me. While living in L.A., I had purchased some cheap stocks and then forgot about them. I sold just about everything to finance my move to New York, but one day my sister called to tell me that Merrill Lynch was trying to reach me; a rep wanted to buy the stock from me for about $9,000. I cashed in the stock and within two weeks, opened my own executive recruiting office at 10 East Fortieth Street. An entrepreneur once again, I soon built this into a very profitable business. I was earning a very comfortable living when I gave it up to start NAFE.

"Know thyself." That's how one wise old Greek philosopher summed up the secret to success in life. My advice to you is a little different: Accept yourself. It's not enough to know and understand your needs and talents. You have to be able to accept them, approve of them, and believe they are worthy of being nurtured. Knowing yourself leads to insight and ideas.

Accepting yourself leads to action. And if there's one priceless lesson that hitting rock bottom can teach you, it's this: If you lose yourself, you've lost everything. Reject yourself, and you'll be rejected.

When job after job blew up in my face, I finally had to accept my fate as an entrepreneur. However demanding this path was, I hadn't chosen it—it had chosen me. When the going gets tough, the tough get tougher. This is when you have to say to yourself, "I'm not going to change who I am in order to survive. *I'm going to find out who I am by surviving.*" Rock bottom may be a lousy place to be, but it isn't really lonely: It's where you meet yourself.

DON'T GET TOO COMFORTABLE— KEEP MOVING!

When you hit the bottom, you really have only two choices. You can either give up and stay there or fight your way out. You can lose yourself or find yourself. Fighting isn't easy. We all have times when we're tempted to take the path of least resistance and give up the struggle. Don't do it! Survive, don't settle! To lose yourself, to fade into anonymity, to make do with what's available—this isn't living, it's just existing. Stay true to yourself. As soon as you hit rock bottom, recognize it for what it is: a way station, a place you're just visiting, not a permanent address. Start searching for a way out. Above all, don't let yourself get too comfortable. That's the kiss of death for an entrepreneur.

Forward motion is everything. So when you're really low, don't slow down; do just the opposite: step on the gas. The single best thing you can do is to try to accomplish something. Take action. Do something that makes you feel good about yourself. No matter how small or simple a step, it will help jump-start your desire and drive. Keep moving, looking, doing, calling, fighting. Be willful! Tenacious! Determined! Adventurous! A pain in the ass, if you have to be!

During one of my low points, I had a friend, Audrey, whom

I both loved and hated. My first call every morning was from Audrey, and the first words out of her mouth were, "Hi, Wendy! What are you going to do today?" I wanted to throttle her! If I said, "I don't know," then she'd reply, "What do you mean, you don't know? Find something to do. Get out and go see somebody. Call Joe and see what he's doing for lunch. Talk to him. I'll call you tonight. I want to know what you did today." Twice a day, every day, Audrey would call and plague me. Sure enough, I'd find someone to talk to about something, even puppy dogs, just so I had something, anything, to tell Audrey that evening. She was a pain, but she never stopped trying to nudge me out into the world where I belonged. Now that's support!

Keep moving and see every situation as a stepping stone to something else. Selling that awful line of petite fashions, getting fired as a franchise rep, losing my recruiting job after only four months—each of these work crises pushed me forward toward something better. Each of them taught me more about who I was and, more important, who I wasn't. Eventually, they led me to my own recruiting business and then to NAFE.

So whatever the mess you're in and however you got there, do something. I don't care what. Don't waste time looking for the right thing: It may take doing 10 things to identify the right thing. The sooner you get started, the sooner you'll find it. When you're in motion, you'll feel better. Don't sit around, doing nothing, and asking yourself, "Is this right? Is this wrong? Is this the sensible thing to do? Am I making a mistake?" Just do *something*. Anything. If you make a mistake, so what? Remember, it's not the something you're doing that counts, it's doing something!

When you're really low, the single greatest temptation you face is giving up on yourself. This is also when you're most susceptible to other people's doubts and negativity. These naysayers are waiting for you with open arms. Beware their siren song!

They want you to settle in at rock bottom.

They'll champion you there.

They'll say, "Join the club."

What took you so long?

Now you're really living!

What were you doing before?

Breaking your neck.

Working 40 hours a day—for what?

What were you trying to prove?

Why don't you relax?

What I'm describing here is a full-fledged support system for failure. If you have something worth doing, there's going to be change involved. There's going to be disturbance. There's going to be conflict, agitation, everything but comfort. Upheaval: That's what creating is all about. That's what new ideas and new products are all about. That's what being an entrepreneur is all about. But all this unsettlement drives 9 out of 10 people crazy. It's simply too much for them to handle. So they're willing to settle for less than they really want out of life. But you don't have to be one of them. You don't have to settle. Why should you?

HANG ON TO YOUR DREAM! IT'S NOT JUST WHAT YOU WANT, IT'S WHO YOU ARE

When you're really struggling to survive, that's when your dream is most important. Remember, dreams often come out of disappointment, crisis, and even anger. Mine did. So when you need to pull yourself out of a depression, start dreaming about better things to come. And whatever *your* dream is, hang on to it at all costs, *because it's not just what you want, it's who you are.* Yes, as an entrepreneur, you're traveling a tough road. Settling for less can be very appealing; it seems a lot easier on your psyche and your stomach. But ask yourself this question: "What can I surrender myself to?"

During my lowest moments—and there were many of them, believe me!—I spent a lot of time being angry. I thought I had something to offer and people couldn't see it. But I never gave up my dream of equality, although I had no idea what to do with it. All I knew was that I wanted to see people treated the same and given a fair chance. To me, my dream was the pot of gold at the end of the rainbow. After I paid my dues, I figured I would have the chance to make that dream come true. To survive, I was willing to put it aside for a while. But I never abandoned it. I knew that my hard times were just temporary and that somehow, someday, I'd find a way to breathe new life into that dream of mine.

But to fulfill my dream, I had to give up my fantasy. I had to let go of the image of myself as a successful, high-paid fashion designer. I also had to let go of the idea of belonging in the traditional, accepted sense. In my loneliest moments, I began to see more clearly. Slowly, I began to understand that the only way I was ever going to fit in anywhere was to build a world of my own—and that's exactly what I did with NAFE.

Believe me, I had absolutely no idea—not a clue!—during my early days in New York that things were going to turn out this way. Who would have thought that Schwundelkopf, that frustrated, lonely kid with just a high-school education, no social background, and no money, would end up being the founder of NAFE—and help lead a movement that touched the lives of hundreds of thousands of women? Not me, that's for sure! But then, why not? This is America! I was a super saleswoman and NAFE was not just a dream, it was the biggest sales job of my career. I was selling women on believing in themselves. That's the wonderful, magical thing about dreams, isn't it? You never know where they'll take you.

PLAYBOY, NAFE, AND ME: THE BIRTH OF A DREAM

It was 1972 and the heyday of the Beatles, bell-bottoms, love-ins, and the women's liberation movement, which was receiving lots of media coverage. I can still see myself sitting at home one evening watching the news, as yet another women's liberation rally flashed across my screen, and thinking, "These 'libbers' are totally off base!" Frankly, it made me upset and angry to hear the way they talked about working women. While I admired their courage in speaking out, I found their message impossible to relate to. They seemed to see women as victims, as powerless, as slaves to an economic system that was busy grinding them into the dust. The battle of the sexes they were describing made the Civil War look like child's play!

At the time, I remember thinking to myself, "Something's wrong here! The women I keep seeing week after week on TV are really missing the boat. They may not know it, but their whole approach is designed to keep women down instead of building them up. What they're creating is a support system for failure, when what women really need is a support system for success." Instead of helping to change the situation, the image of women they were portraying, I felt, was actually making it worse. The more I thought about all this, the madder I got! I had to do something. What, I wasn't sure. But I knew a mission was calling me.

The very next day, I found myself at a friend's house for the weekend. Relaxing in the cozy warmth of her bathtub (which is where I always get my best ideas) I saw an old issue of *Playboy* lying on a shelf and picked it up. Hugh Hefner always had something outrageous to say, and the cartoons were great. As I leafed through the magazine, I was struck by the high-powered, successful image it was trying to sell the men who read it. Page after page of ads offered an exciting, tantalizing array of benefits: Wear Brut and you'll be an irresistible executive male. Drink Schenley's and you'll be a worldly executive male. Buy Swank cufflinks and you'll be a sophisticated executive male. Try these vitamins and you'll be a more manly executive male. Buy this underwear and you'll be a sexy executive male! And on and on.

As I was relaxing in the tub, the thought flashed into my mind: "Executive male this, executive male that! Why not executive *female? Why not* executive female? *Why the hell not* executive female?" I loved the whole idea. The "executive female"—now *there* was an image women could relate to with pride. If women saw themselves as executives, they would begin to identify with success. And once they identified with success, they'd be on the way to economic equality. Suddenly, I was hooked! I didn't know how I was going to do it, but then and there, I knew I was going to bring the "executive female" name to life.

The more I thought about this idea, the more excited I became. If I could convince major corporations that the executive female was an attractive and profitable market, they'd be falling all over each other trying to cater to our needs. They'd be creating products and services for women, just as they did for men. Instead of being crushed, we'd be courted. Instead of victims, we'd be victors. Instead of being put down, we'd be promoted to. Talk about a support system for success!

With all the money women earned, it was incredible to me that not a single major corporation seemed to be reaching out to the women's market. Far from it! We were being ignored.

Things weren't exactly rosy for most working women back in the 1970s. Women in the work force were 31 million strong, but they made up only 33 percent of all managers. Collectively, we were bringing home the bacon in a big way, but individually, even successful working women back then weren't making all that much. The vast majority worked full time and earned just over 60 cents for every dollar a man made. The "two paycheck" family was just beginning to gain visibility, and women's earnings were still considered marginal. As a result, women had a hard time building financial credibility.

To me, gaining financial recognition was where the action was. That's what the "executive female" concept had to be all about: financial independence. Even though we had been working in huge numbers for 10 years or more, as women we found it almost impossible to obtain credit or insurance in our own names. For the most part, credit card companies ignored us. If we wanted to apply for a loan to start or expand a business, except for rare instances, we were out of luck! Our husbands, fathers, brothers, or even our boyfriends had to take out the loan for us or cosign it. Women simply weren't recognized as independent wage earners or family breadwinners. I was going to change all that too!

All that night, the title Executive Female waltzed through my brain, dressed in dollar bills. I even found myself talking aloud to my dad in bed, if you can believe it! I remember wishing I could phone my boyfriend Stanley. I didn't sleep a wink and jumped up at the crack of dawn, filled with energy. I contained myself as long as I could. Stanley wouldn't get to his office until eight o'clock. But Dr. Alan, one of my staunchest supporters, was an early riser. To say that he didn't appreciate my 6:30 A.M. phone call one bit is putting it mildly. As he sipped his first of many cups of coffee, his first words to me were, "What's wrong, Wendy, what's wrong?" "Dr. Alan, I've got it, I've got it! The executive female!" I practically screamed into the phone. "What the hell are you talking about at this hour?" Dr. Alan responded with his customary tact. "The executive female. What the hell is that?"

"Dr. Alan," I bubbled over, almost beside myself, "you

know how I've been talking about creating economic equality for women. The executive female is the idea I've been looking for!" Breathlessly, I told him about *Playboy* magazine and all the executive-type ads it ran for Schenley's and Swank and Brut and so on. I wanted to give women the same opportunities, I said. "Anything in *Playboy* magazine, I agree with," Dr. Alan replied with a laugh.

Undaunted by Dr. Alan's lack of seriousness, I told him I was going to start calling every company I could think of that very morning and begin to sell them on the executive female market. My idea was simple: I wanted to persuade them to create lines, merchandise, credit cards, anything and everything we could dream up with the name "executive female" attached to it, so that women in the work force could start feeling good about themselves. Dr. Alan had never heard me so excited! I wanted to tell him more, but I could tell he wasn't really on my wavelength. Business wasn't his strong suit. It took all my self-control to wait until Stanley arrived at his office. An experienced marketing pro, I just knew he'd love my idea. I called him at 8:00 A.M. on the dot. "Stanley, what do you think of the name, 'executive female'?" I demanded. "I love it," he said, sipping his coffee as he talked, "but I'm late for a meeting!"

"I'm serious, Stanley," I replied. "The only way women are going to feel a sense of equality is if they have the opportunity to earn and spend money the way men do. You know the way companies use merchandise to identify men as executives? I want to do the same thing for women! Who can I call to start making appointments?" I asked him. "I know! I'm going to call American Express!"

Stanley laughed and said, "Good luck! I've got to go. You can tell me all about the exciting progress you've made over lunch. By the way, where did you come up with this idea?"

"*Playboy* magazine, where else?" I answered without skipping a beat. Stanley roared with laughter.

Even Stanley's lukewarm reception to my brainstorm didn't dampen my enthusiasm. I started making call after call. My first was to American Express. Just for the hell of it, I asked for the person in charge of the women's market. Much to my surprise, the secretary who had answered hemmed and hawed and then said, "I think the person you want is John Bennet." As soon as John picked up the phone, I announced that I wanted to meet with him about the executive female market. He didn't hesitate to make an appointment. Little did I know that just that morning, Amex had made the front page of *The Wall Street Journal*— and it wasn't good news. According to the article, women were having a difficult time obtaining credit cards in their own names from American Express and other financial service companies. No wonder John agreed to see me!

After Amex, I called some of the people I'd recruited in the textile business and asked for help in contacting some of the fashion houses. I reached back into my retailing past and called Bill Bloomingdale of Bloomingdale's department store fame, whose brother was the head of Diners Club. I asked Bill to get me an appointment at Diners Club. Having enjoyed a profitable relationship with me during my manufacturing days, he didn't even ask what I wanted. He just said, "Consider it done."

I was on a roll! I had a very busy morning, calling anyone and everyone I could think of. I ran the gamut, from Schenley's to American Plywood, of all places! Why American Plywood? I had no idea what I wanted from them at the time and still don't! I think it was something about a do-it-yourself American Plywood Executive Female wardrobe closet. "Why not?" I said to myself. "You never know what you can find out just by talking to people." And I'll be darned if those plywood people didn't give me an appointment too!

After meeting Stanley at noon, I decided to call Joe, one of my biggest executive search success stories. I had placed him in the top spot at one of the country's leading fashion houses and wanted his advice. I called him and teasingly told him I was on to something and it was too important to talk about over the phone. "I even have a meeting set up with American Express!" I boasted. "When can we have lunch? I need your help." He tried to pry the story out of me, but I was enjoying his curiosity too much to satisfy it. We made a luncheon date for the next day.

By 5:00 P.M., my appointments had piled up and I knew one thing for certain: Major corporations were interested in the female market. I was on to something. I didn't know what, but I knew it was worth pursuing. That same day, I hired a public relations firm, the only one that would take me. Not exactly an A-list firm, for a $750 monthly retainer, these guys would take on anyone as a client. To get my business, Ed Winston, one of the firm's account managers, promised me a press conference. Was I excited! I also made him promise to help me prepare a marketing kit, as soon as I had some ideas ready. Armed with nothing more than this kit, I proceeded to make the rounds of the companies I'd contacted. My first stop? American Express.

   ·   I walked into American Express's fancy suite of offices feeling a little like Dorothy in the Land of Oz. Amex was a hugely successful company with a reputation for creative marketing. I wore my best white pantsuit and my highest stiletto heels— this was the big time, after all! A courtly, impeccably pinstripe-suited John Bennet ushered me into his office and we chatted about the women's market and how attractive it was. After a little more small talk, I decided to bring out my ace in the hole and really knock his socks off. "Mr. Bennet," I asked, "how would American Express feel about creating an Executive Female credit card for women?"

To his everlasting credit, I'm happy to report, John Bennet didn't laugh me out of his office right then and there! Instead, he appeared to ponder this idea for a minute and then politely replied, "That's an interesting proposal, Ms. Rue. At this stage, however, I believe American Express has enough name recognition to survive on its own without a new identity!" Although John burst that bubble pretty quickly, he was still encouraging. The consummate corporate executive, John knew the value of leaving the door open. As our meeting ended, he asked me to keep him posted on my progress. He also said he'd listen to any concrete proposal I came up with. "Not bad!" I thought.

A few weeks later, thanks to my friend Bill Bloomingdale, I arrived for a meeting with Amex's competitor, Diners Club. I was a little late and my marketing kit, with its dime-store plastic cover, had gotten there ahead of me. I became more than a little nervous when I found myself ushered into DC's sumptuous board room, where I was greeted by not one but "five wise men," as I called them, from the company's marketing group. The group was led by a man named Joe Garvey. As I sat down, I saw Joe scanning my marketing kit, which contained what I thought were my brightest ideas: "the Executive Female hotel chain," "the Executive Female health spa," "the Executive Female business club." And so on. Everything in the kit was on a national scale. There was nothing small about this idea! After a quick glance at the kit, Joe Garvey innocently made a comment that changed my life forever: "Wendy, we'd be interested in knowing how many members you have in your club."

A huge, neon lightbulb flashed in my head! "Mr. Garvey," I answered, without skipping a beat, "forming a club is the first project on my agenda! If Diners Club wants to participate, I'll be more than happy to set up another meeting as soon as possible with my financial vice president!" (Translation: I'll drag over my boyfriend, Stanley, whose arm I'll twist!) I was so excited by the way Joe Garvey had instantly zeroed in on my club idea, that I could hardly sit still. Maybe *this* was the hook I was looking for! I wanted to jump up and bounce off the ceiling. I wrapped up the meeting as quickly as I could and raced across town, hitting my P.R. firm like a cyclone.

"I don't like the word *club*," I announced to Ed Winston before he could even open his mouth to say hello. "Is that the reason you burst in here at 10 A.M.? Are you crazy?" he replied. "I'm serious!" I answered. "I don't like the word *club*. Give me a better one." "How about *association?*" Ed offered, as if he were throwing meat to a hungry lion. "I love it!" I answered. "What does it do?" "It has members," Ed replied. "Then that's what I want to be! I want to be the National Association for Female Executives! You're my P.R. firm. Make me an association!" "I can't do that," Ed said. "You have to get a lawyer." "Let me use your phone," I replied.

That same morning, I called a lawyer I knew and said, "I want to be an association. How long will it take to make me one?" "For-profit or not-for-profit?" the lawyer asked. "For-profit, of course!" I answered. "Who goes into business *not* to make money?" All this happened on a Wednesday. By Friday, the National Association for Female Executives, soon to be known as NAFE, was born. It was the first woman's for-profit association in America. With a membership of one. I went back to my P.R. agency, marched into Ed's office, and announced, "I am now the National Association for Female Executives, and you're not going to get paid until I get the press conference you promised me." "What's the association all about?" Ed asked. "Money!" I answered. In that moment, NAFE's credo, "The Dollar Bill Knows No Sex," was coined.

I had my name, my association, and a slogan, and I was ready to tell the world about it. Ed set up a press conference the following week at the Regency Hotel. Things were perking along nicely. Then, suddenly, I got cold feet. I'd never attended a press conference and had no idea what you did at one. To make matters worse, I'd never spoken in public before. I was terrified! "Relax, Wendy!" Ed said. "You have nothing to worry about! You have no members. You have no money. No one's going to attend this thing! If one or two people show up to grab a cup of coffee and a Danish, I'll be amazed. I'll get up and explain what the association is all about. All you have to do is thank the press for attending." "Sounds easy enough," I thought to myself.

At 10 A.M. on the morning of June 28, 1972, I walked into the Regency Hotel to a standing-room-only crowd of media sharks hungry for a red-hot story. Unknown to me, Ed had put out a press release saying that I was anti-women's lib. Every reporter in New York was at the Regency to find out who this crazy woman named Wendy Rue was and what she was up to. There were TV cameras, microphones, tape recorders, and an army of outraged female and bemused male reporters, all ready to pounce. I was absolutely petrified!

Ed walked up to the microphone. Instead of describing NAFE as he'd promised, the sneaky bum pulled a fast one. "Ladies and gentlemen of the press, thank you for coming," he said. "I know you're here today because you're eager to learn what the National Association for Female Executives is all about. So without any further delay, let me turn you over to its founder and president, Wendy Rue." With that, Ed beckoned me to the podium and slipped discreetly out of sight.

I didn't have a clue about what I should say. I had no speech, no notes, nothing. After all, Ed had assured me that all I'd need to do would be to stand up, thank the press, and sit down. I was in a pickle and I knew it. So I did the only thing I could think of, which was to do exactly what Ed had done! He'd dumped the meeting in my lap like a hot potato, so I decided to dump it in the reporters' laps! My knees knocking, I braced myself against the podium, took a deep breath, and said, "Ladies and gentlemen of the press, thank you for coming! I know you're here to learn what NAFE's all about, so let me open the floor to questions!"

The press conference lasted about 2½ hours. By the time I left the hotel, I'd learned more about NAFE from the reporters' questions than they had from grilling me! When I caught myself on TV on the six o'clock news, I looked so scared, my eyes were crossed!

That night, my dad visited me in a dream. "See, Schwundel," he said with a twinkle in his eye, "I taught you right! What women need is financial independence. If they have money, they'll feel like equals and have the emotional freedom to be who they want to be. By the way, I'm proud of you. You did a good job."

The very next morning, all the members of my support team checked in. My first call (at 6:30 in the morning!) was from Dr. Alan. "Hey, kid, you really knocked 'em dead! You're right: Money. That's what all those broads out there need. The press was absolutely full of you!" My next call was from Stanley. "You did a great job!" Next, I heard from Joe Thompson; the conservative type, he was a little less enthusiastic: "Sure, women want money, but don't you think you were a little too tough?" he asked. In the last call of the morning, my sister, Myrna, said, "I haven't the vaguest idea what you were talking about, Wendy. But what the hell! You looked pretty good on TV."

After my round of calls and a quick look at the newspapers, I was on top of the world. The press coverage was incredible! "Women Execs Have Ally"; "Equal Dollar Power Goal of Female Execs"; "Women execs—unite!" "Girls! An Exec Earns 10G; It's to Her Credit"; "New women's group prefers 'par' to 'lib'"; "Dollar Neither Male or Female"; "Them that got, want more"; "Miss Rue: There's Discrimination in What a Woman Gets for Her Money." Headline after headline told the story I wanted people to hear: Women wanted financial equality, and NAFE was going to help them.

Now that my association was on the map, I decided NAFE needed an advisory board. I recruited some key players on my support team as its first members: Dr. Alan Rosenberg, a well-known psychiatrist and lawyer; my boyfriend, Stanley Haltman, who was the executive vice president of a major textile firm and a first-class marketer; Joe Thompson, the president of a public conglomerate; and Ed King, a senior partner at a very conservative accounting firm. I intentionally made the board all male for two reasons. First, I wanted to prove my point that not all men are against women, and second, I felt the executives I selected would give me credibility with the corporate world.

As I think back to that crazy press conference and the first heady days when the "Executive Female" idea began taking shape, it seems almost unreal. What an exciting time this was for me! After struggling so long to give voice to my dream of equality, that dream finally had an identity, the executive female, and a vehicle, a national association. The National Association for Female Executives embodied everything I'd been working toward. It gave me a focus, a purpose, and a way to reach other women and help them in their quest for financial freedom.

Recalling those hectic few weeks, from the time the name Executive Female flashed through my mind to the press conference, I'm struck by how incredibly driven I was. NAFE wasn't a business, it was a happening. And I didn't really create NAFE, it quickly took on a life of its own. I just followed its lead and my own intuition. But though the NAFE story has a very distinctive flavor to it, it also reflects some fundamental truths about entrepreneurial start-ups. And, although NAFE was firmly rooted in the 1970s, its launch offers a powerful model for today's entrepreneur. With this in mind, let me try to capture for you what I learned in founding NAFE:

THE BEST IDEAS ARE FOUND IN THE STRANGEST PLACES

The first spark for what would become NAFE flashed into my head not in a boardroom but in the bathtub! And I wasn't poring over *The New York Times* or *The Wall Street Journal*; I was idly thumbing through an out-of-date, dog-eared copy of *Playboy*. I've told you this not just because it's the absolute truth but because the NAFE story is the best proof I know of to support my theory about where entrepreneurial ideas come from.

Most entrepreneurial ventures have a rough-and-tumble air about them; they're usually far more gritty than glamorous. They're conceived not in MBA classes or conference rooms or think tanks but on the street, where the Arnie Savoys of the world are out snipping chunks of fabric on their lunch hours. In short, most innovative start-ups are part of the fabric of the real, everyday world—not isolated or insulated from it. These ideas emerge from real needs, real problems, real emotions. And more often than not, they are the result not of comfort and control but of confusion and even crisis.

I once heard the director of the Entrepreneurship Institute talk about a study he conducted that totally supports the "kick-in-the-pants" theory of entrepreneurship developed at my alma mater, the School of Hard Knocks. According to his Institute's findings, most successful people make the leap into entrepreneurship only after some kind of upheaval shakes them up and turns their lives upside down and inside out—an unexpected job loss, a family tragedy, a midlife derailment, a period of intense anxiety and soul-searching. In my own case, this is exactly what happened. NAFE emerged at a time when

I was restless, discontented, and searching for some kind of meaning in my life and a way to pursue my dream of equality. The executive recruiting business I had started several years before the idea for NAFE hit me was very lucrative. But I was bored, unfulfilled, and itching to find something to devote myself to that was of real value, not only to myself but to the rest of the world.

If there's one thing I've learned it's that you never know exactly where or when a great idea will hit. Like NAFE, some of my best ideas have come by accident or in unusual places—in a cab, at the races, in my bathtub. For example, I first heard about the recruiting business at my hairdresser's. I happened to sit next to a woman who said she was an executive recruiter and proudly told me that she was making $35,000 a year. I figured that if she could earn that much finding people jobs, then I could earn at least that doing exactly the same thing. That's how I entered recruiting, which led me to my own business and, eventually, to NAFE.

The working women's list that became NAFE's lifeline and its sole source of income for years was conceived after a casual conversation with a venture capitalist. He wasn't willing to underwrite NAFE's start-up, but he suggested that I talk to a man named Warren at *Shopper's Voice,* a consumer marketing publication. This resulted in a meeting in which I came up with the idea to include four simple questions in an issue of *Shopper's Voice* (more on this in Chap. 8). The answers produced the data I needed to create my Executive Female mailing list—the first of its kind.

The idea to set up NAFE networks across the country—still a thriving program today—was sparked by a chat with Susan Strecker, then the editor-in-chief of NAFE's magazine, *The Executive Female.* One day in the office, Susan happened to mention a get-together she'd had with some friends on a weekend trip down to Washington. They'd all caught up on each other's personal lives and then traded stories and advice about their jobs and career goals. Susan told me this same group of women met quite often. "What a wonderful idea!" I remember thinking. As I listened to Susan describe the support and encouragement these friends gave each other, I could see her enthusiasm grow, and the seed for NAFE's networking program took root.

As an entrepreneur, you're a seeker on a quest. You're always searching for an idea or vision that will light a spark. To find it, you have to be totally open and vulnerable to surprise, chance, and whatever the universe happens to throw your way. You also have to be not just willing but also eager to talk and then talk some more—to anyone anywhere about almost anything. Keep your antennae up all the time. Keep reaching out, probing, seeking, expressing your curiosity, trying to understand the world around you better than it understands you. Be alert not just to opportunities but to obstacles. Ask questions. Look for the answers in unexpected places, both exotic and ordinary, and the right idea will find you. And when it does, then the entrepreneurial process really take's flight. Your one idea starts multiplying like rabbits in spring! Once you have that all-important base, your job—and fun—have just begun!

ANGER CAN BE A POWERFUL MOTIVATOR—AND A GREAT SOURCE OF ENTREPRENEURIAL IDEAS

Everyone has ideas, daydreams, and ambitions worthy of pursuing, but we all need something to motivate us to shift from thought to action. More often than not, creative new ventures are born out of frustration not fantasy, and out of anger as much as ambition. I know this is true for me. My greatest emotional motivator has always been anger. This goes back to the days when I started my teen shops because I was steamed about the way most stores treated teenagers. In the case of NAFE, my anger became a living, burning thing in me. I simply could not and would not accept the idea of women being put down and not having a support system that would help them achieve economic parity with men.

For me, being angry involves many feelings, but mainly it

results in a frustrating sense of discomfort and the fear that I won't be able to do anything about it. Personally, it's very hard for me to look at why I'm angry. I'm always questioning whether I have a right to my anger or not. Many other people share this feeling. But whether you have a right to your anger or not, unless you defuse it, you're going to be a very unhappy person. When anger becomes overpowering, it festers until it immobilizes you instead of spurring you to change what's bothering you.

At the time I started NAFE, I was angry at the lack of equality for women, especially when it came to money. I felt it was wrong and unjust. But I was upset in a vague, general sense about the situation women faced. What really triggered my anger in a more focused, direct way was the radical segment of the women's liberation movement. Once my anger had an object, I was able to think about it more concretely and practically—and less emotionally. That pointed me to a solution: creating a support system for success for women.

In my experience, a lot of people—male and female—walk around angry a lot of the time, but they don't know what they're angry about. But the most important thing you can do in handling anger is to recognize what's caused it. Once you understand why you're angry, you can do something to translate your emotional upheaval into positive action. Use your anger! Make it work for you instead of against you. Turn things around. Try to see your anger as a creative, rather than a destructive, force in your life. See it as a wake-up call, a sign, a message from your inner self about what matters most to you. After all, if you didn't care about whatever it is that's burning you up, you wouldn't be mad, would you? What doesn't fit and isn't working? Where are things askew, out of balance, unfair? Who needs help and isn't getting it? What makes you upset and dissatisfied in your everyday life—and why? What makes your life tougher than it should be, and what would make it easier? What do you need but can't find? What makes you frustrated and discontented with your current situation or the way the world works? What would you fix, if you could wave a magic wand?

While anger is a powerful tool for change, it's also one of the emotions that people are most frightened of. It takes real courage to acknowledge and explore your anger, instead of denying it or hiding from it. But if you have the strength to pursue this path, you'll find it very rewarding. Mine your anger for ideas and it can lead you to untold riches and satisfaction.

THE ONLY WAY TO MAKE AN IDEA GROW IS TO SHARE IT

I was sitting with two acquaintances one evening at an impromptu brainstorming session. They had a great idea and wanted my opinion. But as one woman began describing it, she prefaced her remarks by saying, "Wendy, don't tell anyone about this!" After she finally opened up, I recommended a couple of people she might call to run the idea by. "Oh, no!" the two women answered nervously. "We can't do that! Our idea's too good. Someone might steal it!" This hush-hush approach was very hard for me to deal with. I had to restrain myself from saying, "Hey, wait a minute! Right now, you've got absolutely nothing worth taking!"

I've seen this attitude time and time again. It's very damaging—even fatal—to an entrepreneur. People are so frightened about having their ideas stolen that they end up stealing from themselves. Their own fear robs them of the chance to make their idea into something. You've probably seen this kind of fear at work yourself. How many times have you heard a friend or colleague ponder someone else's success story and say, "Gee, I had exactly that same idea for a business a few years ago!" But of course, they never did anything about it, so nothing happened.

I've never been worried about anyone stealing anything from me, because no one could steal my mind or rob me of my creativity. In fact, I've always taken the opposite approach and shared my ideas with anyone and everyone who would listen to them, even at the risk of being a pain in the ass. Being able to share freely is an important skill in sales. When you go to someone and say, "Hey, I have an idea, what do you think?" it makes people feel that you have confidence in their judgment. It also makes them feel important. And people like doing business with people who make them feel good about themselves.

When I had my own retailing business, I was constantly out selling and meeting with customers. Much of my time was spent giving the textile manufacturers I worked with new ideas about how to improve their businesses. One of my fortes was showing them how they could use their existing equipment to produce new fabrics. This willingness to understand my customers' problems and help them find new ways to solve them not only made me more valuable to them, it also gave me more merchandise to sell.

I took exactly this same freewheeling, open approach to launching NAFE, and it taught me an invaluable entrepreneurial lesson: The only way to make an idea grow is to share it. And when you share your idea freely and confidently, the world will help you shape it into something of real value. To me, brainstorming is one of the best-kept secrets of entrepreneurial success. Somehow, when you talk about an idea out loud with other people, the sparks begin flying. You never know what someone else will say that will help make your dream a reality.

People try to nurture their ideas by keeping them under wraps. But this approach is doomed to failure. The longer you keep an idea that really excites you all to yourself, the staler it becomes—until, at some point, it just withers on the vine. If you have a concept or dream that really matters to you, don't hide it! Bring it out into the light of day, where both you and other people can see it. You never know what great contribution someone else will make. But remember, when you do share your idea, especially in its formative stage, do it with care. Be sure you expose it to intelligent, well-informed people who will challenge you but also take you seriously.

When I held my press conference at the Regency Hotel, I had nothing but the name NAFE and a flimsy piece of paper identifying it as a for-profit association. NAFE had no money, no business plan, no project or proposal in the works, no contracts, no clients. There was absolutely nothing to the idea but my belief in its potential. Yet, instead of hiding it away, I decided to put it out in the world to see what would happen. I learned more about NAFE's mission in that 2½-hour press conference than I would have if I had spent six months and umpteen-thousand dollars researching the women's market. Nine out of ten people who had an idea for a venture like NAFE would have been secretive and held it close to the vest. I did the exact opposite and, believe me, it was one of the best decisions I ever made!

LET THE MARKET TELL YOU WHAT IT WANTS

If you are willing to share your idea with the world, then the world will return the favor and help you shape it. If you're open-minded and a good listener, then your market will find you and define your business for you. I know, because that's exactly what happened to me with NAFE. When the name Executive Female first popped into my mind, I had absolutely no idea what form it would take. Not a clue! Because of my sales background, I approached the concept strictly from a marketing angle. I saw the Executive Female name as a merchandising vehicle. When it flashed into my head, a vast array of products and services all geared to working women danced before my eyes.

I thought that by attaching the phrase Executive Female to their merchandise, companies could attract women buyers. And that's exactly what I did in my marketing kit, if you recall. I talked about the Executive Female health club, the Executive Female line of career clothes, the Executive Female hotel chain, the Executive Female briefcase. With this bunch of titles in tow, I began making calls and wandering through the world, looking for a home for my dream.

To my mind, all the merchandising ideas I'd dreamed up seemed very obvious to me. I wasn't sure which one would fly in the marketplace. So I went to each meeting I'd set up with an open mind and a cocked ear. I knew that this was going to be a learning time and that if I listened hard enough, I'd hear what I needed to know. I turned out to be right. And everywhere I went, the lesson was the same. As I suspected, every corporation I talked with wanted to reach the booming working women's market, but no one had the foggiest idea how to go about it. By the time I walked into Joe Garvey's office at the Diners Club, I was ripe and ready to recognize the right hook for the Executive Female name. When Joe asked about my "club," a lightbulb went off in my head. I knew that NAFE was going to be a membership organization. It happened in an instant. Just like that!

I learned about NAFE's mission from my press conference. As I listened to the questions the reporters asked and read their news stories the next day, NAFE's purpose became clear to me. The flood of media coverage my comments created convinced me that I was on the right track. The press zeroed in on NAFE's focus on the bottom line. Article after article talked about NAFE being geared to successful career women—women who were making it and wanted economic equality and more financial opportunities.

The more press I read, the more certain I became about NAFE's purpose. It was to make working women aware of the financial opportunities available to them by convincing major corporations to market financial products and services to them. NAFE was going to offer a support system for success. It was going to put women in the winner's circle. To convince working women that they weren't alone, I planned to give America's largest corporations a vehicle for telling them, "You're important to us and we want your business."

I closed that press conference by putting myself on the line. I promised the reporters crowding the room that within three months NAFE would announce the names of four major corporations that would offer credit cards to women, make them bank loans, offer them insurance or other financial products if they earned $10,000 or more. Never one to do anything by halves, I'd made a commitment and trumpeted my plans to the entire world. There was no turning back. Now, I had to deliver!

CHAPTER

EIGHT

NOBODY'S EVER DONE IT BEFORE? SO WHAT!

Within 24 hours, my press conference and the news stories it generated put NAFE on the map. I was thrilled
and still on cloud nine from all the attention, when I received
a call from Joe Thompson, one of the members of my board of
directors. He thought it would be a good idea to have a private
meeting of the board. Innocently, I agreed. I had no idea that
the key item on the agenda wasn't going to be NAFE but *me*.
As soon as Stanley, Ed, and Dr. Alan were gathered together,
Joe dropped a bombshell in the middle of the table. He turned
to Dr. Alan and said as tactfully as he could, "It looks as if
NAFE is off and running. Now that we may have a success on
our hands, I think Wendy really needs to change her image.
After all, she's looking to be a role model for thousands of
women. She's got to dress and act more conservatively or
NAFE will never make it. You're a psychiatrist, Dr. Alan. Can't
you reprogram her somehow?"

Silence fell over the room. I was absolutely crushed. I
thought everyone was going to be patting me on the back for
the great P.R. job I had done, and instead, my own support
team was trying to grind me into little pieces and turn me into
a corporate clone. Ed King wiggled in his seat and doodled on
his yellow pad. Suddenly, Stanley started roaring with laughter, as if this was the funniest thing he'd ever heard. I waited
breathlessly for Dr. Alan's response. It wasn't long in coming.

He whipped on his thick, black glasses and bellowed with *his* usual tact, "You idiot! Every woman in America would like to be a free spirit like Wendy! She's trying to encourage women to be themselves—that's what they really want. Wendy's right on target and you're off the wall! *You* need to be reprogrammed, not her!"

About a week after this little encounter session, Joe called me and said, "Wendy, I've given it a lot of thought. I really admire what you're doing, but as the president of a public company, I have to be very careful about my image. I think it's best if I resign from the board." Never one to burn my bridges, I asked him to help NAFE behind the scenes, and he agreed. I knew I had to move on, but that board meeting taught me an invaluable lesson: Even though I had the support of Dr. Alan and Stanley, when push came to shove, I was on my own. NAFE had one champion, one anchor, and for the moment, one member: me. Not only was I NAFE's founder and chief executive, I was also its marketing director, sales staff, fundraiser, and P.R. department. To follow my dream, I was going to have to give up everything, even my need for approval. I closed down my thriving and very profitable recruiting business and let go of my beautiful suite of offices in the East Forties. NAFE became my life, my obsession.

At the time, my grand venture consisted of two old shoe boxes filled with dog-eared index cards listing every business contact I could think of. The boxes had a permanent place of honor on the coffee table of my white-and-hot-pink living room in my Upper Eastside apartment, which I couldn't really afford to rent since I wasn't making any money. For almost three years, those two shoe boxes, my telephone, and my dream of financial independence for women were NAFE's sole assets.

"Now what?" I remember asking myself. I knew *what* I wanted to do: build NAFE into a support system for success for working women. I also knew *how* I wanted to do it: by making NAFE a vehicle for helping major financial corporations reach career women with their products and services. But even with all the exposure the press had given NAFE, no one was beating my door down. People in general and would-be friends were saying, "Who is this nut who thinks she's single-handedly going to create equality for women?" Luckily, I was too busy to listen. I had a job to do.

At my press conference, I made a commitment to finding major financial services companies that wanted to reach working women. To me, this goal was by no means mission impossible. Actually, I felt a little like a teacher at a high school dance. The girls were sitting on one side of the gym and the boys on the other. If I could just get a few of them together, soon the floor would be packed! It takes two to tango. First, I needed the right corporate partners, and second, I had to find a way to reach working women and tell them about the benefits NAFE could offer them. I figured I needed four big companies to launch NAFE. "Four sales. Four yeses. That's all I need to get things going," I remember thinking to myself.

Reaching the women I wanted as NAFE members seemed to be no problem (or so I thought). My P.R. agent, Ed Winston, told me I could buy a list of working women. This list would enable NAFE and major corporations to reach our target market via direct mail. Armed with a sheaf of press clips, I decided to revisit American Express. Taking the bull by the horns, I called John Bennet one day and said, "John, I appreciate your interest in NAFE, but I want to talk to your boss—someone who can give me the green light on a major proposal." "Wendy," John said with a laugh, "I *am* the boss! I *am* the decision maker! What's on your mind?"

Whoops! Once the air was cleared, this call was the start of a long and profitable relationship for both American Express and NAFE. At the time, John was Amex's group marketing director. Largely through his willingness to take a chance on me, American Express became NAFE's first corporate sponsor. American Express wanted to attract women with higher-than-average earning power, but didn't know how; they needed a marketing vehicle. NAFE filled the bill perfectly. It had an appealing, upbeat identity and a strong business focus. It also had (or so I thought) access to a list of 250,000 working women's names—something American Express was desperate for.

"The 'geoglyphics' of this list are very desirable," I assured John Bennet, trying to sound savvy about the mysterious world of direct-mail marketing. The term *geoglyphics* really caught John's attention in a big way. Believing that I had access to some exotic new form of marketing data, he became intensely interested in what NAFE had to offer. Only much later, long after we'd cut a deal and were working together, did John learn that geoglyphics was my garbled version of plain old demographics!

I proposed a joint venture: the first cooperative mailing of its kind targeted to the women's market. Through the mailing, women could join NAFE and apply for their own American Express cards if they qualified. I also proposed that American Express pay a portion of the mailing and give NAFE a small percentage of its profit for every new Amex member the campaign produced—a real marketing coup. On top of this, I wanted NAFE to have total control of our mailing and of tracking its results.

"The National Association for Female Executives invites you to apply for an American Express card," was the headline I humbly suggested. The campaign I proposed promised to be a marriage made in economic heaven, creating a win-win sales situation for both parties. "Why do we need NAFE to do this?" John Bennet asked, shifting into his hard-nosed corporate mode. "For two reasons," I answered breezily. "First, for credibility. And second, because I own the mailing list with the proper geoglyphics." "Who else is going to be in the mailing?" he asked. "I'll let you know in a few weeks," I replied.

Easier said than done. Amex was in my corner. Even so, selling three other companies on what NAFE had to offer wasn't as simple as I thought it would be. Day after day, in classic sales style, I worked the phone, calling company after company. My pitch was always the same. As soon as I had some executive on the line (at the time, they were all male, of course!), I'd ask him, "Don't you know the dollar bill knows no sex?! You're only doing business with men, but women have money too!" Believe me, my opening line was a real winner! Mixing money and sex in a business call never failed to gain the undivided attention of my listener. Once I had him hooked, I'd push for an appointment. I always resisted telling the NAFE story over the phone: Face-to-face meetings were what I wanted.

There were many days when I felt like a voice crying in the wilderness. When I talked about the dollar bill knowing no sex, I got people's attention and yet it was like I was speaking a foreign language. Most companies had yet to spend any time, energy, or money finding out who we working women were, where we were, and what we wanted. In 1972, the whole concept of a women's market was foreign to the corporate world. NAFE helped create that market by selling corporations on the idea that women executives with "above average" salaries of $10,000 or more represented a vast, untapped source of buying power that they could ignore at their risk or embrace to their profit.

To make NAFE work, I needed to bridge the gap between working women and corporate America. At the time, there were about 10 million women earning more than $10,000 a year—the magic number for credit card and bank loan acceptability. *Ten million women!* The market was absolutely huge! Even so, it was hard for many executives to grasp the idea that NAFE was a friend, not foe—mainly because of all the bad press corporations were getting from women's lib groups. If I hadn't had Amex on my side, my sales job would have been almost impossible. Amex and my press clips really paved the way.

After a month of calls and a phone bill that shot through the roof, I finally managed to get interviews with about half a dozen companies. Ultimately, Carte Blanche, Hertz, and CTG Insurance decided to invest $10,000 each in my cooperative mailing. Each company supplied its own materials, but on top of each application, once again, I persuaded them to feature that golden headline: "The National Association for Female Executive invites you to...." I was ecstatic! I'd made my first sales for the cost of my phone bill and a few lunches. Even more important, NAFE was in business!

Once I had the OK from my corporate partners, I sent out a press release broadcasting to the world that Amex, Hertz, Carte Blanche, and CTG Insurance were all preparing to do business with the working women's market through NAFE. It was a great moment for me! I was excited and so were my sponsors. American Express and I even held a joint press conference to announce our program. I had a huge NAFE Executive Female membership card made up and was planning to present it to Amex's chairman, Morris Segal. As the conference drew nearer, John Bennet became more and more nervous. How would his boss, whom he thought of as ultraconservative, react to me and my flamboyant style? What could John do to keep me under control? Nothing, was the answer of course, and he knew it.

The day of the conference, I waltzed into one of Amex's fanciest boardrooms radiant in white and dripping with gold jewelry. I walked right up to Morris, put my arms around him, gave him a big kiss on the cheek, and proudly handed him my blowup of an Executive Female membership card, which was as big as a baby elephant. I could see John Bennet quietly groaning to himself from embarrassment. But Morris was as pleased as punch at the great publicity for Amex. He whisked me off to lunch in a limo, and within five minutes, we were old buddies. Morris came from retail, just as I did, and we had lots to talk about. This was the first of many lunches we enjoyed together.

With the joint press conference behind me, I was eager to move ahead with my mailing. I called Ed Winston and said, "Where do I buy my list?" Ed replied, "You don't buy lists, Wendy, you rent them. And by the way, I made a little mistake. There is no list of working women available." In an instant, I saw NAFE's bright future dissolve before my eyes: I had my corporate partners all spruced up and ready to dance, but now I had no way to help them woo the women they wanted to reach. Ed had misled me and I'd misled my sponsors. I could have covered up my problem, but I felt that would be totally dishonest. These companies had trusted me with $40,000 and I wasn't going to snow them. Even though it might mean the difference between NAFE's success and failure, there was only one thing to do: I called my sponsors, told them my tale of woe, and offered to refund their money.

As I mentioned in Chap. 4, telling the truth about this situation was one of the smartest moves I've ever made. My corporate partners learned that I was honest and that they could trust me. To their everlasting credit, all four sponsors told me the press I was giving them was great. They said I should use the money to go forward with my mailing. I'll never forget how much this vote of confidence meant to me at the time. I patched together a list by doing what everyone else was doing: selecting women's names from subscribers to *The Wall Street Journal, Cosmo, Glamour,* and other publications—and hoping they were working women. Not a very promising approach.

Then, to make matters worse, my ever-helpful P.R. firm recommended a direct-mail house whose owner turned out to be a crook! Instead of dropping our mailing by the December 15 deadline, he stole my postage money and used it for his other clients! He figured I was too naive to figure out what he was doing. What a mess! I called Stanley in a panic, made him drop everything, run down to the mailing house, and grab any sacks of NAFE mail he could find. He was able to salvage about 75,000 out of 250,000 mailers, but we had no idea how many, if any, the owner had mailed before ripping me off. This mailing produced about 1700 members for NAFE. Since I didn't know the total size of the mailing, I had no idea what our return rate was—and neither did Amex or Hertz. The whole campaign was a complete disaster. Once again, my sponsors were sympathetic, but I was beside myself. Now what?

Just as I was feeling totally discouraged, Lady Luck turned my way. A venture capitalist I approached about seed money turned me down but told me about a Maryland-based company with a product called *Shopper's Voice,* a household-oriented, market research magazine with a sweepstakes mechanism that reached 4 million households a year. My instincts told me this might be the key to my mailing list dilemma. I called Warren, the company's marketing director, and asked if I could take him to lunch. He agreed. A few discreet inquiries led me to believe that Warren was a latent ladies' man. Thinking he'd be impressed at being wined and dined in royal style, I hustled up my last few dollars, hired a limousine, and drove to Maryland. Over lunch, I persuaded Warren to include four questions aimed at working women in his next *Shopper's Voice*:

- Are you working outside the home?
- Full-time or part-time?
- What best describes your job function?
- What is your salary range?

These four questions, combined with standard data on age, marital status, and so on, gave me a total profile of the women I wanted to reach. I finally had the "geoglyphics" I'd been talking about! The first mailing Warren and I worked on produced about 500,000 names. Once again, I took a joint venture approach: I agreed to pay the owner of *Shopper's Voice* a generous fee for the exclusive right to mass market this working women's segment of its list. In return for a piece of the action, Ed Burnett, a top list broker, agreed to mass market the property. Without spending a penny, the "Executive Female mailing list" was created and it belonged to NAFE. We had created the first list of working women. Even more exciting, NAFE now had a salable product all its own!

From day one, in spite of the high price tag attached to the list—or perhaps because of it—this enterprise was a smashing success. Once we had the Executive Female mailing list up and running, it was easier to attract more corporate sponsors and NAFE really began to take off. But it was always cash poor during its first five years. With every nickel we earned, NAFE would go into the mail again, seeking new members. During these lean years, the Executive Female mailing list was NAFE's lifeline and its only steady source of income.

As NAFE slowly grew, I began to realize that we needed to offer some ongoing benefits to keep the members we recruited. As a first step, I approached Jean Schoonover, the president of a well-known P.R. agency, about putting out a newsletter for NAFE members. Jean wanted to break into the financial services market; in return for introductions to some of my corporate contacts, she agreed to write the newsletter for free, and our four-page quarterly, *The Executive Female Report*, was born.

Unwittingly, Jean also became a bit player in one of my all-time worst business meeting fiascoes. I was at a real low point and wondering if NAFE was really worth it all. I hadn't paid my rent in a month, and I was desperate. Then, out of the blue, I got a call from a Mr. Johnson at Fireman's Fund. I had contacted him ages ago and nothing happened. But suddenly, NAFE's name had cropped up in Fireman's five-year plan and Johnson and some others wanted to fly in to New York and talk. "Fine," I said, "I'll have my corporate team with me." I put in an SOS to Stanley and Ed Burnett. We agreed to hold the meeting in my apartment.

The week before the meeting, the lights in my apartment suddenly went out because I hadn't paid my electric bill. Jean Schoonover gave me the office number of a high honcho at Con Ed. I called him and fussed about a mistake in my bill. Somehow, I persuaded him to turn my lights back on and to give me his home phone number. So far, so good. The Fireman's Fund team arrived, along with Stanley and Ed. We were just sitting down having a few hors d'oeuvres and some cocktails, when *boom!* out went the lights. As soon as I slipped into my bedroom and frantically called Mr. Big, the Con Ed executive, the lights would go on for a while. Then someone down at central switching would turn them off again. This happened on and off throughout the evening.

I finally gave up and lit some candles. When those gave out, I put a flashlight in the middle of the table as if we were having a seance. Given the wacky situation, I wouldn't have been surprised if the Fireman's Fund director had hosed down my bright idea for a program. But he didn't. In the end, the Fund gave me $10,000 to do P.R. on a project they were promoting to working women. I was thrilled to turn over both the project and most of its budget to Jean Schoonover to repay her for all the free P.R. she'd done for NAFE. And thrilled to finally get my lights turned back on!

Despite near-disasters like this, the Executive Female mailing list not only breathed new life into NAFE, it also brought me a business partner. Savvy enough to see the list's potential, Warren, the marketing director from *Shopper's Voice*, offered to work with me. I was broke, but NAFE was growing. There was no way I could begin to afford the expertise Warren had. Always believing that the only good deal is a fair deal, I offered him a full partnership in exchange for his handling NAFE's computer needs, administration, finances, and direct-mail activities. He agreed. I turned over these tasks to him with enormous relief, so I could focus on creative marketing and sales.

A Dapper Dan with an MBA and a wild streak, Warren was a tremendous asset. He was as businesslike and ultraconservative as I was unconventional. He looked like an IBM management trainee; I looked like Auntie Mame. When the two of us walked into meetings, Warren in his pinstriped suit and navy polka dot tie and me in my California whites and stiletto heels, we really grabbed everyone's attention. Most people spent almost as much time trying to figure out what Warren was doing at NAFE as they did listening to our presentations. But that was fine with me; injecting a little mystery into a meeting is never a bad idea.

Most of all, however, Warren's presence gave NAFE a semblance of stability. I continued to run NAFE from my apartment while he operated from an office in an old wooden townhouse in Annapolis. He zipped in to New York once a week to go over finances and attend sales meetings. Our partnership might have been unusual, but it was also very productive. That is, until Warren became a disciple of est. His joining NAFE coincided with a major midlife crisis. Warren decided he'd been repressed in his prior business life and needed to loosen up and build his self-esteem. He enrolled in an est course to become more assertive. As his first project, Warren began trying to manage me. This was his first big mistake.

Once Warren joined NAFE, it was finally possible to start giving members benefits beyond just our *Executive Female Report* and the opportunity to take advantage of a handful of financial products and services. One day, he came up with what I realized was a truly inspired idea. "Let's publish a magazine!" he said to me. "Great!" I replied. "How do we do it?" "Leave it to me," he answered. "I'll put together some projections." I was too embarrassed at the time to ask him how projections worked. To this day, I still don't understand how you can predict sales for something that doesn't even exist yet. Nevertheless, I went along with his plan and we decided to seek out potential investors. After about three months of nibbles but no bites, I said to Warren, "Why not talk to our printer, Bob Rice? We don't really need money—all we need is printing credit."

This turned out to be a great idea, except for the fact that Warren was now involved in est in a big way and was busy taking time-management seminars. He demanded that I set up at least five appointments a day and insisted that each one had to last precisely one hour. He was running me ragged. His next set of seminars was even worse. Its theme: "New Horizons in Sex" (or something along those lines). Warren suddenly became very flirtatious with every secretary he came into contact with. Things really heated up when we approached our printer, Bob Rice, about the magazine idea. We arranged a lunch meeting with Bob, which of course was to last only one hour in keeping with Warren's est training. Bob's girlfriend came along and unbeknownst to me, Warren started playing footsie with her under the table. While she started talking about NAFE and how great it was, I watched the clock and began getting nervous. I tried to cut her off politely, but Warren thought I'd insulted her. He jumped up in the middle of the elegant restaurant where we were lunching and in classic est style, really let me have it: "I'm leaving now," he announced. "But before I go, I want you to know that you're a stupid ass!" I was so embarrassed I bit down on my wine glass and my two front caps popped out! Poor Bob felt so sorry for me that he said, "Hey, Wendy, calm down. I like your magazine idea. You've got yourself a partner." As I've always said there's more than one way to cut a deal! Sadly, however, this new venture was the beginning of the end of my partnership with Warren.

One of NAFE's biggest successes, *The Executive Female* magazine was like magic. It was the thing that instantly made everyone understand what NAFE was all about. It was also a great marketing tool for showcasing our sponsors. Only those companies doing business with NAFE could run their ads in its pages. Our first issue was actually a digest. Karin Abarbanel agreed to pull it together, even though she was busy with a full-time job. She spent all her lunch hours over about three months gathering stories and working with our art director, who was also moonlighting. We weren't able to pay either of them more than sandwich money and carfare, but no one really cared. We were all too excited!

I can still see that first issue as if it appeared just yesterday: In hot-pink type the cover boldly announced our title, *The Executive Female Digest.* An attractive brunette in a flowing cape held a briefcase under one arm as she boldly hailed a cab with the other. What a great feeling to hold that premiere issue in my hands! The articles it featured offered advice on nuts-and-bolts issues like resume writing, job interviewing, and salary negotiation, along with a special "Tools" section on management style. As soon as I saw the magazine, I knew we had a hit. We quickly dropped the word *digest* from its title as we began to persuade friends and experts we knew to write original stories for us. I used brainstorming sessions at my apartment as a way to get new ideas and encourage the corporate executives we worked with to take a deeper interest in NAFE. As issue number two began to take shape, NAFE took a giant leap forward: We found a small office on East Thirty-ninth Street and hired our first full-time employee.

An ordinary want ad brought an extraordinary woman to NAFE: Susan Strecker. What a godsend she turned out to be! For more than eight years, she was not just the magazine's talented editor, she was NAFE's emotional anchor. As editor and later as vice president of NAFE, she hired and nurtured our staff—and shielded them from my whirlwind visits to the office and my intense demands on their time and talents. Somehow she found the energy to put out a bimonthly magazine, run the NAFE office, manage everyone who worked there, and keep me out of trouble. She also had a great sense of humor. At our first convention, she had almost 2,000 women in stitches as she described NAFE's crazy start-up. Her speech was so totally on the mark that I persuaded her to let me include it here:

> Being NAFE's first employee is a dubious distinction at best. But I almost wasn't. When I returned for my second interview, I was greeted at the door by Wendy herself. She shoved a five-dollar bill in my hand and said, "Honey, we're running a little late. Go get us some coffee." And then she shut the door! I stood there thinking to myself, "Well, I could take the money and run, but it's only five dollars, so I wouldn't get very far." So I got the coffee instead. I'd been a teacher and a computer jock—and while *Time* magazine wasn't interested in me, I really wanted to get into publishing. I'm basically a curious person. So in the same way that I'll sit through a bad movie just to see if it will improve, I got Wendy her cup of coffee and dutifully handed back her change. I passed the test.
>
> On the following Monday morning I began to fully participate in the growing pains of an association whose membership files fit in a shoebox. NAFE's first office was way in the back of an old townhouse that had seen more elegant days. It was rather lonely at the top. At the top of four flights of stairs, that is. I got lots of exercise while Wendy worked mainly at home because she hated the office. I sat there wondering what in the world I'd gotten myself into. Well, I didn't exactly sit, because the buzzer on the downstairs door was temperamental, so I was usually running up and down four flights of stairs to let in visitors. I had to go two blocks away for photocopies; no matter how hard I tried, I never could make just one trip, I always had to go back at least once more. Whenever I was out of the office, I used the answering service to make sure we never missed a call. This was vital because I learned very quickly that Wendy considered the telephone her lifeline. Unfortunately, early on the only calls the answering service ever had to report were calls from Wendy wondering if anyone had called!
>
> This townhouse office proved to be impossible and we final-

ly found a real office farther uptown. If the first office was marked by inconvenience, office number two became the target of every bill collector in town. I still wonder how all those collection agencies got *my* name! Anyway, just like any new entrepreneurial venture, we were experiencing cash-flow problems. In fact, one afternoon, someone from the sheriff's office actually tacked a notice up on our door. This notice, though serious in nature, had no religious overtones. It stated that there would soon be an auction of all NAFE's earthly possessions. Wendy remained very calm when I told her. She just looked at me and said, "Quick, get a taxi and take the typewriters home!"

Susan captured NAFE's growing pains and money woes perfectly. NAFE was always sitting on the wrong side of the bottom line. It was seven years before we even saw a profit. As soon as Warren came on board, he set up a separate bank account for NAFE. The checks were yellow, while the personal checks that I'd used in the past to pay both NAFE's bills and my own personal expenses, were blue. For years, those blue checks bounced from one end of Manhattan to the other! It didn't take long for the neighborhood merchants I did business with to catch on to my creative ways with a buck. Whenever I would send them a blue check from my personal account, which was always on the edge of bankruptcy, they would tactfully say, "If you don't mind, could I please have a yellow check instead?"

Yet even with all its financial ups and downs, NAFE prospered. Its growth phase reveals some valuable insights about how to build a successful company on a shoestring budget:

WHEN YOU'RE STARTING SMALL, THINK BIG—AND NEGOTIATE EVEN BIGGER

One woman, one voice, one dream. This pretty much summed up NAFE when I launched it at my press conference in the summer of 1972. Its official name, the National Association for Female Executives, made it sound big and well established, but of course, it wasn't. NAFE had a strong identity, marketing appeal, and a clear mission—all necessary ingredients for a successful entrepreneurial venture. But these were just about all it had. To give NAFE life—to take it from those two boxes on my coffee table and bring it to the marketplace—I needed to think big and negotiate from a position of strength. To survive and grow, I saw that NAFE needed to ally itself with powerful partners who would give it an aura of success in the eyes of the women I wanted to reach.

The strategy I used (if you can call it that, since my decision was intuitive rather than carefully planned out) was simple: In a nutshell, NAFE gained a presence in the marketplace by piggybacking on the success of a high-powered corporate winner, American Express. If my press conference had given NAFE visibility, my relationship with Amex gave it credibility. By allying NAFE with a well-respected and admired company, I catapulted it into the winner's circle. Basking in the reflected power of Amex and my other corporate sponsors, I gave NAFE a marketplace jump start and made it an association that women wanted to belong to. This approach saved me countless marketing dollars and years of toiling in obscurity.

To accomplish this marketing feat, I had to think and act boldly. Many people looking at NAFE and Amex would have seen David trying to woo Goliath. But I never viewed my situation this way. Yes, NAFE was small and new, but it was driven by a big, powerful idea: the need to bridge the gap between the corporate world and working women. That's exactly how I envisioned NAFE and positioned it during my sales meetings: as a bridge, a tool, a marketing vehicle. I had something the companies I approached needed. I had something of value to offer them. In my mind, they needed me as much as I needed them.

The companies I was courting were big, but NAFE was nimble and able to move quickly. They had money, but they had no idea how to reach the women's market and I had the answer: NAFE's list of working women. They had power, but they had no track record in the women's market. They were new kids on the block, just as I was. They could give me credibility in the business world, but NAFE could give them credibility in the women's market. Thinking this way helped me to equalize our positions. It gave me the confidence and chutzpah to negotiate aggressively and set up joint ventures that put NAFE on an even playing field with the corporate giants I worked with, from American Express and AT&T to National Benefit Life and Hertz.

Consider the headline I persuaded John Bennet to allow me to print in our coop mailer: "The National Association for Female Executives invites you to apply for an American Express card." At a stroke, this sentence linked tiny NAFE with one of America's largest and most successful corporations. Even more exciting, it gave NAFE top billing! From my retailing days, I knew how important it was to keep control of a sale. To ensure that NAFE wouldn't be swallowed up by its huge partners, every deal I made gave NAFE control over the mailer we produced and responsibility for tracking the results.

The message in all this for you? Even though you're starting small, as an entrepreneur you have powerful assets at your command. First and foremost, you have a great idea and the vision to bring it to life. It's been said, "There is nothing more powerful than an idea whose time has come." I believe this is absolutely true. NAFE was always bigger than my own needs, the obstacles I faced, or the rejection I encountered. If the idea you're pursuing really compels you, then you have the passion to fuel its growth, just as I did NAFE's. If you've correctly identified a void in the marketplace, then you have the potential to create demand for what you have to offer. You have the ability to move quickly and the flexibility to redirect your path as needed. You have the ability to gather and exploit information resourcefully. You have the freedom to bring your own personal style to the negotiating table.

Approach everything you do and everyone you meet with these assets firmly fixed in your mind and convey them clearly and forcefully, both to the companies you want to do business with and to the customers you want to reach. Only in this way can you negotiate with confidence and from a position of strength. And unless you can do this, your idea, however wonderful and needed it may be, is probably doomed to languish. You have to be a winner in your own mind and heart before you can be a winner in anyone else's eyes. If you have something truly special to offer, there's no one too big or too powerful to want it.

If you approach companies or customers tentatively or with hat in hand, then they'll treat you as a suppliant, not as a partner. And once this happens, they will always see you in this way: as someone who needs something from them rather than as an equal who has something of real value to offer. That's why it's vital that every phone call you make, every meeting you set up, every letter you write, every contract you negotiate is grounded in the knowledge of your idea's value and integrity. This is also why I always favored joint ventures as a way to build NAFE. This approach is based on the idea that two independent parties are coming together because each has something to offer the other and that their combined assets are greater than the sum of their parts. In arrangements like this, the size or relative financial power of the two parties involved isn't a critical issue or even relevant. It's what their combined resources can create that is the key to success.

IF IT DOESN'T EXIST, CREATE IT. IF YOU DON'T HAVE IT, GO OUT AND GET IT

As an entrepreneur, you won't be handed a living. You're almost expected to suffer and sacrifice your way to success. There are a lot of things you're going to need that you may not have. And to bring your idea to life, you're going to have to break new ground, devise innovative marketing and manufacturing techniques, or figure out ways to get what you need quickly and cheaply.

"No one's ever done it before. Why should you be the one to make it work?" I can't tell you how many times I've heard that statement. My response is always the same: Why not me? So I'll be the first. So what? So I'll have to figure things out as

I go. That's nothing new. So I'll make some mistakes. Big deal! So I may get burned. I'll survive. So I may look foolish. I'll live. I've said it before, but I'll say it again: True entrepreneurs aren't discouraged by obstacles and lack of resources; they're inspired and even energized by them. To an entrepreneur, the fact that something doesn't exist is not a problem to solve; it is an opportunity to exploit for fun and profit.

Just as I've never let a good idea pass me by because I was afraid I couldn't handle it, so I've never let the lack of something stop me from pursuing a goal I was committed to. When I founded my teen shops, I created a layaway plan for my customers; no one had ever done that before for teenagers. When I began my executive recruiting business, as a matter of policy, I gave my clients a "money back" guarantee; if a placement didn't work out, I refunded their money with no questions asked. When I first launched NAFE and found out there was no list of working women on the market, I knew I needed to create one and I did. Three different industries, three different approaches, three different "firsts." Yet these situations share one thing in common: The solution I came up with was as simple as it was innovative.

Take the Executive Female mailing list, for example. Morris Segal, the chairman of American Express was a smart, savvy executive. He knew how to hire fine talent and make decisions. Yet in creating NAFE's list of working women, I accomplished something that "all the king's horses and all the king's men (and women!)" at Amex couldn't do. That really knocked Morris's socks off. About once a month, he would take me to lunch. One day, as we were digging into our appetizers, Morris turned to me and said, "Wendy, tell me something. I've spent millions and millions of dollars in my computer department, and I can't get any demographics worth a damn on my members. How did a newcomer like you come up with a complete profile of working women?" I looked him straight in the eye and in all innocence, I said, "Mr. Segal, all I did was ask!" He roared at the simplicity of my answer and said, "Wendy, that's the best idea I've ever heard!"

Look. Listen. Learn. Ask. Then act boldly and innovatively

on the information you gather. Creating a first is as simple—and as complex—as this. The four simple questions I asked women through *Shopper's Voice* were the source of NAFE's working women's list and an invaluable revenue stream for years. I simply saw an information gap in the women's market and moved in to fill it. Gaps like these are everywhere; that's what niche markets are all about. Finding these niches and filling them successfully isn't as mysterious or as difficult as many people think. But this process does demand three things: clarity of vision, the ability to ask the right questions, and the willingness to move quickly and decisively once you have the answers.

BARTER YOUR WAY INTO BUSINESS

As you've read through the way in which NAFE was started and built, I'm sure one thing's become abundantly apparent: NAFE was far from a typical, business-plan type enterprise. Most entrepreneurs are gifted with the ability to beat the obstacles they face, no matter how impossible they seem. And one of the biggest obstacles, of course, is lack of money. Based on my experience, I've found that bartering is a much under-used, but invaluable, tool for making something happen. And it's one that's used not just by entrepreneurs operating on shoestring budgets but by corporate giants as well. No matter how big a company is, the opportunity to do business without spending money is always appealing. It can also keep you out of budget meetings, which can take endless amounts of time and really sap your drive just when you need it most.

Time and again, I used bartering as a tool to get NAFE what was needed when it was needed, even though we had no capital to speak of. I bartered with Jean Schoonover, trading her access to my business contacts in return for the P.R. resources I needed to publish a newsletter for NAFE's very first members. I bartered with *Shopper's Voice,* giving it a new revenue stream in return for the exclusive rights to market the working women's list it generated for me. Ed Burnett also entered into a joint venture with me based on a bartering arrangement. He agreed to absorb start-up computer costs in return for the exclusive right to mass market the list he created, with the profits it generated to be shared equally between his company and NAFE. I learned later that it was almost unheard of for a list broker to share in the profits of a property. I bartered with another vendor, my printer, Bob Rice. In exchange for the extended credit NAFE needed to publish its magazine, I agreed to give him all the direct-mail business NAFE generated, providing he was competitive. At the time, we were mailing over a million pieces a year for NAFE alone, as well as coop mailings with our corporate sponsors.

Even after NAFE really began to take off and we actually had money to spend on projects, I continued to use bartering by choice as one of my primary ways of financing NAFE's development. This helped keep NAFE's overhead surprisingly low and allowed us to successfully weather the financial growing pains we inevitably faced as an entrepreneurial venture. I've always felt that NAFE's consistent and creative use of bartering wasn't just smart business, it also showed the large companies we worked with that we really understood the value of a dollar and were prepared to stretch the dollars they gave us farther than anyone else. Everyone—even the corporate giants of the world—wants to get more bang for the buck. And that's precisely what bartering gives you.

USE PRICING AS A MARKETING TOOL, NOT A COMPETITIVE WEAPON

When it came time to price the Executive Female mailing list, I made a basic decision that transformed that list into a goldmine for NAFE. I've always approached pricing in a unique way. Harking back to my retailing days, I used pricing as a means to attract attention, establish value, and make more money than my counterparts. When Warren and I developed

NAFE's first mailing list of working women, the average list at the time rented for $30 per thousand names. I told Ed Burnett I wanted to price the Executive Female list at $50. Ed said it would never sell. So I came up with an innovative response to his objection. I said to him, "Let's split the difference, market the list at a base price of $40 per thousand, and then romance the demographics by charging $5 for each additional piece of data we offer."

Nobody had ever tried this before, but that's exactly what we did. Our strategy wasn't just unique, it was incredibly profitable. The base list we sold simply provided the names of working women. If buyers wanted to find out who this woman was—her job function or salary range, for example—they had to pay an additional $5 per item. Much to my joy and Ed Burnett's astonishment, this approach brought our average sale up to $65 per thousand, an unheard of fee at the time.

Using pricing creatively is an art that every entrepreneur must master. My pricing philosophy has always been very direct. Be different. Attract attention by pricing high and then deliver the value that your price promises. If you have a unique product, one of the best ways to market it is to price it higher than anything similar to it in order to create curiosity and signal to the marketplace that what you have to sell is special. By charging an additional fee for each descriptive demographic my Executive Female list offered, for example, I announced to the world that my list was so original in content that it had to be packaged and sold differently. Within a very short time, it became the hottest list on the market. In fact, later on, when NAFE was well known in the marketplace and we developed our own list consisting of NAFE members, we priced it at $90 per thousand, which set an all-time record in the list business. To my knowledge, price was never a barrier to a single NAFE list sale. We had something special and people were willing to pay for it. More important, the list delivered the results its users wanted.

Most people establish a price by doing market research, and they try to stay competitive by ensuring that the price for their product falls within a certain range. In short, they run with the herd or they underprice in the hope that they'll attract more business. But just like my dad, I've made it a point never to compete. Instead, I've focused on two things: controlling my product quality and creating a comfort level for my customers about the value that my price reflects. Don't be afraid to stand out from the crowd, even if that means asking your customers to part with more of their hard-earned dollars. Give them a solid reason to do it and most people will. But in applying this approach, always remember that the integrity of your product is the key to its success—that's what establishes its value.

STAY TRUE TO YOUR DREAM— AND YOURSELF

During NAFE's earliest days when I was totally broke, I was approached by one of my first corporate sponsors, CTG Insurance, and offered a $250,000 contract for ongoing promotion. This was an absolutely fantastic sum of money, and I was thrilled. With a budget like this, the sky was the limit! But I soon learned that there was a huge cloud around this silver lining when CTG informed me that it wanted NAFE to market a new cancer insurance product. Not only did I feel the product was poorly planned, I also felt it was designed to exploit an emotional issue for women. Fortunately, I had full rights of approval over any editorial material related to NAFE and refused to agree to CTG's request. The firm hadn't even released the $250,000, but it threatened to sue NAFE for breach of contract. Here I was broke, NAFE wasn't even in business yet, and I already had a lawsuit on my hands! I had nightmares until the contract was finally dissolved, but I've never regretted for a minute my decision not to market a product through NAFE, even though we needed the money desperately.

During the tough times and as your business grows and thrives, you'll often be tempted to stray from your dream.

People will bring you their ideas and want to use your business as their launch vehicle. Or you'll come up with a hot item that you feel will really broaden your business's appeal and franchise. I've had my fair share of these bright and not-so-bright ideas myself—or been persuaded by friends to try them—while I was building NAFE. For a while, we marketed executive gift baskets through our magazine, for example. We also tried to sell stylish blue-and-white bomber jackets with the Executive Female logo emblazoned on the back. I absolutely loved wearing mine, but it was a total bomb with members! This flop didn't stop me from trying again. I was never afraid to put something out into the marketplace if I thought it offered a fair value and might make NAFE a few extra bucks. Why not?

But while I was willing to risk a flier now and then, these ventures were always modest in scale and related in some way to the image NAFE wanted to project. I made every effort to guard NAFE's franchise zealously and turned down numerous offers that I felt would tarnish its reputation or not provide real benefits to our members. I also worked hard to ensure that the products NAFE offered were related to its mission: promoting career and financial independence for women. Over time, this "stick with your knitting" approach proved to be very beneficial to both NAFE's growth and its bottom line. As the company grew, so did its recognition and its reputation. Eventually, NAFE's seal of approval came to have real currency in the marketplace; it allowed me to negotiate progressively bigger and better deals with companies that wanted to be associated with our name and reach our members. Staying true to my dream proved to be a smart business move in every way.

Whenever you're tempted to depart from your original vision in some fundamental way, always ask yourself three questions: Does this damage or dilute my dream? Is the idea or proposition I'm considering unethical or potentially harmful to anyone? If my business goes in this direction, how will I feel about it in five years? If you answer these questions honestly right up front, then you can save yourself an enormous amount of pain and anxiety down the road. I can't tell you how many people I know who've destroyed a vibrant business or short-circuited a venture's success because they were greedy or desperate or because someone brought them a sexy idea they just couldn't resist. Don't make this mistake! The most important thing your product or service has going for it is its integrity and that must never be compromised.

MOVING WITH THE WORLD

At NAFE's first convention, I stood before nearly 2000 women and told them not to be afraid to dream. And then, once again, I told my favorite inspirational story: the birth of NAFE. My message seemed simple enough, but delivering it was one of the high points of my life—and the culmination of many years of struggle. It was also the fulfillment of my own dream, which had come true for me in a way I never could have imagined. As founder and CEO of NAFE, I looked out over an audience of confident, well-educated, well-trained career women. Little did they know at the time that I was none of these things—and the least likely of all people to have created a motivationally oriented business organization for women, the largest of its kind in the country. As the song we played at the convention kept reminding everyone, I did do it *my* way. My education consisted of hard knocks and chutzpah. My business strategies had been scratched on cocktail napkins. My style was anything but conventional. Yet, there I was, telling hundreds of women I'd never met how to be successful.

NAFE had come a long way since its humble beginning in a shoe box on my coffee table. As it entered the 1980s, membership grew to over 90,000; at its peak, more than 200,000 women would join its ranks. We had major corporate sponsors marketing financial service products—a first for the woman's market. Our *Executive Female* magazine, under Susan Strecker's leadership, had become NAFE's most popular and visible benefit. Our staff had grown a little but not much.

People were always astounded to learn that I ran a multimillion-dollar company of NAFE's scale and complexity with only six full-time staff members. There was Susan, of course, whose title was now vice president; her assistant, Susan Kain; Leslie Smith, who directed our networking program; Venice Bartholomew, our comptroller; Michael Korman, who managed direct mail; and his assistant. Managing drove me crazy, and so the rest of the talent we needed—writers, artists, computer experts, and so on—was hired on a freelance basis.

The NAFE networking program was thriving. Inspired by an informal get-together Susan Strecker had enjoyed with some friends, we launched a networking program. To test the idea, we published an article on networking which included a "Count Me In" card that readers could mail back to headquarters. Within weeks, close to 1000 cards flooded the office. Soon there were NAFE groups springing up from coast to coast. By helping women connect with other working women in their own communities, NAFE made the leap from a distant direct-mail organization to a living, breathing association and became a real force in our members' lives.

At the time, most of the networks being formed by other organizations were small and exclusive. NAFE's approach was completely different. We encouraged diversity and openness. Each group was free to shape itself to its members' needs and only the network director in each group had to be a NAFE member. However, our open-door policy proved to be a valuable marketing tool, and our local networks attracted many new women to NAFE. As an incentive, the networks' treasuries received a contribution for each new NAFE member they signed up. At one point, there were more than 2000 NAFE networks meeting and sharing advice across the country. Some consisted of only a few women, though most had about 60 members. A few groups were much larger. When one network director, Rita Calvo, began The Wall Street Women's Network, for instance, it had 15 members. Within a few years, it had grown to 350 women. The energy and excitement these networks created was almost electric. They fulfilled an enormous need for support and companionship.

Whenever a network anywhere in the country reached 100 members, I would make a personal visit to talk about NAFE and the benefits it offered. This was incredibly difficult for me to do: I'm not surprised to hear that speaking in public ranks among the two or three most terrifying experiences for most people, male or female. Terrified! That's exactly what I was every time I had to get up before an audience. I never spoke from notes, so I was forced to work out my own strategy for becoming more comfortable at the podium. Since these get-togethers were usually held at lunch or dinner, I always made it a point to arrive about an hour early. I would wander around during the cocktail hour, talking to members and finding out what their needs were and what they wanted from NAFE. Then I'd tailor my speech to what I'd learned.

I remember one such meeting vividly. Many of the women I chatted with were in transition: either they were housewives moving into the workplace or they were making a career switch. A lot of them were being pressured by husbands or friends who seemed to be giving them a hard time. To show these women I understood what they were going through, I told them about my single toughest critic, my sister Myrna, and a recurring dream I had about her. I would dream that I had just become the president of the United States. When I called Myrna with this thrilling news, her answer was always the same: "That's nice, but more important, who did you go out with last night?" Everyone roared with laughter. Instantly, the women I was addressing knew that I was one of them. This icebreaker helped us all relax and have a good time.

NAFE was growing by leaps and bounds. Not surprisingly, it experienced major growing pains: As NAFE flourished, my partnership with Warren floundered. Much of his energy seemed devoted to reshaping my style and I wasn't willing to change to accommodate him. Things reached the boiling point just after a huge mailing. Membership applications were flowing into Warren's office in Annapolis, which was located in an old wooden house. I used to have nightmares about NAFE's records and all those $29 membership checks going up in smoke. While Warren prided himself on his organizational abilities, I prided myself on my retail background. My father taught me to ask three questions every day:

- How many new members came in?
- How much money do we owe?
- How much money do we have in the bank?

Wherever I was and no matter what I was doing, I always checked in at the end of the day for a status report. The day came when Warren couldn't answer these questions, which made me extremely nervous. Warren and I went out to lunch and had a long talk. We both admitted that we had outgrown our partnership. Though NAFE was still cash poor, I agreed to buy him out over five years and he agreed to ensure a smooth transition and as always, he was true to his word.

I was heartbroken over the breakup of our partnership and scared to death. Handling our creative programs, sales, and customer relations was already more than a full-time job. How on earth was I going to manage NAFE's computer services, direct-mail campaigns, and administration—all areas in which I was uncomfortable and out of my element? At this point, I realized what a mistake I'd made in not being more involved in Warren's end of the business. I called my brother Max in a panic. He flew down from Toronto the next day and offered support. He became a paid consultant to NAFE and spent at least one day a week in New York working with me. Max helped me sort through and manage NAFE's finances, held my hand, and tried to assuage my fears. On his advice, I also hired Paul Lippman, an accountant who specialized in the publishing business.

NAFE may have been experiencing a major upheaval internally, but to the outside world, it was the picture of success. We created an advisory board of dynamic women like Judith Briles, a financial expert; Carole Hyatt, author of a popular book, *The Selling Game*; Fran Gare, a well-known nutritionist and writer; and Fayne Erickson, director of marketing at American Express. NAFE's single-minded philosophy of economic equality and independence was bearing fruit. As NAFE's reach and influence grew, it began winning more and more recognition. I was traveling constantly to networking meetings, and at many of my stops around the country I was now greeted by the mayors and even governors of the cities and states I was visiting. NAFE began receiving proclamations from the state of Connecticut, the state of Ohio, the state of Illinois, the state of New York, the city of Los Angeles, and on and on. A glowing letter even arrived from Mr. New York City himself, then-Mayor Ed Koch!

The best was yet to come. I'll never forget the day that I picked up my mail and found a personal invitation from President Reagan to take part in the Small Business Administration's Interagency Task Force on Women in Business. I was absolutely beside myself. Poor little Schwundelkopf had really hit the big time! I just wished my father could have lived to see it all. For a year, the members of the task force met about once a month. As an entrepreneur, I was fascinated but dismayed by the chance to see our government's bureaucracy in full swing. The SBA officials were totally hung up on the nuts and bolts of procedure, while I just wanted to barrel ahead with our mission: giving financial support to budding women business owners. The big issue was establishing who was qualified to receive an SBA loan. To me, the answer was simple: The loans should be offered to any woman with a sound business plan who was socially and educationally disadvantaged and unable to obtain funds from any other source. Why not open the door to any woman who has a good idea and needs money to launch her venture? I remember how astounded the SBA officials were when I suggested this. They were so preoccupied with quotas, racial issues, and procedures, that they couldn't even agree on their basic mission and how to achieve it. This mystified me the entire time that I worked with the SBA as a pro bono consultant. Eventually, the SBA accepted my general concept and a revitalized loan program began to take shape. Having struggled so many years to make it financially, I found it tremendously rewarding to help make more money available to women with dreams like mine. Being a Washington insider for a while was a big thrill. I even helped present President Reagan with a national business award! Not long after this event, I received a personal commendation from the president. It meant so much to me that I've included his letter in this chapter.

NAFE was growing so quickly that it was making waves beyond the borders of America. For me, this meant that another of my dreams soon came true: I was invited to visit Israel with some of America's most influential women. Only when I arrived after a long trip did I find out, to my great disappointment, that the whole affair was a political ploy on the part of Israel to raise money. After endless lectures and funding appeals consumed the first two days of the trip, I decided to leave the group and discover Israel on my own. I hired a taxi driver who took me to see all the sites, and my excitement soared.

During my time in Washington, I had met Zohar Charte, the women's minister of labor for Israel. I called on her in Israel and she introduced me to Zivia Cohen, the editor of Israel's leading women's magazine. Zivia was a big admirer of NAFE and our *Executive Female* magazine. She and I had fun brainstorming about how to bring some of the information we were giving NAFE members to her readership as well. I finally had an idea which really excited Zivia: I arranged to send her each issue of our magazine's popular "Tools" section, which she then reprinted. Soon after we launched this program, some ambitious women in Israel decided to start NAFE's first overseas network. I couldn't believe it: NAFE was going global! Women in Japan, England, Canada, Australia, and several other countries quickly came on board.

Even though NAFE was launched in 1972, it didn't really get off the ground until 1974, so in 1984 I decided that a 10-year anniversary celebration was in order. Ten years! I wanted to pull out all the stops and put on the biggest, most exciting convention that the Big Apple had ever seen. I nearly drove myself and everyone else at NAFE nuts in the process. The first convention manager I hired was a disaster. But my staff rallied around me and we tried again. Our second manager,

THE WHITE HOUSE

WASHINGTON

October 13, 1983

Dear Ms. Rue:

I am happy to send greetings and congratulations as you are honored for your many contributions to women in business.

As founder of the National Association of Female Executives, you are acutely aware of the need to make executive women aware of the opportunities available, providing them with essential information and assistance in establishing financial independence and success.

In today's economy, it is imperative that all Americans learn to manage their money wisely through diversified financial planning. Your organization is helping to achieve this goal by offering loans, insurance programs, legal services, and two informative magazines—THE EXECUTIVE FEMALE and MORE MONEY. In addition, NAFE will shortly offer its members a special money market and mutual fund.

Today, NAFE is almost 90,000 members strong and has established some 2000 networks nationwide. Your work with major corporations and financial institutions has led them to develop products and services tailored to the needs of the executive woman.

I am pleased to commend you and the very important work you are doing for America's women.

Nancy joins me in wishing you the best for continued success and, again, congratulations.

Sincerely,

Ronald Reagan

Ms. Wendy Rue
Executive Director
The National Association for Female Executives
120 East 56th Street–Suite 1440
New York, New York 10022

Joel Dolci, was a gem. With his help, I decided to make the convention a three-day extravaganza, complete with a big floor-show finale. I even hired a Broadway choreographer, Larry Cherry, to give the event extra pizzazz and polish.

The convention's theme, "Move with the World," was my sister Myrna's inspiration. She had just written a song by that name and sang it one evening at one of her glamorous parties. I was there, along with a few NAFE fans. So was singer Dionne Warwick and her sister, Dee Dee. "Move with the World" had a happy, rocking, toe-tapping beat. As soon as we heard it, my friends and I thought it would be a great song for NAFE's grand finale and a great theme for the convention itself. "Move with the World." I loved the whole idea!

Dee Dee Warwick also was entranced with the song. Dionne encouraged her to record it, which she did. It was released as a single on Roulette Records that same year. Dee Dee also agreed to sing the song at the convention's big floor show.

Then Myrna had another brainstorm. Why not run a "Give a Gal a Break!" contest to find a new, fast-rising young singer? The prize would be a star spot at the convention's evening gala event. I agreed instantly. Swept away by all this excitement, I decided to reward myself by purchasing my first racehorse. His name? "Move with the World," what else? Unfortunately, he never moved all that much!

Myrna took charge of our rising-star contest. She, actor/composer Harvey Fierstein, and producers from CBS and Atlantic Records listened to 300 young hopefuls sing their hearts out in a marathon audition. Eventually, they picked 15 talented singers as finalists. In the end, Andrea Frierson, a lovely young woman with a fabulous voice and a smile to match, won the contest. She sang "I Must Be a Star," another Myrna March original, at the convention and brought down the house. With Myrna's help, Andrea eventually went on to make several records, win *Star Search* six times, and appear on Broadway. What a NAFE success story!

Naturally, I focused all my energy on the convention itself. I wanted a very high-powered keynote speaker for our final evening, someone everyone would admire. My first choice was Barbara Walters and, to my delight, she agreed.

The convention kicked off on a Friday in August at the Hilton Hotel, with Mayor Koch giving a rollicking speech welcoming NAFE members from around the country and the world to New York City. I handed him a huge Executive Female membership card, and he was pleased as punch. His witty welcome set the tone for a happy, lively affair. NAFE's convention proved to be one of the biggest events the Hilton ever hosted, and as one manager told me, "It was more like a love-in than a business meeting." I knew exactly what he meant. There were women, women everywhere! Bright, energetic women, laughing, talking, exchanging business cards, filling the halls, the networking room, the bartering room, and overflowing into my hotel suite! I couldn't walk from one meeting to another, without at least a dozen NAFE members stopping me, throwing their arms around me, and thanking me for everything NAFE had done for them. To receive so much love and support was just incredible. Even today, just thinking about the convention and what it meant to me and everyone who attended brings tears to my eyes.

At NAFE, we had worked nonstop to pull together three days of high-powered seminars that would uplift and energize everyone who attended. We offered expert advice on any topic we thought would be helpful to women on the move. There was something for everyone, from "On-the-Job Negotiating," "The Selling Game," "Networking," and "Strategic Marketing" to "Speaking Techniques," "Leadership Skills," and "Going Back to School." And, of course, we focused on business owners and finance, with seminars like "Three Ways to Get into Business," "Do You Have What It Takes to Be an Entrepreneur?" and "Conquer Your Fear of Financial Risk."

We also made sure that our members played hard as well as worked hard. They networked by day, but partied by night! We offered tickets to half a dozen shows on Broadway and other events. But I soon learned that NAFE members had their own ideas about how to have a good time. The most popular tickets we offered were to the male strip club, Chippendale's!

A meeting of close to 2000 women was a major media event, even in the Big Apple. The coverage was tremendous. Reporters were overwhelmed. They'd never seen a women's convention like this before. The fun, the excitement, the energy our members conveyed were so unusual. But my favorite news story was one I couldn't even read! A small group of members from "JAFE," our Japanese network, attended the convention and so did a news crew from a Japanese magazine. This crew followed me around day and night. I couldn't understand a word anyone said, but everyone was very friendly. Some weeks later, I received a huge article written entirely in Japanese, emblazoned with the headline: "Next Year, Wendy Loo Plans Fifty-Sex Seminars!"

All too soon, the evening of our "Move with the World" gala arrived. Escorted by my two grown sons, Dennis and Harlan, I walked up to the podium to introduce Barbara Walters. As the song "I Did It My Way" floated through the air, I looked down from the stage at table after table of vibrant, smiling women, a festive rainbow of shimmering, glittering color. Beside them sat husbands and boyfriends, handsome and proud in their tuxedos. What a moment of awe and triumph, after so much struggle and disappointment, to look out over a sea of wonderful women and feel their achievement and expectation! "Is there anything we can't do?" I remember asking myself. This moment, so rare and precious, was truly a dream come true. I only wished that my dad and Stanley, who had passed away just six months before, could have shared it with me. But who knows? Perhaps they did.

I glanced over at the table where the NAFE staff sat, proud and excited over the magic in the room and the tremendous sense of togetherness that all their hard work had fostered. NAFE's board members, past and present, were also celebrating with us. Even Joe, who'd resigned from NAFE's board during its start-up because of my unconventional style, was there. Over the roar of the crowd's applause, I could hear Dr. Alan call out in his booming voice, "Well, Joe, what do you think of Wendy's image now?"

I introduced Barbara Walters, who commented on what a

thrill it was for her to be in the company of so many talented women—and so many good-looking men as well! She went on to talk about her own career, the struggles she'd faced as a woman in a tough, competitive field, and some of the things she'd learned along the way. It was a warm, upbeat, inspiring speech delivered straight from the heart, and everyone loved it. Barbara's honesty, success, and femininity symbolized what NAFE was all about.

Then our "Move with the World" floor show began. Dee Dee Warwick kicked things off by literally tripping over some wires and knocking half the sound system out! Nobody cared. She belted out our theme song, and hundreds of women joined in:

> Everybody's got to move with the world and live with the
>   times,
> You can do your thing, but don't put down mine.
> Everybody's got to move with the world and live with the
>   times,
> Respect one another and we'll all get along just fine.
> Open your eyes now and let yourself see,
> We all can be happy when we set ourselves free.

Myrna and her husband, Roufa, joined in, along with our "Give a Gal a Break" winner, Andrea Frierson. A little boy jumped up on the stage and started dancing in time to the music. More people climbed on stage, including me.

Later, as I returned to my table, something wonderful happened, which meant more to me than anything else that evening. At different moments, each of my two sons quietly came up to me, gave me a kiss, and said in his own words, "I finally understand what you're all about, Mother, and why NAFE has always been so important to you." After all the years of sacrifice and struggle, to finally receive this recognition from Dennis and Harlan was so overwhelming, it moved me to tears.

All too soon, this glorious evening of celebration drew to a close, but the audience stayed on and on, talking, dancing, and dreaming until dawn. This was one party none of us wanted to see end! The next day, I took the entire staff out on a yacht excursion around Manhattan to say thank you for everyone's tremendous work. I wanted to sail on and on forever.

Soon after this, I left on a cruise with a good friend, Fran. I found myself crying a lot, not just as a way to release all the tension that had built up during the frenzied months before the convention, but because I knew that something wonderful was ending. The convention was a beautiful, but sad, experience for me. My dream had come true. Now what was I going to do? I was an entrepreneur, not a manager. Building NAFE into a larger and larger organization wasn't for me. I knew it was time to move on, but where and to what?

I had a long talk with my brother, Max. We both agreed that I had taken NAFE as far as I could and that it was time for me to entrust it to other hands. After more than 10 years of preaching about the importance of financial independence to NAFE members, it was also time to take my own advice. Though I was finally enjoying a comfortable income from NAFE, I was far from financially secure. I wanted and needed to feel that my future was taken care of.

After weeks of thinking and planning, Max and I decided to bring on board someone who could both manage NAFE and help orchestrate the company's sale. We finally turned to Joe, my old contact from executive recruiting, who had a strong financial background and plenty of business contacts. Over the next few months, Joe arranged a series of meetings with publishers of all shapes and sizes. They were fascinated with NAFE, but didn't really understand what it was all about. While *The Executive Female* magazine was our most visible asset, NAFE was not a publishing company. It was a membership organization, a direct-mail business, a marketing vehicle, and a valuable "brand name," all rolled into one. Joe finally located some investors from Chicago who weren't in the publishing field but who recognized NAFE's potential. Within a month, the sale was complete, and I came out of it a multimillionaire.

Still, the day that I sold NAFE was the saddest and loneliest day of my life. Joe took the train home to Pound Ridge, my brother flew back to Toronto, and I went home and cried my eyes out. I called my buddy, Dr. Alan, for comfort. "What the hell are you crying for? You have everything you've ever wanted! Stop crying and start celebrating! By tomorrow night, I want you to pull together the biggest party you've ever given!" That's exactly what I did. I hired a four-piece band, blew up balloons, and hung a big banner with the words, "I'm a Millionaire!" across my living room. I invited my family and all my friends, and we had a great time. But while the party was fun, it didn't fill the empty hole in my heart.

I was financially secure at last. At the sale, Max negotiated a substantial consulting contract for me: I was to stay on board as NAFE's president. I thought I could continue contributing to NAFE's growth and still have the time and freedom to pursue other dreams. Looking back, it was foolish of me to believe I could remain part of NAFE once it changed hands. I had never been able to operate in a corporate structure before and NAFE was becoming a corporation. It had reached a new stage in its development and I simply didn't fit in anymore. Within a few months, NAFE and I parted ways.

NAFE had always been so all-consuming and the sale negotiations so demanding, that I made a big mistake: I didn't take time out to dream. If I were to offer some advice to you based on this experience, there are two things I would tell you. First, have the courage to know when your dream has become bigger than you are, and when this happens, don't try to hang on to it: Find the strength to move on. Second, be sure to take time to start dreaming again: Have a new dream (or two or three!) on your horizon before you let your old one go. I learned this lesson early in my career as a fashion designer: Even as I was fitting models for an upcoming fashion show, I was back at my drawing board, planning my next line. Somehow, I forgot all this when I sold NAFE. Dreamers are dreamers above all; they always need a new vision to fill their days and nights with hope and excitement. As this book is being completed, I'm already busy planning my next venture.

Still, what I'd accomplished gave me great satisfaction. My

old dream had been worth fighting for and I had fulfilled it beyond my wildest expectations. When I founded NAFE, most women earned an average of $10,000 a year, couldn't get credit in their own names, and were treated economically as second-class citizens. When I sold the company I'd worked so hard to build, women earned an average of $37,000 a year, had gained equal access to money and credit, and were recognized as valued contributors to the U.S. economy and powerful stakeholders in the American dream. NAFE had played a leadership role in this remarkable change, and I'll always be grateful for the opportunity to help make it all happen.

STRATEGY, SMATEGY: BENDING THE RULES OF BUSINESS

I hate offices. I always have and I always will. There's something about them that makes me feel confined and uncreative. The telephones, the yellow pads, the to-do lists, the meetings, all just distract me. Even when NAFE was growing by leaps and bounds, I avoided the office as much as I could. On a typical day, I'd spend my morning making calls at home and arrive at the office at about 11:30. There, I'd check my messages, touch base with my staff, and leave for a business luncheon. After lunch, I'd check in with the office again, go home, and make more business calls. At night, I'd lie in bed thinking about my plans, wake up at 6 A.M., and start all over again. Not a 9-to-5 business day by any stretch of the imagination.

I've always gotten my best ideas when I'm relaxed and completely removed from a business setting. I've made more business calls and cut more deals in the bathtub than I can remember. And why not? That's just how I am. Instead of fighting my style, I make it work for me. And you should do the same. As an entrepreneur, you have one enormous business advantage that all the money in the world can't buy: control over your time and your life. So find the work style that's best for you and then shape your work environment to enhance and support that style. Remember, for an entrepreneur, there's only one bottom line that counts: getting the job done and making that dream happen, whatever it takes. How you do it, as long as it's legal and doesn't hurt anyone else, doesn't really make a bit of difference. "Now!" That's how an entrepreneur thinks. "How" is strictly a corporate concept.

Success rarely flows in a straight line. Over the years, I've come across many businesses that evolved in unconventional ways—without huge business plans, complicated projections, big staffs, and lots of money. Think about it: The ideas that led to some of the world's corporate giants, like AT&T, Con Ed, and Federal Express, began, not with sales forecasts, but with visionaries dreaming impossible dreams. These pioneers bent the rules, broke them, rewrote them, or ignored them altogether. Let me give you a fun, but enlightening, example:

One of my all-time favorite entrepreneurial success stories is a business called Renta Yenta. Even the name is great, isn't it? It was started back in the late 1970s by two housewives, Lila Greene and Janice (Toby) Brown. After spending years cooking, cleaning, and chauffeuring their kids around, these two dynamic women wanted out of the kitchen and the carpool. Working out of Lila's laundry room, they cooked up a scheme as offbeat and innovative as they were. To announce its birth, they took out an ad in a local paper in Los Angeles. Their claim? "Anything you can't do, we can. Renta Yenta." The response floored even Lila and Toby, and in a matter of days, their venture was off and running. To survive the ups and downs of their first year, they did just about anything you can imagine. When a husband wanted to hire a marching band to serenade his wife up and down the aisles of a supermarket, he called Renta Yenta. When a bashful lover wanted to "pop the question" by having a squad of cheerleaders present his ring, he called Renta Yenta. When a request came in for 50 hot apple pies to be delivered to Congress, Renta Yenta made it happen. A house filled with balloons, strolling minstrels, a visit from Batman, or a romantic breakfast in bed: as long as it was "legal and kind," Renta Yenta was ready for action!

Lila and Toby started with no money. Their husbands, who

were both successful businessmen, thought the idea would wither on the vine and left them to sink or swim. Within five years, Renta Yenta had blossomed into a million-dollar business, with headquarters in L.A. and a dozen franchises. Lila and Toby made *People* magazine and hit the talk-show circuit. Warner Brothers even optioned a book they wrote! "Delivering happiness anywhere"—that was the mission of their business. This simple but compelling idea brought its owners recognition and success. They prospered by combining fun and profit, not by following a fancy, complicated strategy.

Too often people get so hung up on planning and evaluating that they forget about *doing*. That's why any entrepreneur worth her salt absolutely, positively *hates* phrases like, "I'll have to check with my lawyer," "Let's put that idea on hold for a while," or "I'll do it tomorrow." Entrepreneurs live in a world of action and urgency: today, now, this minute, let's do it! This is how they work. When I think of strategy, I think of someone painstakingly mapping out how to get from Point A to Point B to Point C; trying to anticipate how their competition and customers will react to every decision; and trying to cover all the bases so they are not hit by anything from left field. To me, business isn't about all this stuff. It's creative, intuitive, and opportunistic.

When Warren joined NAFE as my partner, he used to spend much of his time making business plans. But as quickly as he designed them, I destroyed them. Not intentionally, of course, but because NAFE was always changing: A promising new program would come up and Warren's latest business plan would go out the window. This isn't to say that NAFE was operated in a totally free-form, anything goes fashion. Some of its key components—its direct-mail program and magazine, for example—were highly structured, with staffs, budgets, deadlines, and yes, even projections! But NAFE's overall direction wasn't planned in advance; it evolved. All I knew was where I wanted to go. Most of the time, I really had no idea how I was going to get there. Like most entrepreneurs, I was guided by one simple rule: If it works, use it. If it doesn't, lose it.

Just about everyone I've ever worked with has commented on my unconventional approach to business. Sometimes it's worked for me and sometimes against me—but it has always set me apart from everyone else. While you're probably not going to run your business from your bathtub, there's no reason why you shouldn't adopt a style of working that's uniquely your own. There's no reason why you can't make doing business with you enjoyable and even unforgettable. And there's no reason why you have to follow anyone else's rules if they aren't in sync with your personality and values. I've spent a lifetime figuring out how to do this. Here are some more ideas on how to succeed without letting other people's rules get in your way:

MAKE BUSINESS FUN

I love business! I enjoy everything about it: thinking up new ideas, meeting new people, launching a new product, making a sale, and watching a project thrive and succeed. To me, all these activities are fun and energizing. I always try to convey my excitement and sense of humor to the executives I work with. I want doing business with me to be pleasant and memorable. When selling, I try to create a relaxed, nonthreatening, noncompetitive atmosphere where people can let their hair down and enjoy themselves. In my experience, this approach is very unusual, even revolutionary.

I have no idea why, but most people seem to feel that working or making money and enjoying themselves are mutually exclusive pursuits. Business is supposed to be all business. I've always fought against this mindset. To me, the traditional business world takes itself far too seriously; it lacks humor. When people lose the ability to laugh at themselves, they're in real trouble. Over the years, my sense of humor has helped me win over many skeptical executives and made me a favorite companion for luncheon dates and as a sounding board. To me, laughter is one of my biggest sales tools. If you can introduce humor into a business setting, then half your battle is over.

Until they get to know me, however, many executives find my informal style very unusual and even a little disconcerting. But I've found that success makes everyone comfortable. As soon as we had an exciting, profitable program under way, even the most conservative business types relaxed. Even so, I always put them just a little on edge. If we were going to a big meeting, they'd often ask me if I'd consider toning down my dress and delivery. I'd just laugh and say, "If I'm too restrained, I won't be myself and nobody will have anything to talk about afterwards. This way, when I have an appointment with you, word goes through the grapevine, via your secretary, and everyone looks forward to seeing what I'm up to."

Corporate executives don't have much free spirit to spare. They're under the gun all the time. Everything comes down to money: how little they have to lay out in order to get back how much. Their job is to minimize risk as much as possible. But this attitude can be very restricting, and you shouldn't let it inhibit you. By creating a relaxed atmosphere, you free the executives you work with to move beyond their self-imposed limits—and to view the opportunities you offer with a fresh eye. One of the best ways to do this is to get people out of their offices and away from their phones, schedules, and desks. I always arrange to meet current or potential clients over lunch or cocktails. It gives me a captive audience, and my prospects are much more likely to let their minds wander and consider an innovative idea (see Chap. 11, tip 5).

MAKE BUSINESS PERSONAL

As an entrepreneur, piercing the corporate veneer to find a common ground isn't easy. One of the most effective ways to do this is to make business not just fun but personal. I've always aimed at making friends out of my clients and genuine-ly tried to get to know them: their backgrounds, who they are, and what they like to do. Some people are very resistant to revealing themselves. They believe in keeping their business and personal lives totally separate. But I try to get beyond this attitude, because to me, business *is* personal. As an entrepreneur, my work and my life are intertwined. So I feel totally comfortable crossing the line between these two areas. In fact, for me, there is no line. Helping your clients and customers begin to think this way and respond to you personally can be very important to your success.

This certainly proved to be the case when I met Fayne Erickson, who inherited NAFE's account when John Bennett left American Express. At the time, Fayne was a typical dress-for-success business school graduate, complete with a little bow tie and briefcase. She was in her twenties, ambitious, and willing to play by the rules to advance up the corporate ladder. Fayne was in total shock when I arrived on her office doorstep. About a month later, she attended a small networking seminar in Kansas, where all the speakers met in my suite. After a few drinks, Fayne announced, "If Wendy didn't have the track record she has, I never would have done business with anyone who looked like her or talked like her."

Fayne was viewing me strictly from a business point of view: I didn't fit the mold, and she didn't like it because I threw her off balance. In her limited business experience, she had never encountered someone like me and didn't know how to handle our relationship. Fayne came to Kansas expecting me to fall flat on my face. But when she saw the warmth and acceptance I received from NAFE members and clients at the seminar, her whole attitude changed. She realized that there were other ways of doing business and that she didn't have to blindly accept the stereotype of the tough, hard-nosed businesswoman in order to succeed. She was very results-oriented, and she saw that I produced—and that how I did it didn't really matter. Eventually, Fayne even joined our advisory board.

Over the years, Fayne did indeed move up the corporate ladder. She also married and started a family. Ultimately, she left the corporate world and joined forces with a partner to start a marketing business. Today, Fayne is a highly successful entrepreneur. She operates out of her home, has no employees, uses her answering machine as a secretary, and works with some of the biggest companies in America. I like to think her contact with NAFE and me opened Fayne up to new ways of thinking and working. She realized that she could relax, be herself, and still build a profitable enterprise.

Just recently, Fayne told me that it was my personal way of doing business that really cemented NAFE's relationship with Amex. At one point, she had to decide between working with NAFE and another women's organization. She chose NAFE because she had gotten to know me personally and felt we understood each other's goals and style of working. Faced with a choice, she continued doing business with someone she knew well. Her comments really drove home to me just how important it is to get beyond the impersonal, detached face most people wear at the office and discover the human beings you're doing business with.

TAKE TIME OUT TO RECHARGE AND REGROUP

One of the nice things about being a boss is that you can afford to follow your instincts without having to worry about being fired. Whenever I run into a tough situation that isn't black-and-white, I always try to resist worrying over it and analyzing it to death. Instead, I make myself promise to set it aside for a couple of days and do something pleasurable to distract me. Whenever I do this, the source of my anxiety just seems to bubble up to the surface naturally. Once I know what's bothering me, I can usually figure out how to handle it. This technique allows my instincts to recharge and kick in again.

Whenever I was in a state of uncontrollable anxiety about NAFE, I knew better than to try to make any major decisions. The only thing to do was to distract myself. My buddy and confidante at the NAFE office was Venice, my comptroller. When I felt the need for a diversion, I would find Venice, make some sort of excuse about a meeting she and I had to attend, and we would take off to my father's favorite playground: the racetrack. As my dad always told me, "Racing is the only sport where you make choices, see the action, and know the result all within a minute. If you win, you feel like a million bucks. If you lose, there's always a brand new game." Somehow, the instant results at the track had a calming effect on me. I could unwind, chat with Venice, and just have fun. This always helped me put my problems in perspective.

Relaxing and renewing yourself shouldn't be seen as a luxury but as a necessity. Most entrepreneurs I know fall very naturally into a work-play rhythm: Intense periods of work alternate with periods of relaxation. This pattern allows you to recharge yourself creatively, handle problems more effectively, and tackle major new projects with zeal and ingenuity. All work and no play doesn't just make you dull: It can stop you from giving your business your best.

COMPETE WITH MEN WITHOUT REJECTING THEM

We had only one male employee at NAFE and we all had to laugh when he refused to make coffee! Things may have come a long way, but let's face it: We still have a long way to go when it comes to male-female dynamics in the workplace. Just one example: A good friend of mine named Jim once spent almost an entire lunch telling me how uncomfortable women made him feel at work. A senior executive and always the perfect gentleman, he was accustomed to opening doors, holding chairs, and even lighting the occasional cigarette. Now, Jim was afraid to say "Hello, honey" to anyone for fear he'd be accused of sexual harassment. I pulled out one of my extralong cigarettes and sat listening to him, waiting patiently. I finally handed him my lighter, and we both began to laugh.

I sympathize with Jim's dilemma because I've always found men to be tremendously helpful and encouraging—often, more so than women. Over the years, in fact, most of the members of my support system have been men. How could I feel that men were against me, when so much of my success flowed from their helping me build my experience, obtain credit, and survive my emotional ups and downs? So, though it may shock you, I'm going to suggest a radical idea that's always worked wonders for me: Try treating men as equals. How, exactly, do you do this? Simple: Don't put them down. Don't accuse them of abusing whatever power they have. Acknowledge their strengths, don't exploit their weaknesses. Applaud them for a job well done. Let them know you appreciate their counsel and ideas. Talk to them about their business needs and how you can be of value to them.

We're all vulnerable. None of us, male or female, wants to be rejected or belittled. We all want to feel respected and valued. Yes, men are men and you're a woman. There's no need to sacrifice your femininity in order to compete or collaborate with men. Give them room to be themselves so that you can succeed without rejecting them. Just as you want to retain your femininity, allow them to retain their masculinity. Radiate confidence when you walk into a meeting with men. Make them aware of your importance to them while giving them credit for their importance to you. Being feminine doesn't mean being helpless or indecisive. Or heartless or hard-nosed. Keep your business style warm and friendly. Yes, you're trying to prove something as an entrepreneur—to yourself, your clients, and the world. But there's no need to do it at someone else's expense.

BEWARE OF MARKET RESEARCH

The road to entrepreneurial success is paved with ideas—good, bad, and almost always unconventional. And not every idea takes off, even if it's a good one—or if market research supports it. The Executive Female doll is a great example. Back in the 1980s, working women were entering and reentering the work force in record numbers. Young women just coming out of college expected to pursue careers, and the number of stay-at-home wives was dwindling. Yet little girls and boys were still playing with the same toys their parents had played with. At NAFE we came up with a super idea: What the world really needed was a doll that helped children understand what Mommy did when she went to work.

NAFE's membership was close to 100,000 at the time, so in the great tradition of conventional market research, we surveyed 10,000 of our members about their views on toys that provided a positive role model for kids. Close to 75 percent of them agreed that an Executive Female doll was an idea whose time had come. "Watch out, Barbie!" I thought to myself.

The media absolutely loved this idea. Reporters from *The New York Times* to local papers across the United States latched on to it and gave NAFE tremendous coverage. Leading toy companies started calling. The doll looked like a winner. Yet somehow, it never made it past the survey stage. It was a tough year for the toy industry and financing was hard to come by. Maybe the idea was just ahead of its time. The executives I had to pitch the doll to were all male, of course, and when it came to putting money into a prototype, they just wouldn't commit. After weeks of meetings and frustration, I had to let the whole idea go. I just couldn't find a manufacturer willing to bet on it. I had the market research, but they just didn't think I had the market. Were these corporate high honchos right or wrong? To this day, I still wonder. But I do know that most Barbie dolls never see the inside of a briefcase and they're still going strong. You figure it out!

HIRE EMPLOYEES WHO'LL LEARN ALONG WITH YOU

As your business grows, you're going to have to build a staff. When you do, don't get too hung up on credentials and past experience. The best choices as employees aren't always people who know far more than you do about a major area of your business. Often, those people are very set in their ways and resistant to new ideas. And their very experience can lull you into complacency and tempt you to abdicate, instead of delegate, your authority. I've generally steered away from "experts" and hired people who were sharp, enthusiastic, hungry for rewarding work, but not very experienced at the job they were asked to perform. I've learned along with them and they've learned along with me. We've grown together, and I didn't have to waste precious energy fighting their entrenched attitudes.

Take Susan Strecker. The editor of NAFE's *Executive Female* magazine, Susan eventually became a vice president of the company, and after I left NAFE, she went on to build another very successful magazine. Susan was a former teacher and computer operator in a bank—a long way from the publishing field. But to me, her desire, intelligence, and enthusiasm outweighed her lack of experience. So I followed my instincts and brought her on board as NAFE's first full-time employee. It was one of the best decisions I ever made. She was a godsend and grew into an incredibly effective and talented executive. The same proved true of Venice Bartholomew, whom I met one evening while I was relaxing at a local watering hole. Venice's cheerful personality and wonderful smile were tremendously appealing. She was a teller at a bank. When I asked if she'd had any bookkeeping experience, she answered, "A little." My antennae shot up. Just the day before, NAFE's accountant had told me that I needed a full-time bookkeeper. When Venice told me what she was earning at her job, I was appalled. On the spur of the moment, I said, "You can't stay there. Those are coolie wages. Come work for me!" Once again, my instincts served me well. Venice turned out to be a gem. She was totally devoted and a quick study. Within six months, she became NAFE's comptroller.

I was very proud of these hiring decisions. In short order, I put together a tiny but very talented staff at NAFE. Whenever people came to visit our office, they always asked where the second floor was. They couldn't believe so few people could accomplish so much! But nothing stays the same forever. One day, Susan sat down with me and said, "Wendy, NAFE needs a full-time manager." This idea made me nervous, because it meant giving up some of my authority, but I knew Susan was right. NAFE was growing so quickly, we needed someone to run it on a day-to-day basis. This employee was not to be found at a local watering hole. I hired a recruiter, ran ads; and Susan and I interviewed dozens of people. We finally decided on Bob, a very sophisticated corporate executive with an MBA and extensive experience with a publishing company. I was very impressed with Bob and even flattered that he would consider joining NAFE. So much so, that I violated my own hiring philosophy.

Instead of hiring someone who would work with me, adapt to my style, and follow through on my instructions, I hired someone who thought he could take charge. But if there's one thing I've learned, it's that in a small, entrepreneurial company, there isn't room for two bosses. Bob was very talented and personable—everyone at NAFE adored him. But the first major decision he made after joining us proved to be his last. He changed the telephone system and removed all the hold buttons, which disconnected me from my staff. This drove me absolutely wild, because the telephone was my lifeline and I simply couldn't tolerate not being able to speak with Susan or Venice whenever I needed to. Once this happened, it became clear to me that while Bob had lots of valuable experience, his corporate background simply wouldn't allow him to understand the mindset of an entrepreneur like me. Both Bob and I quickly realized that he wasn't a good fit. I gave him a glowing recommendation and he moved on to a challenging career in broadcasting.

DON'T LIVE OUT YOUR MISTAKES

I felt very guilty about my hiring fiasco with Bob. I couldn't fault his qualifications, but I had to accept the fact that his style and mine would never mesh. At first I tried to ignore what he was doing, but that gnawing feeling in my stomach wouldn't let me rest. Once I saw things weren't improving, I cut the cord quickly. I had to. My partnership with Warren had taught me that dragging out a relationship that isn't working, or has outlived its usefulness, causes serious problems.

People tend to live out their mistakes way beyond the point that they should. This is especially true when someone they like is involved. One of the biggest errors in judgment that people make—myself included—is thinking that people are going to change. Once they've reached business maturity, the mold is pretty well cast. But we often feel so guilty about our misjudgments that we'd rather live with them than confront them. Resist this weakness! If you make a mistake, admit it! Don't feel you have to wallow in it or live it out to the bitter end. And above all, don't feel you have to sacrifice yourself or your dream to it. Don't play the martyr. Don't beat yourself up for something that's gone wrong. Fix it, learn from it, and move on.

In a small, entrepreneurial business you don't have the luxury of guilt or time or excess. If people aren't pulling their weight, they have to go. If a vendor isn't doing the job, find someone else. If you're in love with a project, but the buyer isn't, dump it. Not every good idea is a winner. I adored the Executive Female doll, for example, but couldn't find a manufacturer who agreed with me, so I had to give it up; I simply couldn't waste time and energy selling something that no one wanted to buy. A big company can afford to hide its mistakes or live with them; a small business can't.

AVOID THE BLAME GAME

It would have done me absolutely no good to blame Bob for the fact that he was ineffective in my company. Thinking he could adapt to a small venture like mine was my mistake and I had to accept responsibility for it. This happened to me many times in building NAFE. When the direct-mail shop handling our first mailer actually stole money from NAFE, I could have had the owner put in jail, but I didn't. I could have blamed my

P.R. firm for giving me a bum steer in recommending him, but I didn't. To me, it was simply a waste of time trying to blame someone else for a situation I was responsible for managing. And to me, looking for sympathy from American Express and the other clients I was working with at the time was also completely unproductive. It would only have tarnished my integrity in their eyes. Instead, I concentrated on the job at hand: salvaging as much of my mailing as I possibly could.

When you play the blame game, the only one who loses is you. Your clients, and even the people you work with, may act sympathetic, but in the end, they'll lose respect for you because you've failed to take responsibility for the choice you made and for your own error in judgment. Believe me, your clients couldn't care less about who did what. Their only concern is the damage that's been done and the impact on them personally and the project they're managing. So instead of blaming someone else—even if he or she is totally at fault—let the buck stop where it belongs, with you. Take responsibility and focus your energy and creativity on figuring out how to solve the problem that's erupted.

DON'T USE OBSTACLES AS EXCUSES FOR FAILURE

I could go on and on about how tough it is to be an entrepreneur. I could tell you lots of war stories about people who tried to launch ventures, but didn't make it. But this book is all about success. So I'm simply going to give you a list of obstacles that people use as excuses to justify their failure:

"I don't have enough money."

"I don't have the right contacts."

"I don't have an MBA or a college degree."

"I don't know how to do projections."

"I don't have enough experience."

"I need more training."

"My lawyer says it won't work."

"My accountant says it won't work."

"My mother says it won't work."

"My husband says it won't work."

"My boyfriend says it won't work."

"Market research came up negative."

"My friends think I'm nuts."

"I can't find anyone to help me."

Do any of these sound familiar? If so, then beware! If these are the kind of rationales you're using for *not* starting a business, then the entrepreneurial life is not for you and you should forget about it completely. Not everyone is intended to be an entrepreneur. If they were, then there would be no big companies. So be yourself and do the best work you can do, whatever it is.

USE BRAINSTORMING AS AN IDEA GENERATOR

Brainstorming is one of my favorite business activities. It's also one of an entrepreneur's most valuable tools. It's informative, inspiring, and inexpensive. And the results can be incredibly powerful. In the early days of NAFE's magazine, we used brainstorming sessions as a way to help us shape each issue. We always held these meetings away from the NAFE office. Over cocktails and dinner, usually at my apartment, the NAFE staff and I would bring together an eclectic bunch of women—and often men—to tell us what they were thinking about—and what they and their friends wanted to read about. We invited writers, clients, vendors, network directors, friends, and interesting people we'd met at conferences. We talked about anything and everything.

Put a bunch of bright, lively people together and let them loose and they're bound to come up with some great ideas. And one idea sparks another. Since the people we invited came from all walks of life, they kept us from becoming too insulated or narrow in our outlook. Their insights also kept the contents of our magazine from becoming stale and repetitive. This diversity helped give our *Executive Female* magazine a sophistication and reach that extended far beyond its small budget and staff. What's more, everyone had fun! The executives at these informal get-togethers had a chance to meet successful people in other industries and exchange ideas with them in a relaxed, noncompetitive environment. They also had the chance to shape a product devoted to helping women advance in their careers. I've used brainstorming sessions like the ones described here in many different situations and they've always been surprisingly effective.

REACH FOR THE TOP

I've always made it a point to go to the top executive in a company whenever I needed action or a decision. In my mind, this is the only way to work. But many fledgling entrepreneurs seem to hesitate about reaching out in this way. First of all, they think it's impossible to get to the top. And second, they think that even if they break through, no one will bother to speak with them or help them. If you're one of these people, then you're wrong on both counts. Yes, you can get to the top, and when you do, you're likely to find a sympathetic ear and swift action—*if you have something of value to offer, that is.*

Whenever I want to do business with top executives, I make it a point to find out their schedules and work styles. Are they in their office before seven or eight o'clock in the morning? Do they work late or catch the 4:55 out to Greenwich? What time do they go to lunch? Once I gather this information from a helpful assistant or secretary, I shift into action. I start calling and keep calling until I reach my target prospect. When I do, I'm well prepared. I have only a few minutes to pique their interest. My goal is usually to persuade them to meet with me over lunch or cocktails—and I'm successful about 80 percent of the time.

When I do make contact, I generally find that these top producers are remarkably relaxed and open to my ideas. After all, they've arrived. They don't have to compete with anyone climbing up the corporate ladder along with them. They don't have to prove anything to anyone—except their stockholders. They don't have to go to anyone else for a decision; they're free to act almost instantly. And that's exactly what they like to do—take action, move ahead, make something happen. That's why they're at the top: They know how to make decisions and make them quickly. This is why working with successful people is so uncomplicated and rewarding: If you can prove to them that you have something of value to offer, you can win powerful allies. So don't waste your time, energy, and resources trying to move from the bottom up. Start at the top. It's faster and easier.

LOOK FOR SIMPLE ANSWERS

Anything that's complicated doesn't work. Anything that's complicated and *does* work is complicated only in its simplicity.

DON'T BE OVERAWED BY LAWYERS AND ACCOUNTANTS

Remember, lawyers and accountants are "hired guns." Their role is to carry out decisions, not to make them. More good deals are broken by lawyers than you can imagine. And no one can undermine whatever confidence you have in your idea more quickly than a good, solid accountant. After all, if these people knew how to think like entrepreneurs, they wouldn't be lawyers and accountants. Use them for what they're professionally qualified to do: keep your legal affairs and your books in order. Give them directions—don't ask for direction from them.

LEARN HOW TO HANDLE REJECTION

Rejection is a basic fact of life and, unfortunately, one of the costs of doing business. And, though this is changing, I believe women still have to cope with more rejection than men do. Despite all the self-help books around, I also think most women still take rejection very personally. This can be very damaging. There are two phases to rejection, according to Dr. Herbert Thomas, a psychiatrist friend of mine who has spent years studying the subject. The first phase is the act of rejection itself, and the second is the response to rejection once it occurs. That response usually involves shame and anger. Women often turn the shame that results from being rejected in on themselves, sometimes to the point of intense physical pain. The pain caused by such shame causes anger. Women often try to wall off and isolate their shame and anger instead of defusing it.

To prevent shame and the anger it produces from building up and doing damage, women have to learn to objectify the person who's rejected them, advises Dr. Thomas. The more they learn about that person and clarify the motives behind a rejection, the less significant it becomes. The goal is to cut the person down to size. The single best way to objectify someone who's rejected you is to talk with other people. Finding out that the person has treated someone else in the same way or that the rejection you encountered is part of a pattern of behavior can really help defuse its impact. If you can't talk with people who actually know the person you're dealing with, then do the next best thing and reach out for your support system. Talk about what's happened and how you feel. Let your team offer advice and war stories about their own rejections. You'll feel a lot stronger and better when you do. Once you handle the pain and shame that a rejection has triggered, your anger will take care of itself.

CELEBRATE AND SHARE YOUR SUCCESSES

If it's important to share rejection, then it's doubly important to share your successes. Everybody loves a winner, and we all enjoy hearing about someone who's beaten the odds. And that's what every successful entrepreneur does: beats the odds. So if things are going well for you, then by all means, blow your horn! Let your staff know. Let your clients and customers know. Let your vendors know. Let the world know. If you don't do it, who will?

You can share your success in many ways. Keeping people up to date on growth and new accounts they've captured is the approach most people take. But often they forget to say thank you to the people who've really made it happen. I've always looked for fun ways to celebrate and say thank you to my staff and clients: cruises, parties, and show tickets, are just a few. One year, I outdid myself and bought fur coats for key members of NAFE's staff. That's right! Fur coats. Why not? I wanted to say thank you in a big way by giving them something I knew they'd never buy for themselves in a million years. This made a big impression, not just on my staff, but on everyone who heard about their furry gifts as well. And believe me, everyone from vendors to clients *did* hear about them!

Oprah Winfrey, one of today's hottest female entrepreneurs, also makes it a point to reward her staff generously. As a way of saying thank you, she treats trusted employees to spa treatments, makeovers, buying sprees, and dream vacations. No wonder they're incredibly hard-working and devoted! Oprah knows how important her staff is, and *she lets them know she knows in ways that touch their lives and hearts.* Give your staff opportunities to grow and then applaud that growth—and you'll be rewarded with loyalty and top performance.

MY TOP 10 SALES TIPS

One day soon after my partner Warren joined NAFE we found ourselves in the New York offices of a major company making a sales presentation. For whatever reason, the executives we were meeting with thought that what we had to sell was very important and we ended up pitching NAFE to five rather conservative businessmen in their very sophisticated boardroom. They were so fascinated with what we had to say that they sat for an hour just listening before they took time out to tell us that we were meeting with the wrong company! Our prospective target was actually run by their cousins, who had the same name on the door but operated from a different address. We all had a good laugh over this mistake in identity, and then one of the executives called his cousin and introduced us, raving about the presentation he had just heard. We jumped into a taxi, arrived at the right office, made our pitch again, and ended up with a new client. Now that's selling!

My single biggest sales tip: If you're starting a business, you have to make sales! If you have a business of your own, then you're in sales: No if, ands, or buts about it. Your dream, whatever it may be, has a price tag attached to it. And without the ability to sell, all dreams, however worthy and wonderful, go down the drain. That's why selling is so incredibly challenging. To me, half the joy and fun of being an entrepreneur is persuading someone else to invest in my vision and its value. My key talent has always been motivating potential buyers: awakening their enthusiasm for the product or service I was offering, whether it was mint-green miniskirts or financial independence for women.

My sales and marketing skills were nurtured by apprenticing with a master salesman, my dad. He regarded sales as a God-given talent, one that could never be learned from books, only improved by experience. To him, business was the great university, and retailing, the world's top graduate school. Perhaps because selling was so much a part of who he was, my father also felt ambivalent about it. He loved the challenge of developing a new product to sell, yet he disdained the lowly salesperson—the mere peddler. Despite my success in all aspects of selling, from creating the first teen dress lines to persuading corporate moguls to recognize the women's market, I too had mixed feelings about my calling. It was years before I would let myself respect my own talent in sales.

That's what I want to do here: help you feel good about selling your dream. I want you to understand and embrace the emotional richness, the drama, and the power of sales. This may be a tough sell, I know. You may absolutely believe in the integrity and value of your product or service but still have mixed feelings about harnessing your skill to sell others what you have to offer. Like many people, you may think of sales as the bottom of the business barrel and a salesperson as someone who sells widgets or haggles over a car deal or makes telemarketing calls in the middle of dinner. That's not the kind of sales I'm talking about here.

I'm talking about the entrepreneur with a vision who's driven to bring a dream to the marketplace. The kind of selling I want to sell you on isn't about pushing a product or beating the competition or cutting the best deal. It's about communicating and educating. It's about understanding the human condition. Crafting a successful, win-win sale, in which the whole is greater than the sum of its parts, is tremendously exciting and emotionally satisfying. It can give you a sense of real strength, importance, and power. Why? Because you are persuading another individual that you have something of real value, something he or she needs. In sales, as nowhere else, the dollar bill knows no sex. In making a sale, you've convinced someone to part with his or her hard-earned or carefully budgeted dollars solely on the basis of your product or service's integrity and your ability to deliver it. To me, that's true equality!

Most people think of sales in terms of evaluating a client's needs, proposing solutions, and closing a deal. But dig deeper, and you'll find there's far more to selling. When a sale is made, that's when your work really begins. Interestingly, the qualities that make a superb salesperson—being a good listener and learner, trusting one's intuition, admitting mistakes freely, and striving to create a win-win situation for all players—are found, more often than not, in women. A good negotiator is like a good mother. She knows what her child needs to grow and she's willing to make it available. A good deal is a lot like a strong, healthy child: It should thrive independently of the strengths and weaknesses of the parties who make it.

If there's one thing my dad taught me, it's that there's only one kind of sale worth making: a good sale. And there's only one way to make a good sale: by delivering what you've promised in a timely, satisfactory fashion so that everyone involved feels whole and happy with the result. How, exactly, do you do this? After years of selling to corporate giants like AT&T, American Express, Hertz, and Ford, I've come to understand how to negotiate a winning sale. I could probably write another whole book on the subject, but I've captured my best sales tips for you here:

1. IN A GOOD SALE, THERE AREN'T TWO SIDES TO THE BARGAINING TABLE, ONLY ONE

To craft a win-win sale, you and your customer must find a common ground: the place where his or her need dovetails with the value and benefits your product or service offers. You must find this place together, as partners and not as adversaries. Leading your clients to their emotional comfort zone is one of the keys to selling. And it isn't easy. You have to be willing to understand their world: their needs, the pressures they face, the failures they fear, the successes they yearn to achieve. You have to approach this new world like Columbus, sailing an uncharted sea but with your product or service as a compass to guide you.

When I first began approaching major companies about NAFE, I found myself in unfamiliar territory. It was as if I had landed in Russia or China and had to master a new language, new customs, and a new culture. I had been a highly successful recruiter in the fashion industry, but selling to sophisticated corporate decision makers like John Bennett at American Express was a whole new level of selling for me. I really had only one thing I could count on: my belief in the integrity of NAFE and the value it offered the women I wanted to reach.

Along the way, I found that the hardest sale is the first one. Once you persuade a creditable company to buy what you're offering, you've overcome your biggest barrier to future sales. The next time around, new prospects can no longer point to your lack of a track record as a reason for not striking a deal. Instead, they have to base their go/no-go decision solely on their own insecurities about whether they think you can work effectively with them. In short, they have to make a decision about investing in you. How do you overcome their doubts? By fostering their comfort and confidence not just in your product or service, but also in your ability to deliver what you promise. That's why being direct and honest is so critical in sales.

As soon as my corporate clients met me, they knew where they stood: I had no secrets, no hidden agendas, no ace up my sleeve. I never bothered with grandstanding or one-upmanship. There was no mystery to the way I operated. If I wanted something from them, I told them what it was and what I had to offer in return. If I didn't know something, I asked questions until I understood it. If I made a mistake, I admitted it. If someone on the corporate end made a mistake, I didn't try to exploit it for my own advantage but tried to help fix it. If I felt something was off track, I spoke up about it quickly and forcefully. I did this not to make waves, but because I knew that a runaway train would run over everyone: me, my client, and our customers. If something worked, I took my fair share of credit but was quick to spread the praise and profits around. My corporate friends have told me time and again how refreshing and reassuring my straightforward style was for them. They knew they were on firm ground when they negotiated with me—and that made them comfortable.

2. KEEP YOUR EYES OPEN, YOUR MOUTH MOSTLY SHUT, AND YOUR EARS COCKED

Listen, L-i-s-t-e-n, LISTEN! Listening is probably your single most important key to decoding a client's world and mindset as a buyer. As my father knew so well, selling doesn't take any special credentials or a fancy title: Anyone who has a healthy respect for other points of view can become a great salesperson. But you may have to overcome the negative image of a salesperson as a high-pressure con artist. The best way to separate yourself from this image is to make clients partners in your joint success.

How do you do this? By encouraging potential clients to talk to you and by listening to what they say. Ask questions. Solicit feedback. Assess their needs and the demands they face with the fresh perspective of a friendly outsider. Identify their fears and limits, not so you can exploit them but so you can help overcome them to your mutual benefit. Boost their corporate stock by giving them the means to make their company stronger. Probe their attitude toward risk. Understand their idea of success. Let the sales opportunity you are looking for evolve out of a give-and-take discussion rather than trying to engineer it.

I enter every sales meeting with the same goal: finding out how to help my prospects discover new ways to create additional business and profit. What can I offer of real value? That's the question I aim to answer at the end of every sales meeting. Careful, creative listening inevitably reveals to me how to meet a client's needs—and how I can adjust (not change!) what I have to offer to ensure the best possible fit at the lowest possible risk. Once I understand how my clients operate and what they want, it's relatively easy to shape a program that provides us both a good chance for success.

Actively listening to clients has an added benefit: It can provide you with exciting new ideas for building your business. You'd be surprised how many great entrepreneurial pearls of wisdom clients have dropped at my feet. Many corporate executives are frustrated dreamers themselves. You'll find they admire your spunk and chutzpah in chasing after your own personal rainbow—and will give freely of their experience and creativity. Don't be shy about taking advantage of the precious insights and ideas these talented business people can offer you.

3. NEVER TRIP OVER YOUR EGO— OR LET IT GET IN THE WAY OF MAKING A SALE

I pride myself on never tripping over my ego—or trying to buck the system unless it's absolutely necessary. Getting the job done that I've set out to do in the best possible way is all I care about. And short of mayhem or murder, I'm willing to do whatever it takes to reach my goal. To succeed in your entrepreneurial venture, you'll need this same kind of single-minded commitment. That means checking your ego at the door when you go into a sales meeting. I learned this very early in my career.

Back in the 1970s, for example, I was a novelty in the executive recruiting industry: I was the only woman in the field who was running her own agency and not working as an agent for a male employer. I was recruiting at the top: My clients were the CEOs and presidents of leading textile firms who wanted help in locating senior executives. They were also all male, of course. In order to make these high-powered decision makers more open to working with me, I took on a male partner, Ed Burns.

Many women at the time would probably have called this a cop-out, a compromise, and even sexist. But I was interested in making a sale, not making a point. Ed wasn't much of a producer, but he made my clients feel more comfortable because they were used to dealing with men. Quite frankly, it was much easier for me to have a man in the office than it was to prove whatever it was I was supposed to prove by trying to run my business alone as a woman. I've always focused my energy and talent on being successful rather than dissipated it by trying to prove something to someone else. I couldn't have cared less at the time about whether men accepted or didn't accept women. I kept my eye on my own personal bottom line: making the sale, caring for my family, and achieving financial security.

When launching NAFE, I also avoided the need to make a grand statement about women's equality or inequality. For my dream to succeed, the corporate executives I wanted to work with needed to feel relaxed and on familiar ground. That's why I always took Stanley or Joe along with me to my first sales meeting with a potential client. I chose Warren, another man with a traditional business background, as my partner in building NAFE for exactly the same reason. Having a man with me broke the ice and made prospects more receptive to my sales presentations. After a first meeting, I was firmly in control.

Did it bother me that I had to rely on having a man in tow to make a sale? Hell no! I spent my time finding a void in the marketplace and filling it—not proving how important or unique I was. In a sales meeting, my attitude toward a prospect is never "Here's what I have to offer you—see how valuable it is?" but "What do you need? How can I help you get it? How can we work together?" The buyer always comes first. Trip over your ego and you'll go flying out your prospect's door before you ever get a chance to make your pitch.

4. MAKE IT EASY FOR THE PERSON YOU'RE SELLING TO SAY YES

If you create an offer that's irresistibly attractive to your clients, then selling them on its value is a piece of cake. How do you make it easy for your clients to say yes and just about impossible for them to turn you down? First, by bringing them a product, service, or program that offers new business potential. Second, and equally important, by keeping their up-front investment so low that you just about eliminate any risk involved. Let me show you what I mean.

When I first started NAFE, I needed money to launch a direct-mail campaign to recruit members. To find these start-up dollars and win credibility in the marketplace, I had to work with major corporations. To sell them on investing in NAFE, I always proposed that they underwrite a low-risk, low-budget test mailing. The test was so modest that most executives could sign off on it without waiting for a new budget cycle or going to a million people for approval. Even more enticing, I always shared the risk with my clients by going into the mail with them. They would pay the cost of the printed material and postage, and NAFE would pay the cost of mailing and tracking. This approach appealed to clients because it gave them NAFE's endorsement. It also saved them the hassle of setting up a separate tracking system. At the same time, it allowed NAFE to keep control of the mailing.

This strategy gave me a much better chance of closing an initial sale than if I had designed a huge, complicated program with a gilt-edged budget to match. If the test succeeded, then NAFE had a track record with the client and finding more money for a bigger, more elaborate program was relatively painless. If, for some reason, the test bombed, I always stood behind NAFE's value. I'd say, "Hey, Don (or Joe), I think I know what went wrong. Let's try it this way." The client usually agreed to a second test, and we ironed out the kinks together.

Whatever you're selling, your immediate goal is getting a foothold in your client's business. To do this, you must make it painless and relatively safe for a buyer to invest in what you have to offer. The easiest way to do this is to offer a low-risk, low-budget proposal to your clients. This approach has many advantages. By operating outside a company's budget, you bypass its lead-footed bureaucracy and gain the chance to move into the marketplace quickly. By keeping clients' initial investment low, you reduce their exposure and lower the psychological barrier to working with your company.

Equally important, by taking this approach, you signal your confidence in the project you're selling and position yourself as an equal partner in the project's success. You also establish yourself as a businessperson with integrity—someone who's willing to share not just the revenues and rewards of a project but its responsibilities and risks as well. In fact, you may not even have to underwrite part of the start-up yourself. Once you have a firm dollar commitment from a client, you can easily go to vendors you plan to work with and persuade them to extend you credit for printing or computer services in return for future business.

5. KEEP CONTROL OF THE SALE IN YOUR HANDS

Keeping control of a sale is critical to success, yet many people unwittingly surrender this control early in the selling process. Actively manage the sales process by knowing your clients' work habits and taking the lead in establishing communications with them. Find out what time prospective or current clients arrive in the morning and call them as early as possible, before they plunge into their workday. Most top executives are at their desks at least half an hour to an hour before their staffs arrive. If you call at this time, you increase the chances of reaching them directly, their offices are relatively quiet, they have a little time to plan and reflect—and are far more likely to respond positively to you.

Always initiate calls yourself so you don't waste time waiting for call backs. If you reach a secretary, resist any request to leave a message and number. Just say something like, "I'll be out all day, so I'll give Mr./Ms. So-and-So a call back later in the afternoon. What's the best time to reach him/her today?" When you speak with a prospect, as I said earlier, always aim for a face-to-face meeting, preferably over lunch. If you take the client out, always pick up the lunch tab—even if you're selling to a man. That's one of the keys to maintaining control of a sale: keeping control of the purse strings. To eliminate hassling over the check, make yourself known to the staffs of several high-profile lunch spots. On the day of a sales luncheon, arrive 5 or 10 minutes early and hand the waiter your credit card in advance. This way, no bill appears at the table. This impresses clients and lets them know you mean business.

When you meet with clients, as I said in Chap. 10, try to make your encounter with them both fun and personal. Create a friendly, open climate. Don't overwhelm or try to dazzle anyone with your business savvy; let your style speak for itself. Be enthusiastic about what you have to offer without being too effusive or overeager. Good selling is a collaborative, not a competitive, process. Give your clients breathing space and time to think and digest the benefits of working with you. Keep the atmosphere light: Tell a funny story and indulge your sense of humor.

6. PACE YOUR PITCH FOR MAXIMUM IMPACT AND KEEP IT OPEN-ENDED

Every sale has a natural rhythm and you mustn't tamper with it. Most people think of sales in terms of a buyer-seller relationship. I see it differently. My goal is always to transform a client into a participant, *a giver*. Exchanging ideas back and forth is much more rewarding and revealing than going to a client with a preconceived, prepackaged program. In my experience, overpreparation often kills a sale.

As a meeting winds down, I'll say, "Think over what we've talked about. Nothing is etched in stone. If there's anything you want added or adjusted, I'm open to it—as long as we keep the basic program intact." I usually keep a few ideas in reserve, instead of "giving away the candy store." This leaves the door open for future meetings and allows me to make a call back without being a pest. Sometimes, I'll phone a client and say, "You know, I was thinking about our program. If we add such and such, we'll get a better result." I've also never hesitated to tamper with a project in the execution stage. Until a mailing was out the door or a conference was under way, it was subject to change. This would drive my staff at NAFE crazy, but if making a change would improve a product's chances for success, then I wanted it made.

7. ACT AS A RESOURCE FOR YOUR CLIENTS BY ENCOURAGING THEM TO DEPEND ON YOU

Sharing is an important part of sales. As I said in Chap. 7, I've always shared my ideas freely and never been afraid that someone would steal them from me. In fact, I view the ability to share as a terrific sales tool—one that's often ignored and undervalued. If you make a sincere effort to understand your clients' problems and offer suggestions for solving them, you become more than just a vendor to them; you become an adviser and confidante.

Once you get to know a client, for example, you might find out that he or she needs a good administrator. If you know someone appropriate, you can pass the name along. If you see information about a new product or service that could affect your client, then get it to the right person quickly. Make a habit of doing this and your clients will automatically think of you as a resource. Every time they reach for you, your value to them increases. The more you know about your clients' businesses, the more opportunities you can create to enhance their success—and your own.

In some cases, you can even teach a client a thing or two! That's what happened with Bob, the CEO of one of the major publishing companies NAFE worked with. Every couple of weeks, Bob and I would go out to lunch and he'd cajole me into telling him my latest brainstorms for building NAFE. One day, I happened to mention an idea that really blew his mind: automatic renewals. I had worked out an arrangement with major credit-card companies that allowed NAFE to automatically bill cardholders for annual membership renewals. "Don't you get hundreds of angry women calling you up and complaining about this?" Bob asked in amazement. "Far from it," I answered. "Most members like the convenience of not having to fill out another form. If anyone objects, we just cheerfully refund their money." Bob pondered my chutzpah in putting this concept to work for me. P.S. Not long after our lunch, he developed an automatic renewal program for his readership. If only I'd asked for a commission!

8. INVEST IN TOMORROW BY CREATING RELATIONSHIPS, NOT DEALS

Once I've sold someone on a product or project, my goal is always to turn the deal we've made into a relationship. I want to expand our work together so that the client begins to think of me as someone with the power to contribute to his or her success in a whole range of ways. I also want clients to become more involved in my venture, so that they have a growing financial—and psychological—stake in my business's success. The way in which NAFE's program with AT&T evolved is a good example.

Imagine my surprise when Anna Walden, a marketing executive from AT&T, called me up one day. Old habits die hard: I was sure NAFE was late paying its phone bill! Far from it! NAFE was finally being wooed by a Fortune 500 company. AT&T was trying to encourage long-distance calling by promoting the phone calls as a networking tool. Anna knew about NAFE's networks and wanted to take me to lunch (I still picked up the tab!) to see whether we could work together. What a great feeling to be at the other end of a sale! We brainstormed and quickly created a small promotion.

We launched our relationship with a modest mailing insert offering NAFE members a special AT&T incentive. Then I shifted into overdrive and began thinking up creative ways to encourage AT&T's further involvement with NAFE. First, I suggested that it underwrite an informational brochure offering NAFE members successful tips for networking—including advice on networking by phone. Second, AT&T agreed to run ongoing ads in our *Executive Female* magazine.

Even more exciting, AT&T agreed to become a corporate sponsor for NAFE's "Move with the World" conference. In return for its endorsement, we invited one of AT&T's top executives to be a key luncheon speaker on the theme of changing technology. We also created a corporate membership program offering AT&T's female executives and staff a special rate for joining NAFE. Eventually, many of these women formed their own NAFE network—which created a strong internal base of support for our programs. This corporate membership concept proved so popular that we introduced it to other clients as well.

Moving from a deal mentality to relationship building takes a major investment of time and creativity on your part. To make it work, you can't live on yesterday's ideas. You have to be prepared to build your business on two fronts at once: improving on what you have and finding new avenues for expansion. I've always been very proud of the fact that NAFE never lost a client. As we grew, we added new sponsors, but our old friends stayed with us, mainly because we always had something new to offer them.

When fostering long-term relationships, never underestimate the importance of hand holding. Nurture your clients' commitment by keeping them up to date on a joint program, alerting them to any roadblocks, and building on your joint successes. Hand holding makes the executives you work with feel important and minimizes the chance that they will face any unpleasant surprises that they may have to justify to higher-ups. And it gives you the kind of continuing contact you need to move from a client to a friend and from a deal to a relationship.

9. ASK YOUR CLIENTS FOR HELP IN BUILDING YOUR BUSINESS

Enlist your clients as part of your support system for success whenever you can. Once you've developed a strong relationship, request their assistance with referrals. I've never hesitated to ask someone to open a door or two for me. Being able to make a call and say, "Joe (or John) at AT&T (or Ford) suggested I get in touch with you," means half my sales job is done. Most of my contacts have been happy to pave the way by letting me use their names; in some cases, they've even made advance calls to introduce me.

This is one more reason why it's so important to do business with people at the top. They are not going to recommend someone to a friend or colleague unless they feel that the two people they are bringing together have a strong chance to work together successfully. Their referral isn't just a vote of confidence in you; it also conveys a message to one of their own: "Here's someone it's worth your while to talk to." Then it's up to you to deliver. Of course, cold calling is still likely to be part of your business repertoire, and you never know who you'll find at the other end of the line. After all, my call to John Bennet at American Express changed my life! Just remember, even in a cold call, try to find out the name and title of the person you're contacting. You'll be amazed at the difference calling someone by name will make.

10. KNOW WHEN YOU'VE COMPLETED YOUR SALE—AND QUIT WHILE YOU'RE AHEAD

I've been surprised time and again at how many people make one of the deadliest mistakes in business communications: continuing to sell long after a sale has been made. They are so eager to please and so infatuated with what they have to offer that they oversell—and often lose a deal as a result. Avoid this mistake at all costs! Once again, the key to success is listening. Listen carefully to a client's cues and you'll know whether to press forward with your proposal or whether you've completed your sale. Once your prospect agrees on the key elements of your deal, move quickly to discussing its execution. If you can shift your client from talking about *what* you want to do to the nuts and bolts of *how* to make it happen, you're home free.

Well, that's 10 sales tips. But just because I'm such a good salesperson and so convinced of the value of what I'm offering you here, I'm going to give you an extra piece of sales advice:

11. REMEMBER, CLOSING A SALE IS JUST THE BEGINNING OF A SALE

I never consider a sale closed until I know that my buyer is absolutely satisfied, and then I keep close tabs on our project as it moves forward. I learned the importance of follow-through back in my recruiting days. My agency was the first in the business to offer clients a 60-day guarantee. This gave them time to see if there was a good match between their needs and a candidate I had found for them. Many people relax too much during the follow-through phase of a sale—or worse still, ignore it all together. This can be a recipe for disaster. I've always been very careful about delegating the details of a program—and you should be, too. Anything you haven't done yourself needs to be checked and rechecked.

So, there you have it: the secrets of my selling success. When I think about how to put all of this together, one of my all-time favorite sales comes to mind. If there's one quality I have that's really helped me in sales—and in life!—it's my determination. When I made a decision to offer a loans-by-mail benefit to NAFE members, I wanted the best and heard that National Pacific had the most reputable and well-established program of this kind. One day, I picked up the phone and asked for the head of National's loans-by-mail business. Fortunately for me, the man of the hour turned out to be a friendly, easygoing, and very savvy Irishman named Denny O'Brien.

I spent a few minutes pitching NAFE and the creditworthiness of the women's market to Denny. He was polite, but I could feel his skepticism flowing over the phone line. Then and there, I made a crucial decision. I told him I was so convinced we should be doing business together that I was going to fly out to California on my own dime and take him to lunch. Try as he might, he couldn't refuse this offer. Before hanging up, I said, "I'm not flying across the country to sit in a stuffy office. Please make a reservation at your favorite lunch spot. I'm going to wine and dine you in style!" Denny laughed and said, "It's a deal! I'll take you to the best damn restaurant you've ever seen! I'm really looking forward to meeting you!"

We met about a week later, and after a cocktail and a short chat, I knew I'd made a friend. Denny was relaxed, cordial, and most important, open to new ideas. After I described NAFE's demographics to him, he began to express some enthusiasm. He was impressed with NAFE's clients, but he still felt women were too mobile and too busy searching for their niche in the business world to be good candidates for a loans-by-mail campaign. I overcame this reservation by using my "Let's test the market" strategy. Denny agreed to a modest test in which his only investment was to print up applications for a "NAFE invites you" mailing of 100,000 and pay for postage. In return for paying for the mailing and tracking, NAFE would receive a percentage for each loan that was approved. We wrote up the contract right then and there at our table on a cocktail napkin! Denny was totally shocked when I paid our lunch bill. I told him, "When the program's a big success and you come to New York to celebrate, lunch will be on you." "Wendy, you're really a class act," he replied.

We both got a big charge out of the high-powered deal we'd made and Denny actually photocopied the cocktail napkin for me at his office. Later on, he had it framed! Denny soon saw he had a winner on his hands. NAFE members quickly became his best accounts, because women were so protective of their credit standing that they generally repaid their loans before the due date! Even today, I love telling the story of my cocktail-napkin negotiation. This sale has everything: a strong marketing pitch, a win-win proposal, fun, drama, trust, and most important, it was a huge success!

PUTTING YOUR DREAMS TO WORK

Dear Reader,

We've reached the end of our journey together. In writing this book, we've shared with you some of the joys and hardships of entrepreneurship, survival secrets and tips on successful selling, and the strong belief that emotional freedom and economic independence go hand in hand. But most of all, this book is about dreams and dreamers.

It takes courage to be a dreamer. Most of the people you'll meet in life are afraid to dream because they fear that their dreams won't come true and that the very act of dreaming will make them dissatisfied. So they'd rather pretend that an ordinary life without too many demands or disappointments is really what they want.

But you're not like that. If you were, you wouldn't be reading this book. We believe you know all about dreams. You know that sometimes a dream sleeps quietly within you, gathering strength and support. And sometimes it drives you, restlessly and recklessly, across a sea of unfulfilled desire. Sometimes it demands complete devotion and sometimes it asks only for your belief in its value and the promise that, though it may be put aside for a time, it will never be abandoned.

Dreams aren't miracles. They're opportunities. Entrepreneurs aren't just dreamers, they're doers. And they're not just dream shapers, they're also dream sharers. Yes, they dare to dream alone, but they don't *do* alone. They share their dreams with others and persuade those around them—against all odds—to help their dream find a life of its own out in the world.

Each of the enterprises described here was born out of the emotion of anger and a dream of equality. Every success and failure, every up and down, every business lesson we've talked about in these pages was a stepping stone to the creation of NAFE. Twenty-five years ago, women couldn't obtain credit cards, loans, or insurance in their own names. However successful they were in their careers, economically they were treated as second-class citizens. NAFE found a way to change all that and proudly continues to meet the changing needs of career women.

Today, NAFE is a national institution and a powerful social force with 200,000 members—more than half of whom work for themselves, as business owners, self-employed professionals, or entrepreneurs. Today, NAFE offers sophisticated investment and retirement programs and reaches tens of thousands of women each year through satellite conferences beamed across the country. And today, through the NAFE Women's Foundation's innovative and widely praised Esteem Team program, it is helping successful career women to encourage and inspire teenage girls from New York to L.A. to pursue *their* dreams. NAFE may have begun as one woman's vision, but like all powerful dreams, it has grown far beyond its dreamer. We applaud its ongoing accomplishments and offer our best wishes for NAFE's 25th anniversary and future.

Dreams have a way of reinventing and renewing themselves. Writing this book has been a wonderful experience: It's allowed us to share a unique approach to entrepreneurship and lessons learned, especially from NAFE's growth, with many more women. We hope you've found your own personal support system for success within these pages. We also hope that the ideas, advice, and strategies offered here will encourage you to follow your dream and fulfill your vision as an entrepreneur.

Above all, we hope we've emboldened you to reach out for help and share your dream with those who believe in you.

Dreams may be born of sleepless nights, but they grow and blossom by day and through the devotion of not one dreamer but many doers. Yes, you may fear rejection; but with support, you can push past that fear. Yes, you may taste failure; but with support, you can find the strength to fight another day. Yes, you may lose a sale or even a business; but with support, you'll never lose heart. Never fall into the trap of believing you have to go it alone: You don't and you can't.

Our dream for this book is that it will offer you the helping hand you need to move forward with courage and confidence. We wish for you all the fruits of success and the rich sense of satisfaction that making your dream come true can bring. And we remind you that the biggest obstacle you face is *you*. Dare to dream and you can accomplish anything. Dare to believe in yourself and you will. Good luck!

Sincerely,

Wendy Rue & Karin Abarbanel

P.S. Always remember, the dollar bill knows no sex!

INDEX

Index note: The initials WR refer to Wendy Rue.

The ENTERTAINMENT
FUNCTIONS of TELEVISION

The ENTERTAINMENT FUNCTIONS of TELEVISION

Sponsored by the Social Science Research Council

Edited by

PERCY H. TANNENBAUM
University of California, Berkeley

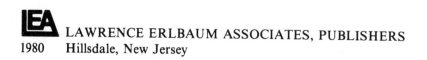

LAWRENCE ERLBAUM ASSOCIATES, PUBLISHERS
1980   Hillsdale, New Jersey

Lawrence Erlbaum Associates, Inc., Publishers
365 Broadway
Hillsdale, New Jersey 07642

Library of Congress Cataloging in Publication Data

Main entry under title:
The entertainment functions of television.

Papers based on a conference organized by the
Committee on Television and Social Behavior of the Social
Science Research Council.
Includes bibliographies and indexes.
1. Television—Psychological aspects—Congresses.
I. Tannenbaum, Percy H., 1972–   II. Social Science
Research Council. Committee on Television and Social
Behavior.
PN1992.6.E57   301.16′1   79-24637
ISBN 0-89859-013-2

Printed in the United States of America

Contents

Acknowledgments

The principal acknowledgments in a collective work of original chapters by a variety of authors are to the authors themselves and to their various sources of support and assistance. These are indicated, wherever appropriate, as acknowledgments in the individual chapters.

But the whole is different than the sum of its parts, and its existence as an entity should be appropriately acknowledged as well. From its inception in 1973, the activities of the Social Science Research Council (SSRC) Committee on Television and Social Behavior, of which this volume is a product, was supported by a grant (No. 5 R12 MH 24522-03) from the Behavioral Sciences Program of the National Institute of Mental Health. NIMH and its main officer on the grant, Joel Goldstein, are to be commended for the supportive and facilitative manner with which the grant was administered. Ronald P. Abeles, formerly of the SSRC, was the principal staff person for the Committee and played a central, constructive role in all its deliberations. He provided particular support to the editor of this volume in helping to shepherd it through some rather trying periods. Robert A. Gates assumed this role in the later stages of manuscript preparation. Katharina Varney and Deirdre Kessner helped with the typing and editing chores in Berkeley.

PERCY H. TANNENBAUM

1 An Unstructured Introduction to an Amorphous Area

Percy H. Tannenbaum
University of California, Berkeley

While most of the research dealing with the mass media generally, and television in particular, has focused on direct or mediated learning from communications messages—from factual materials as such, or lessons and generalizations derived from fictional presentations—one of the more salient facts of media consumption has been overlooked. Most of the deliberate exposure of most people to TV is motivated less to seek information, as such, but in search of something generally referred to as "entertainment." This cardinal fact is reflected with great consistency in audience ratings in the United States, in similar data from other countries, and in the perennial popularity of certain American and British programs across diverse foreign cultures. It is also reflected in some of the data contained in the "uses and gratifications" type of research wherein respondents are asked to reflect on why they use the medium. Although there is reason to suspect some of the data collected in the latter type of research—if anything they probably inflate the actual incidence of active information seeking and deflate the entertainment function—there is still abundant support for a significant incentive to be "entertained."

There has, nevertheless, been very little research on the entertainment functions of the media—indeed, a paucity of research on the significance of entertainment in everyday life, quite apart from the media per se. It is one of those phenomena that is around us all the time, a kind of activity shared by most individuals on almost a universal basis, and yet it continues to be neglected. Scholars of television, particularly, avoid this phenomenon at their own peril—in terms of understanding why so many people use television to

such a great extent and what some of the main influences of the medium are on vast numbers of individuals.

This volume is an indirect product of the activities of the Committee on Television and Social Behavior of the Social Science Research Council (SSRC). Although its main activities were directed elsewhere, the Committee recognized fairly early in its deliberations that among the neglected items on the communication research agenda was the great appeal of the public media in general and television in particular as means of disseminating entertainment fare on a broad basis. In focusing on TV as a socializing device forging attitudes and behavior patterns (see, for example, the companion volume edited by Withey and Abeles, 1980), the Committee did not completely forget the entertainment content of the medium, but the nature and form of that content, its apparent appeal, its antecedents and its consequences—in short, the entertainment function of television —was hardly touched on.

The Committee collectively realized that if we are to more fully understand and appreciate the television medium and its functions in our contemporary society, a more systematic study of its role as a popular entertainment device is called for. Indeed, one wonders how it has been so neglected for so long, especially considering how dominant sheer entertainment is on television and that, one way or another, the effect of television has probably been among the most researched social science phenomena to date. The time had clearly come, to use the phrase of Elihu Katz (1977), "to take entertainment seriously."

It is not the practice of the SSRC to undertake and conduct research. Rather, its main role is as a mediator, initiator, and broker. It functions through its constituent committees to foster and promote established and potential new areas of social research, primarily by assembling involved scholars with mutual interests at conferences and through the publication of appropriate books—conference reports, research compendia, theoretical speculations, etc.—for dissemination to the social research community at large.

That was the pattern followed in the present case as well. The Committee first convened a small conference of interested researchers. This volume is a direct development of that conference.

BACKGROUND TO THE CONFERENCE

As with most other such gatherings, there were two issues that had to be addressed early in our planning for the conference: an appropriate agenda and who to invite. Clearly the two are not independent.

Participation

Regarding the composition, we opted for a relatively small group made up primarily of social psychologists who had demonstrated an interest in and/or had conducted research on some aspect of entertainment in the media. We had earlier discussed the desirability of a more broadly based collection of scholars who would address the issue of entertainment from the perspectives of a wider variety of disciplines. However, the judgment was that a more narrowly focused collectivity of psychologists and sociologists—reflecting the composition of the SSRC Committee and, in fact, substantially overlapping with it—was more appropriate for such an initial undertaking. As is often the case with such events, not everyone invited could attend—most unfortunately, perhaps the two foremost workers in this fledgling area were prohibited from participating due to illness—and we ended up with a group of 14 participants almost equally divided between those invited from the outside and Committee members.[1]

Agenda

Given the amorphous nature of the concept to begin with, it was apparent that even a relatively homogeneous group of scholars reflected a substantial diversity of interests and approaches. This made setting a formal agenda somewhat questionable. Accordingly, we settled for a relatively loose procedure aiming at modest goals. We sought to get the "lay of the land," so to speak, by attempting to address the following issues which I, at least, thought to be of sufficient general concern:

1. There was, first of all, the perennial definition issue. What do we mean by "entertainment"? What is to be included and what excluded under this rubric?
2. The motivational issue could not be overlooked. What is it about entertaining materials that provides positive incentives for people to seek it out, often at the expense of other desired or more preferred activities? What "rewards" does it provide for individuals in different settings (e.g., the

---

[1]The participants included Ronald Abeles, SSRC Staff; Leo Bogart, Newspaper Advertising Bureau; Aimée Dorr, then at Harvard University, now at the University of Southern California; Paul Ekman, University of California, San Francisco; Seymour Feshback, University of California, Los Angeles; Hilde Himmelweit, London School of Economics; Gerald Lesser, Harvard University; William McGuire, Yale University; Jack McLeod, University of Wisconsin; Harold Mendelsohn, University of Denver; Jerome Singer, Yale University; Percy Tannenbaum, University of California, Berkeley; Steven Withey, University of Michigan; and Dolf Zillmann, Indiana University.

isolated)? Is there anything special about television that enhances these positive functions (other than the obvious fact that it provides a less costly—in terms of time and energy as well as money—means of access)?

3. The nature of the experience: What are the by-products of "being entertained," particularly of its emotional components? Is the experience a set of conditioned responses such that we react in predictable emotional ways to certain patterns of stimuli, or is it something more intrinsic? Is it merely a question (as if that were not enough) of affect, or are other experiential phenomena involved?

4. The question of consequences, perhaps most important: What are its immediate and long-term effects? Is it something that is experienced and labeled for the moment and then promptly set aside, or do its effects tend to linger on and influence us later? Can the positive emotional responses associated with certain entertaining materials be stored in memory so that some of its excitatory and pleasing components can be experienced upon retrieval?

5. Not least, in what way, if any, does the purely entertaining function help or hinder the mediation of other effects of the message and other subsequent behavior?

CONFERENCE PROCEEDINGS

If the main purpose of the gathering was to assess "the lay of the land," we found a rather littered landscape. We could not quite come to mutually agreed terms with the various questions posed but did manage to generate a considerable variety of assorted terminology, approaches, concepts, and methods for a conference lasting a day and a half. There certainly was little evidence of any integrating theory or consensus—not an unexpected occurrence at this stage of the game, even if it were considered desirable.

It was, of course, no accident that the relative emphases and different foci appeared to be so diverse among the participants. As noted earlier, there were fundamental differences in how the assembled individuals addressed the subject matter and agenda questions. But just as social scientists have learned to extract some conceptual order out of the relative chaos of assorted data arrays through multivariate techniques, it was possible to extract some degree of latent organization from the relatively unstructured nature of our proceedings.[2] Our limited sample probably reflects a similar distribution of

---

[2]All too often, multivariate analysis is employed blindly as a poor substitute for a decent theory. Better than factor analysis or some such technique, one is fortunate to be blessed with the insight of clever, conscientious colleagues. Bill McGuire is one such colleague, and the following analysis owes much to his assessment of what the conference "churned up" in him.

these underlying factors in the profession at large—in kind, if not necessarily in relative degree—so they are worth considering in some detail.

Conceptual Approaches

There are basically three dimensions that distinguish the conceptual space defined by the "television and entertainment" rubric, when considered in terms of the motives of the investigator. One emphasizes the television medium and is thus more independent-variable oriented. A second is preoccupied with entertainment as a behavioral phenomenon and can be considered to be more dependent-variable oriented. The third focuses on some other social psychological phenomenon (e.g., fantasy), which has some relationship to both TV and entertainment.

TV Focus.   Some investigators are primarily interested in the topic at hand as part of their preoccupation with the effects of television, only one of which is entertainment. They usually are concerned with other potential TV effects such as violence, prosocial behavior, political socialization, etc., and somewhere along the line became aware that a main social function of television and keystone of its economic basis lies in its contribution to human entertainment. But such a mediacentric focus is not without its costs, and those with primary interest in the television medium, as such, begin to get uncomfortable when their more dependent-variable-oriented colleagues start talking about the appeals of the ballet, or of participation in sports, or what makes for a popular novel, etc., on the grounds that these other topics distract them from their central point of departure: the impact of television and not of entertainment more generally.

Entertainment Focus.   The opposite holds true for those who are attracted to the area via its dependent variable. Such individuals are more preoccupied with what constitutes entertainment and its motivational properties. Obviously, television as a major source of entertainment in our society comes in for some share of attention, but those social scientists with this primary interest tend to feel constrained by confining their thoughts only to those forms of entertainment which are possible through that medium. They roam readily and easily to other forms of entertainment, such as participation in or direct observation of sports, outdoor recreation, music, literature, etc. They avoid addressing other effects of television (e.g., violence, socialization, stimulation of cognitive development, etc.) which have little to do with entertainment per se. They would prefer to grapple with the complexities of entertainment as a common, if not universal, behavioral phenomenon.

Focus on Related Phenomena. The third dimension is represented by scholars with primary concerns in topics and concepts other than TV or entertainment (e.g., the development and function of fantasy, humor, arousal, recreation, aesthetics, sex, and other prime motives). Any one such emphasis may eventually lead toward a consideration of TV and/or entertainment. For some, the dominant paradigm is one where the focal phenomenon mediates between TV and entertainment. For others, it is seen as the primary motive system behind entertainment behavior, or of TV viewing. At times, the phenomenon becomes the main dependent variable and TV and/or entertainment are merely part of an array of antecedent conditions. Either way, such individuals tend to shun considerations of other possible effects of TV which do not particularly involve their central concern, and the same applies to discussions of entertainment where other processes are the main object of interest.

Conceptual Mapping

Given these three main avenues of approach, the conference participants also engaged in identifying constructive means of filling in the defined conceptual space. Although the discussion vacillated between the ponderous and the flippant—as much akin to a parlor game as to an academic committee meeting—we can again discern three underlying directions.

Subdividing the Field. All agreed the "Television and Entertainment" topic was vast and complex. To avoid being overwhelmed it is useful to break down the field into manageable size by sorting and classifying the various entertainment materials available on television into a convenient taxonomy. The relevant questions generated by this activity include:

1. What are the main types of entertainment programs and what are the variants within these typologies?

2. Do the conventional categories of the TV trade (soap opera, adventure story, situation comedy, sports, etc.) serve for the audience as well, and do they match the kind of entertainment experienced?

3. Instead of a content point of view, would it be better to approach the topic of types of television entertainment from the perspective of the different wants and needs which might be met and gratified?

4. How would one go about cataloguing type of television entertainment so as to have the divisions be optimally useful for suggesting novel research problems?

Provocative Contrasts. It is often a useful activity in itself and provocative to further conceptualization to search out the seeming contradictions in the current intellectual ferment of a given area. There was

no shortage of such paradoxes in our relatively short meeting. The following represents a variety of such heuristically provocative dialectics that emerged and that are probably quite common in this area. The questions are obviously raised not for an answer in favor of one or the other alternative but to stimulate appreciation of the complexities of television entertainment.

1. Does television entertainment involve the individual's "getting outside" of themselves, or does it involve intensifying, enriching one's self-consciousness?

2. Does television entertainment involve escaping from one's problems or getting wrapped up in new problems? Is it best explained in terms of negative escapism—getting away from things—or more positively by the attractiveness of the entertaining material?

3. Does television entertain by calming or exciting, either or both?

4. Is a given entertainment experience more intense when the person is isolated or in a social context (e.g., is watching football on television more pleasurable than at the stadium)?

5. How does one explain the paradoxical attraction of seemingly negative material, such as being entertained by suspense and puzzles, by horror shows, by tragedies and tear-jerkers? More generally, why are some people attracted by the exertion, pain, danger, etc., involved in vigorous sports and dangerous recreation?

6. Is what is entertaining socially defined, or is it determined by the intrinsic needs of the individual? How much of the selection of TV entertainment is a matter of deliberate choice and how much is incidental, even accidental.

7. To what extent does entertainment involve novelty versus confirmation of expectedness, as in the ritualized depictions of comedy situations versus the unexpected punch line, etc.?

8. What is the relative appeal of spectator versus participant entertainment?

9. Is TV entertainment mostly a matter of momentary diversion or does it involve more remote, in time and/or place, reoccurrences and fantasies?

10. What are the neurophysiological correlates of using the TV medium, as such, and do they differ with certain entertainment content? Does it primarily involve left hemisphere or right hemisphere functions, or both in some mix?

Terms and Constructs. Not surprisingly, a good deal of the discussion tended to be in terms of other social science concepts that are partially but not fully associated with either TV or entertainment. The following is a somewhat incomplete and haphazard (that is to say, alphabetical) listing, merely to give some insight into the vast range of constructs that are elicited when one pries open the black box represented by the concept of entertainment. The fact that

many of these terms are not better defined than that of entertainment per se certainly does not help our task any.

aesthetics	fun
affect	gratification
amusement	humor
arousal	instrumental acts
art	interest
autotelic activity	leisure
ceremony	novelty
content/style formats	pleasure
diversion	quality of life
empathy	recreation
enjoyment	ritual
escapism	symbolism
excitement	vicarious experience
fantasy/make-believe	volition

Methodological Considerations

In the course of our discussions, a wide variety of research methods were mentioned in passing, some in connection with brief reports of ongoing research, others as potential tools for exploring new problems. The following represents a selective culling of those that were mentioned, along with the kind of problem to which a given method might be applied:

1. Propositional inventory of related fields (sports, popular culture, literary criticism, movie producers, etc.) giving the accumulated wisdom (some of which may not be all that wise) of what entertains, as judged by a wide variety of people, especially those in the entertainment business who serve gatekeeper roles.

2. Multidimensional scaling techniques that would help us determine how various types of programs cluster, or the judgmental factors characterizing entertainment programs, in order to get some insight into the dimensions of television entertainment.

3. Open-ended interviews of both producers and consumers of television trying to get at what entertains, when the respondent may well be unaware of and unable to articulate feelings about this generic question.

4. Thought experiments, involving imagining how entertainment would be in a different world (e.g., before television, or without print and literature, etc.).

5. Look for the categorizing and relative use of various entertainment materials by different subpopulations (e.g., children, the elderly, the secluded, men and women separately, different social classes, etc.).

6. Use actors, directors, television administrators, etc., as resource people to suggest the main entertainment variables (i.e., those that they belive make a difference in the entertainment value, and hence popularity, of a program, and then test by survey and experimental manipulation.

7. Analyze television entertainment from each of several different perspectives that appear to have some bearing on it (e.g., the psychology of humor, quality of life, factors in best sellers, popular culture, literary criticism, aesthetics, sociology of sports, leisure studies, etc.).

8. Secondary analyses of the Nielsen TV ratings, focusing on program content analysis, demographic characteristics of the depicted roles, etc., to try to isolate certain correlates of relative program popularity. This could readily be duplicated across several countries—where similar, even superior, popularity data are readily available—to look for cultural generality or specificity.

9. Use of "concept-testing" approach used by networks and advertisers as a convenient way of studying the hypothetical variables involved in television entertainment.

10. Study how people choose the programs which they view on TV. Study also the actual patterns of viewing/listening (as in "watching children watch television") in order to zero in on precise viewing patterns and get insights into the determinants of these patterns.

11. Study the effort people are willing to expend to watch one versus another type of program, by imposing certain devices (e.g., static, with a switch depressor to cancel it, or a treadmill, etc.) between the viewer and the TV set.

12. Study joint choice regarding program preferences to get insights into the meaning of patterns of preference typologies among individuals (e.g., are they likely to address the same or different needs?).

THE PRESENT VOLUME

The diversity represented by the foregoing mosaic of ideas and methods was not totally without its rewards. The conference did provide a useful forum for a once-over-quickly exchange of conceptual approaches, updated reports on current and expected personal lines of research, and the like. Although displeased with the unstructured nature of our deliberations and the lack of a consensus on priorities, we all felt that was an unavoidable feature at this stage of the game and that it was preferable to encourage investigators to pursue their own.

The assembly was also asked to address alternative activities from the perspective of the Committee and its concern with stimulating researchers in the field, other than those present, to pursue ideas in the general area under consideration. What emerged from this discussion was an agreement that the

field could benefit from a more detailed airing of the type and range of activity these various investigators, each pursuing an individual interest under this very broad rubric, could provide. The conference accordingly recommended that the Committee arrange to publish such a volume by asking the conference participants and other suggested individuals to set down their thoughts and use their own research to illustrate what kinds of problems could be addressed, some useful approaches to such problems, and the methodological as well as conceptual difficulties that prevail. Diversified as such a volume was bound to be, it was felt that this could have the desired stimulating effect on potential researchers.

The present book is the result. It is not exactly what we had in mind when the publication venture was first launched, but the best we could muster from a limited group of busy scholars within an already extended period of time. A number of potential contributors did not join in the undertaking at the outset due to existing commitments, whereas several others who did originally agree to participate fell by the wayside as other pressing duties intervened.

The result is somewhat of a potpourri, as it was bound to be from the outset. With no agreement on a sufficiently compelling single model at hand, we purposely opted for each contributor to "do his own thing" and prepare an individually appropriate chapter. As editor of the volume, I did try to impose some commonality of approach, requesting each author to outline a particular theoretical perspective to some aspect of entertainment and television, and to describe issues and problems involved in that approach, using findings from actual research to illustrate salient points.

Clearly, the authors adhered more to the first dictum than to the request for a more systematic approach. One or two chapters are essentially reports of research with the theoretical stance secondary to the presentation of results. Others address an aspect of the entertainment area directly, whereas several make only oblique references to it. Although the total result is not of a single pattern, each contributor does introduce the interested reader to some intriguing speculative ideas, several provocative theoretical formulations, and the results of actual research. Since most of these have not been widely circulated until now, the book may turn out to be the source of fresh ideas it was meant to be.

Organization of the Volume

Since this is a free-lance volume rather than a systematic treatment of the subject, no fixed sequence of chapters is clearly suggested. There appear to be two main classifications of topics—one dealing with more general theoretical speculations, the other focused on more specific TV-content areas—and, lacking any other guide, this is how the materials are organized.

Accordingly, I chose to lead with the Mendelsohn and Spetnagel chapter, largely because it gives a broad, if still selective, historical perspective within which contemporary issues may be examined. All too often, we tend to forget that many phenomena do have a long past, with earlier critical occurrences helping shape, if not determine, subsequent development, as this account of the growth of popular entertainment suggests. They thus provide a sobering counterperspective to the more psychological approach that marks most of the rest of the volume. At some points, it even offers provocative alternative explanations to account for some already observed research results, such as with the arousal research.

There follows the equally broad-ranging though more psychologically oriented chapter by Jerry Singer. One of the more prolific researchers on the use of television by children, Singer has here chosen to introduce the reader to a wider array of psychological theorizing, including man as an information-processing animal, the notion of affect, and ongoing tendencies for the use of imagination. In the process he reports not only on his own research dealing with fantasy, children's learning through entertainment formats, and the like, but also on the brain-hemisphere theory separating logically reasoned, linear intellectual processes from more spontaneous, emotionally tinged neural activity. It is a chapter rich with speculation that any neophyte in the area should find replete with research ideas.

The empirical chapter of Hilde Himmelweit, Betty Smith, and Marianne Jaeger Biberian directs attention to the categories, and their underlying judgmental dimensions, of selected entertainment programming from the viewer's perspective. The subjects are various programs on British television, on which the authors thoughtfully provide descriptive comments to aid the reader in matching the judgmental data to certain content/format characteristics. The rating of various popular entertainment programs as being exciting and stimulating have echoes elsewhere in the volume.

My own account of coming to grips with the field of media entertainment rounds out this more general section. I borrow from personal experiences in developing a set of theoretical ideas centered on the role of emotional arousal through communication. This type of reasoning, coupled with opportunities for production-related research, has led me to a number of applications in actual TV-programming settings. These are touched on, each rather briefly, in an attempt to convey the variety of interesting, often fascinating, problems that greet the investigator in this area.

Dolf Zillmann takes the arousal model several steps further in his contribution. His extension of Schachter's (1964) theory of emotional states to the so-called "emotional transfer" model has spawned a prolific and wide-ranging series of experiments investigating different entertainment content areas (e.g., aggression, humor, sports), with consistent support for the

theoretical paradigm. Here he tackles the very significant but usually neglected issue of suspense content, developing a tightly reasoned conceptual rationale and reporting some intriguing experimental findings in detail.

Operating from a somewhat different theoretical stance, Tom Scheff and Stephen C. Scheele direct their attention at the apparent appeal and consequences of humor and laughter. Along with the Tannenbaum and Zillman offerings, they too invoke a physiological mechanism. They report actual research findings tending to support their theoretical predictions, again providing further speculative grist for the research mill.

The humor theme is also the focus of Paul McGhee's offering. Here, his concern is less with humor as such but the role it—and, by extension, entertainment fare generally—can play in aiding and abetting the use of the television medium as a learning device. His reports of research findings from both children and adult programming sets the stage for a number of hypotheses regarding the use of the amusement in the service of deliberate training.

Somewhat of a change of pace and conceptual focus is introduced in Leo Bogart's final chapter. His specific issue here is the informational function of television, particularly as represented by news shows. His particular concern is with how such programming has become diluted, if not trivialized, by the introduction of "show biz," audience-developing techniques and formats in order to promote higher ratings. His discussion of how such treatments may influence the viewer's distinction between—and possibly the blurring of—reality and nonreality, and the relationship between information and entertainment in shaping such orientations, leads to a substantial agenda for research on TV news.

REFERENCES

Katz, E. Can authentic cultures survive new media? *Journal of Communications*, 1977, *27*, 113–121.

Schachter, S. The interaction of cognitive and physiological determinants of emotional state. In L. Berkowitz (Ed.), *Advances in experimental social psychology* (Vol. 1). New York: Academic Press, 1964.

Withey, S., & Abeles, R. (Eds.). *Television and social behavior*. Hillsdale, N.J.: Lawrence Erlbaum Associates, 1980.

2 Entertainment as a Sociological Enterprise

Harold Mendelsohn
H. T. Spetnagel
University of Denver

To understand entertainment properly, it is important not to focus solely on individualistic pleasure-seeking behavior. Entertainment phenomena do not take place in vacuua; thus they are not likely to occur in laboratory-like situations where historical, aesthetic, and social influences are considered to be either inoperative or unimportant. Rather, entertainment occurs within a context of complex interactions that involve institutions, social norms, group behaviors, and traditions—all of which can be considered to comprise a sociological enterprise.

Further, the sociological enterprise does not function without historical anchorages and aesthetic milieux. Consequently, it is essential to use insights from sociological and aesthetic theory against a backdrop of history in order to provide a comprehensive perspective.

The analytic perspective we provide here is based on five propositions:

1. Audiences for entertainment emerged late in the seventeenth century as a consequence of the break-up of feudalism.

2. As Western society became more and more stratified different social classes vied for visibility in entertainment fare; visibility being equated with legitimacy.

3. The stratification that occurred in the West was ultimately reflected in diverse markets for diverse entertainment fare.

4. As differentiations in tastes emerged, specialized art and entertainment institutions and technologies were designed to satisfy them.

5. Gratifications derived from exposure to entertainment fare are both psychological and social in nature; psychological analysis perhaps serving as necessary but not sufficient conditions for interpretation.

Aiding in making a case from the five propositions are theories derived from the sociology of collective behavior, social structure and social organization theory, social change and diffusion theory, history of ideas, literary, art, and music criticism, and use-gratification theory.

The blending of such a diverse array of observation, theory, and speculation can be expected to produce neither empirical data nor empirically grounded generalizations at this time. What is offered here is an attempt to mobilize historical evidence to support a number of hypotheses relating to entertainment as a sociological enterprise.

HISTORICAL TRENDS

In viewing entertainment from a sociohistorical perspective, it is essential to consider the fact that other than in the simplest societies, "entertainment" is neither monolithic or monotonic. That is to say, as different subgroups attain participatory status in society, they develop and manifest their own unique aesthetic standards, tastes, and expectations. The less stratified a society is, the fewer will be its aesthetic standards, tastes, expectations, and entertainment modes. The more complex the social structure, the more complex will be a given society's entertainment enterprise.

The Sacred and the Vernacular

Prior to the middle of the seventeenth century, the social order of Western civilization was divinely prescribed. Basically, there were only two kinds of people: those who mattered and those who did not. Those who mattered—the aristocracy of the church and state—lived at the apex of the social pyramid, and their lives, their ceremonies, their arts and entertainments were tinged by the sacred. Those who did not matter—the peasants and tradesmen—lived at the base, and their lives were considered vulgar and profane. Their arts and entertainments were less worthy, primarily because they were tainted by a vernacular expression.

For those who mattered, the "sacred" arts and entertainments were forms through which they expressed both their solidarity with the divine and, simultaneously, their aloofness from the lower classes. For those who did not matter, the vernacular arts and entertainments provided simple temporary respite from toil and an opportunity to socialize on special occasions. Because of the participatory character of the vernacular entertainments—singing, dancing, and games—they served to maintain solidarity with others of similar status, whereas their religious roots served to assert the continuity of the participants' tenuous and ritualistic linkages to the divine.

Although it is true that differences between elite and folk arts and entertainments can be described functionally, both the sacred and vernacular

arts and entertainments shared one similarity in that they always have been manifestations of human pleasure-seeking behavior. The distinctive qualitative differences between the two appear, historically, to have been the consequence of extreme differences in the material condition of audiences rather than, as many would maintain, the result of inherent differences either in the intent or function of sacred and vernacular entertainments.

From earliest antiquity, entertainment has functioned consistently to provide pleasurable reassurance to audiences by satisfying their deep-felt desires for distinctive reflections of their own lives. By structuring content in conventional forms that assert a continuity of the audiences' culture, traditions, norms, tastes, and values, entertainment offers gratificiations that are quite unlike those that are afforded by art. Where art aims for universals, entertainment is totally culture-bound.

The degree to which entertainment fare reflects what the in-group audience finds desirable and, simultaneously, projects what is considered undesirable in the out-group, will determine the gratifications that audiences receive from such fare. Thus, for example, while the "Grand operas" of eighteenth-century Italy tended to reinforce the value systems of a beleaguered aristocracy, the English "ballad operas" of the same period not only placed the "common man" on the stage, but at the same time, they parodied the elitist-oriented Italian works.

Rise of the Middle Class

The simple duality of social structure that dictated Western society's orientation to and involvement in the arts for centuries was abruptly shattered by the emergence of a totally new participatory social force in the seventeenth century—the bourgeoisie.

The middle class offered an unprecedented addendum to the traditional basic social structure of master–servant. It was an addendum that was to have the most consequential impact on the arts until the present time, for the bourgeoisie had acquired the numbers, finances, and literacy that made them a dominant force both in society and in the arts.

With the rise of the middle class, the two ancient social roles of servant and master were replaced by a variety of middle-class roles that audiences wanted to see portrayed in theatres and in the novel. The literacy of the middle classes gave them access to the printed word, and new institutions such as publishing firms, lending libraries, and the postal service sprang into being to facilitate that access. Their literacy was also a "cultured" literacy which ultimately opened the doors to opera, public musical performance, reading clubs, and salons.

The economic changes that took place produced a rather large social cohort that had money to spend. The spending power of the bourgeoisie enabled them to compete with the royal court for the services of writers,

musicians, and painters for the first time and thus was able to influence the form and content of what was written, composed, performed, and painted. In a relatively short time, the status of the artist/entertainer changed from that of a servant at court whose services could be dispensed with at whim to that of a professional/entrepreneur for hire.

In the political sphere, when the hierarchic order dissolved a new system of social control had to be developed to make policy and keep order as replacement for the old order. Art and entertainment which had previously functioned rather matter of factly in accord with their place in the divine order of things now required rational regulation. Because both art and entertainment could confer and preserve status simply by giving visibility to social groups, attempts to regulate the arts became a more important part of the agenda for the state, and the arts and entertainment became institutionalized for the first time.

The consequence of the changes in the philosophical underpinnings of society that took place was a radically new way of looking at the world. As John Donne said, the "New Philosophy calls all in doubt." It was apparent that another principle had to be developed and that principle was reason.

The result was remarkable. In the space of about 200 years a hierarchic conception of a social system with power emanating from the top had begun to be replaced by an atomic–mechanical model where power was dependent on aggregations of individuals and their social, economic, and political interactions and on the relatively new phenomenon of "public opinion." By the early eighteenth century, art and entertainment had become a commodity, and the artist/entrepreneur's survival depended on offering various publics what they wanted to buy. It was a different world, and although the basic pleasure-giving functions of the arts and entertainment had not changed, their emergence as institutions managed by cadres of professionals and supported by technicians represented a different state of affairs indeed.

By the time the massive migrations from the villages of Western Europe to its cities had reached its peak in the early eighteenth century, a new and powerful aesthetic standard of quality had been added to the prevailing elite and folk standards—the aesthetic standard of the emerging burgeoisie.

The fact that a totally new sociological entity had emerged on the European scene not only was revolutionary in the economic and political sense, but its appearance marked significant changes in the arts—in how they were produced, disseminated, patronized, and criticized. In particular the notion of "entertainment" itself as a form of common acceptable social behavior came into some prominence at this time.[1]

---

[1]The *Oxford English Dictionary* notes the earliest usages of "entertainment," "amusement," and "escape" to convey their contemporary meanings as occurring in the seventeenth century.

Unlike the nobility, the bourgeoisie were neither bound to a particular geographic domain nor to the overwhelming costliness of waging wars either to protect or to expand physical turf. Neither were they few in number. Similarly, unlike the peasants, the bourgeoisie were literate, educated, monied, and lived contiguously to each other rather than in geographic isolation. In brief, the bourgeoisie was an urbanized, literate, educated, and cosmopolitan social force that thrust itself into the fabric of Western society on the basis of its numbers, wealth, knowledge, and disdain for geographic boundaries. As such the new middle-class constituted a powerful vested interest not only in the political sense but in the cultural one as well.

In order to protect its advantageous economic position, the bourgeoisie first attempted to work through established political institutions of the monarchy, church, courts, and parliament. On the cultural level, the middle class was forced to develop totally new institutions in order to guarantee that its cultural interests would be served according to *its* standards and not those either of the nobility or the peasantry. For the first time, then, we see the development of a "market" for cultural fare. This new market was comprised of relatively large numbers (a mass market) who demanded a "popular" culture or a culture that fitted its very own standards rather than those of others. And as previously noted, the middle-class was able to pay for what it wanted. The institutional responses to the cultural requirements of the emergent middle-class were nothing short of explosive.

Consider just a sampling of the developments that took place between the 1600s and 1800s as cases in point:

1. 1607, Monteverdi's opera *Orfeo* is performed, and by 1613 four theatres in Venice alone offer musical entertainment to a paying public.
2. 1672, John Banister gives violin concerts to a paying public in his London home.
3. 1730–1750, secondhand bookstores, subscription and lending libraries, postal services, reading clubs, and coffee houses come into existence.
4. Mideighteenth-century London taverns such as Sadler's Wells offer public entertainment by paid comedians and singers—entertainment that foreshadows the music hall, vaudeville, "revue," muscial comedy, and "variety" show.

Never before and never since has there been such a high degree of social ferment surrounding the pursuit of "nonserious" social activity. It is in this period that entertainment first becomes the focus of serious intellectual and social concern. From classical antiquity through the patristic and scholastic thinkers of the Middle Ages, aesthetics was treated either as Plato and

Aristotle treated it—as an inferior form of thought—or it was largely ignored. The attack on entertainment that grew out of the institutionalization of art and entertainment during the seventeenth and eighteenth centuries is still with us and has been discussed at length elsewhere (Mendelsohn, 1966).

What is important to note here is the residue of psychological unease that these attacks have bequeathed to contemporary middle-class audiences of mass entertainment. Oftentimes, modern middle-class audiences will express guilt over their own pursuit of the vernacular vis-à-vis the divine in the arts, reflecting personalized reactions to what originated as social criticism. Perhaps, the pleasure that contemporary middle-class audiences derive from the entertaining arts rests to an important extent in the very defiance of the social critics. In other words, the arousal phenomenon that psychologists have been noting as an entertainment "effect" may be as much a manifestation of traditional social-norms defiance as it is of purely physiological occurrences.

Returning to the events of the seventeenth and eighteenth centuries, we note once more that for the first time large numbers of relatively sophisticated and affluent individuals participated more and more as paying audiences for entertainment fare. And, over time, these paying audiences comprised a market of substantial proportions. The effects of these developments were most consequential for the arts, the aritsts, and the audiences.

Hans Speier (1950) observes succinctly that:

During the 18th century popular religious literature was gradually replaced by secular reading materials. Content and style of fiction changed in the process. The novel of manners and the epistolary novel, both primarily addressed to women, made their appearance, and the moral concern of the readers was shared by their authors. It became possible for them to earn a livelihood by writing. The professionalization of writing was furthered by the breakdown of the patronage system and its replacement by the collective patronage of the anonymous public. Parallel with the formation of a broader literary public, the middle classes transformed musical life. Public concerts to which an anonymous audience paid admission fees took the place of concerts given by the personal orchestras at the courts of European rulers and in the luxurious residences of distinguished aristocrats.

The expansion of the reading public was accompanied by the development of related social institutions such as reading societies, reading clubs, circulating libraries, and secondhand book stores. The establishment of the first circulating library in London coincided with the publication of Richardson's *Pamela*. Secondhand book stores appeared in London during the last third of the 18th century. European reading societies were influenced by the model of the American subscription libraries, the earliest of which was founded by Franklin in Philadelphia in 1732 [pp. 376–388].

AUDIENCES:
A RELATIVELY RECENT SOCIAL DEVELOPMENT

Much has been written about the impacts that the new bourgeoisie produced on artist, art form, and art content. But very few scholars have addressed themselves to the changes that took place in the very ways that middle-class people learned to seek out entertainment as well as in the manner that gratification was to be experienced from entertainment fare.

Basically the new middle-class audiences learned that there was an extremely important social component to the gratification dynamic that went considerably beyond an individualized "response" to a pleasurable "stimulus." This social component was, and still remains, three-pronged in that:

1. It is socially normative (e.g., there are rules governing the times at which entertainment is to be attended, where it is to be presented, and what the proper attire is for the occasion).

2. It involves social interactions (e.g., attending a particular entertainment is so much a social event that the entertainment stimulus can be used as an occasion for carrying out a courtship, sealing a business deal, or exhibiting one's desirable social status as much as for simply deriving subjective pleasure from exposure to its offerings).

3. It is repeated at regular intervals (e.g., one develops a "social" habit of going on to an entertainment, say for example, every Saturday evening at eight).

Because the pursuit of entertainment required a socially interactive milieu and occurred with regularity under socially prescribed conditions, it became ritualized and functional within dominant segments of society, and so it remains today. The notion that the pursuit of entertainment reflects some sort of deviant behavior on the part of the "masses" is an absurd one. From the seventeenth century onward, engagement in entertainment pursuits has been as normally functional as eating, worshipping, or working. And the very fact that engaging in entertainment is indeed functional from both an individual and societal perspective (i.e., the "relaxed" citizen is a more productive citizen) makes the entertainment experience itself that much more pleasurable.

Entertainment Versus Art

In one respect, considering the three sociological aspects of audience mentioned above helps us to differentiate the experience of pleasure that may be derived from entertainment versus art:

1. Recognizing the existence of exceptions in either case, one generally can derive maximum pleasure from a painting, a book, or an architectual form in near total social isolation. On the other hand imagine yourself as an audience of one in an opera house, a theatre, or a music hall.

2. Similarly, there are no standards of conduct governing the reading of a book or the viewing of a painting or piece of sculpture. But think of all the rules and folkways that govern attendance at a live "entertainment": rules and folkways regarding prompt arrival, refraining from conversation once it is under way, laughing in unison with others, manifesting approval in an enthusiastic way (again in unison with others), but restraining open disapproval, and so on.

3. Finally, other than coping with the restraints of opening and closing times of libraries, book stores, museums, and galleries, the pursuit of art is not time-bound. One can read a poem, a serious novel, or an essay simply when one wishes to. The same applies to viewing a work of art. Here, developing habits of repeated exposure are purely personal and are socially dictated in only an indirect fashion. Entertainments, on the other hand, occur in designated places and on schedules that are originated by the entertainers and not by audiences. Thus, audiences are required to develop or modify personal entertainment habits to fit in with social requirements.

As a full and powerful participant in society, the middle-class individual had displaced the aristocracy of earlier times as a prime audience element in the elite arts (e.g., as frequenters of "serious" theatre and opera and the new public concert halls) as well as in the popular arts (e.g., as readers of romantic novels and as frequenters of "music halls," "burlesques," and "variety theatres").

Publics as Audiences

It was becoming apparent, even at this time, that the middle class was neither homogeneous nor monotonic. No one entertainment institution by itself could be expected to accommodate the varying needs and tastes of the varying subpopulations that make up the middle class. One cannot help but wonder whether a truly "mass" audience ever did exist. As society becomes more complex it becomes more differentiated, and unique social aggregates reflecting their own particular values, experiences, and interests begin to form, not as groups or organizations but as audiences that are joined together by common preferences.

Drawing upon general societal values and norms regarding form and substance and combining these with their own notions, each audience ultimately develops unique standards for choosing what it considers to be the most desirable means for satisfying its pleasure needs. These standards are

often referred to as "tastes." Most frequently diversity in public tastes sires diversity in the public dissemination of information, art, and entertainment, and not, as many contemporary critics argue, the other way around.

In one important sense, then, audiences can be considered to be vested interest publics, with each public battling to have its own particular tastes for art or entertainment satisfied via its own unique institutions. Although, as we have seen, the tastes of one given public may dominate a society at any given time, as social participation and division of labor broaden, social consensus regarding what artistic and entertainment materials should be made available breaks down. Just as the purveyors of entertainment begin to compete for their "share" of the consuming market, so do the various audiences making up that market pressure creators and disseminators to offer fare that is suitable only to their own particular tastes.

The ultimate consolidation of the middle classes in the early ninteenth century was most consequential in a number of ways:

1. In the arts it completed the trend away from patron-orientation. Drawing upon the rights of the aristocratic patrons of the arts to determine form, substance, and means of dissemination, the self-confident middle class took on itself the very same rights, but now as a collectivity. By threatening and actually witholding its purchases, by enacting censorship laws in its legislatures, and by moral suasion, the middle class became the all-powerful repository of entertainment tastes. Because it was both numerous and affluent, the middle class and not the aristocracy, was now catered to by the suppliers of art, information, and entertainment. The market place had shifted from the salon to the parlor.

2. A thoroughly new criterion for judging the success of an entertainment enterprise was established—sales.

3. Sales could be increased through adopting cost-saving technological innovations, by making improvements in business practices, and, most importantly, by giving customers "what they wanted."

4. In order to accommodate the new market, a new breed of entertainment entrepreneurs began to emerge. Entertainment entrepreneurs now looked upon what they were offering for sale as a variety of audience tastes. Social communications no longer were magically "sacred." They were of this world, for this world; that is, almost exclusively, "vernacular."

5. In order to protect their own selfish taste interests, middle-class audiences began to urge varying forms of censorship on the vehicles that did not conform. Essentially, censorship on behalf of bourgeois self-interest was offered as a solution to meeting minority needs in a growing pluralistic society under the guise of protecting the state or under the pretense of protecting the "good taste," cultural integrity, or morality of its citizens.

Beginnings of a Mass Audience

No sooner was the bourgeoisie's preeminence as the audience for entertainment firmly established than it came under severe pressure from the emergence in the midnineteenth century of a previous to this time insignificant and neglected audience. Among other consequences, the Industrial Revolution spawned a relatively literate, publicly educated market of proprietors and wage earners comprised of small shopkeepers, clerks, foremen, and workers. In a relatively short period of time, as the petite bourgeoisie and proletariat achieved a degree of political and economic participation in Western society, changes in the traditional modes of entertainment occurred; and, abetted by technology, once again totally new modes appeared. Perhaps the most significant shift that occurred here related to the development of the mass media as the principal (and least expensive) vehicles of entertainment: the "penny paper," the "dime novel," and the "nickelodeon" motion picture machine.

By way of review, we have noted that as different social classes move into power positions that result in their increased social participation, they demand visibility, and in achieving acknowledgment they ultimately win control over the structure, form, and content of entertainment, until challenged by successive audiences. As each new audience emerges as a significant one, it "borrows" standards from the old and always initiates unique changes of its own. Curiously, older forms may be displaced but rarely do they disappear entirely.

This process can best be illustrated by Fig. 2.1, which sketches the progression of musical drama from pre-Christian sacred ceremonials to modern musical comedy as responses to both cultural borrowing and innovations that result from the development of differential audience tastes and demands. Importantly, Fig. 2.1 shows that as audience tastes shifted away from the divine to the moralistic sentimental as well as to the vernacular, muscial drama entertainment followed suit. Roughly similar processes occurred with regard to narrative literature and spoken drama as well.

Fundamentally, as the petite bourgeoisie/proletariat was enjoying the songs and jokes that best reflected their ways, bourgeois audiences could still enjoy the romanticized sentimentality that mirrored their own value system.

It is in the area of the vernacular that we note the greater amount of innovation. What Fig. 2.1 does not indicate are the many subdifferentiations and overlappings that have occurred in response to the various permutations in audience tastes that have been developing over time, such as those, for example, of unsentimental middle-class audiences, or of romantically oriented proletarians, or of still another subset—the relatively few but culturally significant intellectuals.

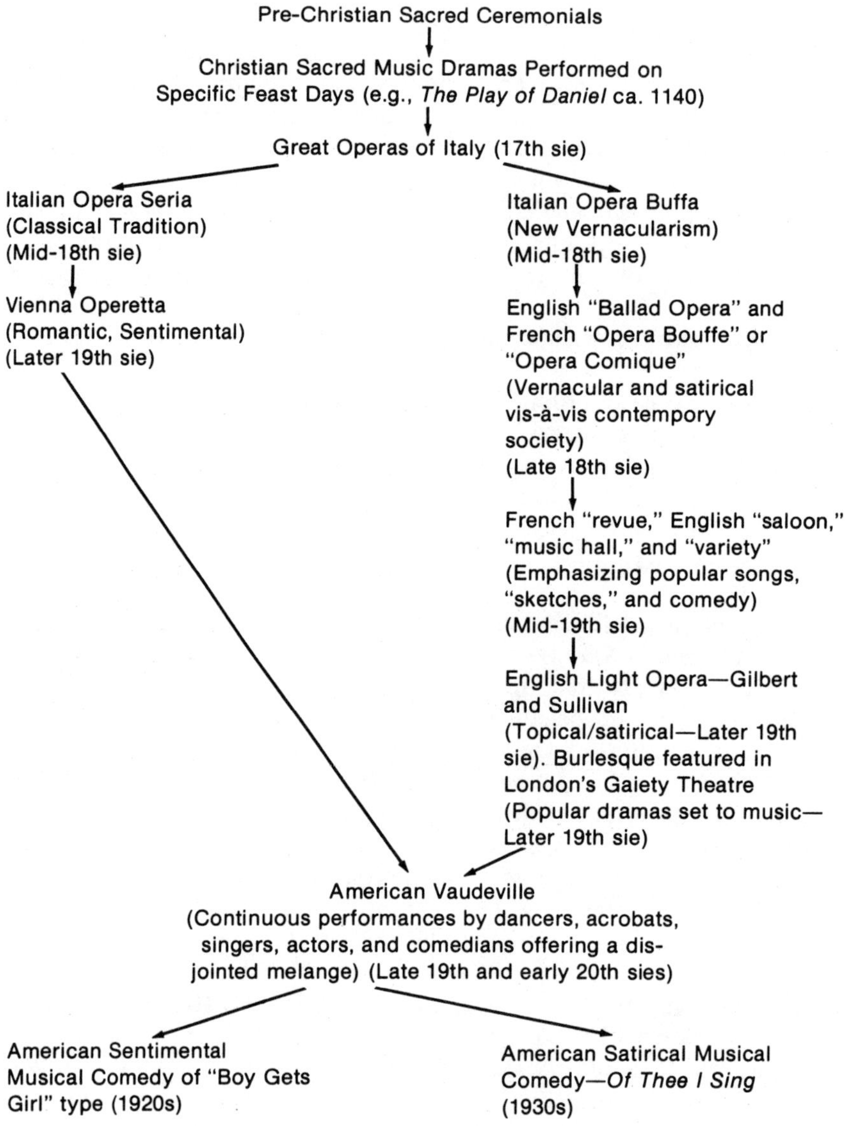

Pre-Christian Sacred Ceremonials

↓

Christian Sacred Music Dramas Performed on
Specific Feast Days (e.g., *The Play of Daniel* ca. 1140)

↓

Great Operas of Italy (17th sie)

Italian Opera Seria
(Classical Tradition)
(Mid-18th sie)

↓

Vienna Operetta
(Romantic, Sentimental)
(Later 19th sie)

Italian Opera Buffa
(New Vernacularism)
(Mid-18th sie)

↓

English "Ballad Opera" and
French "Opera Bouffe" or
"Opera Comique"
(Vernacular and satirical
vis-à-vis contempory
society)
(Late 18th sie)

↓

French "revue," English "saloon,"
"music hall," and "variety"
(Emphasizing popular songs,
"sketches," and comedy)
(Mid-19th sie)

↓

English Light Opera—Gilbert
and Sullivan
(Topical/satirical—Later 19th
sie). Burlesque featured in
London's Gaiety Theatre
(Popular dramas set to music—
Later 19th sie)

American Vaudeville
(Continuous performances by dancers, acrobats,
singers, actors, and comedians offering a dis-
jointed melange) (Late 19th and early 20th sies)

American Sentimental
Musical Comedy of "Boy Gets
Girl" type (1920s)

American Satirical Musical
Comedy—*Of Thee I Sing*
(1930s)

FIG. 2.1. Changes in musical drama as a result of "borrowing."

23

THE CONVENTIONS OF ENTERTAINMENT

As the previous subsection points out, modern societies have become increasingly heterogeneous and pluralistic in structure. As a result, the conventions of entertainment have become similarly diverse. Of necessity, entertainments are composed of ritualized conventional elements known to audience and entertainer alike. The function of entertainment conventions is twofold: They provide audiences with images of their own lives as distinct from the lives of others, and, at the same time, conventional elements assert audiences' continuity of relationship with members of their society and culture.

Two general types of entertainment conventions can be described:

1. Formulaic conventions, which are audience/culture-specific methods for structuring cultural products (Cawelti, 1976).
2. Technological conventions, which modify the temporal and spatial character of entertainment events.

Formulaic Conventions

At first glance it would seem that Homer's *Odyssey*, Joyce's *Ulysses*, Haley's *Roots*, and Lucas's *Star Wars* would have very little in common. A closer examination reveals that all four stories concern themselves with the protagonists' place in society. The basis of all four stories is a concern with lineage and identity—of Odysseus, Stephen Daedalus, Kunta Kinte, and Luke Skywalker. Thus all four stories are specific manifestations of the human concern with social identity as generally conceived in Western culture.

If the quest for identity is the basis of the action in the *Odyssey, Ulysses, Roots,* and *Star Wars,* it is of some interest to note the implications of the specific formulaic treatment of the identity quest in each story.

The hierarchic world view held by the Greeks and later by European monarchists meant that the king was superior, by nature, to those he ruled. Therefore lineage remained a crucial issue. Of the four, Homer's *Odyssey* is the only version with a king as the protagonist. *Odyssey* is the story of Odysseus' (the King of Ithaca) attempt to return home after the Trojan War, to take his rightful place on the throne beside his wife Penelope and as the father of Telemachus. But because Odysseus was delayed, it was decided to identify and to legitimize his successor by gauging those aspiring to leadership against their ability to string and shoot Odysseus' bow. The idea was that he who could string the bow of a superior man was also superior and, therefore, fit to rule. Of course, Odysseus returns in time, slays the pretenders, and legitimate order is restored.

The importance of the contest to the well-being of Ithaca was that it provided a means whereby the best leader—for a primitive society, that is—the strongest, could be selected. It is interesting to note that the Olympic games grew out of similar contests which were held as funeral rites to determine who would inherit the possessions of the dead. These games, as well as the later Olympics, were based on an institutionalized view of hierarchy which prescribes that as long as the rules are in force the best athlete will win. For the spectator, these contests were and are important because the games demonstrate that there is order and continuity in nature and in the affairs of human beings.

The rules of athletic contests which govern the resolution of conflict are functionally similar to the formulaic conventions of entertainment. They insure that on the playing field, as well as in the metaphoric world of entertainment, there exists an acceptable and reassuring social order—providing that order and reassurance is what entertainers have always done for their audiences. Homer's *Odyssey* locates the concern about social identity in the hierarchic context and, at the end of his story, assures us that all is as it should be.

James Joyce's *Ulysses,* although dealing with the same quest for identity, is based on a wholly different set of conventions, acknowledging the social emergence of the common man. Joyce's book of 1922 also embodies the conventions of an early twentieth-century intellectualism occupied with a systematic fight against conventional means of expression. The book suffers from an inherent contradiction in the position of the artist who tries to make himself understood while he destroys conventional forms of communication.

But there was in this period an elite audience so preoccupied with the convention of invention that they were willing to attempt to follow Leopold Bloom and Stephen Daedalus in their identity quests. And this audience was reassured to find that there was in Joyce an alternative to the novels of his contemporaries—John Galsworthy, H. G. Wells, and Arnold Bennet. Joyce, unlike his more "commercial" contemporaries, evoked a sensibility consistent with his audience's aesthetic intellectualism.

Compared with *Ulysses,* Alex Haley's *Roots* is a more conservative work. As popular-book and television entertainment it is an embodiment of the melodramatic formulae of middle-class entertainment, although it seemingly focuses on the problems of an emerging black peasantry/proletariat. Although *Roots* seems at first glance to be remarkable because the good guys are all black and the bad guys are all white, what makes it conventional and, therefore, reassuring to large television audiences is that it embodies the fundamental middle-class sentimental view of the importance of the family.

The book and the television show are based on an interesting reversal of the governing convention of Edgar Rice Burroughs' *Tarzan.* Instead of the

urbane Lord Greystoke rejecting family to live as natural man, we have natural man, assimilating family ties to become a part of the complex American mainstream. *Roots*, then, can be described as a pastiche of sentimental middle-class conventions, reassuring and accessible to large numbers of a book-buying and television-viewing audience.

George Lucas' *Star Wars* is, like the other three narratives, based on a quest for social identity. Luke Skywalker is an orphan living on a futuristic farm who discovers that his heritage is that of the heroic Jedai Knights. The conventions of the story are the conventions of heroic fantasy and science fiction. And as a motion picture, the appeal of the film can be attributed to its elaborations of the conventions of earlier science-fiction fantasy films. However, audiences are attracted not only by the conventional characters, settings, and situations of science fiction and fantasy formulae; they are also attracted by *Star Wars'* allusive evocation of the films that they recall pleasurably. Finally, *Star Wars* makes creatures like the Laurel-and-Hardy robots "Artoo Detoo" and "Threepio" as well as extra-terrestrials like the "Wookie," members of the family of man. Perhaps the portrayal of robots in a symbiotic social relationship with human beings suggests a concern on the part of audiences about their relationship with their technological servants.

The demands of new audiences in the eighteenth and nineteenth centuries spurred major changes in the formulaic conventions of entertainment. As the brief discussion of *The Odyssey, Ulysses, Roots,* and *Star Wars* suggests, the formulations of the problem of social identity become very different as we move from an hierarchic society to one first dominated by the middle classes and then by the petite bourgeoisie/proletariat. As new audiences emerged, they required that conventional problems be formulated in the specific terms of their own lives, tastes, and values. The consequence was not only change but also a new diversity in formulaic conventions.

A major contribution of the twentieth century has been to provide technological solutions to the problems of entertainment access and distribution. The consequence has been the alteration of the entertainment experience by the conventions of technology.

Technological Conventions

An important technocratic principle is that as technical solutions to problems are discovered, new technical problems are created which demand further technical solutions. In moving a musical performance from the "sacred" court to the "vernacular" concert hall, important technical, spatial, and temporal characteristics of the entertainment event are changed. In order to serve its function as a gathering place for audiences, a concert hall must have specific spatial and structural characteristics.

Further, once the performances are no longer held at the whim of the king, the event becomes subject to specific scheduling and durational constraints necessary to insure audience access. These changes in the spatial and temporal character of entertainment pose new technical problems for the entertainer.

A commissioned work for a nobleman was usually intended for a single performance, whereas a concert piece is written for as many performances as possible. As a consequence, after the eighteenth century music had to be written more carefully and dramatically, and it had to be performed in a more exacting fashion. Beethoven wrote substantially fewer symphonies than did Mozart or Hayden.

Moving musical performances into larger halls and eventually into the recording studio required the technological development of variety of musical instruments and eventually, of electronic amplification and recording techniques. Today it would seem that the experience of contemporary popular music is almost wholly dependent on technological convention rather than on its form or even content. Regardless of formulaic content, contemporary popular music cannot be performed adequately without sophisticated sound recording, amplification, and mixing apparatus.

In much the same way, recording the dramatic performance on motion picture film and moving it from the proscenium arch to the silver screen required modifications in the techniques of dramatic writing and performance. Providing access to larger audiences required that the drama and spectacle in motion pictures be elaborated and amplified through the techniques of montage, color, sound, wide screen, and other special effects. *Macbeth*, as performed in the theatre, is very different from Polanski's *Macbeth* as realized on the motion picture screen. This is due, *only in part*, to what McLuhan and others have described as inherent technological differences among media. Equally important are differences in the technological norms established for performances and expected by audiences in various situations.

Since the release of the *Poseidon Adventure* in 1972, the technological conventions of remarkable special effects have become an increasingly important component of the audience experience of motion pictures. For example, *The Exorcist* (1973), *Earthquake* (1974), *Towering Inferno* and *Jaws* (1975), *King Kong* and *Star Wars* (1977), all rely on the conventions of special-effects technology for their success.

In solving problems of access and distribution, technology has added a variety of important special effects to the entertainment experience. As suggested earlier in the discussion of *Star Wars*, part of the appeal of the film lies in its power to evoke pleasurable recollections of other film experiences. Thus it seems that in addition to the gratifications derivable from content, formula, and social situation, contemporary entertainment provides

audiences with gratifications directly derived from the experience of the conventional use of sophisticated technologies. To see a special-effects movie on a big screen is a technological pleasure. The appeal of a "live" concert over a recording is, in an important respect, a function of the impact of the electronic technology of concert performance. Still, as technology solves problems, it raises new problems.

The development and refinement of the technologies of printing, photography, sound reproduction, and broadcasting in response to audience demand for convenient access to entertainment has provided that access. Cable television and video-recording technologies promise to give every man, woman, and child the prerogatives of a monarch over his servant–entertainers. However, that same technology has tended to diminish the social component of entertainment activity. With monarchic power comes regal isolation.

For example, attending a motion picture is governed by fewer social norms than attending a live theatrical performance. Films are presented more frequently and in more locations; and, in some respects, the filmgoer is alone in the dark. Similarly, listening to the stereo can be an entirely individual experience governed by none of the social norms of attending a concert.

Early television provided for access to entertainment without the necessity of leaving home and hearth. Still, in the age of one set per household, television viewing had a social dimension. The technology of miniaturization made it possible for each family member to have individual access to television entertainment. The same process affected radio listening a generation ago.

Although it is true that, at present, television-network programming does not live up to the technological promise of individual-television access, as the pressure for increased access to television by various groups attests, network programming does not and cannot provide a sufficient diversity of images to satisfy the desires of all individuals for images of their own unique lives. This provides the impetus for further technological innovation.

At present the institution of American television is undergoing a technological metamorphosis. The cause of the change lies in the discrepancy between the promise of its technology and the present inability of programming to satisfy the desires of an increasingly segmentalized audience. Eventually, television will, like publishing, be able to provide a greater variety of fare, ranging from simple diversions to elite art.

If the entertainment experience is characterized by a social component, an assertion of a relationship with others, it is likely that the future of television holds only limited entertainment potential. As television technology confers the access and manipulative powers of the king and the artist on ordinary individuals, its audiences can be expected to turn more and more to entertainments which provide greater opportunities for social participation.

As electronic technology has individualized access to television entertainments, major metropolitan population centers have upgraded their facilities in order to accommodate the increasing crowds of people who assemble at entertainments ranging from athletic events to concerts. We have suggested here that entertainment has an important social interaction component. Future research could tell us why it is that all these people come to the stadium instead of watching the game on television or listening to the stereo. We have tried to suggest that to understand entertainment is to understand more than individual psychological gratifications and taste content, and we have presented what promises to be a fruitful approach to understanding entertainment as a sociological enterprise.

REFERENCES

Cawelti, J. *Adventure, mystery and romance.* Chicago: University of Chicago Press, 1976.

Mendelsohn, H. *Mass entertainment.* New Haven, Conn.: College and University Press Services, Inc., 1966.

Speier, H. "Historical development of public opinion." *American Journal of Sociology*, 1950, *LV*(4), 376–388.

3 The Power and Limitations of Television: A Cognitive–Affective Analysis

Jerome L. Singer
Yale University

The television set is a unique new factor in the human environment, as important in its way as the development of written language or the invention of the printing press. Occasionally it is used by a hundred million viewers in the United States as a source of significant local, national, or world information or as a guide in periods of temporary natural crises such as floods or blizzards. However, it is mainly a form of entertainment, a daily resource for pleasure seeking and distraction. As an entertainment medium in a relatively affluent society in which considerable leisure time is available to a large majority of the population it must compete with card playing, attending movies, theatres, sports events, athletic activities, dancing, and bar-hopping. Aside from its obvious convenience (availability in the home) and remarkable affordability, what special appeal does television have for us? Why do we turn the set on almost automatically on awakening in the morning or on returning home from school or work? What special characteristics does the television medium have to draw our attention and to compete as a leisure activity with reading or card playing or conversation? A recent popular book (Winn, 1977) sets forth the thesis that TV viewing has all the properties of an addiction, and at least some evidence is adduced therein to support this extreme position. If television does have at least some of the power that Winn asserts can we find a theoretical approach to the psychological reason for its attraction?

The present chapter attempts to look at the television medium from the standpoint of the current status of cognitive–affective theory in psychology. The 1960s and 1970s of this century have witnessed a major shift in psychological theory and research, away from the reductionism of stimulus-response theories of learning or drive-reduction models in personality and

psychoanalysis toward a cognitive orientation that attempts to integrate human information-processing capacities with the experience and expression of emotion (Tomkins, 1962, 1963). This broader perspective on human behavior takes seriously the image-making capacities of our species, and it opens the way for an understanding of the attraction and also the information-processing limitations of the television medium. From what we now know about the major dimensions of the cognitive system and the differentiated affect system (Izard, 1977) can we draw some inferences or suggest some research approaches for examining the psychology of the television-viewing process and also for comparing its impact on storing and evaluating information with the process of reading? This comparison is especially important when one considers the possibility that at least some portion of the three hours daily that children, especially of the middle socioeconomic levels, are spending in front of the television set were in the 1900s to 1940s spent in *reading,* a skill that clearly requires continued practice. Is it possible that recent indications of a drop in SAT-examination scores may reflect the fact that children simply spend less time reading?

SOME GENERAL IMPLICATIONS
OF THE COGNITIVE POINT OF VIEW

The Role of the Environment

In the paradigm shift that has characterized the change from S-R to cognitive models in psychology it is intriguing that environmental inputs are now assigned more importance than they were in the behaviorist years. Watson and Hull along with their opponents in psychoanalysis assigned motivation to "tissue-needs," to presumed basic biological drives such as hunger, thirst, and sex and, sometimes, aggression. With Tolman, Lewin, and Piaget as pioneers, the eventual research and theoretical analyses of Hebb, Tomkins, White, and Hunt among others have forced us to look more carefully at the characteristics of environmental stimulation as it intersects with the information-processing capacities and predisposing sets of the individual. Growing out of the many experiments on sensory deprivation has come increasing indication that all of us *require* some kind of input from the outside world in order to keep ourselves alert, reasonably content, and free from either the hyperrestlessness occasioned by boredom or from extreme apathy.

We have learned, in addition, that some individuals can tolerate great reductions in external stimulation much better than others. People who do especially well under such conditions of limited input from the physical environment are people who already have developed their imaginative capacities. That is, they can, by drawing on their memories and fantasies,

create through their imagination a lively and engaging environment that can substitute for the lack of new stimulation from the outside. The reports of individuals who have been kept prisoners in solitary confinement confirm this finding from the sensory-deprivation experiments. The architect Herman Field (a prisoner of the communists in Czechoslovakia) wrote a novel in his mind as a means of dealing with extended solitary confinement designed to force him to confess that he was an American agent. The Nazi war criminal, Albert Speer, who spent a quarter of a century in Spandau Prison, preserved his sanity, he reports, by imagining himself walking around the world.

Just as we require considerable sensory stimulation from the environment, we also are frequently confronted with situations in which too much information is being presented, and therefore cannot be processed. As a matter of fact, in almost any ordinary environment one is confronted with a vast multitude of possible kinds of information that could be attended to. In effect, we must learn to screen out, or filter, a great deal of what is presented to our senses if we are to maintain any reasonable direction of movement, or if we are to concentrate on particular information that is especially valuable.

If you are driving down a busy midtown avenue, it is easy to be distracted by the shop windows, the interesting passers-by, the music that may be pealing forth from a nearby department store, or by the sight of an altercation between a policeman and another motorist. If, while driving, you allowed yourself to dwell for too great a length on any of these sights or sounds, you would risk bumping right into the car in front of you or not noticing that the traffic light had changed.

The human information-processing situation is made even more complex by the fact that one's private thoughts, one's worries, fears, or wishes, also have some of the force of an alternative environment and therefore might come into play in the process—unless they too are screened out by a filtering system. In a sense it can be argued that we must maneuver ourselves through life while attending to two environments, the external region of sounds, sights, and social interactions and the inner region of our memories and fantasies (Singer, 1975a,b).

The environment thus presents elements of complexity and of different degrees of attractiveness and stimulation. It can also present situations of ambiguity, such as occasions when you cannot quite hear what others are saying or cannot quite make out through fog or dimming light the pattern of an approaching vehicle. The ambiguities or indeterminacies of particular environments, physical as well as social, play a key role in how much priority we assign to processing material drawn from our own memory systems, our wishes, or our hopes.

This same set of complexities prevails even in the more relaxed occasions when one decides to read a book, newspaper, or magazine, or to watch television. We have all had numerous occasions in which loud noises from

other rooms, distracting interactions between children, or the loud blare of a stereo in a neighboring apartment may make it difficult for us to concentrate on what we are reading or viewing on television, even leading us to remark, "I can't hear myself think!"

The Individual as an Active Participant

As psychologists have understood with greater precision the influence of the environment, they have been forced to change their view of the individual human being from that of a stimulus–response organism to that of a more active participant in the information-acquisition and processing situation. Today, psychology regards a human being as playing an active and *selective* role in how he or she approaches each new environment. There is much greater emphasis on the fact that individuals bring to each environment preestablished schema or what might be called "preparatory plans," based, of course, on previous experience about what may be expected in a situation. These schema have been built up over dozens of previous interactions with the environment, or on the basis of other kinds of learning experience. Some of our schema are more complex and *differentiated* than others. If someone were to ask me for information about the history of psychoanalysis or about great figures in American baseball, I could go on for hours expanding on the highly differentiated schema I have stored in my brain in these areas. If someone were to ask me about the workings of the engine of my car, I do not think I could get much more than two or three minutes of material out of my stored schema on that subject.

The various schema we have stored and organized in our brain also are in part dependent on the developmental stage we are at in life. Children in general have been exposed to far less information than adults and also lack certain kinds of organizing and interpretive skills. It takes them longer to grasp certain kinds of concepts when they are very young, or indeed, there are some types of notions that they cannot make sense of at all before they have reached certain age levels. Much of the impressive career of Jean Piaget has been devoted to explicating the stages of developmental cognitive capacities of children and showing how certain notions of time, space, or morality are beyond their grasp before certain levels of development. Research on reading or on television viewing has made it clear that it is not *only* limitations in vocabulary that impede children of preschool age from grasping materials that may be presented. They simply lack the fundamental integrative capacities to put together certain kinds of information into meaningful groupings that are obvious to older children or adults.

Another major contribution of cognitive psychology has been the recognition that each person brings to a new situation a complex set of plans, private images, and anticipations. Indeed, this is one of the major ways in

which we manage to avoid being completely bombarded by the tremendous range of stimulation available to any new situation. When we come into a room, although we may take a quick glance around, we focus primarily on the main persons we have come to talk with, or walk directly to the desk of the individual with whom we have an appointment. If, on coming into a room, one were to spend the time studying the layout of the furniture, the patterning of the drapes, the relative value of various antiques, one would simply never get one's business done. Thus we come into the room with some set toward effective action and move fairly rapidly in that direction. We still have enough of what we call in psychology "channel capacity" to permit some kind of swift, sweeping review of the room. But, by and large, we need to waste little time on that because we have already set up some plan of action.

Of course, sometimes the images or plans we have prepared are inadequate for what actually faces us in the room. If we walk directly over to the desk of the person with whom one has an appointment only to find seated there a gorilla, then one's reaction would be one of startle and perhaps terror. Here is a case where one's private plans or anticipatory images are completely confounded by the novely of this new sight. Most of the time, however, our anticipations are not that far afield, and we can steer ourselves effectively through many environments by such active anticipation.

One can see, however, that the fact that we must rely so much on our own imagination and anticipation in order to move through the environment can lead to some occasionally serious misunderstandings or confusions. In American television, the attempt is made to build up the viewer's anticipation through excitement, violence, and chases so that the viewer will be looking forward to the next event or outcome of some action or comedy sequence. At this point, one is interrupted with the presentation of a commercial. Presumably since anticipation has led one to be glued to the set, the attention will be maintained for whatever commercial then appears, and the message of that commercial will come across effectively.

This approach presupposes that viewers will not have developed an alternative private strategy for television viewing that would have emerged perhaps out of years of experience at being interrupted in viewing. This has led many viewers to "turn off" when the commercial actually appears. Many people get up and go to the toilet or get some food or simply look down at some reading material they have in their lap whenever the commercials come on. Others simply seem to be able to tune them out mentally by gazing blankly at the set. Of course, the advertisers count on the fact that not everyone will have developed such strategies, and therefore they will get at least some fraction of the audience who will carefully attend to the commercial message presented.

Another aspect of psychology's view of the role of an active organism in the information-processing situation emphasizes the fact that all of us carry on

privately an extended stream of thought. Our minds are probably never inactive. It is likely that the brain stores material not by dropping it into one or two or three locations, as one might find in a computer data bank. Rather, the brain seems to be constantly playing and replaying material that has been stored. This contributes what might be called a "noise," the actual distraction we may experience from our own thoughts and memories while we are engaged in some other task (Singer, 1977).

Such ongoing thought, however, is more than just an extraneous element in the information-processing system. Rather, it is an important part of the way we learn and reorganize the material which we have taken in from the environment. It is a form of "instant replay" and also of continuing replay or rehearsal of the events of the past. As we replay this material mentally in the form of memories, or as we try out alternative possibilities of these same events through imagery and daydreaming, we are creating even new memory schemes and organizations of this information. In other words, our ongoing thought and our daydreaming play a rather important role in how we organize information and in how we begin to set up new plans and anticipations for our future behaviors. In the course of such continuous mental activity, we are clearly also laying the groundwork for carrying forward our major motives and values. *We are creating intentions that have decision making and action implications.*

In summary, then, the modern view of the human as an information processor is not simply of a passive recipient of information through the senses. Rather, the view is of an organism that is actively approaching each new situation, already anticipating certain consequences, prepared to screen out as much irrelevant information as possible, searching for information that will mesh with previous plans and expectations, and, at the same time, attracted by moderate degrees of novelty to engage in further exploration. In the light of this view of an active organism, it may be worthwhile to look more carefully at the specific mechanisms which an individual employs in attending to, delimiting, and finally storing the information presented through various media such as television or books and newspapers.

BASIC COGNITIVE PROCESSES

Sensory Capacities

Of the five major senses of the human being, vision and audition are the most developed and critical. We are drawn most especially to sights and sounds in our environment and are much less responsive to slight fluctuations in smell, taste, or touch. Indeed, it is often noted that as we grow up we tend to lose some of the quality of clarity of smell and touch that seem much more important to children. Part of developing our own aesthetic capacities as

adults comes from rediscovering the beauties of a refined palate, which permits us to discriminate between wines or reexperience the delight of smelling the different scents of the forest or of a flower garden (Schachtel, 1959; Singer, 1975b).

By and large, then, most people are predominantly oriented toward watching and listening, and we know that perhaps the single most effective form of stimulation is a movement in the environment, which leads our eyes to track it. There seems little question that one of the major powers of television as a medium is the fact that it does involve movement and thus attracts our attention even when we are not interested in the program. If one is engaged in conversation in a room while the television set is turned one, no matter how intense the conversation, it is hard to avoid one's eyes wandering toward the TV set and the activities depicted thereon.

Although vision and audition are governed by somewhat separate and clearly defined brain systems, the fact is that in many circumstances when we are engaged in listening intently to someone we may miss the details of a visual experience. Conversely, if we are involved in considerable effort to study something visually, we may not hear clearly words spoken at the same time. We also know that if one is engaged in thinking about a scene from the past while at the same time listening to sounds or words, one is less likely to notice visual materials in the environment. The same effect occurs if we are recalling sounds or conversations from the past. We may be less likely to notice words spoken to us but not lose any information from the visual environment. This is important to keep in mind since many messages presented, particularly on television, involve not only visual activity but also a "voice-over" communicating a message, and indeed frequently a printed message which adds still a further limitation to the information-processing capacities through the sensory modality.

Attention and Orientation Reflex

Another basic mechanism for processing information grows out of our ability to focus our attention on a specific and delimited area of the environment. This can, of course, be sight or a sound, or some combination of both, excluding, however, a great many other sources of stimulation that may be occurring simultaneously. Human beings are, in effect, "wired up" to make a response to any sudden, new, and unexpected stimulation that occurs in the environment. This is called the "orienting reflex" and insures our safety since it makes certain that we will react suddenly and effectively to any major change that confronts us. Just as we do respond by a quick orientation, we also quickly habituate once the situation can be assimilated into preestablished schema. This assures the fact that we will then be ready to respond to some *new* stimulus, should it occur.

The introduction of sudden novelty is, of course, a key feature in television. The program "Sesame Street" was devised with particular efforts to hold the attention of the extremely distractible 3- and 4-year-old child. The technique used was similar to that employed by the program "Laugh-in": the use of quick blackouts, or cuts, from one sequence to the next. Indeed it was possible to demonstrate that by this method chidren's eyes were kept glued to the set, since about every 30 seconds a new sequence of events and new little story line was being presented (Lesser, 1974). For adults, of course, such extremely rapid shifts are not as necessary for the maintenance of attention to the set. But much of the same strategy does exist in television. Writers of adventure shows realize that they must introduce action sequences within a matter of minutes; they feel they may lose their audience when there is any kind of extended conversation or plot development.

Short- and Long-Term Memory Systems

Psychologists have come to recognize that because there is so much information in the environment we have to find ways of holding onto some of it for a while if we are going to store it eventually in the brain. The short-term memory system is a recently discovered mechanism of our mind that permits a kind of brief—within seconds—replay of sights and sounds during which time, if there is further attention paid to the material, it will be transferred to more permanent memory. It is possible to show that if one does not attend to the material during those few seconds when it is in the short-term memory system, it will never be registered and subject to any further recognition or recall. The timing for material to stay in the short-term memory system is extremely delicate and subject to considerable interference from new material that is presented.

   Thus it is possible to see that the pressures of attention to novel stimulation can actually interfere with our ability to store. Here again, the active role of the individual is one in which he or she must make an almost instant decision to stay with certain new material and mentally replay it for a few seconds if there is going to be any likelihood of remembering it. In some respects, a "crowded" medium such as television establishes conditions in which there is somewhat less likelihood that a good deal of the content presented will be transferred from short-term memory to the long-term memory system. By the very "busyness" of the presentation of material, it interferes with the possibilities of replay. This is a situation to which we shall return shortly.

Limited Capacity for Processing

Although on the one hand it is amazing how much information we can store in our brain and draw upon in a great variety of situations, it is also true that

our capacities for processing information at any given time remain limited. This is one of the reasons why we need anticipations and strategies for dealing with new material. We have already noted in relation to the sensory capacities of the individual the differential effects of auditory and visual material when occurring at the same time. It is entirely possible that a system can easily become overloaded so that one experiences a blur, cannot take the time for replaying so that information can go from short- to long-term, and indeed, cannot make precise discriminations between the sights and sounds presented.

There is an experiment now widely used in cognition called the *dichotic listening experiment with shadowing.* A person has two different sets of sounds or words piped into each ear simultaneously. The person is instructed to "shadow" the sounds coming in the *right* ear. This means the listener must repeat each of the sounds as the person hears it by saying it out loud. Under such circumstances, one can show that practically nothing that is being piped into the *left* ear ever gets noticed or remembered. There are, however, important sets of coding strategies that alert us to certain specalized material. The filter is one that has rules for particular words. Thus, if one's own name is said into the left ear while one is shadowing material from the right ear, one indeed will hear it. The same can be shown from time to time for other personally meaningful or psychologically important material.

The limited capacities of the organism for processing new information are also associated with two different kinds of methods of processing. Some processing follows a sequential form. That is, one listens to a sound, then shifts to viewing some image, then shifts back to listening. This is called sequential activity. It is also possible to describe certain processes as involving parallel activities, where we can show that even though two sets of events occurred simultaneously, it was possible for the individual to process both and acquire information from both. Probably more human activity does involve sequential processing of new information, but it is certainly possible to demonstrate that one can listen intently to a radio broadcast or carry on a CB conversation while driving a car and going through the complex visual and motor activities necessary for operating a vehicle and still process complex information at the same time. The system has limits, however, and one would not recommend becoming involved in an extremely passionate conversation with a member of the opposite sex via the CB radio when driving in very heavy traffic. What would be happening under such circumstances would be that although one might be viewing the street and road ahead and other vehicles, one might also be visualizing the charms of the other person, and also experiencing physical sensations associated with sexual arousal. This visualization and tactile imagery would overload the system and lead to the likelihood that one could miss important visual cues leading to an accident.

Encoding Strategies and Brain Asymmetry

One of the things we have learned in very recent years about how the organism can efficiently separate out different kinds of information and set up strategies for storing the material for effective retrieval and re-use later on is that there are different kinds of what are called "encoding strategies." Certain materials can be stored in the form of words or fairly abstract concepts. An abstract term such as "liberty" applies to a great variety of possible situations and in a sense is a very efficient means of describing literally dozens of specific life events. Words such as "table" and "chair" encompass hundreds of examples of specific tables and chairs we have seen in our lifetime.

When we are confronted with new situations, we learn to form words that will characterize these events and subsequently allow us, very quickly, to retrieve occurrences in brief expressions. The verbal encoding system, because of the very nature of our language, is a *sequential* system. That means that sentences or groups of words occur one after another over a period of time.

This system therefore has different properties from a system of encoding events in terms of the way they look to us, or in terms of their actual sound. If we see a sight and then visualize it, attempting to reproduce more or less what it looks like, we are processing the material in what is called a *parallel* form. This involves trying to encompass a range of events within the same time span, as when we look straight ahead at a complex stimulus.

We have come to realize that human beings use both verbal- and imagery-coding systems. Some situations are more easily coded verbally, others more easily coded visually, and many situations are coded in *both* systems. There is increasing research evidence to suggest that the most efficient kind of recall occurs when we store an event by labeling it verbally and also by fixing it in our minds; that is, transferring from short- to long-term memory a complex pictorial or tonal representation of the event as well as the label in words (Seamon, 1973).

We have also begun to find out much more about the fact that the brain itself is specialized for processing these different kinds of encoding strategies. The left side of the brain in most right-handed, and indeed in some left-handed people, is highly specialized for encoding words, numbers, and other concepts such as mathematics that require sequential processing. The right side of the brain seems more highly specialized for encoding images, sounds, smells, and is also more closely associated with the evocation of emotional characteristics associated with particular events (Gazzaniga, 1970). As a matter of fact, we now know that boys and girls differ from very early ages in the degree to which their brains are specialized. Girls' brains are more equally efficient in processing both types of material, whereas boys' brains seem to be more clearly differentiated between the left hemisphere and the right

hemisphere, with the left emphasizing verbal and the right, spatial and imagery encoding strategies. This early difference may account for the fact that boys are more susceptible to reading or speech defects than girls. To anticipate—our own research suggests that girls, especially the brighter ones, are much more likely than boys to grasp the more subtle content or messages presented in "Sesame Street."

We are also beginning to find out that many people favor one or another coding strategy in the way they process information. This may also lead them to develop to a greater degree one or another side of the brain, so that some individuals are particularly likely to shift their eyes right (suggesting greater left brain activity since neural connections of eyes and brain are controlled contralaterally) when thinking about a problem, whereas others are much more likely to shift their eyes to the left (suggesting right brain activity) when concentrating. A whole series of studies has now been carried out exploring personality differences and information-processing differences as a function of the type of encoding strategies, and presumed emphasis on left or right brain function, that characterizes given individuals.

An important aspect of these findings relates to the relative effectiveness of one or another storage strategy. In many ways, the verbal–sequential system associated with left-brain activity is extremely efficient if we want to recall certain events quickly. If, on the other hand, we want to provide a detailed description of a situation and also to characterize its emotional tone, we might have to rely more on *visualization* or *pictorial* reactions, which are more likely to be processed through the right side of the brain.

For example, if you are asked a question such as, "Does your house have windows?" or "Do you have casement or picture windows?" you can usually answer this very quickly with words that are almost literally at the tip of your tongue. If on the other hand you are asked "How many windows are there in your house or apartment?" you cannot answer that question without visually taking a trip from room to room in your house. Of course, if you have recently had occasion to buy storm windows and therefore had to count the windows at some point, you would have stored a number (presumably processed on the left side of the brain, therefore). Then you could retrieve the answer to the question almost instantaneously with a word.

If you are asked a question about the name of someone, you may be able to come up with that relatively easily. But if you are asked to describe the person in detail, then you must visualize the face of the individual, and this seems much more likely (from research) to be processed through the right side of the brain. In general, faces seem to be linked to right-side-of-brain activity.

One of the important differences between the left and the right side types of processing is that material on the right side tends to be grasped in a form that we call "holistic"; that is, it is not delineated with great precision ordinarily, but organized in huge chunks. Thus, whereas the processing through parallel

means has certain advantages, it also has certain limitations for most people, since it lacks some of the precision of organization and labeling that can come only if one also has geared words to the information that has been processed. That is why the ideal kinds of information presented ought to include opportunities both for verbal labeling and for detailed visualization or organization into auditory images.

Recognition and Recall Functions in Memory

One of the consequences of the different encoding strategies is that we have different ways of retrieving information once it has been stored. It is likely that information that has been stored through the holistic "right-brain" parallel processing system is best suited for what is called *recognition* memory. It has been possible to demonstrate in research that we have the capacity to store a fantastic amount of information with just quick review of the material by this method (Shepherd, 1967). For example, Guatemalan peasants who were shown a Sears-Roebuck–like catalogue depicting objects and implements with which they had no personal familiarity were able a few months afterwards to pick out with almost perfect accuracy these same objects from an array of similar but different ones they had never seen. In other words, one quick glance was enough to assure some long-term recognition value.

The problem with recognition memory is that it is not useful when one does not have the object before one for identification. Thus, in the many kinds of decision-making situations we face, we need the advantages of the verbal- and organized-coding strategy in order to retrieve the information. Simple exposure to material cannot assure its efficient retrieval. Retrieval usually requires a more active process that is associated with taking the time to examine the material, perhaps to label is verbally, and then, also to replay it mentally in the form of some thought about decision processes.

These differences in encoding strategy and implications for recall suggest that passive kinds of information presentation will yield considerable recognition memory without efficient retrieval. Rapid retrieval is usually best established through a more active kind of learning process, one that has engaged more attempts at devising combinations of words *and* images to increase the likelihood that connections can be made (Seamon, 1974).

Mental Rehearsal and the Stream of Consciousness

As suggested, our brain is constantly active. Even at night during sleep it can be demonstrated (and awakenings through the night reveal) that people have been engaged in a very large number of thought processes from the most vivid visual dreaming to simply more structured "thought-like" rumination. For

various reasons not yet fully understood, we remember perhaps one dream in the morning upon awakening despite the fact that we have been engaging in a great deal of thought, as far as can be determined, throughout the night. This same process of continuous activity undoubtedly goes on during the day as well. Research on daydreaming suggests that most people daydream every day. Experiments which interrupt people during the pursuit of specific tasks reveal again and again what a great amount of material is being processed privately even in the midst of active processing of new information from the environment (Singer, 1975a).

All of this activity plays a role in how we store material, and also in how we increase the likelihood of later recall and retrieval. Our intentions, wishes, and hopes determine a good deal of the direction of our daydreaming and fantasy. We play and replay a great many events from the past, sometimes trying to reshape them into better forms, sometimes using the material from the past to anticipate more successful outcomes in the future, sometimes simply trying to escape from unpleasant or boring current situations by creating "castles in Spain."

We also know that there are great individual differences in how extensively and effectively people can tune in and out of this ongoing inner stream of consciousness. There is increasing reason to believe that for both children and adults the capacity to make use of one's daydreams and pretending capacities represents a major cognitive ability, one that can be useful in developing one's own effectiveness in a variety of intellectual and interpersonal situations.

One of the major questions that needs to be addressed in relation to the role of televison viewing versus reading as a part of the intellectual development of children has to do with the possibility that television viewing may itself substitute for the active practice of one's own imagery skills. Reading, on the other hand, provides a medium by which one must fill in, through resort to one's own memories and images, the material suggested by words on a page. Thus it is likely that reading provides more extensive practice for imagery capacity, whereas television has the potential merely for stimulating specific image content, but not for providing the opportunity for independent practice of such skills, since it substitutes an external image that one can passively lean on rather than forming one's own.

To sum up: The new cognitive view of human behavior and information processing emphasizes a series of subsystems beginning with the specific properties of the sensory organs at their periphery and their relationship to the visual or auditory systems of the brain, which can only process limited amounts of information concurrently. Similarly, there is an emphasis on attention as a system, or on the short- and long-term memory system, on other aspects of the necessity for selectivity, and the limited channel capacity for processing of the brain. Another major system has to do with the encoding strategies available to the human being, with greater awareness of the two

major systems of encoding—visual–serial associated with the left hemisphere of the brain and imagery–parallel associated with the right hemisphere of the brain. The evidence increasingly suggests that truly effective retention of material in a form that makes it suitable for effective use in decision making requires a combination of the two encoding strategies as information is initially processed. The system of storing material in the brain also requires a constant replay of new material as well as material from long-term storage, and this is at least in part related to the stream of consciousness and the psychology of daydreams and dreams in which a great deal of material from the past is reenacted and reshaped, establishing new schema and new potentialities for action.

Differential Affect Theory

I have so far emphasized the purely cognitive aspects of organizing experience. It is increasingly clear that human beings are motivated by emotional experiences, however, and that emotions are themselves closely related to the information-processing capacities of the individual. The period since the early 1960s has witnessed the emergence of differentiated affect theory developed originally by Silvan Tomkins (1962, 1963) and elaborated through extensive empirical research by Ekman (Ekman, Friesen, & Ellsworth, 1971) and Izard (1971, 1977) among others.

Tomkins's position represents a Darwinian view that the human being has evolved a specific set of emotions, presumably more than other animal species, that provide the individual with information about the individual's own motivational structure and that also, through manifestations primarily from facial expression and more general body postures, communicate to others potentially motivating information.

Tomkins's theory proposes that affects or emotions are one of five basic systems which combine to determine an individual's behavior: *the homeostatic-autonomic regulatory system, the drive system, the affect system, cognition, and the motor system.* Although drives may in most instances be essential for survival, their primary role in human motivation is thought to serve as a signal of the presence of deprivation states. It is the affect system that is viewed in Tomkins's theory as the major motivating system. Affects may amplify drive signals or may in their own right provide the organism with rewarding or punishing experiences. Affects themselves, however, are subject to the information-processing activities of the brain and particularly the rate and complexity with which new material has to be processed. Information has ultimately to be assimilated to established schema or new schema need to be formed.

In Tomkins's position a limited number of affects may be triggered by fairly specific differences in the information-processing tasks that a person confronts. For example, massive inputs of new or unassimilable information

produce startle or fear responses; moderate rates of new information generate interest or excitement, which are positive affects; and the sudden reduction of high levels of seemingly unassimilated information (as in delayed recognition of an old friend, seeing the point of a joke, or finding good new when opening a letter) leads to the positive experiences of joy or laughter. High rates of unassimilable or complex information persisting over long periods of time lead to the negative affects of anger, despair, and sadness. Thus, the flow of information, the readiness of the individual based on past experience, cognitive style, anticipation of a situation, or planning for the situation—all these play an important role in whether negative, punishing affects emerge or whether the positive rewarding affects of interest (a moderately rising gradient of new information) or joy (a moderately declining gradient from a high level of novelty) are expereinced.

Tomkins employs the term *"density of neural firing,"* which implies the degree to which there is a massive involvement of neural activity from various brain areas. Since this is not an easily measured variable, I have preferred to translate it into assimilability of information. If the doorbell rings and one goes to the door and it is a child returning from school at the usual and expected time, then that information is easily assimilated since it was largely anticipated in advance. If, on the other hand, the doorbell rings and a long-lost relative, a gorilla, or two FBI men are there, one is most likely to respond with a startle reaction. After the initial startle response, recognition of the relative should lead to the experience of joy and much smiling. In the case of the gorilla and the FBI men, a great deal depends on what follows from the situation, but the changes of a persisting high level of density of neural firing and, hence, negative affect are much greater.

This theory suggests therefore that at least one attraction of television is that it presents a good deal of novel information, particularly sudden changes, yet all set within a little box so that we respond not with startle or fear but with the positive affect of moderate interest. The repetitiveness of material permits us many matches between new material and established schema and evokes a smugly pleasant affect. Only if a strange face were to appear suddenly on the TV and start denouncing the viewer personally could one expect the negative affects of fear-terror, anger, or distress!

CHARACTERISTICS OF
THE INFORMATION MEDIA

The Power of Television

A little more than a century ago the vast majority of the population of the earth was illiterate and relied for most information on word-of-mouth communication. A minority of the population, making up the small middle

and upper classes of society, government officials, or the priesthood in various countries, controlled the written literature and enjoyed its possibilities. Today, through the medium of increased literacy, and perhaps even more through the availability of relatively inexpensive television sets, the average citizen of the world is exposed to a range and complexity of information beyond anything ever known before in human history. More people are reading more books, magazines, and newspapers all over the world than ever before and are seeing and hearing through television and radio actual events or fictional representations, a range of information beyond anything that could have been dreamed of at the turn of the century. Let us keep this tremendous acceleration in the availability of information for the masses of the world population in mind when we move too hastily to criticize the limitations of the popular media.

From a cognitive standpoint, the television medium has an especially powerful appeal. As noted earlier, the human brain appears organized to respond to movement in the environment, perhaps as a survival of adaptive evolutionary self-defense or hunting tendencies. We find the moving picture very difficult to ignore, and in the presence of a television set we cannot resist our eyes wandering in its direction. The most insipid game show or stereotyped-cowboy movie can still draw the attention of almost anybody who is somewhere near a television set. The constant movement and pattern of change that characterize the screen produces a continuous series of orienting reflexes in us, and it is hard to habituate to the set (the way we can to other sounds or sights) because of the great variations in degree of movement and in the appearance and reappearance of various characters.

If one is engaged in reading while the television set is on before one, no matter how important the written material or intense the concentration, it is difficult to resist looking up at the set occasionally and being at least briefly captured by even a fleeting "trailer." This is one of the major powers of television, and this power has been recognized commercially in the United States.

If one has a message to communicate (such as the introduction of a new product which as not been heard of before), then the television medium is the best device we know for such an introduction, because if there are a sufficient number of presentations of the stimulus, at least some of them are bound to reach even the reluctant viewer.

Because it relies primarily on the visual-sensory system, television also has an important affect on the learning process. The human brain is capable of storing a tremendous amount of visual material. This is perhaps also related to the "holistic" or "Gestalt" qualities of the right brain, where visual imagery is processed. Thus, material seen just a few times on television, without any significant effort at learning it, can be recognized if it is re-presented at a later time. The passive quality of our viewing of television thus makes us

susceptible through the constant representation of visual material to storing a surprising amount of what is presented (e.g., pictures of faces of performers, cereal boxes, or other packaging characteristics, all of which will later be recognized if they are shown in a group of hitherto unseen objects, by even the most casual viewer).

Another important power of the television medium is the fact that it is, in itself, a small social world. It provides "company" for the solitary viewer and peoples his or her world, at least temporarily. Thus, the material presented on television can elicit empathic reactions, identifications, and a host of emotional reactions, also associated with the power of imagery in the human brain. Since all of us have ailments of one kind or another and fear death, we are much drawn to the warm and protective image of a Dr. Marcus Welby. If the National Association of Broadcasters (N.A.B.) code were to permit this fictional Dr. Welby to appear at the end of a program to advertise a health food or medication, we would be hard put to resist noticing and going out to purchase what he recommends. The fact that there is industry self-regulation, both through the N.A.B. codes and the National Advertising Division activities of the Better Business Bureaus attests to awareness of the unfairness of a selling technique that capitalizes too much on the tremendous and inherent power of the TV medium. Such an orientation is also reflected in the guidelines developed by the Children's Review Unit of the Council of Better Business Bureaus.

Still another important factor of television is that in a certain sense it does our thinking for us. At times when we are weary or distraught by pressures of the many unfinished details in our daily routine, we might want to find a distracting source of stimulation. Daydreaming and one's imagination might serve, but it often would not prevent our thoughts drifting back to the many unfinished tasks of our lives. Television provides a series of packaged fantasies, an alternative that has immediacy. Of course, reading, whether newspapers or books or magazines, also serves to distract one from the complexities of one's daily life. Indeed, I believe a great many of the compulsive morning readers of the *New York Times* are persons who are learning more than they can ever want to know about the previous day's events, simply as a form of distracting themselves from confronting what they personally have to become involved with later on in their work or interpersonal relationships.

In a preradio, pretelevision era, when there was already a sizable literacy rate in this country and in Europe, hundreds of small magazines, the "pulps," purveyed stories of love and adventure for the masses. Even comic books, however scorned, did require some practice of reading skills to keep up with the dialogue. Television removes the effort that the less well-educated or indeed that almost anybody has to put into the reading process by presenting its packaged diversion and fantasy. There seems little doubt to me that one of

a number of reasons for the drop in reading comprehension scores as measured by national tests over the past generation reflects the fact that the one or two hours a night in which people previously sought diversion through reading "light fiction"—thereby inevitably *practicing* their reading skills—is now taken up by television viewing which minimizes reading capacity.

If one contrasts the act of reading with television viewing, the reason for TV's relative power is obvious. If we are reading and hit on an unfamiliar word, we must stop and examine it in context or perhaps even consult the dictionary to try to figure out what it means. Material presented in written matter requires us to draw upon our own memories and fantasies, to take the time to try to follow the drift of a writer, and to conjure up by ourselves exotic settings, sights, and sounds suggested in the text. Simple introspection indicates that this is obviously a more difficult task than watching events unfold before us on the screen.

Television and Affect

Let us take a closer look at the relative entertainment power of television and reading from the standpoint of the differentiated affect theory. Tomkins has proposed that human beings seek to enhance positive-affective experience, minimize negative affect, express affects, and also control their expression. These four possibilities provide the basic motivations for action. Interest (evoked by moderate amounts of novel stimulation in the environment) and joy (evoked by reduction of a high level of arousal or assimilation of novel or complex material into established schema) are the primary positive affects. The TV set attracts us by movement, by conversation and music, by presenting us chiefly with that most significant of all environmental stimuli, the human face (or its caricatured exaggeration in cartoons for children). It thus plays on our orienting response and the inherent pleasure we get from manageable doses of novelty, neatly packaged in a relatively small box. Even if it titillates or begins to threaten by presenting strange monsters or violence, anyone can look away, turn off the set, or (except for very small children) quickly reassure oneself that the danger or complexity is coming from far away or at best resides in that little box.

The entertainment value of TV or the reading of, say, detective stories, lies then in part in the ability of these media to intrigue us without threat, to arouse interest and then joy as the strange or menacing becomes readily assimilated into our established schema as "just TV" or "just a story." The movies, by contrast, because of the large screen and because of the fact that one views them outside the security of one's home, evoke much greater extremes of affect. It is almost certain that movies such as *The Exorcist* or *Jaws* have produced more persisting emotional reactions among adults and adolescents than have television representations of frightening scenes. Only

relatively young children seem to show much recurrence of nightmares after viewing frightening material on TV whereas adults and adolescents thrive on "Creature Features" or a gothic soap opera like "Dark Shadows"—shows which while suspenseful or violent are still clearly "in the box" and easily assimilable.

Reading, of course, has even less power to evoke such extremes of emotion. One can, surely, put a book down easily. In addition it takes some serious effort to be truly caught up in a book, the effort of generating visual and auditory images. If one has little skill at reading, then some of the most powerful potential effects of reading are not available since these depend on the complex vocabulary of a writer. When hundreds wept on reading of the death of Little Nell in Dickens's serial of *The Old Curiosity Shop*, reading was a relatively *new* and exciting experience for the emerging educated classes of Victorian England. There was no competition of mass media then. And as New York's Mayor Jimmy Walker is reported to have said, "No woman was ever ruined by a book." Even Dante's Francesca Da Rimini, who might be the sole exception, was reading alongside her lover when her passions were roused by the story of Lancelot and Elaine.

Television and, to a somewhat lesser extent, reading have the potential for reducing negative affect. The naturally exploratory child confined to the house on a wintry afternoon or evening must create its own novel environment through make-believe or risk a series of unpleasant confrontations with parents or older siblings if he or she moves around too much, tries out others' possessions, nags for attention or asks too many questions. Since children differ in their predispositions to make-believe play or in the tolerance of such play or direct encouragement by parents, reading or television viewing become useful alternatives, ready escapes from an unpleasant environment. But reading especially for the very young or for children who receive little parental support is simply more difficult than watching TV. The research we are carrying out indicates that 3- and 4-year-old boys are encouraged by parents to watch more TV on weekends whereas girls are more likely to be engaged in quiet play, pre-reading activities such as coloring or cut-outs, or even helping mother to go about chores.

For the older child or adult TV can also serve to reduce the negative affect produced by the recurrent mental contemplation of one's unfinished schoolwork, household chores, bills to pay, or the complexities of work and love. If TV has a potential addictive power it arises from the fact that it reduces negative affect (see Ikard & Tomkins, 1973, on smoking addiction) by substituting somebody else's thoughts for your own. After a day of hectic business activity, mistakes of fellow workers, complaints from customers, forms for central office or the government still not completely filled, the supermarket manager comes home with a head spinning with unpleasant thoughts. Only someone else's fictional troubles or adventures or *almost*

anything midly novel and not directly reminding one of unfinished business or of one's failures or limitations or helplessness will suffice. Where card playing, reading light fiction, or listening to the radio once served, television now performs this escapist function. It is simply the easiest, most nondemanding resource ever available for shifting one's attention away from contemplating one's miseries. As advertisers of vitamins, laxatives, and Geritol well know, millions of the elderly who might have to struggle to read or to walk down the stairs to a nearby park bench for companionship can turn away from loneliness or their own fears or frustrations by watching an afternoon game show.

Television is of course a companion. It does tell interesting stories and does permit the expression of emotions. One may not weep but one feels *concerned.* There is always an element of control in the experience of vicarious emotion. Accounts of the daily lives of the urban poor call attention frequently to the amount of time spent by women in discussing the adventures of characters in TV soap operas. Television provides—on a far more extensive basis for the broad masses of society—those vicarious and controlled emotional responses that upper-class ladies and gentlemen obtained chiefly from reading *Thaddeus of Warsaw* or later (1850-1940), that the middle classes obtained from hundreds of popular novels and magazines,

In effect, television is almost irresistable because it does meet essential affective criteria for motivation. It reduces negative affects and can for long periods substitute another's brain for one's own, thus minimizing painful private rehearsals of one's own problems. It enhances the positive affects of interest and joy or laughter, it permits some expression of emotions but also, by its very box-like structure, allows for control of affect. Reading can accomplish the same thing, but that medium simply demands more effort or skill for most people not only in manipulating the vocabulary but in producing the necessary private imagery that makes the reading experience so valuable.

THE LIMITATIONS OF
TELEVISION VIEWING

Cognitive Overload

Inherent in the very power of the television medium, its visual attractiveness, its use of auditory communication as well as written material, are its limitations. The TV set, and particularly commercial television with its clever use of constantly changing short sequences, holds our attention by a constant sensory bombardment that maximizes orienting responses. That is, we are constantly drawn back to the set and to processing each new sequence of

information as it is presented. In effect, this technique, so well understood by the television industry, works in some ways against the communication of complex messages. *The set trains us merely to watch it.* It does not provide us, as a rule, with a psychological situation that permits us to process the information presented in a manner that will allow us the most efficient later use of what we have seen. The rapid shifts of focus, the quick 30-second commercial, and the speed of dialogue hold our attention almost too well.

There was a well-known experimental observation that a monkey whose brain had been surgically altered was so drawn to external stimulation that if he was offered a grape, he would seize it and start to bring it to his mouth. Before he got it into his mouth, a new grape was offered him. He would drop the one in his hand and reach for the new one. In effect, he never did get to taste a grape. In a sense, television provides a somewhat comparable psychological situation. If we are to make sense of information that is being presented and organize the material both visually and in terms of a verbal-labeling system that says, "Oh that's the name of the product. Let me make a note of that so that the next time I go to the store I'll want to buy it," then such activity requires time. We have to replay what we have seen, think about it, and go through the *sequential* verbal process as well as the parallel processing of the images themselves. Too often, the brevity of presentation of complex new material rules out the possibility of effective encoding for later uesful retrieval.

In terms of how well information can be organized by us, *more* is not necessarily *better*. A slower, somewhat repetitive and longer-lasting commercial is much more likely to be susceptible to intelligent processing than a lively, rapid-fire presentation that has passed before one even identifies with it. It is very likely that advertisers who are paying large sums for many 30-second commercials would get more useful effects from fewer but longer-lasting and more clearly delineated content presented in their commercial messages.

Obviously the same principle applies to serious news or information programming. To the extent that intercutting is the rule (as it is chiefly in U.S. television and less so in other countries), the medium is becoming the *only* message for it is hard to remember any content. As suggested earlier, human beings are more active in the way they approach the information-processing situation. They anticipate events. They check new material against material drawn from their long-term memories.

An individual who is viewing an episode on television that is especially involving is reluctant to switch attention from that material to the commercial at the point of a sudden break. Instead, what is often likely the case is that the person will continue to rethink or re-imagine the scene just viewed or play out some of its implications through the mind's eye or mind's ear. Television, by the rapidity or novelty it presents, works against imaginative replay. By

bombarding the senses, it necessitates either a failure of storage of current material being presented, or it forces the viewer into, in effect, "tuning out" one of the sensory modalities through which the television message must be processed.

Our research evidence indicates that even when confronted with a moving stimulus, it is possible while daydreaming to blot out the natural "tracking movements" of the eye by letting them go out of focus or staring straight ahead at the same time as processing visual material mentally. Thus commercial messages that follow hard on scenes of considerable power or involvement are likely not to be seen at all. Even if they do have sufficient liveliness or vividness to attract the listener, they are more likely to evoke an angry reaction, since the natural tendency to replay the emotional and vivid scene just completed is interfered with and a temporary confusion may result. If the commercial succeeds in keeping the viewer's eyes glued to the set after a particularly effective story sequence, a scene of beauty, or lovely song, it does so at the risk of arousing considerable negative emotion, something the advertiser scarcely would want associated with the presentation of his product.

The evidence from children's research suggests that although preschoolers cannot clearly discriminate commercials from the program content, by the period between 6 and 9 years such discrimination is readily made, and within a few years beyond that there emerges a somewhat cynical and distrustful attitude toward the commercial content on the part of the children. It is hard to believe that advertisers can long be satisfied with, in effect, creating a generation that is hostile and cynical about the messages they seek to communicate.

The sensory overload of the television medium has other unfortunate implications for efforts to communicate somewhat more complicated messages. Although many television advertisers may emphasize the fact that a TV commercial presents its message in "sight, motion, sound, and print," this very complexity of presentation presents an information-processing difficulty. The channel capacity of the brain, although perhaps greater than often recognized, is nevertheless limited. A moving picture which also has a rapid-fire "voice-over" providing what the advertiser hopes is a significant additional aspect of information, and then the presentation of a written message in addition on the screen may simply be beyond our capacities for effective processing. The very power of the movement effect of television may mitigate against the storage of the name–label, which is of course so central to the advertising or other informational message, or to the processing of the label whether presented to the auditory sense or to the visual sense in a printed form. The filtering capacities of our sensory and cognitive systems are such that we simply will learn to ignore important messages that may be overloading the system, or that may appear to be competing with other

information we are trying to process at the same time. If we add this to the point mentioned above, the individual's need to replay mentally in one or another modality a just-experienced stimulus, then we can see that television may in many respects be an extremely inefficient medium for communicating any kind of fairly complex information.

A good example that points up the limitations of verbal labeling in competition with new visual information is the situation of a cocktail party where one is introduced in sequence to seven or eight new people. As you reach out to shake hands with each individual, look at his or her face, and take in their form, you are also presented with a vocally expressed verbal label. Unless you have experience as a politician and take the time to repeat mentally the name of each individual and try to tie that name to a particular face and form, you will find that by the end of the brief series of introductions you will be at loss to recall a single name. If you walk out of the room and walk back in, you will instantly recognize a person to whom you have been introduced but will be unable to recall the name at all. Thus verbal information, because of its sequential structure, takes time for processing, and if the system is already involved in processing complex movement, such as the shaking of a hand or the smile on a face, then something simply never gets stored.

This is a basic problem with the television medium. It is in effect introducing us constantly to new material before we have had a chance to grasp either the printed or verbal and auditory material being presented, and as a result it yields a high rate of information loss. Such loss may be made up in a dramatic show out of subsequent cues presented in related content. But the advertiser or educator who is seeking to describe the special advantages of a particular product or to make an informational point in 30 seconds is often engaged in a self-defeating exercise.

The television medium also presents important limitations for the viewer, depending on the viewer's developmental level and mental age. There is now a small body of research that indicates that preschool children process remarkably little of the complex information presented to them in certain programs. Indeed, in evaluating a number of standard shows, investigators found that preschoolers could keep track of less than 50% of the content of brief sequences (Collins, 1970, 1975). Important aspects of messages designed specifically to provide information of importance to the children were not grasped at all or recalled. This is a consequence in part of the fact that children have not yet developed sufficient complex cognitive schema so that they can anticipate what will be shown on the screen and therefore have time to process the new material. Also, changes in the content presented too rapidly will not allow them to make connections with their limited vocabularies and to realize that a word or phrase used in somewhat different context has the same meaning as the one they originally heard from parents. Our own recent

research on specially designed children's programs such as "Sesame Street" and "Mister Rogers" also supports these conclusions (Tower, Singer, Singer, & Biggs, 1979).

Even with older individuals who have limited vocabulary or limited reading skills and limited anticipation of certain settings and social structures which are being represented, the effort to process such new material may mean that they are a few seconds behind what is being presented on the rapidly shifting television screen. The result often is that they have missed important nuances in human relationships, missed important phrases that were used by characters, and as a result have put together only a garbled-memory schema of the material they were viewing.

Television's prime technique, the "quick cut" or blackout as a means of holding attention on the screen, thus seems to present serious difficulties for the child or adult of limited intelligence or experience who seeks to make sense of what is being presented. A dramatic case in point is represented by the program "Sesame Street," which deserves much praise for its serious effort to prepare preschoolers for reading, but which also provides some serious problems for the growing child. One of the major premises of the "Sesame Street" program is that preschoolers are easily distracted and will allow their eyes to roam from the set or will themselves get up and walk around the room. Since the intention of the program at the outset was to encourage the learning of letters and numbers, it was important to keep the child's attention fixed on the set. This was accomplished by the introduction of rapid-fire "show-biz" techniques. Quick sequences, like those pioneered by the program "Laugh-In," were used extensively, and it could be demonstrated experimentally that such sequences did indeed keep the child's eyes focused on the set. This was a maximizing use of the orienting response as suggested earlier.

The problem presented by this approach, however, is that too often the children simply failed to *follow* the material being presented from one sequence to the next. The necessary time for mental replay was not allotted, and there was insufficient repetition, except possibly for the repeated presentation of a given letter or number throughout an hour's program. Indeed, this rapid-fire presentation led a number of child psychiatrists and psychologists to call attention to the phenomenon of the "hyped-up" child, an excessively jumpy, lively child who was increasingly seen in mental hygiene clinics during the period after "Sesame Street" had been introduced (Halpern, 1975). In contrast to "Sesame Street," other programming for children has often been inclined to be slower paced. "Captain Kangaroo" and especially "Mr. Rogers' Neighborhood" represent much greater awareness of the child's need for repetitive, slowly, and carefully presented materials. Careful research on children's comprehension based on a Piagetian analysis has led German investigators to propose that directors make use of much longer action sequences and fewer shifts of focus (Sturm, 1977).

In recent research we have compared the response of nursery school children to viewing either "Mr. Rogers' Neighborhood" or "Sesame Street." Immediately after the viewing the children were taken into another room and provided with a series of questions about the content of the programming. The children's attention was held more firmly by "Sesame Street." Those children watching "Mr. Rogers'" had tended to look around the room or wander away from the set for brief periods. If anything, however, "Mr. Rogers'" had some advantage in what was actually recalled about the half-hour sequence. Indeed indications were that even for recognition memory, which is the easiest type of measure, those children who were less intelligent suffered more from exposure to "Sesame Street," purportedly designed for the educationally disadvantaged.

One of the programs in the series we studied involved an attempt on the part of the producers of "Sesame Street" to demonstrate the notion of deafness to children. A group of deaf children were introduced and they engaged in a series of activities, including suggesting letters through their body postures. Despite the production effort and undeniable sensitivity of the show (at least from the perspective of an adult), only 1 of the preschoolers in our sample of 60 who viewed this program grasped that the children on the screen *could not hear*. In effect thousands of dollars went into the production which failed completely to communicate its major message to the preschooler target-viewing audience.

Other research on children's comprehension of programming suggests that wherever there is an attempt to link action to its consequences and to its motives, young children failed to grasp the writer's or director's intention. Preschoolers and even early school-age children often do not show an ability to link action and motives for action or their consequences for much television programming. This is one of the reasons why television has certain inherent dangers for children. Children are attracted by rapid movement and violent actions. Those children already predisposed to being aggressive and violent and therefore who have never internalized a code of self-control are often unable to see the connection between action, motivation, and consequence that is represented in a TV show. The result is that they imitate the violent action, and as a result television is susceptible to the criticism that it increases the level of violence among children. The research evidence is fairly conclusive on this point (Comstock et al., 1978). Those children particularly predisposed to aggressive behavior who view aggressive television *do* subsequently become more aggressive. Even if this group amounted to only 10% of all children viewing (and child audiences run between 4 and 6 million), one could still argue that the high degree of violence presented on the medium was creating a national increase in the likelihood of violent action by children. More recent studies (Tannenbaum & Zillmann, 1975; Watt & Krull, 1977) also suggest that the "hyped-up" quality, the very

form of TV presentation, may generate hyperactivity or aggression. Our current research following preschoolers over a year indicates that those who watch hyperactive shows like "The Gong Show" as well as violent cartoons or detective shows are more aggressive in nursery school.

Still another major problem presented by the television medium is the fact that it is in effect training children mainly to watch the set. Although all children can benefit from the imagination stimulation provided by TV, as well as by reading and by the stories told to them by adults, the TV viewer becomes "hooked" to the set. We have increasing reason to believe that make-believe and imaginative play are very important parts of the growth experience of children and are closely tied to the development of cognitive, emotional, and interpersonal skills (Singer, 1973; Singer & Singer, 1976c). Quite a number of studies have now shown that additional training of children in make-believe by adults can increase the children's capacity to tolerate delays, to move more smoothly into the school situation, to empathize with other children's feelings, to increase the level of their verbal fluency, and to become more effective in social interaction. Imitation of imaginative material on television can play a role along this line, but unfortunately the television set by its very power holds the child fixed to the set and thus prevents it from the quiet periods of practicing make-believe that are essential for stimulating this process as a part of the child's behavioral repertoire.

Our research suggests that children are eager to play make-believe games and need just a very small amount of stimulation from adults before launching out to practice this material on their own and enjoying it immensely (Singer & Singer, 1976 a, b, c; Tower, Singer, Singer, & Biggs, 1979). The television set precludes such practice because it substitutes itself for the child's own resourceful activity. In those instances where parents have consciously forbidden children to watch television over periods of time, a frequent observation is an increase in imaginativeness of play and generally greater enjoyment of solitary play behavior. Again, therefore, the very power of the television medium in stimulating imaginative potential is mitigated by its own demand-character, which prevents the child from breaking away easily and internalizing the imaginative possibilities as part of its own skill.

The ease with which the child can watch television, its frequent use by adults as a baby sitter, gradually creates a certain passive style that can present serious problems in later life. Already in the high schools and colleges instructors complain of students who demand that they be entertained. The lecturer who held the respect of students in the past, not so much by his style of delivery as by the logical unfolding of complex content, cannot survive today. Instead showmanship, visual aids, and a kind of carnival-like atmosphere are often required on the lecture platform. In a sense, the TV set creates a mood of "learned helplessness," a passive yielding to the power of the set that also evokes an underlying mood of cynicism. Again, one has to

question how effective any fairly complex message presented relatively briefly can be, confronted with this combination of passivity, helplessness, and cynicism on the part of the viewer.

In fairness one should mention the emergence of film-making as a genuine art form in the 1960s and 1970s. Almost certainly this reflects the high degree of visual orientation that characterizes young people who grow up in a television world. But is this gain at a cost in literary art?

THE PROCESS OF READING

The very process of reading occurs, on the whole, in a strikingly different context from that of viewing television. To initiate a TV viewing one needs but the smallest flick of a switch. Reading, however, requires one to settle oneself into a situation that is relatively free of other visual or auditory distraction. To initiate a reading situation requires a fairly conscious intention and a sequence of motor acts that involve adequate preparation for the task.

Written material can capture us to some extent as we notice when we are seated next to someone on a train or bus who is absorbed in what looks like an interesting novel or magazine. We may find our eyes drifting over and beginning to follow the text, only to be annoyed when the individual flips the page before we are ready. By and large, however, we engage in the act of reading out of much more conscious choice and out of much more active and voluntary engagement with the material.

The process of reading itself is a much more complicated act than that of viewing television. What is presented to us on the whole are a series of visually represented printed words. We must read the words, translate them into a different encoding system and then in the course of the reading itself, we must make use of both the verbal and visual or auditory imagery systems for maximum appreciation of the material. If we are reading the account of a conversation between two individuals in a foreign country, we are likely not only to be taking in the words but also to some extent to be imagining the two people in their strange costumes, hearing in our mind's ear their voices as they speak, and creating our own private movie or play. Thus the reading act engages the brain, it would appear, in a more complex way than does the more passive viewing.

There is only a small amount of research that bears on the question as yet. Some individual studies of the amount of brain activity carried out during viewing television as against reading suggest more extensive and diffuse brain activity during reading. There are also indications of greater and more frequent involvement of the autonomic nervous system once one has become absorbed in an extended pattern of reading (Krugman, 1971, 1976). There are

suggestions of somewhat more effective storage of material and comprehension from material that has been read. By and large the major research comparing the two media remains to be done.

Nevertheless it is clear that one advantage of reading is that it is a self-paced activity. Much of the evidence on how we learn effectively indicates that we learn best if we can cut the material up into reasonably modest parts and then rehearse it mentally. Reading allows one to move along the page and then go back and re-read material if we seem to have missed the point along the way. It also permits us to stop for a period and think over the implication of a particular statement for a dramatic scene. Our autonomy in the reading situation also permits the possibility of relying on one's own memories and images to flesh out the events represented. If one is reading about a particular event that has occurred in a distant city, we may take a few seconds to rethink our own experience visiting that city. We may make a connection between the author's reference and the location of certain events and our own private encounters and observations about the setting. Such replay and rehearsal, often leading to even more extended thinking and daydreaming about the material, increases the likelihood of greater associative connections between the material read and our own memory-storage system. Thus the reading situation, although obviously slower paced, by its very deliberation provides the opportunity for greater integration of the material with our own pattern of memories, wishes, and intentions.

For certain kinds of practical material even the best writing may not suffice to convey a message. Magazines will often present a coupling of words and pictures. Again the effect is quite different from that of coupling word and picture on the television. The fact that the medium is not moving may not be as exciting to the viewer in the case of reading, but it permits a more systematic juxtaposition of word and image than is possible under the sensory-bombarding conditions of the television set. In this case the entire brain is being used. The reader has been presented with a series of verbal labels and processes these sequentially with the left side of the brain, at the same time having been presented with a picture or two that makes for more effective parallel processing. The combination of the two, the opportunity to read and re-read or reexamine the material, increases the likelihood that the verbal label and the image will be linked and also associated in subsequent thought with other material. Thus the reading individual is maximizing his information-processing capacity and brain potential in this exercise.

The heavy emphasis on the sequential verbal materials that is part of the reading process makes for especially effective retrieval possibilities. Although television clearly has an advantage when issues of recognition-memory are at a premium, situations in which one must voluntarily call up material that has been previously learned are maximized if one has in effect stored this material in two locations—in the verbal encoding system *and* in the visual system. There is considerable research suggesting that learning occurs best when

combinations of words and imagery are linked (Paivio, 1971; Seamon, 1974). If one wishes to convey a message that requires some degree of logical understanding and thought, and to have this message retrieved later on, then the use of words has a distinct advantage.

There is now an increasing body of research that points out that verbal processes, although limited because of their sequential nature, are also critical for adding a logical direction to thought. A message that involves a responsible comparison or listing of advantages and disadvantages of certain products will be most effectively stored and retrieved if it is presented in a combined verbal and visual medium. The reading situation far exceeds the possibilities of the television medium for presenting a more complex message and also for insuring the likelihood that it can be retrieved when it is needed by the individual as part of a later decision-making circumstance.

An important point raised in our earlier discussion of general cognitive processes has to do with an ongoing stream of consciousness. It was proposed that our stream of thought represents a critical method by which we examine the various unfinished tasks that lie ahead of us and relate these to memories and sets of anticipations of future events, thereby creating new organizations of memories and plans for the future as well (Singer, 1975a,b). The task of reading is one in which the reader allows for time to be taken out to relate such material to the ongoing stream of thought. If the individual has been thinking about the possibilities of a vacation while reading, such vacation images may occur and then may prepare the individual further for the appearance of an advertisement or article concerning a particular vacation resort. There follows, then, an opportunity for thinking through a possible visit to this advertised resort in relation to one's fantasy. In many cases the advertised or touted location may not fit with one's anticipations and fantasies and thus may be discarded. If a mesh is made then a new cognitive structure gets organized—a relatively conscious intention to explore this possibility further or actually to make direct use of the information given about the vacation. The reading process becomes a part of a more general decision-making process of the individual, and in this respect again reflects a very different psychological situation from that experienced by the television viewer.

In effect print sits still and it makes a richness of detail available for the interested individual. Here the notion of "contact" introduced by Krugman (1972) is especially relevant. The individual who already has some set of anticipations about a particular ultimate decision may find opportunities for checking these out in the course of reading. Indeed, the person can turn back a dozen pages and review a particular article or advertisement and then carry this further into the ongoing thought process. The overload effect that characterizes television is simply not a part of the reading situation.

An important aspect of the reading situation is the fact that with the increased specialization of interest-oriented magazines, readers come to the material already with some ideas about what they expect to find. Readers of a

"tennis" magazine will expect to find material concerning equipment or training opportunities. One searches actively for these. In print one may be able to get a kind of detail and discriminating information about products not available from watching a tennis match with some related advertising on television.

There is, finally, a factor that cannot be minimized. People, particularly those that are relatively well educated, trust print materials more. The very detail presented and lack of show-biz quality make a tremendous difference in their reliance on what they see in print as against what they view on television. The combination of voluntarily chosen reading material, the special-interest nature of magazines, the quality of the editorial content of the magazine, all combine to create an atmostphere of respect in the select, the "magazine-imperative" viewer. Reading, by being self-paced, by engaging the total brain, and by relating itself to the decisional attitudes and more active, self-generated fantasies of the viewer, provides special opportunities for the communication of complex messages that will be retrieved later in a decision-making context.

CONCLUSIONS AND RESEARCH IMPLICATIONS

A cognitive–affective point of view can help one to understand the special attractiveness and hold of the television medium on the "unprepared" viewer. It maximizes orienting responses, reduces some of the painful self-awareness that confront us through our own recollections and mental rehearsals when we have returned from work or school or are at home alone, and it provides some moderate novelty and opportunity for emotional expression in a reasonably controlled fashion. I have not dealt with some of the dynamic implications of TV as a fantasy medium—the opportunities to identify with heroic characters, to experience vicarious travel or magical solutions of one's sexual, dependency, or aggressive inclinations. These factors may play a role in determining why certain programs attract larger audiences or why certain characters such as Dr. Welby, Lucy, Archie Bunker, Kojak, the Fonz, the Six Million Dollar Man, or Bionic Woman have special appeal. The amazing audience attraction to "Roots" deserves mention because it reflects the complexity of the appeal a given show may have—identification by blacks, a mystical almost archetypal search for origins of self and continuity with species, the appeal of a well-told, suspenseful story, the exploration of guilt or prejudice by many concerned whites, the psychological contagion of word-of-mouth reports.

But the entertainment and informational effectiveness of a fairly well-produced program on an inherently significant theme such as "Roots" or the Watergate hearings reflect only a tiny fraction of the day-to-day

programming that attracts scores of millions of viewers every evening of the year in the United States. Thus, although individual dynamic motives might determine who watches what show regularly, the more general attractiveness of the medium itself seems more explicable along the lines of the cognitive analysis proposed earlier.

As entertainment television works by appealing to the lowest common denominator of cognitive–affective systems, a value judgment may not be out of place here by suggesting that whereas our dominant visual mechanism and the escape from our thoughts are exploited by the medium, our potential for more extended reflection, for retention of information, and for careful, critical evaluation of information are minimized. Gerbner (1977) has argued on the basis of repeated studies that heavy television watchers may be classified as more unnecessarily fearful, conservative, and confused about facts than light viewers. The medium (at least in the United States), by maximizing quick cuts, which permit little critical analysis, and the visual presentation of violence or disaster, assures retention of global imagery content (right-brain functions?) at the cost of the more orderly and logical verbal and analytic processes (left brain?). Reading, by contrast, can present equally sensational information (as in pulp magazines or "yellow" journalism), but it requires a more active stance by the reader who must project his or her own imagery onto a more orderly array of verbal information. The self-pacing of reading at least gives the reader some chance to reflect, perhaps critically, on what has been presented, whereas in television a sensational item may be followed at once by another one, or by a commercial, or by a humorous bit of news of "show-business" effect that prevents the viewer from mulling over what was first presented.

Although the problem of adequate information processing through the TV medium is more acute for young children, I believe the same principles obtain through the age range. There is a need for television producers to address seriously the value of longer drawn-out sequences, of some repetition, of opportunies for child or adult to be able to "talk back" to the set, at least mentally. Much of the present frenetic quality of the medium in the United States is attributable to its excessive commercialization. TV sells products and local station sales managers who live in a capitalistic society can scarcely be faulted for trying to put on as many ads as they can. Indeed it can be argued that most of the content of television, the attention-getting laughs, chases or shoot-outs are there to keep your eyes on the set so you will see the commercials which pop up just at those points. TV may be an overly expensive and wasteful medium for many kinds of ads because so much fails to be processed and therefore ad campaigns must rely on expensive saturation campaigns. It may well be that advertisers could get more for their money if ads were presented at special times permitting longer sequences of programming. Longer ads, more thoroughly developed, and geared more to

specialized viewing audiences might prove more effective than the scattershot approach of 30-second commercials which now prevails.

If television can modify its mode of presentation to permit longer sequences it can open the way to an aesthetic development of the medium now largely precluded by the format (except on Public Television). This can also be a step of great value for children's programming where there is reason to believe that the quick-cut, black-out techniques so favored on "Sesame Street" are not useful or desirable for children.

Many of the assertions made in this chapter cannot yet be supported directly by research evidence. We need more specific studies comparing the differential processing potential for children or adults of material presented on TV or in print. We need more careful studies of whether simultaneous "voice-overs" or print along with visual effects produce interference in processing. We need experiments on length of sequences and their relationship to retention of content or intelligent *comprehension* of content. The cognitive–affective factors of *format* of presentation need more extensive exploration (Watt & Krull, 1977).

Research with adults can take a number of forms. In the laboratory one might examine controlled TV viewing, monitoring eye movements, facial affect, and brain-wave activity. To what extent do typically fast-paced entertainment or action shows primarily engage the right side of the brain? How effective is comprehension after such shows when processing has indeed involved typically holistic "right-brain" viewing? Alternate, slower-paced formats might be considered and tested to see if entertainment value (as measured by viewer ratings and facial affect) varies systematically with the pace of a show and its encodability.

More naturalistic experiments are also possible. Our current research suggests that with training parents can monitor children's viewing patterns quite reliably. Spouses could be trained to check each others' viewing patterns, and systematic interviews might then pursue issues of comprehension and entertainment value. Recent research on the stream of consciousness (Pope & Singer, 1978) has made increasing use of intermittent self-recording of ongoing thought in the context of normal daily activities. Individuals carry electronic "beepers" of the type used by physicians which go off randomly and call for reports at once. Such devices could be employed to tap in on daily TV viewing with the viewer recording reactions to shows, affect, and comprehension. A little ingenuity can open striking vistas for new directions in research that will seek to capture what special qualities TV viewing generally and individual shows in particular have for different personalities.

Our own current research at the Yale University Family TV Research and Consultation Center is examining the socialization of preschool children into

a television culture. We find that already by age 3 regular-viewing patterns are established and almost 3 hours a day (over and above attendance at nursery school and day care center) are spent before the set. Strong identifications with characters are being established, "Six Million Dollar Man" or "Batman" for boys, "Bionic Woman" for many girls. Although "worthwhile" programs such as "Sesame Street," "Mr. Rogers' Neighborhood," or "The Electric Company" are at the top of the list of frequently watched shows for a middle-class sample, when the weather turns nicer children go out to play during the hours such shows are on and come back to watch cartoons or more adult-oriented programs later in the evening. It remains to be seen as we follow 3- and 4-year-old children over a year or two just how early-established viewing patterns are reflected in the spontaneous imaginative or aggressive behavior of the children during free-play periods.

One of the major issues demanding research on the role of television as child entertainment has to do with parent or adult involvement. Our earlier studies (Singer & Singer, 1976a, b; Tower, Singer, Singer, & Biggs, 1979) suggested the value of an adult model viewing along with children as an aid to their concentration or as an enhancing factor for their own development of spontaneous imaginative play or prosocial behaviors. It may be that using the TV set primarily as a mindless baby sitter (something most parents admit to doing at least some of the time) trains the young child for viewing at the lowest common denominator of cognitive-affective response, as suggested above. We need more studies on whether parents can be helped to recognize the risks of using the TV as sitter, the advantages of joint parent–child viewing, and, indeed, the potential social and educational value of parent–child interaction around particular programming. Our own research is examining the possibilities of parent-training procedures in this respect, but studies of other approaches including the use of print materials (perhaps distributed weekly) built around programs jointly watched by parent and child need systematic examination.

A concluding speculation: One of the great human capacities is the ability to combine memory and imagination. A wonderful experience—a beautiful sunset, a tender, shared interlude of intimacy, an exciting sports event, a moving performance of a Beethoven sonata—is valuable to us not just as we participate in it, because we can replay it mentally and can embellish it, or elaborate on it, or play it in our imagination, among other possibilities. What would life be like if we awoke every morning unable to remember what happened the night before—as sometimes occurs after one has drunk too much at a party? In a sense, television as presented in this country throws so much at us so fast with so many interruptions that we cannot savor and replay mentally that we have seen very often. If producers and broadcasters have any pride in their work why not recognize that the present format plays against

our own cognitive capacities to retain and truly enjoy what we see. Entertainment comes not only in the immediacy of watching but in the many private hours of mental rehearsal that make experiences richer.

REFERENCES

Collins, A. Learning of media content: A developmental study. *Child Development,* 1970, *41,* 1133–1142.

Collins, A. The developing child as viewer. *Journal of Communications,* 1975, *25,* 35–44.

Comstock, G., Chaffee, S., Katzman, N., McCombs, M., & Roberts, D. *Television and Human Behavior.* New York: Columbia University Press, 1978.

Ekman, P., Friesen, W. V., & Ellsworth, P. *Emotions in the human face: Guidelines for research and a review of findings.* New York: Pergamon, 1971.

Gazzaniga, M. S. *The bisected brain.* New York: Appleton-Century-Crofts, 1970.

Gerbner, G. *Television and the family.* Paper presented at the Prix Jeunesse Seminar, Munich, West Germany, June 1977.

Halpern, W. I. Turned-on toddlers. *Journal of Communications,* 1975, 25, 66–70.

Ikard, F. F., & Tomkins, S. S. The experience of affect as a determinant of smoking behavior: A series of validity studies. *Journal of Abnormal Psychology,* 1973, *81,* 172–181.

Izard, C. E. *The face of emotion.* New York: Appleton-Century-Crofts, 1971.

Izard, C. E. *Human emotions.* New York: Plenum, 1977.

Krugman, H. E. Brain wave measures of media involvement. *Journal of Advertising Research,* 1971, *11,* 3–9.

Krugman, H. E. Why three exposures may be enough. *Journal of Advertising Research,* 1972, *12,* 11–14.

Krugman, H. E. *Long-range social implications of the new developments in television technology.* Address to the American Association of Public Opinion Research, Asheville, North Carolina, 1976.

Lesser, G. S. *Children and television* New York: Random House, 1974.

Paivio, A. Imagery and language. In S. Segal (Ed.), *The adaptive function of imagery.* New York: Academic Press, 1971. (Paper read at 3rd annual conference of the Center for Research in Cognition and Affect, City University of New York, June 1970.)

Pope, K. S., & Singer, J. L. (Eds.), *The stream of consciousness.* New York: Plenum, 1978.

Schachtel, E. *Metamorphosis.* New York: Basic Books, 1959.

Seamon, J. G. Retrieval processes for organized long-term storage. *Journal of Experimental Psychology,* 1973, *97,* 170–176.

Seamon, J. G. Coding and retrieval processes and the hemispheres of the brain. In S. J. Dimond & J. G. Beaumont (Eds.), *Hemisphere function in the human brain.* New York: Wiley, 1974.

Shepherd, R. N. Recognition memory for words, sentences and pictures. *Journal of Verbal Learning and Verbal Behavior,* 1967, *6,* 156–163.

Singer, D. G., & Singer, J. L. Family television viewing habits and the spontaneous play of preschool children. *American Journal of Orthopsychiatry* 1976, *46*(3), 496–502. (a)

Singer, J. L. *The child's world of make-believe: Experimental studies in imaginative play.* New York: Academic Press, 1973.

Singer, J. L. Navigating the stream of consciousness: Research in daydreaming and related inner experience. *American Psychologist,* 1975, *30,* 727–738. (a)

Singer, J. L. *The inner world of daydreaming.* New York: Harper & Row, 1975. (b)

Singer, J. L. Ongoing thought: The normative baseline for alternate states of consciousness. In N. Zinberg (Ed.), *Alternate states of consciousness.* New York: Free Press, 1977.

Singer, J. L., & Singer, D. G. Can TV stimulate imaginative play? *Journal of Communications,* 1976, *26,* 74–80. (b)

Singer, J. L., & Singer, D. G. Imaginative play and pretending in early childhood: Some experimental approaches. In A. Davids (Ed.), *Child personality and psychopathology: Current topics* (Vol. 3). New York: Wiley, 1976. (c)

Sturm, H. *Practical conclusions from the perspective of the scientist.* Paper presented at the Prix Jeunesse Seminar, Munich, West Germany, June 1977.

Tannenbaum, P. H., & Zillman, D. Emotional arousal in the facilitation of aggression through communication. *Advances in Experimental Social Psychology,* 1975, *8,* 149–192.

Tomkins, S. S. *Affect, imagery, consciousness* (Vols. I and II). New York: Springer, 1962, 1963.

Tower, R., Singer, D. G., Singer, J. L., & Biggs, A. Differential effects of television programming on preschoolers' cognition, imagination, and social play. *American Journal of Orthopsychiatry,* 1979, *49*(2), 265–281.

Watt, J. H., & Krull, R. An examination of three models of television viewing and aggression. *Human Communications Research,* 1977, *3*(2), 99–112.

Winn, M. *The plug-in drug: Television, children, and the family.* New York: The Viking Press, 1977.

4 The Audience as Critic: A Conceptual Analysis of Television Entertainment

Hilde T. Himmelweit
London School of Economics

Betty Swift
Open University

Marianne E. Jaeger
London School of Economics

> *The stage but echoes back the public voice.*
> *The drama's laws the drama's patrons give*
> *For we that live to please, must please to live.*
> —Samuel Johnson

These lines are part of the Prologue written for the opening of the Drury Lane Theatre, London, in 1747. They could equally serve as a motto for television entertainment today, especially in those countries where the industry depends on advertising revenue based on audience size and where many channels compete for the same public.

The importance of holding large audiences is particularly great at peak viewing times. Here failure bites deepest. One way of minimizing risks is for the industry to create long-running series based on well-tried formulae of action and adventure (Westerns, crime, and science fiction) or on comedy or romance (soap operas). The public is not told in advance how many episodes there will be; generally the producer does not know either. All depends on the ratings. Once a series has been successfully established, it seems to have a life of its own. To kill it becomes cruel, almost bizarre, and as risky as the decision to start the series.

We decided to look more closely at this form of entertainment, not only because it takes up so much air time and is a distinct and important genre, but also because the many episodes that make up a series ensure that nearly every viewer is sufficiently familiar with the series to answer questions about them. Self-selection is therefore less of a factor than would be the case with single, one-off plays.

Previous studies of this form of entertainment seem to fall into three types: first, content analyses, describing themes, types of characters, and changes in these over time (Gerbner, 1972), as well as content analyses of particular events or modes of presentation; e.g., the presentation of violence (British Broadcasting Corporation, 1972; Gerbner, 1977). The second type of study involves the effects on the viewer: generally potentially harmful effects; e.g., in leading to violence in real life (Lefkowitz et al., 1972) or, in the case of a comedy series, "Till Death Us Do Part" (or its American counterpart, "All in the Family") to racial prejudice (British Broadcasting Corporation, 1974/1975; Vidmar & Rokeach, 1974; Brigham & Giesbrecht, 1976). The third type of study deals with uses and gratifications, of which Herzog's (1944) study of women's uses of radio daytime serials remains the classic.

Studies of entertainment by social scientists are primarily concerned with an examination of input or content and with the entertainment's influence on cognitions and/or behavior. By contrast, literary criticism is more concerned with charting and explaining the emotional responses that a play or program evokes. The emphasis is on the evaluative. Since almost any subject can be trivialized or made absorbing, television or drama critics characteristically devote little time to a description of content or plot. Instead, they describe their own reactions, whether they were bored, moved, amused, and then seek to account for these feelings in terms of certain stylistic attributes (violent, brutal, funny), or in terms of the script, the production, or the actors' performances. Although the critic might be judged to be more informed about drama than the public for whom he writes, the underlying assumption is that the two have sufficient in common for the critic's reactions to serve as a useful guide to the prospective theatergoer. Although this might be so where the public is relatively homogeneous and not too different from the critic, this is unlikely in the case of television with a public of millions.

For the television producer the task of empathizing with the audience is far harder than it is for the theater producer, doubly so since the television producer cannot, as is the case in theater, be present when the audience watches the program. A television producer, therefore, neither experiences the joy that comes from that strange "loud" silence that sometimes occurs between the lowering of the curtain and the onset of applause, nor the sadness when jokes misfire or a tender scene makes the audience laugh.

Given the immense difficulty of the task, the absence of feedback, and the importance in television entertainment of satisfying the public, it is surprising

that producers themselves have not asked for studies to examine why some series succeed and others fail. Neither ratings nor the relatively crude audience-appreciation indices used by the broadcasters in Britain are sufficiently sensitive, in-depth indicators. We could not find any studies, other than those asking viewers to rate the amount of violence of given programs (British Broadcasting Corporation, 1972; Greenberg & Gordon, 1972), which canvassed in any depth the public's responses to entertainment programs. It is as if the producers have a rather schizoid attitude to their public. On the one hand, they are much influenced by the ratings. The viewer is king; his turning of the knob decides what will, and will not, be shown, what will, or will not, be imitated. On the other hand, studies of audience reactions, conducted by broadcasting companies seem to see the public as incapable of any subtle judgments.

We take a different view. We believe, as the study reported here demonstrates, that an audience has views about programs, can express them, and much can be learned from such descriptions.

In our study, then, the audience becomes the critic and rates popular television series on attributes commonly used in literary criticism.[1] Since the success or failure of a program depends on a particular mix of characteristics rather than the presence or absence of any one, the viewers were asked to rate each program on many attributes. To understand one program we need to compare it with others of a similar genre. We therefore asked the viewers to rate many programs, using for each the same set of attributes. These ratings, coupled with a measure of the viewers' "overall" enjoyment of each program, provide the building blocks for the investigation.

UNDERLYING PROPOSITIONS

The purpose of our study was to see whether we could develop general principles about television entertainment, using the viewers' reactions as source material. It is essentially a phenomenological approach based on the individuals' experiences. We examined a series of propositions. The first of these was developed, not by a literary critic, but by one of the world's greatest dramatists:

> One's aroused by this, another finds that fits;
> Each loves the play for what he brings to it.
> —*Faust, Part I* (Goethe, 1808)

---

[1]The link between the two traditions comes from the continuing interest of the first two authors in the study of literature in which they took their first degrees.

For Goethe, it is not so much the play as the viewers' needs and interests which affect their responses. How true is this? How varied are the responses? We suggest the reactions to a program by the audience might be described as lying on a continuum, one end of which represents the demand characteristics of the play and the other, those of the audience. Where on this continuum a particular reaction is located would depend on: (1) the program; (2) the particular attribute; and (3) the heterogeneity of relevant characteristics in the audience.

1. The programs: we predicted that uniformity of reactions would be greater for program series built on clear-cut formulae as, for instance, crime and detective series, than for those dealing primarily with human relations (e.g., soap operas), and, further, that agreement would be greater for long-running series which might have produced a shared stereotyped picture of the series as a whole. Finally, agreement would be greater for programs which had a strong appeal than for those where enjoyment was more tepid, bordering on indifference.

2. We expected uniformity of reactions to vary with the attribute and for agreement to be greater when the audience described objective aspects of the program (e.g., its violence), compared with rating its emotional impact (e.g., moving, absorbing, etc.).

3. We further expected that the different circumstances in which the viewers lived their lives, as well as their outlook and values, might affect both enjoyment and sensitivity to different attributes (i.e., that some variation in response would be due to the social and psychological characteristics of the viewers). Katz and Gurevitch (1976) have shown that people seek different gratifications from the same medium. We extended their approach to see how far the audience's view of television and its role influenced reactions to specific programs. Television is always "on tap." In the case of other entertainment, where more effort is required to sample it, people express fairly clear-cut preferences on which they act: they go to listen to a particular type of music or to see a particular type of film. What about the television viewer? Does he have clear-cut preferences for given content (humor, crime stories), for styles of presentation aimed at generating different levels of emotional arousal ("I can enjoy a story with a really sad ending."), or for dealing with the amount of intellectual effort required to follow a story line ("I prefer programs which you can understand without much effort.")?

We expected such preferences to relate to one another in a meaningful way—capable of being expressed in terms of a small number of dimensions or factors. We also predicted a concordance between individuals' general and stylistic preferences and their rating of related attributes in a program. For instance, those very concerned about violence on television and those who

disliked programs containing violence would be more sensitive to—and therefore more inclined to rate as more violent—action programs than would those not so concerned or who liked "scary" programs.

A second focus aimed at assessing the relevance of given characteristics to the enjoyment of the total program. To do so, we related individuals' ratings of particular attributes to their overall liking for a program. We were interested in seeing whether there were certain essential attributes which were always present when a program was liked or whether there was no regularity at all. In the case of the crime and detective series, we were particularly interested in the role played by violence. To what extent was violence important and to what extent did its role depend, in turn, on the presence or absence of other attributes?

The third step involved going beyond the study of individual programs to an examination of the relation of attributes and programs. For this purpose we used a statistical technique called Multidimensional Unfolding (Green & Carmone, 1972) which determines, first, whether there is an ordered relationship or structure among the judgments (e.g., whether the rating *realistic* tends to go with ratings of *absorbing* or *moving*). Provided the ratings can be ordered, a relatively small number of dimensions suffice to represent the richness of the "meaning world" or "cognitive map" of the subject. Once this has been done, each program is placed in the best fitting or "ideal point" within the attribute space. By inspecting the attributes which fall within the same regions of that space and by noting the position of each program within it, we can see what reactions the program evokes and which, if any, of the other programs evoke similar reactions. It enables us, for example, to see how far similarity (i.e., occupying an adjacent position in the attribute space) is a function of the type of program such that all crime programs occupy a similar space, or to what extent it is a function of certain attributes shared by programs of different content.

This type of phenomenological approach, using the viewers' experiences as data and analyzing these by multidimensional scaling methods, has already been successfully employed in the field of aesthetics. For example, Berlyne and Ogilvie (1974) studied paintings and Hare (in press) works of music employing techniques which have shown that aesthetic judgments made about works of art can be successfully expressed in terms of a small number of dimensions. To our knowledge, this method has not previously been used to study perceptions of television programs. It must be emphasized that we are using here the viewers' reactions to generate hypotheses about television entertainment, the validity and generality of which would have to be tested in subsequent studies.

The fourth and final step involves relating the programs' popularity to their position on the attribute space. If the programs' popularity relates in an ordered fashion to their position in the attribute space, then we have at least

the beginnings of a theory about television entertainment. In presenting the main findings of our study, we first examine the viewers' perception of programs and move from that to the findings of the multidimensional analysis of the ratings. A subsequent section describes individuals' attitudes toward television and their stylistic preferences, examines the structure, and relates these measures to the viewers' responses to specific programs. Limitations of space allow only a brief mention of the development of the measures and their relation to the social and psychological characteristics of the viewer. The final section discusses the implications of the findings and makes suggestions for further work.

METHODOLOGY AND PROCEDURE

The Sample

The study required a sample large enough to bring out differences due to social and other characteristics. In addition, it was necessary that the sample be composed of people sufficiently interested in television to be willing to undertake the work involved with the study. The British Broadcasting Corporation (BBC) viewing panel fulfilled both requirements. This is a volunteer sample which the BBC recruits; the panel's reactions form the basis of the BBC audience-appreciation indices of programs. There were equal numbers of men and women represented as well as a good age spread. As is usual in volunteer studies, there were more middle- than working-class respondents. However, since the total sample was over 1000, we still had a sample of 352 working-class respondents, sufficient to bring out differences based on social factors where these existed. The study reported here was added to a two-phase enquiry into people's attitudes to the Common Market, carried out before and after the vote in Parliament in 1971 (which decided on Britain's entry). There were two advantages to being a part of a larger study. First, we could draw on the demographic and psychological measures of the larger enquiry. Especially relevant were measures of self as powerless or efficacious and of the importance attached to each of five goals: living up to one's standards, being successful, leading a quiet life, opportunity for self-expression, the desire to understand society. In an earlier longitudinal study of over 200 young men first studied in adolescence (Himmelweit & Swift, 1976), we had found a relationship between these measures and measures of enjoyment of television and of liking for particular programs.

The second advantage comes from the fact that the larger study used two closely matched subsamples.[2] This made it possible to test the reliability of

---

[2]Matching on age, sex, social class, vote, and attitude to the Common Market was done on an individual case-by-case basis.

some of our findings, which we found to be astonishingly high. There were few significant differences between the samples on any of the measures. Also, by asking the two samples to react to the *same* program but providing each with a *different* list of attributes, more characteristics could be examined than would have been possible with only one sample.

The Programs and Their Characteristics

Both samples were asked to indicate how often they had viewed each of 20 programs and to rate their liking for each, using a 3-point scale (like a lot, a little, or not at all). A list of ten attributes was arranged alongside the name of each program, and the subjects asked to rate the program on each attribute, selecting the most appropriate response category from the following four: (1) applied not at all; (2) very little; (3) somewhat; (4) very much. The 200 observations were made on a single sheet—a Herculean task which required high motivation. Although few managed to make an entry on every observation, the number of replies for any given attribute on any given program was very high.

The Choice of Programs

Because of the need for full information about the programs, we had to select programs which the majority were likely to have seen. This precluded single, one-off plays and restricted the choice to programs shown repeatedly at peak viewing times on the two main channels (BBC1 and ITV). Within this range, 11 of the 20 programs were adventure, police, detective, and science fiction series. We included such a large number of action series both because this type of program does in fact occupy a great deal of peak viewing time, and also because of the public's concern about the violence shown on them. We hoped to contribute to the debate about violence, first by seeing to what extent the audience agreed in its rating of the violence of programs compared with the ratings of other characteristics, and second, by examining whether liking for the programs depended more on their violence or on a mixture of attributes in which violence might or might not figure prominently. Finally, following Greenberg and Gordon (1972), we wanted to see whether those viewers who were concerned about the effects of TV violence perceived more of it in these programs than did those less concerned, and whether viewers who enjoyed such programs might be *less* sensitive to their violence.

Comedy was represented by four programs (one of which was given to the second, or B, sample only). Soap opera, historical, costume, and contemporary drama were each represented by one popular series. These were "Coronation Street" (a soap opera, the saga of the inhabitants of a street in a typical working-class area in the North of England), "The Six Wives of Henry VIII," "Forsyte Saga," and "The Troubleshooters" (the last is a series about an international oil company based in London).

Two nonfiction programs were included: "The News" and a long-running BBC current affairs program, "Panorama." Since news and current affairs programs also contain violent material, we thought much could be learned by including them as "marker variables" to see to what extent reactions differed when the violence was known to be real or fictional.

By restricting our choice in this way, we provided an opportunity for testing two predictions. The first is that the long-playing series might have such a strong public image that *individuated* responses to them would not occur. We were able also to test the second prediction, namely, that viewers would respond differentially to individual programs within a given genre. We carefully chose within each genre programs that differed stylistically with regard to some attribute (e.g., in degree of realism, violence, glamour) and, as far as possible, with regard to a combination of attributes (e.g., realistic and violent vs. realistic and not violent, glamorous and violent vs. not glamorous and violent).

In the case of the action series, we chose British and American programs: some programs centered on the police ("Softly, Softly," "Hawaii Five-O," "Dixon of Dock Green," and "A Man Called Ironside ["Ironside"]), others on private investigators or lone heroes ("The Avengers" and "The Saint"). We also included one Western, two science fiction series, and one late-night series, "The Guardians." "The Guardians" is a British series representing life-conditions in Orwell's *Nineteen Eighty-Four* in some unspecified country, dealing with the brutal suppression of dissidents by a totalitarian regime. What distinguishes the program from others is not only its fascist overtones and brutality, but also the complex characterization of the dissidents and the dictators. The program was generally not liked. By comparing it with other, more popular series containing violence, we hoped to learn more about the mixture of attributes which go with dislike rather than enjoyment.

The number of programs within each category is not the same. Since this was an exploratory study, it seemed best to concentrate on one genre in detail. If adequate differentiation of attributes within the crime and detective series were to be found, a later study could usefully concentrate on looking for different reactions within other types of entertainment programs.

Table 4.1 provides a brief description of the 20 programs, arranged within type of program in descending order of popularity (based on the samples' mean liking score for that program). American programs are indicated by a superscript *b*.

The Choice of Attributes

Compiling a balanced and comprehensive list proved to be no easy task. Returning to our discussion of professional critics, we find at times that they are explicit about stylistic features of a play, saying that the play is

TABLE 4.1
List of Programs within Program Type in Descending Order of Popularity[a]

Mean Liking	Program Type
	Current Affairs Programs
1.20	"News"
1.69	"Panorama" (weekly BBC current affairs program)
	Comedy Series
1.27	"The Morecambe and Wise Show" (featuring two popular comedians)
1.41	"Steptoe and Son" (sitaution comedy: father and son rag-and-bone merchants)
1.63	"Up Pompeii" (noted for its sexual innuendos; centered on popular comedian)
1.64	"Please Sir" (humorous saga, young teacher with his adolescent class)
	Action Series
1.40	"Softly, Softly" (realistic, British police series, with focus on social problems)
1.59	"A Man Called Ironside" (sensitive former cop and team solve crime and social problems)[b]
1.71	"The Saint" (modern-day, glamorous "Robin Hood")
1.72	"Dixon of Dock Green" (police sergeant—archetypical British "bobby")
1.75	"Mission Impossible" (team with strange powers combat evil/danger)[b]
1.75	"The Avengers" (upper-class, glamorous British investigators, improbable, humorous, sexy)
1.82	"Hawaii Five O" (police series in Hawaii)[b]
	Science Fiction/Futuristic
1.86	"Star Trek" (children/adult science fiction; "to boldly go where no man has gone before")[b]
2.06	"Dr. Who" (children/adult science fiction: the Doctor and his female companion solve problems in different places, centuries, and guises)
2.40	"The Guardians" (Orwellian-type fascist takeover; late-night program)
	Drama Series/Soap Opera
1.32	"The Six Wives of Henry VIII" (historical drama)
1.32	"Forsyte Saga" (costume drama)
1.62	"The Troubleshooters" (problems of international oil company based in London)
2.08	"Coronation Street" (saga of the inhabitants of a working-class street in a northern city, presented three times weekly)
	Western
1.73	"The Virginians" (Western soap opera)[b]

[a]In front of each program is its score. The lower the score, the more popular the program (1 = like a lot; 2 = like somewhat; and 3 = do not like at all).

[b]American series.

lighthearted or brutal, at other times characteristics are implied by describing the impact the play made on the critic. Since both approaches seemed valid, our final list of 17 attributes included both types: attributes judged to express primarily impact reactions—were informative, moving, exciting, disturbing, trivial, annoying, convincing, and absorbing. Those expressing stylistic features,—were violent, brutal, realistic, funny, lighthearted, glamorous, sexy, unpredictable, and complex. (In practice, the distinction between the two types of attributes is far from clear.)

Three of the 17 attributes—informative, violent, and disturbing—were presented to both samples and the remainder were split between the two subsamples. The A sample rated attributes which were concerned with *emotional* impact and those which helped to clarify the role played by violence. These attributes were exciting, brutal, moving, realistic, trivial, sexy, and funny. The B sample rated attributes primarily concerned with the *intellectual* impact of a program or its absence: unpredictable, convincing, complex, as well as such characteristics as lighthearted, glamorous, and annoying.

By presenting three of the attributes to both samples, we were able to see how far their rating was influenced by context (i.e., by the other attributes on the list). In fact the influence proved to be remarkably small: out of 60 possible comparisons, only 11 were significant at the 1% level (a rather low number given the size of the sample), and these differences formed no coherent pattern. In no case did the difference shift the placement of the mean rating on one of the four response categories.

PERCEPTION OF PROGRAMS

Aggregate Judgments

At the beginning of the chapter, we suggested that the audience might agree more in their ratings of descriptive attributes such as violent or brutal than in those characterizing impact, for example, moving or absorbing. To test this hypothesis, we computed the mean of the standard deviation for each attribute across all 20 programs (the size of the standard deviation provides a measure of degree of agreement: the larger it is the more varied the response).

In the following we give the five attributes with the largest and the five with the smallest means of the standard deviation:

Attributes with means of s.d. below 0.80	Attributes with means of s.d. above 0.90
violent	convincing
brutal	absorbing

sexy	moving
funny	unpredictable
disturbing	trivial

Our expectation was generally confirmed. Three of the five attributes about which there was more agreement were basically descriptive and the other two (funny, disturbing) fall somewhere between description and reaction. By contrast, among the five on which there was least agreement, four expressed reactions to the program rather than described a particular feature.

Individual Programs

In addition, we carried out similar computations for each program across all attributes, rather than for one attribute across programs. Those programs with the smallest and largest means of the s.d. of the ratings are shown in the following list:

Programs with means of s.d. below 0.80	Programs with means of s.d. above 0.90
"The News"	"The Avengers"
"The Morecambe and Wise Show"	"Star Trek"
"Please Sir"	"Mission Impossible"
"Softly, Softly"	"The Guardians"
"The Six Wives of Henry VIII"	

Contrary to our prediction, the element that distinguishes programs which generate uniform rather than varied reactions is not the simple plot based on well-known formulae of law breaking and law enforcement, nor familiarity bred from long-running series; if anything the opposite is true. Only our third prediction is confirmed: it is the strongly liked programs which evoke more uniform reactions. Four of the five programs about which there was most agreement were among the five most popular programs and all were among the top 10. No other program on the list came anywhere near them in popularity. This could be be because moderately liked programs tend to present flat, stereotyped stories which, through their very indistinctness, make less impact and are therefore more open to projection of the viewer's own predispositions. In the case of high quality, nonstereotyped short-run series, which are something of an event, it is the programs that impose themselves on the viewer. The only long-running series which evoked uniform reactions was the British police series, "Softly, Softly," a very popular and well-scripted story without the customary stock characters and plots.

Support for the view that it is the popular program which imposes itself comes from the attribute profiles of the programs, which clearly showed that

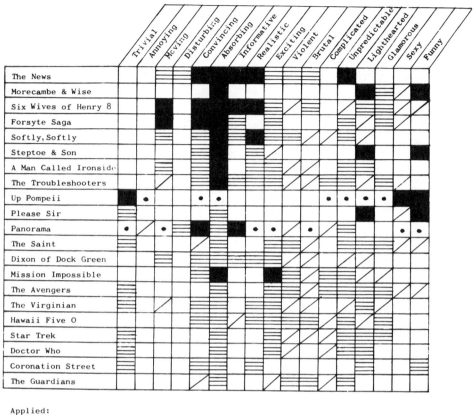

Applied:

■ Very much ☰ Somewhat ◪ Very little ☐ Not at all

● Measures not available

FIG. 4.1. Program profiles: plot of modal responses on 17 stylistic attributes. The programs are arranged in descending order of mean liking.

viewers were sensitive to stylistic differences *within,* as well as to similarities of style *across,* program types. Figure 4.1 shows, for each attribute of the 20 programs, the modal or most frequent category selected from the 4 response choices (does not apply at all, applies very little, applies somewhat, applies very much). For purposes of discussion of the profile we treat the responses "applies not at all" and "applies very little" as equivalent. The programs are arranged in decreasing order of popularity.

Inspection of the profiles provides interesting insights. The "News," included to act as a "marker," was rated not only very informative, realistic and unpredictable, somewhat brutal and violent, but also as making an

impact by being very convincing and absorbing, somewhat moving, exciting, and disturbing. As a program, therefore, it makes a strong impact at both the cognitive and emotional level. Significantly, this is the program that is also most liked.

The stylistic profile of "Softly, Softly" resembles less the more stereotyped crime series than it does the "News." Like the "News" it was judged realistic, absorbing, and violent, but somewhat less informative and convincing. "A Man Called Ironside," the most popular of the American series, represents a muted version of "Softly, Softly": less realistic, less violent and informative, but liked also for being somewhat lighthearted. On the other hand, the British "bobby" series, "Dixon of Dock Green," had no strong positive features to recommend it. Where "The News" was very unpredictable and "Softly, Softly" and "Ironside" somewhat unpredictable, "Dixon of Dock Green" was seen as predictable—neither violent, brutal, lighthearted, nor glamorous. The ratings also show that as impact decreases so does popularity.

After "The News," the second most popular program was "The Morecambe and Wise Show," a weekly comedy show featuring two top comedians. Indeed, all comedy programs were well liked. All were rated as very funny, lighthearted, and absorbing, though there were differences with regard to secondary attributes.

Two other programs warrant more discussion than we have space for— "The Six Wives of Henry VIII" and "Forsyte Saga"—the third and fourth most popular programs on our list. Noteworthy here is the number and range of stylistic attributes on which these two programs seem to have positive ratings. Both were found to very absorbing, convincing, and moving. Additionally, "The Six Wives of Henry VIII" was seen as realistic and informative, somewhat brutal, as well as lighthearted and glamorous. The "Forsyte Saga" was rated as somewhat informative, unpredictable, and glamorous. Whereas the two top favorites, "The News" and "The Morecambe and Wise Show," each have specialized appeal—realism and information in the one case, and comedy in the other—these programs may well be popular because of the diversity and richness of their stylistic content. Figure 4.1 shows that liking increases with richness of stylistic profile: "The Troubleshooters," for example, has a "rich" profile; the soap opera, "Coronation Street," an empty one. "Coronation Street" is seen as realistic without being informative, somewhat convincing and absorbing, yet trivial, neither moving nor exciting. The same principle—liking being associated with richness of style—also operates within the subset of violent programs.

Regression Analysis

To understand better the mixture of attributes that describe a well-liked program we carried out multiple regression analyses, using the ratings of the

attributes to "predict" liking for that program. Two separate analyses were done for each program: one on the attributes presented to the A sample, the other on those presented to the B sample. These analyses tell us first how well the attributes account for liking: the higher the percentage variance accounted for, the better the fit. For both analyses, the percentage was relatively high for all the fictional programs (on average over 40% and some well over 50%).[3] This is evidence that the ratings express features or reactions that go with enjoyment, indifference, or dislike.

The analyses also show which attributes contribute in what strength and at what stage to the combination of attributes that make up liking. Adjectives expressive of the individual's *emotional reactions* made the largest contribution; the more the viewer felt involved in a program, the more he enjoyed it. Among the attributes in list B, absorbing appears to be the most important attribute for 13 out of 20 programs, its place in the A list being taken by exciting (most of the correlations of these two variables with liking were over 0.60). Cognitive responses appeared in second place: informative, realistic, not trivial, with unpredictability and complexity entering as desirable features at the third stage. (The correlations between cognitive attributes and liking were between 0.30 and 0.50).

Enjoyment was increased when the program was thought to have some attribute *not* commonly associated with the genre: exciting in the case of comedy series such as "Please Sir" and "Up Pompeii"; funny in the case of "The Avengers," and informative in the case of "Hawaii Five-O."

These analyses also show whether given stylistic features like violent or glamorous, even if they themselves correlated little with liking, made a contribution when linked to other attributes. We were particularly interested in the role of violence. Rather to our surprise, it made a very minimal contribution at the final stage, and then only in 4 out of the 11 action series. In the case of "Softly, Softly," and "Dr. Who," violence detracted, whereas in the case of the American series "Hawaii Five-O" and "Mission Impossible") it marginally added to enjoyment.

Correlations cannot, of course, tell us about the direction of causality. But other evidence—the attribute profile and the relatively high measure of agreement in the ratings across the sample—suggests that the ratings express features inherent in the program. Otherwise there would not have been so much agreement in the rating of violence in programs by people who differed in their liking of them.

---

[3]Not surprisingly, "The News" was less well predicted, largely because liking was uniformly high (without sufficient variance in the dependent variable, no prediction is possible), but also because the attributes were more appropriate for television entertainment than for the rating of "The News" or documentaries.

Attributes
AB Absorbing
AN Annoying
 B Brutal
CM Complicated
CN Convincing
 D Disturbing
 E Exciting
 F Funny
 G Glamorous
IN Informative
 L Lighthearted
 M Moving
 R Realistic
 S Sexy
 T Trivial
 V Violent
 U Unpredictable

Programs
 1. "News"
 2. "Morecambe"
 3. "Forsyte Saga"
 4. "Six Wives"
 5. "Softly"
 6. "Steptoe"
 7. "Please Sir"
 8. "Ironside"
 9. "Troubleshooters"
10. "Mission Imp."
11. "Saint"
12. "Avengers"
13. "Dixon"
14. "Hawaii Five-O"
15. "Virginians"
16. "Star Trek"
17. "Dr. Who"
18. "Coronation St."
19. "Guardians"

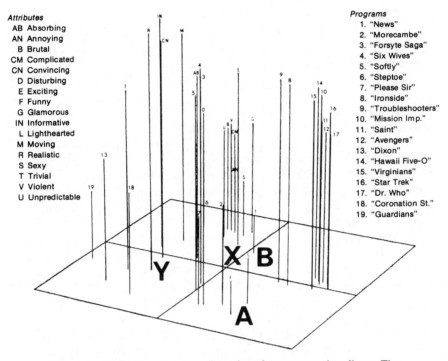

FIG. 4.2.   Three-dimensional configuration of programs and attributes. The regions are indicated by : A, B, X, Y. The level of arousal is indicated by the distance of program or attribute from the base.

PROGRAM STYLES AND THEIR MEANING:
THE COGNITIVE WORLD OF THE VIEWER

In the previous section we have shown that viewers, like critics, are sensitive to stylistic attributes of individual programs and that these affect their liking. By relating the attributes of all programs to one another, we now try to reconstruct the cognitive or "meaning" world that lies behind viewers' ratings of all the characteristics.

The statistical technique used is that of multidimensional unfolding. For such an analysis to be informative, ratings of a large number of attributes are needed. This was achieved by merging the two samples and using as data the mean rating of each attribute.[4] There were ratings of 17 attributes for each of

---

[4]Taking the mean of the evaluations of those who had rated the program as an indicator is common practice. The BBC and ITV do the same in arriving at their appreciation indices.

19 programs. ("Up Pompeii," a comedy series, and the current affaris program, "Panorama," had to be excluded since they were rated by one sample only.) The results of the unfolding analysis will be described more fully elsewhere; here we concentrate on salient findings.

The analysis showed that judgments about stylistic attributes were highly structured. The two-dimensional solution was fairly satisfactory and the three-dimensional one highly so.[5] This suggests that viewers evaluate programs in similar terms to those used by critics. It also suggests that there is a shared understanding, perhaps implicit, of the meaning of these terms, and that the reactions can be adequately and parsimoniously expressed by means of a small number of dimensions. Figures 4.2 and 4.3 present the three-dimensional solution. In Fig. 4.2, each line represents either an attribute or a program. The length of each line indicates the positions of the program or the attribute within the space.

Moving from left to right in Fig. 4.2, we move from realism to an absence of realism. This dimension is characterized at one end by the attributes realistic and informative and at the other end by the attribute trivial. Since all of the programs except for the "News," are fictional, this dimension does not describe whether a given story is factual or not, but whether the viewer perceives the plot and characterization as being true to life.

The space further divides into four regions. Regions A and B are regions of low tension. Region A (humor) is characterized by attributes such as funny and lighthearted. Region B, a rather empty area, is defined by only one attribute, trivial. Opposite Region A is Region X, one of unease and disquiet defined by the attributes disturbing, violent, brutal, unpredictable, complicated, sexy, and annoying. Opposite Region B lies Region Y; this represents positive involvement, characterized by such attributes as absorbing, convincing, moving, realistic, and informative.

Within the regions we can distinguish four levels of arousal (Tannenbaum and Zillmann, 1974), which vary qualitatively as well quantitatively. Level 1 is an area of low arousal. Feelings at this level are low key, trivial or annoying, funny or lighthearted. Levels 2 and 3 represent stronger reactions: negative and unpleasant at Level 2, and positive and satisfying at Level 3. Level 4 deals with cognitive rather than emotional arousal as indicated by such attributes as informative, realistic, and convincing.

Next we examine the ideal points which locate the programs within the attribute space. Figure 4.3 provides a schematic three-dimensional

---

[5]In multidimensional unfolding analyses, the dimensionality of the solution represents the complexity of the structure underlying the judgments—the less-well structured the judgments, the more dimensions are needed to express the complexity of the data.

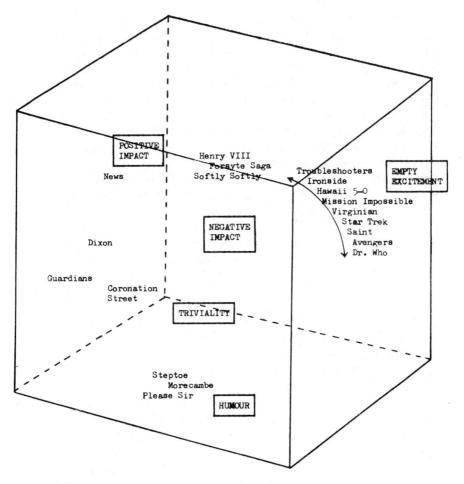

FIG. 4.3. Schematic representation of programs and regions in a three-dimensional space.

representation of the regions and levels just described, together with the position of the programs.

The position of "The News" and the three humorous programs comes as no surprise. "The News" falls directly within the positive impact field, whereas the "Morecambe and Wise Show," "Steptoe and Son," and "Please Sir" are clearly in the lighthearted humor field.

The positioning of the other 15 programs highlights not only the particular appeal of each, but has relevance for a fuller understanding of what the viewer finds entertaining. First let us look at the programs that lie close to Region Y

where the attribute clusters suggest cognitive and emotional arousal. The three popular series which have "rich" stylistic profiles are found at Level 3 in the fiction portion of the space ("The Six Wives of Henry VIII," "Forsyte Saga" and "Softly, Softly"). Two other fictional programs, "Dixon of Dock Green" and "Coronation Street," i.e., a police series and a soap opera, form a loose cluster on another fringe of Region Y; however, at Level 2 (realistic, but trivial and not informative), they generate little involvement. "The Guardians," the rather brutal Orwellian-type series shown late at night, is again at the periphery of this region; it is closer to the negative impact area than are the others. Surprisingly, despite its brutality it lies in Level 1 (i.e., it aroused little emotion). The viewers were not disturbed by the program, probably because they did not empathize with the characters, a necessary condition for feeling involved.

The other 11 programs—all "violent" except for the contemporary drama series, "The Troubleshooters"—arrange themselves in an arc. At one end of the arc are unrealistic, rather trivial, glamorous action series ("Dr. Who," "The Avengers," "The Saint," and "Star Trek"), and at the other end lie the more realistic and convincing ones ("The Troubleshooters" and "Ironside"). All of these are located at Level 3, the latter programs at a higher point within that level than the former group. They are all seen as exciting. However, unlike the cluster formed by "Softly, Softly," "Forsyte Saga," and "The Six Wives of Henry VIII," they lack other qualities. This group of programs were also not seen as disturbing, either because the plots and characters bear little relation to real life or because the viewers have become so habituated to the violence that forms such an integral, stereotyped part of these long-running series that they no longer react to it. We labeled this area "empty excitement": empty because it neither absorbed nor disturbed.

So far we have considered the viewers' ratings of the programs. It now remains to relate liking for the programs (see Table 4.1) to their position within the attribute space. The relation is a close one and the pattern very clear. The most highly popular programs are either in the strong positive impact or in the humor field sections. Programs elsewhere fare less well. In particular, the empty excitement sector is filled with programs that are little liked. "The Guardians," the only program to be described as brutal, is the least popular.

It seems clear that viewers want programs which make a strong positive impact or else are humorous. Empty excitement is tolerated rather than liked. They reject programs which while disturbing and unpredictable have no compensating features. The "News," by contrast, is very popular even though it disturbs, just because it is informative and realistic.

THE RELATION OF ATTITUDES
AND STYLISTIC PREFERENCES
TO SPECIFIC PROGRAMS

Earlier we examined reactions to programs; here we move from a consideration of programs to a consideration of the viewer. Has the viewer well-defined preferences for given styles of programs, and how do these preferences predict enjoyment of those programs which, on the face of it, match the viewer's preferences? We saw such preferences—not operating in a vacuum, but related to the gratifications that the viewer sought from television, to the viewer's attitude toward television, and the role assigned to it. We therefore devised instruments to assess these attitudes.

Attitudes Toward Television

We asked a number of agree-disagree questions concerning the individual's attitude toward different aspects of television. A factor analysis yielded three distinct factors: (1) concern about TV violence; (2) perception of bias in news and current affairs programs; and (3) perception of television as broadening the individual's interest and knowledge.

To gain a better picture of the role viewers assign to television in their own lives and in the country, we asked them to imagine what the effects would be *if television were to stop for good.* A semantic differential format was used.[6] The factor analysis of the statements of *the effects on self* yielded three factors: (1) mood; (2) level of activity in and outside the home; (3) and knowledge (having a more accurate picture of the world). The four factors obtained from replies to the statements about the *effects on the country* concerned: (1) people's well-being; (2) interest in cultural and social matters; (3) effects on social stability or unrest; and (4) compassion and social conscience.

Appendix A lists the items making up each factor, together with the distribution of replies. These point to an ambivalent attitude toward television. The great majority agreed that television enriches, stimulates, interests, makes people more informed, and would be greatly missed. At the same time, a life without television—at least in theory—meant that people would go out more, do more, and take a greater interest in community affairs. Attitudes toward the amount, and effects, of violence shown on television were divided, as were views about bias in the presentation of news. More

---

[6]With bipolar statements separated by a 5-point scale, 1 and 5 indicated a definite effect with regard to either of the two statements, 2 and 4 a possible effect, and 3 no effect.

agreed than disagreed that demonstrations would be more peaceful without television, and that TV tends to blow up the importance of isolated scuffles. What was striking was the general consensus that television made little impact on the real problems of our society: crime, delinquency, and class divisions. The minority who thought TV had an influence were evenly divided as to whether it reduced or aggravated such problems.

Stylistic Preferences

Preferences for types of content, characterizations, settings or styles of production were assessed again using the semantic differential format. The distribution of the replies shows that for 20 of the 23 bipolar statements, the great majority (three-quarters of the sample) expressed clear and definite preferences. At no time did this percentage drop to below 50%.

Nor were the reactions idiosyncratic. Factor analysis of these preferences yielded five factors: (1) avoidance of potentially arousing or upsetting content, whether humor, tragedy, or passion; (2) wanting to be involved (liking to think about a program once it is finished); (3) preference for clear-cut stories requiring little effort to understand; (4) preference for glamorous and escapist programs rather than down-to-earth, realistic ones; (5) and preference for excitement, action—thrillers. (Appendix B lists the items that comprise the factors and the replies.)[7]

Not surprisingly, those wanting to avoid arousing or upsetting programs disliked scary thrillers or unpredictability and preferred programs requiring little effort to understand. Those who liked to think about the characters and content of a program preferred series about people with whom they could identify.

Attitude–Style Relations

To test our prediction that there would be a link between the individual's attitude toward television in general and his preference for different stylistic characteristics, we carried out a *metafactor analysis*—so called because we used as data the factor scores derived from the four analyses just described. The varimax solution yielded five factors. As anticipated, every one of the five style scores loaded significantly on three of the factors which expressed the individual's general view of the role of television (Table 4.2).[8] The first factor brings together dislike for high level of arousal (of humor, passion, tragedy,

---

[7]To make sure that the specific program did not influence the answers to the preference questions, questions about these were asked first.

[8]The other two factors were concerned with the effects of television on activity in and out of the home and on social concern.

or in scary thrillers) [S1 and S5] with the perception of TV as too violent (A1) and as contributing to disharmony in society and in the home (EC3). The third factor singles out those who like programs whose characters appear to be real people (S2 and S4) and see television as enriching their lives (A3). For such viewers, television drama is indeed the "symbolic reality" to which Gerbner (1972; Gerbner et al., 1977) refers, a reality with which they identify and from which they feel they learn. Finally, those who felt they would do more if television were to stop (ES2), enjoyed television programs that excite and disturb. They sought a high level of emotional as well as intellectual arousal, preferring the unpredictable to the cut and dried (S1 and S3). Preferences then for given styles of programs relate to broader attitudes toward the medium and its role.

What determines these views? We found them first to be related to the amount of time that the individual viewed television. One obvious finding was that those who viewed a lot were more involved with television than those who viewed little (r = .28), a correlation which remained even after the effects of education and social status had been partialled out. But which comes first: the viewing and hence the involvement, or the involvement and hence the viewing? We can gain some insight by examining which characteristics, if any, differentiated the involved and frequent viewer from the more aloof and less assiduous viewer. Just as the older and the less-educated felt more enriched through television and more dependent on it, so did a particular outlook within the different age and educational groups favor such attitudes. Those who valued a quiet life, liked conformity, and saw themselves as powerless, were more involved. The younger and more-educated viewers and, in particular, those who wished to understand society and to feel free to express themselves, viewed less and were more critical of, and aloof from, television. They exhibited a love-hate relationship with television; they gave time to viewing, yet resented doing so.

These results are in striking agreement with those of the longitudinal study discussed earlier (Himmelweit & Swift, 1976). In that study a sample of young men were studied over an 11 year period, starting in adolescence, thus making it possible to pinpoint the course of the relationship between background, outlook, and attitude toward television. The direction is clear; it is the social environment, the skills and outlook of the individual, which help shape the response both to the presence of television in the home as well as to its content. Television does not influence basic goals and values.

Genre Preferences and Program Enjoyment

So far we have established and provided some evidence for an argument which contends that stylistic preferences relate meaningfully to general views about television and as well as to outlook and life experiences. The next step

TABLE 4.2

Meta Factor Analysis of Factor Scores of Attitudes to Television and of Factor Scores of Stylistic Preferences

Factor Scores	Meta Factors[a]				
	I *Concern About Violence*	II *Increases Social Concern*	III *TV as Enricher*	IV *Decreases Activity*	V *TV as Stimulator*
Stylistic Preferences					
S1 Approach to or *avoidance* of potentially upsetting stimuli	.36[c]	-.15	-.06	.05	-.54
S2 Aloofness or *involvement* *in programs*	-.06	-.11	.59	.06	-.17
S3 Preference for low/*high* cognitive effort	-.08	.02	.05	.15	.44
S4 Preference for real vs. *fantasy* content/ presentation	.03	-.01	-.32	.04	-.19
S5 Liking for thriller/ action content	.36	-.02	.04	.17	-.09

Attitudes

A1	Concern about TV violence	-.69	.07	.03	-.03	.13
A2	Bias or neutrality of TV news and documentaries	-.31	.15	-.21	.05	.11
A3	TV enriches	-.03	-.18	-.65	.09	.14

Effects on Country

EC1	*Negative* effects on people's well-being	-.36	.44	-.10	.24	-.12
EC2	*Negative* effects on interest in cultural and social matters	-.12	.47	.08	.55	.09
EC3	*Negative* effects on social stability or unrest	.66	-.03	.01	-.08	-.02
EC4	*Negative* effects on social conscience	-.01	.60	.07	.13	.08

Effects on Self

ES1	*Positive* effects on mood	.27	-.38	-.34	-.02	.32
ES2	*Negative* effects on activity	.08	.03	.00	.57	.08
ES3	*Negative* effects on knowledge and thought	-.05	.52	-.09	-.05	.05

[a]After VARIMAX rotation.
[b]High scores are italicized.
[c]Factor loadings over .30 are italicized.

in the analysis consists of seeing whether expressed preferences for a genre predict enjoyment of particular programs. To what extent, for example, does preferring everyday characters to glamorous or oversized heroes accompany enjoyment of "Coronation Street" and "Softly, Softly" as opposed to the liking of "The Avengers" or "The Saint"?

To examine this question we carried out multiple regression analyses, once again to predict liking for a program, this time from attitudinal and preference measures as well as from frequency of viewing, age, sex, social status, and education. Since the demographic variables related both to the liking of specific programs and to the style scores, we had to show that the stylistic preferences added to the prediction over and above that due to the demographic variables alone. This indeed proved to be the case. The improvement was significant, though small, with the stylistic preferences which contributed to the prediction matching the main ingredients of the programs. Similarities and differences among and between the crime and violence series discussed earlier were reflected in the combinations of tastes which best predicted liking for the individual programs. Most of the series were linked by those who preferred thriller action with stories and heroes larger-than-life. The only exceptions were the rather "cozy" police series: "Dixon of Dock Green" and "Ironside" were liked by those who preferred realistic content, avoided upsetting content, and preferred a story line that could be understood with little effort. By contrast, "Steptoe and Son," a comedy series featuring two complex working-class characters (the American imitation was called "Sanford and Son"), was liked better by those with a preference for off-beat humor and for programs which were potentially upsetting.

Sensitivity to Violence

Goethe, it will be remembered, suggests that an audience, depending on their needs, will differ in their sensitivity to different attributes of a play. Greenberg and Gordon (1972) support this view. They found, for instance, that critics who viewed programs from the vantage point of the professional observer (concerned about the potentially harmful effects of TV violence) rated programs as *more* violent than did the ordinary viewer. In our study we examined whether similar differences existed within the viewing public, depending on their concern about TV violence and their stylistic preferences.

We predicted that those concerned about TV violence (Meta factor 1) and those who disliked thrillers or programs which scare or disturb (S1 and S5) would see the programs as *more* violent and brutal. This prediction was not supported, nor was the opposite prediction, namely, that those who liked such programs would tend to *discount* their violent content. None of the correlations was significant. These negative findings are important and

throw serious doubt on the view frequently expressed that perception of violence is so greatly influenced by subjective factors that little reliance can be placed on such perceptions (British Broadcasting Corporation, 1972). Indeed, as we have already shown in an earlier section, there was more agreement in the ratings of programs for their violence and brutality than for almost any other characteristic.[9]

However, stylistic preferences did relate to the perception of other attributes (those relating to the impact of a program and its level of arousal). The viewers who wished to avoid upsetting stimuli and for whom television was enriching tended to rate programs as more moving, more realistic, and more informative than did the others. This was particularly true in the case of the long-running stereotyped series ("The Virginians," "Ironside," "Hawaii Five-O," "Coronation Street" and "Dixon of Dock Green"). In the case of other highly popular programs such as "The Six Wives of Henry VIII," "Forsyte Saga," and "Softly, Softly" no such relation was found.

This is probably because certain programs impose themselves on the viewer, whereas others, as Goethe suggested, offer opportunities for projections of the viewer's own needs. A program makes a relatively stronger impact the richer its stylistic profile—the more plot, character, and presentation move, absorb, or amuse. The more a series depends on well-tried formulae and stock characters, the less it is enjoyed and the more it is that the description of its characteristics influenced is by the viewer's own predispositions.

IMPLICATIONS

The television industry aspires "to create delight" (Wheldon, 1975). The practical necessity is to produce programs which attract a large audience. This is particularly important at peak viewing times. Most resources are poured into entertainment programs shown then.

A combination of high risk and high stakes are the very conditions under which, in the absence of proper feedback, the folklore about the audience's taste and reactions are likely to fluorish. Judging from the schedules of the television services, one way of minimizing risks is for the industry to create long-running series, generally based on the well-tried formulae of action and adventure. Unlike plays or the special drama series, "Forsyte Saga" or "I, Claudius," which are adaptations of novels, these series are not written as a

---

[9]Viewers had little difficulty in agreeing on the relative violence contained in programs. Comparing the means, we find that "The Guardians" was judged the most violent, followed by "Hawaii Five-O" and "The Avengers." These shows were followed by "Softly, Softly," "Mission Impossible," and "The Saint;" "Ironside" and "Dixon of Dock Green" were rated as least violent.

unit. Instead they consist of one-episode vignettes, complete in themselves. The continuity is provided by the central character and his retinue (as in "Kojak"), or through series of stories about particular characters all living in a small town ("Coronation Street," "Peyton Place"), continued at snail's pace from episode to episode.

Sir Huw Wheldon (1975) suggested that a series should stop when the author has nothing more to say, as had been done in the case of "Till Death Do Us Part." This is a suggestion not often followed, certainly not in the case of the American imitation, "All in the Family," or that of the British soap opera, "Coronation Street." The script for most series is written not by one writer or a team of writers, but by successive teams whose assignment includes writing in such a way that there is no discontinuity in style or characterization.

The longevity of series is disturbing. Although the study reported here was carried out 7 years ago (in 1971), 9 of the 16 series we studied (4 American and 5 British) were still being shown within the last two years, with three continuing to this writing to make their weekly appearance.

Does the public really have such an insatiable appetite for sameness? TV managements argue that the fact that several of the series continue to feature among the top 20 testifies to their popularity: not necessarily. As Goodhardt, Ehrenberg, and Collins (1975) have shown the phenomenon is as much a testimony to scheduling and to social habit. But all this is a far cry from viewing the series because they are really enjoyed. Our study shows that three series which continue to make their regular weekly appearances, "Hawaii Five-O," "Dr. Who," and "Coronation Street" were, seven years ago, the least popular (with the exception of "The Guardians," included as "marker variable" precisely because the series had been unpopular).

It would seem that provided a series does not "grate" (i.e., is not actively disliked), it is viewed. The familiar is habit forming: above all, the habit of turning on the set. Many viewers develop what the industry calls loyalty to a channel. It may equally be inertia. We do not know whether the audience likes what is shown on the channel which they view, cannot be bothered to experiment, or stays put because they believe—having experimented—that television is so much of the same cloth that the other channels are unlikely to have anything more attractive. These findings make it even more difficult to understand why television companies have done so little research in an attempt to learn about differences in reactions to series or about the ingredients which contribute to enjoyment. It is hoped that our demonstration of the ability of the public to take the role of the critic will encourage companies to be more venturesome.

The phenomenological approach to the study of entertainment reported here proved more promising than we had expected. This was due to a number of reasons, but first and foremost to the impressive way in which the viewers

took to the task. Their willingness and ability to rate programs on a wide range of attributes showed that although the industry tends to think in terms of genres, the public looks at each program in its own right and not merely as a member of a family of programs. Second, there was sufficient agreement as to the meaning of the attributes to be rated by viewers. The third reason lies in the fact that there was an underlying orderly pattern among the perceptions of attributes of programs linked to the viewers' enjoyment of them.

The study consisted of two parts, both necessary for the development of principles of entertainment. The first concentrated on the characteristics of the programs and the second on those characteristics of the viewer which might account for differences in reactions: attitude toward television generally, stylistic preferences, and the extent to which these relate to outlook and social characteristics on the one hand and to the manner in which a viewer responds to individual programs on the other. Whatever their education, viewers had clear stylistic preferences. These were not uniform. Some wanted programs which made a strong emotional impact, others avoided these. Some wanted the heroes and settings to be glamorous, others the opportunity to identify with real-life characters and situations. Some liked scary thrillers, others did not. Some wanted to let the story unfold, others preferred the unpredictable to the cut-and-dried. We showed that these preferences, in turn, related to the enjoyment of programs with matching attributes.

One finding in particular should give the industry cause for reflection. Within each educational level, the men and women who were the more forward-looking and more interested in understanding society, were the most critical of television. They viewed less, valued television less for themselves, and saw it as less enriching for others than those more willing to conform and to lead a quiet life.

The viewers' reactions suggest two avenues to successful entertainment: either through humor (as in the case of "Steptoe and Son," "Please Sir," and the "Morecambe and Wise Show"), or through stylistically "rich" programs which evoke a whole range of reactions. It is tempting to speculate that such results might explain why the American copies of two highly popular British programs fared so differently. "Sanford and Son" was highly successful, possibly because good jokes and repartee made their impact even without reproducing the complex relationship between father and son in the British prototype. In the case of the drama series "Beacon Hill" (to many a version of the British series "Upstairs, Downstairs"), the imitation failed, possibly because too little attention was paid to creating empathy for certain characters, concentrating instead on the trappings of wealth and on social class differences. The producers of "Beacon Hill" might have learned much about the ingredients necessary for producing a successful copy had they first studied in depth viewers' reactions to the highly popular prototype. Some of

the very popular police series, for example "Softly, Softly," had attribute profiles almost as varied as those of the special drama series. As the profiles become more barren, so enjoyment apparently decreases.

Our study suggests that the enjoyment of a program depends on the kind of arousal it evokes: at the first level, absence of, or release from, tension is enjoyable where it is funny, and boring, where it is trivial. At the stronger, second level, the arousal is associated with enjoyment when it is moving, absorbing and, exciting, but unpleasant when it is disturbing, brutal, and unpredictable. There is a level of intermediate arousal (both cognitive and emotional) where the disturbing and unpredictable are more acceptable, probably because they are informative and realistic. The relation of the rating of *disturbing* to enjoyment clearly shows that it is the "Gestalt" or mix of attributes which determines the impact of each.

A further test of the value of our approach came from the detailed study of one genre, and in particular, of a genre where one content character (in this case violence) featured prominently. Our fear that such a study would be meaningless because the rating of violence would be linked to enjoyment proved unfounded. In fact it was neither unduly emphasized nor discounted by those who felt differently about the effects of violence on television or about action series generally. Although the rating of violence was rather uniform across the sample, by choosing a range of action series differing in setting, mood, and amount of violence, we could examine to what extent the violence present related to enjoyment, and, furthermore, how much enjoyment would vary depending on the presence of other characteristics.

We found that violence contributed relatively little to enjoyment. Although it correlated 0.75 with brutal, it correlated very little with exciting, absorbing, or moving, the very attributes which relate closely to enjoyment of a program. In two of the American action series it added marginally to enjoyment, and detracted marginally from enjoyment in the case of the two British series. For the remaining seven action series it was largely irrelevant. The not uncommon view that audiences like action series because of their violence may well be one of the baseless folklores of the industry.

It is quite possible that violence matters so little just because the killings, beatings, car crashes, and broken bodies come to represent a ritual manner of providing links in an action series; a choreography of violence which because repeated so frequently no longer "disturbs." This was not true in all cases: it was related to disturbing where characters in a play came sufficiently to life for the viewers to empathize. "The News" rated the most violent program was also found to be very disturbing.

Our discussion here deals solely with viewers' reactions to violence in these series, not with the consequences of a continuous diet of violence. Just as one additional shot in a Western adds little to either excitement or impact, so here one more beating or one more killing may make little difference. That this is

so is an indictment both of the use of violence in the series, of the poverty of the story line, and of the flatness of the charcterizations. In some way, these findings should cause more concern than if we had found that violence had disturbed: violence ought to shock and disturb, especially in those series that emphasize the realism of plot and setting.

What, then, does the study suggest as possible strategies for making a series more popular? The producer of an "empty excitement" action series, in particular, faces a dilemma. Strong stimuli, such as strange happenings, violence, brutality, and bizarre characters, elicit less excitement over time. People can become habituated to beatings and car chases as they can to barbiturates. The producer might be tempted to increase the dosage and opt for even more violent happenings. Yet, not only is there social pressure to reduce violence, but it could also be self-defeating since habituation to the new level might soon set it.

Nor is extravaganza alone enough: a successful series tends to spawn many close copies. From the "Six Million Dollar Man" we move to the "Bionic Woman," from one beautiful "Policewoman" to three beautiful women investigators ("Charlie's Angels"), from exploits in outer space ("Star Trek") to those below sea level ("Man from Atlantis"). Endless expensive changes are rung around the same theme, but they are unlikely to be effective if characterization remains flat.

One solution is that adopted in "Kojak," where there is an almost caricaturing of the original idea with an overemphasis on one or more characteristics of the "hero" to a point where this becomes humorous or endearing. An alternative, also seen in "Kojak," is to make the policeman sensitive to motive and to act as a commentator on crimes. Through him the public may develop empathy, not for the crime, but for the social problems of the city that led to the crime. Here too there are dangers; the mixture between toughness, humor, and sensitivity as exemplified by the hero needs to be carefully varied or else "Kojak" becomes the "Ironside" of New York and thus becomes less popular (which may already be happening). Although there have been successful "exciting" series which are also humorous ("The Avengers"), the balance may be very difficult to strike. Humor is tension-releasing, whereas excitement depends on a buildup of tension. Another solution, to enlarge the roles of minor characters once the main one is no longer sufficient to carry the series, can also backfire. Diversification through introducing "stock" characters may increase interest in the short but not in the long run since it may reduce identification with the central character.

Where the series depends on continuity, using one investigator or a team as the link, the characters need to be readily recognizable from their mannerisms or their particular brand of investigating. Although we do not learn anything about the lives of the officers of the law, we learn much about their style (whether it is Kojak embracing the criminal when he apprehends him to

demonstrate that the criminal is in fact the victim of the social problems of the city or the terrier technique of Lieutenant Colombo). The writers face an almost impossible task. They are given insufficient time to sketch the solution of, and the motives for, the crime and the characters involved in it.

The findings of our study point to the need to involve viewers; this requires stylistic diversity rather than unidimensionality. The criteria for good television entertainment are the same as those for the theater and the novel: the ability to create characters with whom the viewer can identify and to whose reasoning and motives he can resonate, however fantastic the setting or plot. A good script is essential. The public is well able to distinguish between the work of a craftsman and mass-produced imitations.

Where competition is keenest and the stakes are high, the number of series continues to be high. This may well be one of the reasons for the growing disenchantment with television observed in the United States (Bower, 1973) and in Britain (British Broadcasting Corporation, 1974/1975). One would have to have a passion for sameness, amounting to mania if after six years of viewing "Coronation Street," or "Hawaii Five-O," one still looked forward eagerly to the next episode. Few people suffer from this form of mania, yet such shows continue to be popular enough to be extended.

Given the resources of the broadcasting industry, it seems a short-sighted policy not to experiment more with new types of programs. Also, one wonders whether sufficient "risk money" is deployed to ensure that a new generation of writers is given the opportunity to put on plays or for such plays to be tried out elsewhere. It is outside the scope of this chapter to examine under what conditions (i.e., under what structural arrangements) broadcasting will be particularly prone to play safe or to encourage new talent.

Arnold Goodman (1977), discussing financial support for the arts, points out that if you do not venture, "go over the edge, the risk will always be that you will remain too far from the edge." Both the American and the British broadcasting services may well be playing the game too safe. The study reported here shows that the public is more sophisticated than the broadcasters probably believe and might well be ready for departures from the well-trodden path.

This was an exploratory study. We should like to see such a study repeated, with different attributes drawn from viewers' own suggestions. Also, we should like the producers to rate the same programs to see whether there are consistent differences, and whether ratings by professionals are more uniform than those of the laymen. This method is also very suitable for testing the correctness of the producers' images of the public. A set of producers might be asked to rate the programs not as they themselves would rate them, but to predict the ratings of audiences from different educational backgrounds.

   In this study we concentrated mainly on long-run series and on one particular genre; a similar exercise, using suitable attributes, could be undertaken for other types of programs (e.g., comedy series or variety shows). One could also carry out a comparative study of children's programs using children of different ages to act as raters. Earlier we discussed test results that showed that the least enjoyed series are the ones which continue the longest. Periodic ratings of the series at yearly intervals might assist management to decide whether to continue a series or allow it to die.

   Goffman's (1974) frame analysis stresses the way each individual encapsulates his experiences; here we looked for dimensions shared across the sample of viewers to explain different reactions to television programs. Like Goffman we used the viewers' experiences as data and later, with the help of multidimensional scaling, brought out shared characteristics or dimensions. A similar approach could be used to study other forms of entertainment, such as films or plays.

APPENDIX A

Attitudes to TV

	Agree (%)	Uncertain (%)	Disagree (%)
A1. Concern About TV Violence			
In general there is too much violence on TV.	44	19	37
If there were less violence on TV, there would be less violence in the world.	23	24	52
Leave things as they are: There is a lot of fuss about nothing (against cutting violence now).	35	28	37
Far from making people more aggressive, violent TV programs act as a "safety valve" for people's feelings.[a]	21	40	39
TV plants the seeds of delinquency in a child's mind.	17	27	56
People overestimate how much children are upset by what they see on TV.[a]	50	22	28
A2. Bias or Neutrality of TV News and Documentaries			
TV news tends to pick on isolated scuffles at demonstrations and blow them up out of proportion.	53	18	29
TV news tends to exaggerate the amount of conflict there is in the world today.	30	13	57
There's too much misery thrust at you on TV these days.	30	20	50
Television tends to "bend over backwards" to colored[b] people and other minority groups.	45	27	28
Television does not present an accurate picture of working-class life.	45	25	30
A3. TV Enriches			
News and current-affairs programs give you a real insight into the problems of society.	82	10	8
Through TV I've increased my range of interests.	73	10	17
Some of the characters on TV seem like real friends to me.	62	13	25

[a]Replies to these items have been reversed in the computation of further scores.
[b]The term 'colored' in Britain covers West Indians, Pakistanis, Indians as well as Africans.

Effects on Country If TV Were to Stop

	Definitely/ Possibly (%)	No Effect (%)	Possibly/ Definitely (%)	
EC1. Effects on People's Well-being				
Family life would be better.	60	20	20	Family life would not be as good.
People would be more content.	24	39	37	People would be less content.
EC2. Effects on Interest in Cultural and Social Matters				
People would work more.	53	42	5	People would work less.
People would take more interest in the arts.	50	30	20	People would take less interest in the arts.
People would be more interested in educating themselves.	51	27	22	People would be less interested in educating themselves.
People would take more interest in community activities.	80	16	4	People would take less interest in community activities.

(continued)

Effects on Country If TV Were to Stop

EC3. Effects on Social Stability or Unrest

Juvenile delinquency would increase.	24	50	26	Juvenile delinquency would decrease.
There would be more violent crime.	12	58	27	There would be less violent crime.
There would be more industrial unrest.	9	71	20	There would be less industrial unrest.
People would think more about sex.	27	49	24	People would think less about sex.
Demonstrations would be less peaceful.[a]	9	57	34	Demonstrations would be more peaceful.

EC4. Effects on Social Conscience

People would be more understanding of other people's problems.	22	36	42	People would be less understanding of other people's problems.
People would take more interest in the disabled and others in need.	27	44	29	People would take less interest in the disabled and others in need.
People would be less class-conscious.	17	64	19	People would be more class-conscious.

[a]On the questionnaire itself, the bipolar statement has been reversed.

Effects on Self If TV Were to Stop

I would:	Definitely/ Possibly (%)	No Effect (%)	Possibly/ Definitely (%)	I would:
ES1. Effects on Mood				
feel at a loose end.	53	20	26	welcome having more free time.
feel a real sense of loss.	60	24	16	feel I had gained something.
find it harder to relax in the evening.	52	33	15	find it easier to relax in the evening.
ES2. Effects on Activity in and Outside the Home				
go out more.	57	41	2	go out less.
do more around the house.	62	35	3	do less around the house.
spend more time talking to my family.	63	35	2	spend less time talking to my family.
ES3. Effects on Knowledge and Thought				
have a more accurate picture of the world.	9	25	76	have a less accurate picture of the world.
have more to think about.	34	33	34	have less to think about.

APPENDIX B

Stylistic Preferences

	Close to My View (%)	Both Equally Close/ Undecided (%)	Close to My View (%)	
S1. Approach to or Avoidance of Potentially Upsetting Stimuli				
I can "enjoy" a joke that is a bit "off color."	69	17	14	I never enjoy jokes that are a bit "off color."
I prefer plays about strong passions between the sexes.	25	43	32	I prefer plays that stress the romantic side of love.
I prefer programs that are "real" even if good doesn't always triumph.[a]	60	20	20	I prefer programs where everything comes out well in the end.
I prefer humor that is a bit "off-beat."[a]	56	22	22	I prefer humor that is straightforward.
I can "enjoy" a story with a really sad ending.	56	20	24	A sad ending just makes me feel miserable.

S2. Aloofness or Involvement in Programs

I seldom find myself thinking about a program once it's finished.	65	15	20	I very often find myself thinking about a program once it's finished.
I prefer programs that appeal to my head.	37	36	27	I prefer programs that appeal to my heart.
People in TV series usually seem like actors playing a part.	22	22	56	People in TV series often seem like real people to me.
I prefer series (a complete story each week).	18	29	63	I prefer serials (story continuing from week to week).
In selecting a program I look first at what it's about.	66	15	19	In selecting a program I look first at who's in it.

S3. Preference for Low/High Cognitive Effort

I prefer programs you can understand without too much effort.[a]	34	24	42	I prefer programs that you have got to make a real effort to understand.
I prefer programs that are quite clear-cut in their meaning.	61	18	21	I prefer programs whose meaning is not so cut-and-dried.

(continued)

Stylistic Preferences

S4. Preference for Real/Realistic Vs. Fantasy/Escapist Content and Presentation

I prefer heroes who are down to earth.	61	25	14	I prefer heroes who are larger than life.
I prefer programs where the characters are like people I know.	36	41	23	I prefer programs where the characters are quite unlike the people I know.
I prefer programs that tell me about the world and its problems.	54	24	22	I prefer programs that help me forget the world and its problems.
I prefer programs set in everyday surroundings.	26	42	32	I prefer programs set in glamorous surroundings.
I would like more programs dealing with the kind of problems I face.	41	48	11	If anything there are too many programs dealing with the problems I face.

S5. Liking for Thriller/Action Content

I prefer programs where you are kept guessing from moment to moment.[a]	3	21	77	I prefer programs where you know what to expect.
I prefer thrillers that really scare me.	48	20	32	I prefer mild thrillers.
What makes a plot interesting is the action.	40	30	30	What makes a plot interesting is the people.

[a] On the questionnaire itself, the bipolar statement has been reversed.

ACKNOWLEDGMENTS

The authors are indebted to the Markle Foundation and the Television Research Committee for financial support and to Dr. Patrick Humphreys for his statistical advice. The authors are very grateful to Brian Emmet and David Newell of the BBC Audience Research Department for permission to use the BBC viewing panel as subjects, for printing and distributing the questionnaires, and for their assistance at many stages of the study.

REFERENCES

Berlyne, D. E., & Ogilvie, J. G. Dimensions of perception of paintings. In D. E. Berlyne (Ed.), *Studies in the new experimental aesthetics.* New York: Wiley, 1974.

Bower, R. T. *Television and the public.* New York: Holt, Rinehart & Winston, 1973.

Brigham, J. C., & Giesbrecht, L. W. All in the Family: Racial attitudes. *Journal of Communication,* Autumn 1976, 26.

British Broadcasting Corporation. Audience Research Department. *Violence on television: Programme content and viewer perception.* London: BBC Publications, 1972.

British Broadcasting Corporation. Audience Research Department. *BBC Audience Research Findings Annual Review,* London: BBC Publications, 1974/1975.

Gerbner, G. Mass media and human communication theory. In D. McQuail (Ed.), *Sociology of mass communications: Selected readings.* London: Penguin, 1972.

Gerbner, G., Gross, L., Eleey, M. F., Jackson-Beek, M., Jeffries-Fox, S., & Signorielli, N. Violence Profile No. 8: The highlights. *Journal of Communication,* 1977, *27,* 171–180.

Goffman, E. *Frame analysis: An essay on the organization of experience.* Cambridge, Mass.: Harvard University Press, 1974.

Goodhardt, G. J., Ehrenberg, A. S. C., & Collins, M. A. *The television audience: Patterns of viewing.* London: Saxon House, 1975.

Goodman, A. State subsidy and artistic freedom. In *A symposium on culture and society. Great ideas of today.* Encyclopaedia Britannica, Inc., 1977.

Green, P. E., & Carmone, F. J. *Multidimensional scaling and related techniques in marketing analysis.* Boston: Allyn & Bacon, 1972.

Greenberg, B. S., & Gordon, T. F. Perceptions of violence in television programmes: Critics and the public. In G. A. Comstock & E. A. Rubinstein (Eds.), *Television and social behavior. Vol. I: Media content and control.* Washington, D. C.: U.S. Government Printing Office, 1972.

Hare, F. G. Dimensions of music perception. *Scientific Aesthetics,* in press.

Herzog, H. *What do we really know about daytime serial listeners?* In P. F. Lazarsfeld & F. N. Stanton (Eds.), *Radio research 1942–1943.* New York: Duell, Sloan & Pearce, 1944.

Himmelweit, H. T., & Swift, B. Continuity and discontinuity in media usage and taste: A longitudinal study. *Journal of Social Issues,* 1976, *32,* 133–156.

Katz, E., & Gurevitch, M. *The secularization of leisure: Culture and communication in Israel.* London: Faber & Faber, 1976.

Lefkowitz, M. M., Eron, L. D., Walder, L. O., & Rowell Huesman, L. Television violence and child aggression: A follow-up study. In *Television and Social Behavior. Vol. III: Report to the Surgeon General.* New York: Department of Health, Education and Welfare, 1972.

Tannenbaum, P. H., & Zillmann, D. Emotional arousal in the facilitation of aggression through communication. In L. Berkowitz (Ed.), *Advances in experimental social psychology.* New York: Academic Press, 1974.

Vidmar, N., & Rokeach, M. Archie Bunker's bigotry: A study in selective perception and exposure. *Journal of Communication,* 1974, *1*(24), 36–47.

Wheldon, Sir H. British experiences in television. *Dimbleby Lecture,* 1975.

5 Entertainment as Vicarious Emotional Experience

Percy H. Tannenbaum
University of California, Berkeley

Most people alive today (at least in the industrialized countries, if not quite universally) have spent a good deal of the waking, nonworking hours—that is to say, their leisure time—receiving mediated communications messages. I refer not only to the so-called "television generation" (i.e., roughly those born post-World War II) but also to the current middle-aged and elderly generations. The growth of available leisure time in the twentieth century was matched by a rapid growth in literacy and education and a more ready availability of printed matter, not to mention the later technological marvels of radio, motion pictures, and then television. In ever-increasing numbers— and apparently also for increasing proportions of the daily hours—people read, listened, watched, sometimes all at once.

It is not an idle intellectual activity to speculate on the reasons for such growth in popularity and use of the mass media, culminating in the present preoccupation with the average use of TV for more than four hours daily in the average U.S. home. Part of the explanation may lie in the changing work pattern. In a real sense, more leisure meant more hours to be filled with some activity, and the media, by their sheer accessibility and inexpensiveness, were ready, nontaxing (else, of what value leisure?) candidates for the role. In addition, the mere dynamics of the situation was also a factor: Supply can create a demand. As more materials become available, especially novel ones presented in novel ways, a greater consumption followed.

But the demand side of the equation must be satisfied as well for an acceptable explanation. Surely, the avid, expanding consumption of media products must do some things for the recipient for it to be maintained at such a level. It is the thesis of this chapter that while part of this activity meets

obviously informational, even life-sustaining needs, a good deal has the perhaps less "important" but no less functional role of adding some spice, some of "life's minor pleasures," to that existence. This is certainly not a novel formulation but it bears repeating, especially in the present context.

SOME PERSONAL PERSPECTIVES

I first address this thesis from several different lines of approach that have guided my work in this aspect of communication behavior in recent years. These somewhat random speculations have led to a set of propositions—not related systematically enough to justify the label of a theory—for research and application that has occupied me for more than a decade, and which I briefly report on subsequently. They represent only one man's views, of course, but it is hoped that the limitations of subjectivity are somewhat offset by the intimacy of detail.

A Retrospective View

I happen to be of that middle-aged group who grew up in the prewar days without television. Looking back with the advantages of hindsight I now feel fortunate that my early media experience was mainly through books. This is not to belittle what TV can and possibly does achieve for contemporary children, but merely to point out that once I learned to read, it turned into an exciting experience that I regarded with awe and wonder even then. With the guidance of a stern but devoted local librarian who took her position and responsibility seriously, I was able to enter a vast new world I had no other way of reaching. Some of it was the world of experience but a good deal of it was that of imagination.

The Yiddish writer, Isaac Bashevis Singer, recently commented on this stage of development, in his remarks on accepting the 1978 Nobel Prize for Literature. Among other things, he said he prefers to write for children because they like a good story, accept the use of imps, demons, and heroes equally because they contribute to the story, do not look for redeeming social significance, and probably would not recognize it if it were there.

I became a voracious reader of both fiction and nonfiction, tending to prefer the former as I too reveled in the sheer story-telling. I readily learned, as noted earlier, to suspend reality and participate vicariously, delighting in being able to "transport" myself to other realms, to accomplish wonderful feats of physical and mental daring. It does not require a deep psychoanalytic conceptualization to determine that a goodly part of my motivation was pure escapism. I think it is important to recognize, however, that there exists not only the impetus to escape from one's own limited environment but also to

escape to new worlds, new situations, new companions, new dilemmas, new adventures, even if—indeed, probably because—it is all fantasy.

Such reading activity was matched, on a more selective basis, by the availability of radio. There were certain programs (e.g., weekly opera broadcasts) I was forced to listen to because the were "good" for me. Favorites I followed week to week, even in day-to-day serialized formats, as plots unfolded and favorite characters coped with perilous problems, with me seemingly right alongside them. Radio did not diminish my reading activity, and probably abetted it. Together they stimulated imagination, even at the risk of being misled by accepting the world of fiction as reality. This concern, so much in vogue today, is not new of course and was in fact a source of some consternation then. But the perceived benefits of reading and radio listening were generally regarded as outweighing the risks. Fortunately for me, there was relatively little learned social science research available in those days to convince my parents or well-meaning officials otherwise. It would have denied me many precious hours of simple pleasure and food for thought and fantasy.

Television was not available then but motion pictures were—except not to children below the age of 16. The alleged excuse was that theaters were fire traps, but it was mostly that the authorities (particularly the religious ones) thought films would be bad for our morals. This naturally gave rise to the familiar "forbidden fruit" phenomenon: Largely because it was denied us, we spent an inordinate amount of time and effort finding ways around the obstacles and, on the few occasions when we were successful, the resulting experience was regarded as all the more rewarding. These early exposures to film were relatively sparse and limited, but once films became more accessible I was converted into a "movie freak," a condition that persists to this day. I am not certain, but I think a major part of the enjoyment of cinema (perhaps of the live theater too) is the darkened setting, where one can be less public with thoughts and emotions, can laugh or cry, feel sad or elated, sense danger or relief, in relative privacy.

This not atypical experience suggests to me that such media behavior must have intrinsic rewards—not only for some possible later purpose but for here and now, in and of itself. All too often learned treatises about media behavior do not give enough credit to this obvious fact—that it is a desirable activity in terms of its immediate rewards—and in fact they often deplore it. Can anything that is so sought after repeatedly, for its own sake and not necessarily in the service of some other worthwhile cause, be all good?

It seems obvious that the reward we get from such fictional materials is largely emotional in character, that is, it involves undergoing various emotional states, albeit at a removed, vicarious level. The reverse reasoning is probably more true: Emotional behavior plays a significant part in our lives and provides a major source of motivation for much of our communication

behavior. This suggests that the attempt to satisfy such desires on a widespread (and, hence, possibly a diluted, shallow) basis is why so much of our popular media content is geared to entertainment, and why such emotionally arousing TV-entertainment programs are consistently and repeatedly among the most popular in different countries.

An Evolutionary Perspective

Switching from such a subjective, ontogenetic approach, it is possible to reach a similar set of conclusions using an approach based on phylogeny (if also a somewhat subjective view). From a survival standpoint, it can be argued that the human species has certain built in disadvantages. Its members enter this world apparently stripped of many of the inherent, autonomous mechanisms—"instincts," if you will—that allow other species to survive with little choice and effort. They are also born "prematurely" in the sense that they are ill-equipped to cope for themselves at birth and have to spend a substantial, possibly inordinate proportion of their life span developing and learning to survive on their own.

The species' evolutionary advantages are its intellect and capacity to convert incoming data to information and to process that information into knowledge. Along with other related attributes, the ability to receive, process, store, and retrieve information and sort it into meaningful relationships provides man with the capacity to learn to adopt and adapt (i.e., with the means of survival). Of critical importance is the fact that not only can he learn by direct, proximal, trial-and-error experience but also through indirect, remote—in place and/or time—already tested, vicarious experience. To use Bandura's (1965) cogent phrase, the latter represents a true case of "no trial learning" and operates by virtue of our capacity to communicate.

But man does not live by intellect alone, but with emotion and feeling. Whether or not we have emotional "needs," as such, the fact remains that we have emotional wants and that we are quite willing, often at great sacrifice of time, energy, and money, to pursue these desires. Again, these are met both by proximal and distal experiences. Just as a communication capacity allows us to learn vicariously, so too can we become emotionally involved vicariously. One of the powerful attractions of the mass media, more specifically of television, is that they can provide so many with so much emotional experience at so little personal cost.

To be sure, indirect vicarious experience is not the "real thing." It can compensate for, possibly substitute for, but cannot always totally replace both direct intellectual and emotional experience. Certain skills (e.g., learning to ride a bicycle or to swim) can apparently only be acquired by experience (as well as with information). On the emotional level, purely vicarious experience can pack all the thrill of kissing someone over the telephone, although there is

abundant evidence that books, films, music, etc. can make people cry and laugh, feel elation and despair, love and hate with intensity.

One important advantage of vicarious experience is its relative safety over real practice, which can often involve elements of direct threat and danger to the individual. This difference was neatly summed up in a taunting expression of my youth. "Sticks and stones can break my bones but names will never harm me." By the same token, threatening situations depicted in book, film, or TV fiction can be very involving emotionally but their intrinsically dangerous elements can be considerably muted by the simple realization that it is "only a story." This condition, also developed in Dolf Zillmann's subsequent chapter, can readily place the viewer into a situation of having his cake and eating it too: he can undergo the excitation of the threat and suspense without actually facing the danger. He can invest of himself emotionally while suspending reality, but by merely switching the reality as circumstances warrant, he can actually have "the best of both worlds."

A Precipitating Event

That one may not always be so able to retrieve reality in a fiction situation was brought home to me most vividly when I attended Expo '67 in Montreal, Canada. I had been a film aficionado (i.e., a fan but not a connoisseur) for many years by then, but I was unprepared for the myriad of inventive uses of the medium shown there. The simultaneous projection of sequential and otherwise related events on several different screens, the blending of film with live theater, attempts at audience participation by having it select story developments at critical plot junctures, etc., truly boggled the mind.

One film—oddly enough, a rather banal one in terms of pure content—really stimulated me. This was a Disney Studio production, a Canadian travelogue of sorts, in which nine cameras mounted in a circular arrangement were used to film the scenes which were then projected on nine screens in a similar circular arrangement. The audience, some 300 at a time, stood in the middle of a large hall with the screens all around it.

The opening scene set the stage for me when I first viewed the production. It featured a parade of Royal Canadian Mounted Police atop their horses—cantering Mounties in front, back, and to either side of you. It was difficult to avoid the impression that you were in the very middle of the parade on your own horse, bouncing along with the rest of them.

However, the crucial scene for me featured a car chase down a busy city street with the cameras mounted on the second car, depicting the action as you would see it if you were actually riding in the car. The film shows the first automobile making a sharp turn at high speed and, seconds later, the car in which you seem to be riding goes into the same sharp turn, tires screeching and car tilting precariously. All 300 people, myself very much included, issued

an involuntary screech at this point, and I sensed a distinctly uncomfortable feeling in the pit of my stomach—literally, a gut response.

When the film was over some minutes later, the memory of these events and of my uncontrolled reaction lingered on and bothered me. I was annoyed that I had so readily succumbed to a film's obvious manipulations. After all, if I knew it was a film, that I was not actually in the car, why did I react as I did?

Determined not to be seduced again, I stayed on for the next showing. Now forewarned, I was presumably forearmed to avoid screaming out. As the car went into the slanting turn, 299 unknowing souls did scream while I in fact did not. But I was still very much bothered: Although I could control the overt response, I had the same sickening visceral feeling in the stomach. Being a dedicated researcher (not to say a glutton for punishment) I stayed on for six more showings of the same film, waiting for the critical moment to see if I could fully control the gut response but never fully succeeding, although the effect did diminish somewhat with time.

An unsettling personal experience, this proved to be a stimulating one professionally. In part I was curious: Was this a special, possibly unique event, or was the fact that awareness was an inadequate defense against visceral side effects a more generalizable phenomenon?[1] The experience also made me particularly sensitive to the physiological component of vicarious emotional experience. Within a year, I was getting acquainted with psychophysiological measurement techniques, checking through equipment manuals and negotiating to install a laboratory. I wish somebody had warned me about what I was getting into.

A TV-Medium Perspective

While I am on the subject of physiological reactions, with or without awareness, permit me another personal confession. Among life's more embarrassing moments have been countless occasions when I am engaged in conversation in a room while a TV set is on, and I cannot for the life of me stop from periodically glancing over to the screen. This occurs not only during dull conversations but during reasonably interesting ones just as well. Judging from the behavior of the people with whom I was talking at the time and from reports of friends and colleagues, I am far from alone in this behavior and its accompanying chagrin.

---

[1]One answer is apparently that the sense of loss of balance—balance control being located in the inner ear—is particularly susceptible to such manipulation, although there are probably other such behavior phenomena which are equally vulnerable. It is nevertheless particularly impressive that the visual cues, along with supporting auditory ones, were so powerful as to overcome the veto power to full awareness. It is probably one of our built in adaptive reactions that we carry with us from birth, as if the body does not allow for the possibility of a mistake.

What explains it? Are we all so conditioned to the tube that we literally cannot take our eyes off it for very long? Is it the screen, or what is being shown thereon? I have yet to come across a convincing explanation of this phenomenon.

One promising suggestion some colleagues and I have entertained is that it is the flicker pattern—the alternating bursts of light and darkness that make up the TV picture—that is responsible. There are other such phenomena to which we seem strangely attracted: The play of light on moving waters or the flames in a fireplace appear to have a similar mesmerizing effect. One element these have in common is the flickering of the image: rapid internal change within a constant overall perceptual pattern, which can be physiologically arousing in and of itself. This is only a hypothesis on which we have no confirming data, but it seems an attractive enough idea worth pursuing.

If true it suggests some intrinsic appeal to the TV medium per se quite apart from the content. On a more general level, this distinction has been a somewhat bedeviling issue which our linguistic conventions serve to obscure. Most often when we speak of the "effects of television" we are referring to aspects of the portrayed content rather than to the nature of the image on the screen. This is particularly true of those critics of television who hold the medium at least partially accountable for a number of personal and social ills (e.g., attributing increased social aggression or fear of one's immediate environment to the frequency of violent content on TV; attributing improper social models of women and minority groups to the way they are depicted in programing; etc.).

These are, of course, real enough concerns that merit attention. At the same time, however, it would be useful to investigate the influence of the *medium qua medium*. Better still, the relationship between the two—combinations of depicting certain materials in the different ways the medium allows and makes possible—seems a most promising locus for research.

Perhaps an illustration will help clarify the point I am advocating here. In my judgment, the power of TV is best realized at present in its depiction of live sporting events. TV not only gives you the best seat in the house right on the 50-yard line, but—far better than actually being in a fixed location in the stands—it can provide you with the multiple perspectives of several different cameras in different locations.

Of even greater impact are the wonders introduced by TV technology. One such development is the zoom lens which allows for a close-up perspective from a distance, singling out one aspect of a game for particular attention. How nice it would have been if nature had endowed us with such a device, even for just one eye! As if that were not enough, current TV technology even allows those of us with feeble immediate memories to recapture a just-happened event with the instant replay. Add to that doing it in slow-motion,

often shown from several perspectives, and the medium puts human perceptual capacity to shame.

What is surprising is how infrequently these or other such techniques are applied to nonsports content. It is quite possible that these distinctive tools of the TV trade lend themselves uniquely to action sports where perception of movement and countermovement are so critical for appreciation. If so, they should apply to other movement-related activities such as dance (and in fact they are sometimes employed in modern dance and ballet presentations but only occasionally).[2] Could such techniques be effectively employed with other content, for example, drama? In part these are questions of the art of the TV medium, perhaps best left for the producers to judge their suitability. But they are also empirical, if not theoretical, questions of concern to the researchers.

A TV-Industry Perspective

In recommending more study of the medium, I refer not only to TV in the sense of the electronic image but also in terms of the TV industry of large-scale, profit-oriented competitive organizations (at least in the United States) operating under relatively loose government regulation. Such an extension in range of coverage obviously introduces many complicating elements but is necessary if one is concerned with investigating the medium as it actually operates—and as it can operate—rather than in some abstract representation.

This added perspective brings us close to the realm of communication policy, another focus much in vogue today, but one which cannot be accorded its full and proper treatment in the present context. However, several characteristics of the structure and function of the medium do deserve mention in relation to the medium's entertainment functions:

1. The fundamental virtue—and problem—of television and the other mass media is their capacity to deliver uniform messages to vast but heterogeneous publics. This, along with their basis in advertising as their main economic support in this country, dictate the pursuit of large audiences for the same kinds of programs; hence a preoccupation with the so-called

---

[2]The juxtaposition of art and technology may introduce an incompatibility of form and presentation as seen by the different parties. I have in mind an episode in which a film maker actually shot a pas de deux in slow-motion and then spent a number of years trying to find a suitable piece of music (obviously the original would not do) to match the new dance. Finally successful in this quest, he arranged a showing which included the performing dancers and several of their colleagues, all of whom castigated the film maker for making mockery of their art. A given dance, they claimed, was made to "go with," even to interpret, a particular piece of music, and by altering the music in the final product he was demeaning and contaminating their original dance. He thought he was making a film, using the medium to give another perspective to his subject; to the performers it was a dance to be shown on film.

"lowest common denominator" approach to broadcasting. Perhaps the most common of the denominators in our type of pluralistic society is popular entertainment, and it is no accident that TV features so much low-grade, repetitive entertainment fare over so much of its schedule. The industry is adept at producing it relatively inexpensively, many individuals can tolerate, accept, and understand it, and the medium lends itself readily to its widespread dissemination.

2. The competitive nature of the industry, among other considerations, makes program popularity, as indexed by ratings, a governing criterion for program selection. (Interestingly, there is as much of a preoccupation with ratings in countries without TV advertising.) Although program selection is made by vested authorities—either professionals, designated centralized officials, or business executives, depending on the country and system—the audience's past and anticipated record of selection plays a significant role.[3]

What the audience does prefer from among what is available is possible to discern from ratings. What it will like in the future is a matter of guesswork, if not divine revelation. Uncertainty, competition, and reliable production capability all too readily make for a decision situation where the past is the best model for the future. The same plot lines, presentation formats, characterizations, and production gimmicks, all tend to be repeated until somebody produces something different. If this turns out to be successful (more often it does not), the innovation too gets to be limited and repeated. Adding to this pattern of redundancy is the tendency toward spin-off shows (programs developing out of secondary characters in successful shows).

If this scenario is anything close to the truth, it is again no surprise that current TV fare is so geared to common entertainment fare presented in conventionalized formats. For American programs especially, the economics of the situation are such that initial showings may recoup production expenses, but the real profit comes from reruns and foreign sales. It is to be expected, then, that such extended audiences will feature heavily in calculating the chances for a new program.

3. There is little objection to popular entertainment as such among TV's critics, except that its overwhelming presence tends to drive out quality programming. In addition, there is considerable concern and controversy outside and inside broadcasting organizations in different countries

---

[3]It is important to distinguish individual or household TV-viewing behavior (as indexed by automatic recorders on the TV set) from the more commonly employed aggregate compilations. Applied to a weekly series, for example, the former often reveal a glass half-full/half-empty phenomenon: only 50% or so of one week's audience tunes in the same series the following week, the remaining half participating in other activities or watching a different TV program. The remarkable sociopsychological fact is that the overall audience for the series stays about the same in terms of size and demographic composition. One set of incoming viewers substitutes for the departing set: they are the same type of person but not the same individual.

regarding possible negative effects of the latent influences of TV fiction. There are a number of grounds for such concern, and various theoretical models exist that attempt to explain such influences (see Withey & Abeles, 1980, among others).

One formulation that invites more systematic investigation suggests that just because fiction programs are entertaining, the viewer is preoccupied and distracted and hence is more vulnerable to be influenced by the "message" implicit in the program content. An opposite conceputalization would hold that the viewer clearly recognizes the difference between fact and fiction, takes each for what it is, and does not confuse the issue. The evidence in favor of one or the other formulation is hardly convincing or decisive, so we can expect the controversy to continue unabated. The coupling of a significant social policy issue with one or more intriguing theoretical models involving entertainment on TV makes the prospect of research in this area even more alluring.

GENESIS OF A THEORETICAL MODEL

From the preceding set of facts and speculations, it is possible to derive the beginnings of a theory of TV entertainment. At this stage, I regard it as premature to develop a formal theory. It is sufficient for our purposes here to suggest a set of related propositions that can serve to generate a research agenda:

1. A link has been established between television, entertainment, and the evocation of emotional experiences. Entertainment is the stuff of which much of TV is composed and forms a substantial basis of its appeal. It serves its audience in various ways—by providing escapism, amusement, fantasy, and diversion—all of which has a common element of some sort of emotional arousal.

2. Most of the time for most people the arousal produced by TV entertainment is of a low-level or modest dosage (enough to titillate without really exciting), but under most everyday circumstances such "mild emotional jogs" have positive valence in and of themselves. Moreover, in comparison with other forms of entertainment, TV is reliable, readily at hand, and requires little in the way of effort or expenditure. Thus, its reward/effort quotient or benefit/cost ratio, although not very high, is more favorable than other means of amusement and diversion.

3. Current psychological theory concerning the nature of emotional experience is far from established, but it seems most sensible to begin with the two-component, two-stage model suggested by Schachter (1964) and others.

An incoming stimulus initially triggers a set of physiological responses, probably all mediated by an initial release of adrenalin. It is assumed most such responses are acquired in the course of experience (probably originally associated with simple hedonistic types of behavior), but there is a likelihood that some are innate. An individual so aroused is presumed to be somewhat aware of the internal physiological changes, even if unable to assess them in detail. Being alert to such modifications in physiological equilibrium, the person then seeks to find an appropriate explanation, something to which to attribute the arousal. This second stage, then, is a cognitive activity, one of identifying the cause and labeling the felt state in some reasonable manner. It is as if the subject asks, "Why am I excited?" and then scans the environment to find a likely cause.

4. What is particularly important in such a model is that once a given state of physiological arousal is labeled, the individual then behaves in accord with the attributed cause. It may be in fact the real one, but often, as in studies where the arousal is induced surreptitiously through drugs, it may be a misattributed one. In this manner, the model posits a generalized physiological arousal state rather than linking specific emotional states with specific causes, and it does not link the actual cause with any subsequent behavioral effect. The content and format of communication messages can serve to induce the generalized physiological excitation and can provide cues—sometimes the true ones but often "misleading" ones—for interpretation by the individual.

5. Of additional significance is the suggestion that when an individual is in a state of heightened arousal and is called upon to perform in a certain manner, the individual will do so more readily and with more intensity. The important point here is that the person responds more intensely because of the state of emotional arousal, independent of the actual reasons for that arousal and the actual behavior the person is called on to perform.

6. The above somewhat primitive model focusing on arousal per se induced by the communication can be further refined by including cognitive attributes of the situation. The essential notion here is that the excitation guaranteed by one source—here, exciting episodes in TV-entertainment programs—can be transferred and then "mis-attributed" to any likely source (e.g., somebody who had previously provoked the subject). In this sense, we can speak of an "emotional transfer": Communication-induced arousal can come to be employed in the service of some other cause.

A Note on Methodology

In assessing the effects of entertainment we are thus concerned with an assortment of responses. Methodological problems abound here as they do in any social science area. For example, one reason the controversy about the

effects of televised aggression persists is that we lack the appropriate means of determining cause–effect relationships with the requisite degree of certainty (although one must say that does not seem to deter investigators from applying the same inadequate measures repeatedly).

Equally serious is the absence of convincing, reliable measures of the kinds of effects we wish to assess. Again, the case of aggression provides a useful example: Ruling out opportunities to provoke direct measures of violent behavior for obvious reasons, we are forced to resort to indirect indices (e.g., simulated electric shocks ostensibly to provide negative feedback in a learning situation, teacher and peer reports of student hostility, etc.). The same inadequacy holds for other response areas, such as humor or fright.

There are two additional measurement problems that, although not restricted to the field of TV entertainment, are apt to arise in such research with some frequency. These are psychophysiological assessments and the measurement of preferences, and it would be well to consider these briefly before proceeding to the actual research applications.

Physiological Measures. Since the model ascribes a significant role to degree of emotional arousal as both an effect of entertainment and a mediator of subsequent behavior, there will be many occasions where one would want an accurate assessment. Although there is a fairly well-developed instrumentation and technology for determining various psychophysiological parameters, the neophyte to the area would be well advised to think twice before venturing into it. The equipment is not inexpensive, it has to be mastered, and the obtained data, usually in analogue form, has to be converted to the digital for processing. There is also the issue of which parameters to use, more than slightly complicated by considerable individual differences in locus of arousal. Additional difficulties result from the fact that applying the actual measurement procedure while the subject is being exposed to a TV program may interfere with both the viewing and the measurements. This fact that subjects vary considerably from one another and have to be tested individually, or at best in small groups, suggests the use of repeated measure designs in which each subject can be his own control and experiments with relatively small numbers of subjects.

Preferential Measures. There are many occasions when the investigator will want to compare choices between programs or between different versions of the same program. Questionnaires and comparative ratings are adequate for some purposes, but are not fully satisfactory; as one who is never certain of his own actual choices, I tend to distrust others' expressed preferences and would rather have them revealed in more behaviorally operational measures. Giving people actual choices and seeing what they do watch appears to be a more reliable index.

I have recently attempted to measure preferences by determining how much energy subjects are willing to expend for different programs or program segments. The basic instrument is an exercycle which has to be pedaled at a (variable) preset rate, below which picture and/or sound will become difficult to perceive.[4] We have found that individuals will pedal harder and longer for some materials than for others and will generally stay with the task for the length of a given segment.

A chance happening in the laboratory suggested another useful index. One day in the middle of viewing a detective drama, the apparatus broke down. Subjects were asked to wait if they liked (they were free to leave at any time of course) until a repair technician could be located. When quite a few people chose to wait up to two hours to see the ending of the program we felt we could use waiting time as another index of interest. We now stage breakdowns at preselected points in a program and determine the waiting time from that point.

SOME RESEARCH APPLICATIONS

Over the past decade or so, I and a number of students and colleagues have undertaken a series of experiments testing implications of the theoretical model (presented above in bare outline form) in a number of communication contexts. In its earlier stages, the theory sought to address questions of television violence but rapidly spread to other areas of entertainment.

Violence. There is a considerable number of experiments in the literature reporting on a greater tendency toward aggressive behavior following exposure to film or TV violence. Most investigators and commentators attribute such results to the aggressive content of the message. This is a plausible enough assumption if one invokes a so-called "modeling" type of theory (i.e., the observer tends to emulate the depicted behavior), but becomes less convincing when the postexposure behavior (e.g., the supposed delivery of electric shocks to another subject) is quite different in kind from the portrayed violence (a prizefight scene).

---

[4]Again, a personal experience stimulated the use of such a device. Some years ago, I acquired an exercycle which I positioned in my study facing a blank wall. After reaching a standard operating level of pedaling for a half-hour or so a day, I found it a most boring task and tried to relieve the monotony somewhat by imagining I was riding along a sylvan lane through a forest instead of staring at a blank wall. Fearful that such illusions might become hallucinatory, I hit on another solution: I placed the bike before the TV set and pedaled merrily away while watching the national TV news (but I failed to analyze whether my activity ebbed and flowed with the nature of the news). From there it was an easy transition to the laboratory.

Applied to this situation, the emotional arousal theory, at least in the primitive form presented earlier, does not invoke the specific nature of the content. Instead, it concentrates on the arousal produced by that, or any other, content. It merely suggests that the person, once aroused, will behave with more intensity, no matter what type of response he is called on to make. For example, if one pitted a more arousing (as measured physiologically) but less aggressive (in terms of content) film against a less arousing but more aggressive film, the arousal theory would predict the first stimulus to produce a higher level of subsequent aggressive behavior (as measured by the preselected intensity of an alleged electric shock), whereas a content-based theory would tend to favor the latter stimulus.

This is exactly what was found in one key study that used sexual content as the more arousing communication and the usual prizefight as the more aggressive one. In fact, in more than a dozen studies to date, where we have varied the content to include humor, music, even "content-free" abstract symbols and movement, we consistently found more aggression following the more arousing though less aggressive content.

However, as matters developed, our accumulated findings suggested that one should not neglect content-based factors entirely. Thus we find a film that is both emotionally arousing and violent leads to more aggression than one which is equally arousing (again, when measured by physiological means) but nonaggressive. This has led, in turn, to the more sophisticated version of the emotional arousal paradigm that posits an interaction between the emotional and cognitive aspects of the message under particular circumstances (see Tannenbaum & Zillmann, 1975).

It is to be noted that these results obtain only when the subject must make some kind of aggressive response, the individual's only choice being how intense (or frequent, or long, etc.) to make it. Unlike other theories in this area, the emotional-arousal model does not predict spontaneous aggressive behavior in response to an aggressive stimulus, and this is in fact what is found in most of the research in this area. In a systematic series of studies, we found that in order for aggression to occur, a necessary feature was the legitimization of a target "deserving" of the aggressive response (usually someone who had somehow angered the subject earlier). Even when we allow the subject to first vent the aggressive feelings, then inform the individual that there had been some error and the shock had mistakenly gone to an innocent third party, the subject subsequently will administer as much shock to the proper, deserving target party as if the previous aggressive behavior had not occurred.

Humor. As already noted, the simple arousal model does not link the nature of the content with the specific response to be evoked. Accordingly, we have used both violent and relatively nonviolent communication messages with a variety of possible behavioral responses. One in particular concerned

humor—this time as the response to aggressive content rather than as the arousing stimulus for aggressive behavior.

Again, in several studies we find support for the arousal model. Humor appears to be a desirable commodity for a wide variety of people, but they find it funnier and appreciate it more under conditions of higher, rather than lower, emotional excitation. This holds true whether or not the earlier arousal is produced by material that is funny, and even obtains when it is of a violent nature, the seeming opposite of a humorous tone.

Suspenseful Cliff Hangers.   Here is another staple of contemporary media fare; yet almost all theories of media behavior either do not address the issue entirely or are hard-pressed to account for the popularity of cliff hanging, perilous situations. On the face of it, having favorite characters, especially ones you identify with, be faced with danger, their fate hanging by the flimsiest of threads, is not particularly enticing. Children often show signs of fear and trepidation, even cry at such depictions—presumably feelings and behaviors that one seeks to avoid normally—yet keep returning for more each time they are available.

Zillmann (Chapter 6, this volume) presents a thorough review of the several theoretical speculations that tend to explain this appeal in terms of the experienced viewer who has learned that such situations always work out satisfactorily in the end. Berlyne (1973) reiterates this hypothesis. Our approach is not in conflict with such formulations but concentrates on some additional elements. It emphasizes firstly the sheer reward value of the emotional experience itself: Suspense content is inherently arousing, which, according to the theory, is desirable in its own right. Moreover, as we noted earlier, it is a "safe risk": The viewer can invest deeply in the danger of the depicted situation knowing full well that retreat from the situation is always open, and realizing that, after all, it is only a story. Its appeal can be likened to the reassuring feeling one experiences when awakening from a terrible nightmare and realizing it was "only a dream."

Again, we have some experimental data supporting such contentions, mostly cliffhanger contexts, where the tension is built up to a pitch and then there is a break—variously, for the length of a commercial break, or for one day, or for one week—before the story is resumed. Additional support for the particular application of the emotional transfer model to this area of content is provided in Zillmann's thorough account.

PRODUCTION-RELATED RESEARCH

Some years ago, I had occasion to speak about my research on arousal and aggression before a group of Scandinavian film makers. During the question period I was asked (by a well-known film maker, I learned later) to name the

most vicious, violent film I had ever seen. After I could not come up with a good example, my interrogator told me his choice: an old movie featuring Richard Widmark as a demented young man and Ethel Barrymore as a crippled old woman in a wheelchair. He proceeded to describe a climactic scene in graphic, shot-by-shot detail: The camera, shooting over Widmark's shoulder, shows him pushing the wheelchair to the head of the staircase. He then shoves it forcefully down the stairs, the camera following the tumbling chair and body all the way down. The camera then pans in for a close-up shot of the crumpled body beside the shattered wheelchair. There was a quick cut—remember, this is a film producer telling the story—and the camera retraces the staircase in reverse, stair by stair, closing with a tight shot of the leering face of Richard Widmark filling the screen.

I reacted with suitable horror, shuddering at the poor old woman, the broken wheelchair, etc. "No, No," said the producer vehemently, "Not the old woman! Richard Widmark's face!" He proceeded to state that if he had Widmark's face to work with, he would purposely make a violent film because "it would be a shame not to make full use of it." Whereas I was preoccupied with content, he was concerned with building a whole film around a particularly cinematic ingredient. Such are the differences between a creative media producer and a mere social researcher.

The lesson of that story has remained with me during various opportunities I have had to work with film and TV producers in recent years. These sessions were sometimes an attempt to provide feedback on the consequences of earlier decisions, at other times an opportunity for so-called "formative" research during the production of a program, and at still others were simply occasions to try out some ideas.

Contextual Effects

Particularly in the public visual media, where explicitness of presentation is most likely, there has been continual concern with regulating both the content and the format of certain materials, especially those involving sex and violence. Sometimes this is a matter of self-regulation among the producers and distributors, at other times it is embodied in some centralized, usually governmentally appointed, authority. Several issues arising in this regulatory context and involving various presentational formats were subjected to research to determine whether the desired effect is in fact realized.

Justification of Violence. As a partial defense to the relatively high rate of violence on American television, the TV networks at one time offered the argument that since the depicted aggression is usually presented as a justified act (e.g., the shooting of a known murderer by a sheriff, an act of revenge, or self-defense), the viewer is not affected by the violence as such. An opposing

argument can be made that just because the violence is justified, the viewer (especially the impressionable child) can "learn the lesson" of ends justifying means and apply it to his own environment by exhibiting more readiness to use violence to achieve goals that are justified in the child's own eyes.

A half-dozen or so separate experiments have systematically varied the context of justification, by kind and degree, in which the same acts of aggression are committed. The findings consistently support the notion that the greater the degree of justification, the higher the probability of more intense, subsequent aggressive behavior. In this instance, at least, the actual effect of a consistent, if not fully regulated, format was the opposite of that presumed.

Sanitization of Aggression.   More the subject of direct regulation is the issue of the detail accompanying violent acts. Most media organizations tend to avoid certain explicit detail (such as showing blood and gore, dwelling on the faces of dead people, etc.) on the assumption that it is too revolting and possibly too stimulating. Again, the opposite can be argued: the inclusion of such negative detail in association with violence lowers the probability that aggression would be subsequently employed.

The findings here are less consistent across several studies but are clear in suggesting that the inclusion of such "forbidden" detail would not lead to more aggression. If anything, they support the conclusion that there will be a dampening in aggressive tendency. Here again, then, we find that a well-meaning policy decision may well have consequences contrary to what was intended.

Selective Deletions.   "Censorship" is a pejorative term most everywhere, but in many ways, official and otherwise, it is practiced everywhere. Any decisions involving criteria of inclusion and exclusion of certain content can be construed as acts of censorship. The example cited earlier on the sanitization issue in one such case. Another such case occurs when certain explicit scenes are deliberately omitted from a film or TV program because they are considered too provocative. I became involved in one such situation in an actual court case, where all I had to offer was that I did not know what effect the suggested deletion would have, that it might have quite an opposite effect than the one intended, and that the issue was a matter for empirical determination rather than expert testimony. I decided to heed my own advice and embarked on a series of studies to examine such cases more systematically.

The issue is interesting both as a policy matter and for theoretical reasons. Most often when explicit deletions are advocated there are enough cues in the antecedent and subsequent content to provide information as to the nature of the deleted material. Thus the viewer can readily "fill in" the missing detail for

himself. Under such circumstances, what he fills in may well be more vivid (and possibly more arousing) than what was there originally. More significant from a psychological view point is that by engaging in such filling-in activity, the viewer can become more emotionally involved in the drama. The result of this added emotional engrossment should be an even higher level of arousal than would be present initially.

In a number of experiments just such an effect was in fact realized, with higher physiological excitation resulting when a particular segment was deleted rather than included. An important consideration here are the cues regarding the missing material: the more explicit the antecedent and consequent cues, the higher the arousal. In several studies it was also found that subsequent behavior (e.g., the application of electric shocks) correspondingly increased in intensity.

Also of particular interest was the question of differential recall between the group provided with the original scenes and the one provided with a cut version. Both groups scored equally high on identifying five still photographs of scenes that were common to the two groups, equally low on five other scenes that neither group saw, and—surprisingly—equally high on five photos from the censored material, this despite the fact that one group did not actually see these scenes. Apparently the filling-in behavior is so vivid and suitable (again, given appropriate cues) that the scenes are taken for granted as actually having been seen.

We have further such evidence of increases in arousal under conditions where the action is implicitly rather than explicitly presented (e.g., all the sound but only a little of the sight of a fistfight shot through a restricted doorway or in a darkened hallway). These can have an important influence on production decisions, as in children's programs where the violence is sometimes deliberately set to take place offscreen rather than before the camera. In this case, producers and TV executives may be caught in a genuine dilemma as to the correct treatment: They are pulled in one direction by certain critics who advise them to "clean up their act" and make possibly objectionable detail less explicit, while there is the research discussed earlier suggesting this may well be counterproductive.

The case of children's TV raises other such issues. Is the possible impact of the relentless aggression of animal cartoon programs vitiated by the fact that they are animated rather than acted, featuring animal characters rather than humans? Can the humor often accompanying such violence also have a muting effect, or will the two in combination be even more arousing? In general, is obviously nonreal, fantasy material, such as science fiction, animated monsters or supernatural beings, etc., apt to be less provoking? These are the types of questions on which decisions are regularly made in the course of individual program production, but are as yet poorly if at all informed by appropriate research.

Producer/Research Partnership

I recently had the extraordinary good fortune to spend the better part of a year doing research in conjunction with a variety of people concerning a number of different production decisions at the British Broadcasting Corporation (BBC). At the BBC, too, a number of production dilemmas are faced on each program, and in the absence of any better information, producers are naturally inclined to use their judgment, rely on previous experiences, or on those treatments they have seen others employ.

Probably most TV producers, whether at the BBC, NBC, or PBS, much prefer to have such decisions left entirely for them to make. This is, after all, what they are there for, and what "professionalism" and "creative freedom" are all about. They certainly do not want the empiricists, experimentalists, quantitative types, messing around with their programs. To them, it can only lead to production by formula and computer (which is not to say that many of the decisions they do make are any less predictable). I am actually quite sensitive to such views and believe they should be honored, just as I would not particularly relish these individuals puttering around in my research; it is really the essence of artistic and academic freedom.

However, on occasion there are producers who feel they can use the help of researchers and do not feel threatened by them. Equally important, there are those researchers who are likewise willing to cast their lot with producers. During the course of the year with the BBC, I was able to work together with the producers of three main programs, while handling a number of other "quick and dirty" issues that came up during the year on which a researcher's input might be useful.[5]

One of the collaborative efforts focused on a series dealing with Britain as a multiracial society. The producer got me intimately involved in the planning of the series and several of its component programs, including such issues as whether lightly satiric, humorous treatment would be more successful in getting certain points across than a more conventional, straight documentary approach. We had actually designed a study to test this proposition but had to abandon it when production resources within the department were inadequate for the task of doing the humorous version convincingly.

---

[5]On a number of such questions that arose, I was able to suggest solutions based on research that had already been done (usually outside the television context) and that appeared generalizable to the issue at hand. On other occasions, it was obvious that we lacked the means or techniques to be able to inform the issue at all with research (this was perhaps the most appreciated response). On still others, it was an empirical (occasionally also theoretical) problem that could be researched but there were no resources nor was there adequate time to accommodate it. In all cases, the research was only there to "inform"or "suggest"; the decisions were always left to the producer or broadcasting management representative.

The actual research was on a seemingly more mundane topic, yet of no less significance to the producer. One of the programs dealt with the West Indian community in Bristol, and was filmed as if the camera was reflecting the community's viewpoint. The question arose whether to use a conventional BBC announcer reading the conventional voice-over narration, or would the use of a West Indian announcer doing a West Indian narration be more convincing and fitting to the film? Videotapes of the various possible permutations and combinations of conditions were tested with potential audiences. The results were rather surpisingly consistent, favoring the more "compatible" film-and-commentary versions, and this proved to have a significant influence throughout the subsequent production of the series. A separate study varied the race and tone of the interviewers of a community activist, and found similar support for the more compatible combinations. Of added significance from a production policy standpoint, we also obtained the reactions of other vested interest groups (e.g., a West Indian community group, members of a national racial equality council) to the pilot material. These are groups whose opinions and judgments are of obvious importance to the producer, and hence their responses provided further input in the production process.

Another program series dealt with "numeracy" (i.e., the understanding and use of numbers in simple everyday purposes, designed for individuals who had difficulties in this respect). Again, there was an intimate producer-researcher interaction as the series went through its various stages of planning: to what subaudience to direct it, what aspects of matematics were most in need of presentation, which lent themselves best to television, whether to emphasize concepts or numerical operations, etc.

Among the major choices was whether to adopt a more-or-less didactic teaching approach, or whether to use an entertainment format, featuring well-known celebrities as individuals with numerical difficulties accompanied by animated examples. Appropriate versions of the test program were prepared and used with groups who were thought to be likely candidates for such a program. The results were somewhat vitiated by the necessary nonrandom assignment of already intact groups of subjects (such are the inherent vagaries of actual field research). Nevertheless, the tests clearly suggested that certain features of the approach geared to the celebrity had obvious shortcomings that either had to be accommodated in some way or the format had to be dropped entirely. Whether or not such a conclusion could have been reached without the research per se remains a moot question.

The most ambitious research was conducted in connection with a one-off special program dealing with the social effects of TV and focusing on the main and side effects of TV fare relating to crime. It so happened that earlier in the year there had been an open conflict between the head of the Criminal

Investigation Division (the famous Scotland Yard) and the BBC over a number of such programs in which the police detectives were portrayed in an unfavorable light. One series called "Law and Order" came in for attention particularly because it was of the so-called "docudrama" variety—a dramatized version of alleged documented cases, put together with an appropriate dose of creative license.

Both sides in the controversy—and other parties as well, since in Britain television is regarded as a cultural commodity worthy of reviews in the daily newspapers, and its problems are commented upon openly—made various claims regarding how "the public" would, and subsequently did, react to such a series, whether the public would be "taken in" by the docudrama technique, etc. The argument, which was somewhat heated at times, included threats of noncooperation and censorship and was totally uninformed by the actual reactions of the viewing audience. The Audience Research Department of the BBC provided some information on this issue via a survey among its regular viewer panel, and we also decided to conduct a typical before-after experiment under controlled viewing conditions. One of the features of the experiment examined how the same program was identified and introduced: as essentially a documentary, a drama, or without any such identification (as the program was actually shown on the air). In an effort to keep this treatment as realistic as possible, the identification consisted of a very brief, 10-second audio introduction, unfortunately done in an improvised manner. Thus we cannot be certain that the general lack of differences seemingly tied to this variation were genuine or not.

The other results showed that although most viewers took the program for what it was, there were some notable changes in their conception of the detective force and other elements of the criminal justice system touched on in the test program. As with other such issues, there is the question of how much of a change in how many people occur for the issue to be regarded as of significant policy concern. This is essentially a political matter for a given society to decide. In any event, these and other findings, relating to an actual program that became a minor cause célèbre, provided significant input for the subsequent BBC documentary on the social effects of television.

REPETITIVE EXPOSURES

It is a relatively short leap from the British to the Canadian Broadcasting Corporation, although Canadian television, like most other Canadian institutions, is more American than British. The major factor is that most of the population is concentrated along the U.S. border, within easy reach of American TV stations through an extensive cable system. This makes Canada

a most interesting laboratory for a variety of broadcasting research problems, among them one that shed additional light on the nature of the seeking and gratification of entertainment fare.

Some years ago, for competitive reasons, the Canadian Broadcasting Corporation carried the first run of a situation comedy series on Thursday evenings, with exactly the same weekly episode being shown on an American network the following Monday. In the city of Toronto, where most homes have cable TV, and thus could easily receive the Monday show, it was found that over 40% of the Monday audience for that program had already seen exactly the same show four nights previously (this, I might add, despite the fact that some 11 additional channels were available at that time to cable TV subscribers).

This was such an unbelievable, unexpected finding that the survey was repeated, with the same results. When a subsample of the program's fans were interviewed, they did not think it incredulous but quite acceptable for them to prefer a program they had already seen shortly before. They apparently were seeking not novelty but familiarity. They still found the featured situations and jokes amusing. It was a safe, certain form of entertainment as compared to the uncertainty of new programs with unknown plots and characters.

Although most of us would probably not engage in such behavior constantly, there is most likely a tendency toward this type of activity in each of us. It is certainly obvious in young children, as any suffering parent can attest. In most homes there is a repertoire of bedtime stories, each of which the child has heard numerous times but which he wants to hear again and again. Certainly it is not a memory problem: If one stops in the middle of a story, the child will readily fill in the following lines with ease, as if there were a script. The story-telling chore—the same stories told in exactly the same ways—may be a bore for the parent but the child remains very interested in these same tales.

The phenomenon occurs with adults as well, if in a more modulated and selective fashion. There are those who will re-read a coveted book several times, go to see the same films repeatedly, etc. Perhaps it is most apparent with those who have collections of favorite music which are played repeatedly (oftentimes, as in my case, particular selections are played to suit certain moods) rather than buy new discs and tapes. This is the case with opera as well, where we tend to favor familiar ones to new operas.

Some students and I have attempted to examine further this phenomenon of the attractiveness of repetition. We have found, for example, that football fans, presented with a choice of watching a replay of an exciting championship match that their favorite team won some years ago or a live game being played that day are more likely to choose the former (not surprisingly, the exact opposite is true for fans of the losing team!).

In another study, we used the previous mentioned exercycle apparatus to determine whether individuals would exert effort and time for both the initial

and repeated exposure to a "Kojak" detective-adventure program. In the first round, the required minimal pedaling level (for the picture and sound to be sustained at an acceptable level) were gradually increased through the course of the program, with a particular extra output required at the climactic point of the plot some minutes before the program's ending. No subjects dropped out of the experiment despite the required efforts.

Within a three-week period, all subjects were again exposed to the same program. This time, however, the apparatus was made to malfunction just at the critical point. The participating subjects were invited either to wait until the apparatus was repaired in order to see the remaining resolution of the plot or to leave (they were paid the same rate in each case), with the waiting period deliberately left open-ended. We were startled to find a mean waiting time of over an hour, with quite a few subjects waiting up to three hours—all this to see the ending of a TV program (rather predictable to begin with in our judgment) that each had already seen within the last few weeks.

It can be argued that our subjects, mostly retired, older people, had nothing better to do or waited just to fulfill an implicit obligation assumed when agreeing to participate in the experiment. The fact remains, however, that they wait more for some programs than others—hence the index of relative program popularity—both on initial viewing or on repeated exposures. In the present case, a plurality of subjects both pedaled harder and waited longer for the rerun of "Kojak" than another, less familiar detective story they were seeing for the first time. Greater commitment hath no fan than a true "Kojak" aficionado!

CONCLUDING COMMENTS

Having organized this chapter around personal observations, it is fitting that I close it in a similar manner. I firmly believe we have too long neglected the obvious appeal of a medium like television to provide a reliable, constant diet of entertainment. As noted earlier, it is my guess that a main part of that appeal is that it provides a "cheap thrill," an inexpensive form of mild arousal; its convenience may be its greatest asset. On the rare occasions when it covers some special live event—a landing on the moon, a Sadat visit to Jerusalem, a World Cup final in Argentina—it is unsurpassed in its power to capture both the cognitive and the emotional rolled into one, real live drama in its truest sense. Most of the time, it offers a fairly bland diet but apparently with enough of a jag, a bit of excitement to whet the appetite for more. At least most people do come back for more most of the time.

In its fiction content it has a mixed record in most countries, with some peaks of dramatic excellence set against many troughs of repetitive formula programs. If people are willing to forget the world of reality for a while, to invest moderately of themselves for an hour or two, they can at times, even

with the relatively bland content offered, get some significant emotional input in return. If watching TV (or going to a movie or reading a book) is a physically passive undertaking, it can be emotionally and even intellectually active and, in a sense, participatory—and that cannot be an altogether bad thing.

Such easy-to-come-by, if mild, rewards may become more desired, possibly even needed, under certain conditions. For example, it is not uncommon for people to state that after a "long day at the office" or a "busy day coping with the kids at home," that they want nothing else but to sit down in front of the TV, to be diverted from their travails and concerns. We have recently begun some research in which we systematically vary a full day's activity (e.g., with chores that are either physically demanding or relatively indolent or continuing tasks that are mentally boring or interesting and challenging) and then see what communication behavior individuals select to engage in under limited choice conditions.

Our findings to date suggest considerable differences between, but consistency within, individual preferences under such varying antecedent experiences. By and large, physically and/or intellectually demanding activity has to be associated with more seemingly passive later behavior, with television viewing being among the more prominent (far more than radio, music listening, reading, or playing competitive games). When the TV choices are restricted (roughly) to between informative (fact) vs. entertainment (fiction) programming, there is consistently more preference for the latter, but the difference is more marked under conditions of more demanding antecedent activity. Within the fiction category, preexisting, individual preferences tend to dominate, with as much choice for adventure, action drama as for sports and comedy (although comedy was notably more popular after a do-nothing, boring day). There is more than a suggestion that, at least under such prevailing circumstances, people tend to use the vicarious activity of the TV as a means of adapting themselves to the rigors of the day, and, in one pilot study, to the anticipated demands of the following day. I am sure such choices are not without their intellectual or emotional "costs"—few things in life are—but they clearly serve some purpose which would be folly for us to ignore in seeking an understanding of why people are so fond of a medium like television and why the prevailing patterns of preference persist.

REFERENCES

Bandura, A. Vicarious processes: A case of no-trial learning. In L. Berkowitz (Ed.), *Advances in experimental social psychology* (Vol. II). New York: Academic Press, 1965.

Berlyne, D. E. The vicissitudes of aplopathematic and thelematoscopic pneumatology (or the hydrography of hedonism). In D. E. Berlyne & K. B. Madsen (Eds.), *Pleasure, reward, preference: Their nature determinants, and role behavior.* New York: Academic Press, 1973.

Schachter, S. The interaction of cognitive and physiological determinants of emotional states. In L. Berkowitz (Ed.), *Advances in experimental social psychology* (Vol. I). New York: Academic Press, 1964.

Tannenbaum, P. H., & Zillmann, D. Emotional arousal in the facilitation of aggression through communication. In L. Berkowitz (Ed.), *Advances in experimental social psychology* (Vol. VIII). New York: Academic Press, 1975.

Withey, S., & Abeles, R. (Eds.). *Television and social behavior.* Hillsdale, N.J.: Lawrence Erlbaum Associates, 1980.

6 Anatomy of Suspense

Dolf Zillmann
Indiana University

> *The trouble with suspense is that few people know what it is.*
> —Alfred Hitchcock

In this chapter, we examine the phenomenon of suspense in drama and delineate the principal conditions that control the enjoyment of suspenseful drama. Suspense is analyzed in conceptual terms, and the apparent paradox in the enjoyment of mostly negatively toned affective reactions to suspenseful drama is detailed. Some theoretical resolutions of this paradox are then offered, and a theory of the enjoyment of suspenseful drama is outlined. Recent experimental research on suspense is reported, and the adequacy of the proposed suspense theory is evaluated in the light of the evidence. Finally, some implications of this theory for the development of personal preferences for suspenseful drama are discussed.

THE CONCEPTUALIZATION OF SUSPENSE

According to dictionary definitions, which presumably reflect the common denotative if not connotative usage of words, the concept "suspense" has at least three shades of meaning. Suspense is said to be: (1) a state of uncertainty in the sense of doubtfulness and indecision; (2) a state of anxiety-like uncertainty; and (3) a state of pleasant excitement about an expected event. Suspense, then, is viewed as an experience of uncertainty, mainly, whose hedonic properties can vary from noxious to pleasant; and the uncertainty

involved apparently applies to any decisional dilemma as well as to the likely or unlikely behavior of others and environmental happenings that produce consequences which have affective significance for the respondent.

The usefulness of such general definitions is quite limited; the conceptualization they express is very ambiguous. For one thing, it would seem desirable to exclude the experience of ambivalence about entirely certain outcomes from consideration and to restrict the concept "suspense" to *apprehension about future events*. If, for example, a young man finds himself in a dilemma over which of two equally excellent, highly desirable cars (whose future performance is not at all in doubt) he should buy, it seems pointless to regard him to be in a state of suspense about the choice. But more importantly, the view that uncertainty can assume any conceivable hedonic valence is troublesome. Uncertainty about a future event is obviously more pronounced the closer the subjective probability of its occurrence is to that of its nonoccurrence. Uncertainty is thus at a maximum when the odds for a desired or a feared outcome are 50:50. In the face of such even odds, the experience of uncertainty about a desired outcome should prove noxious because of the relatively high perceived likelihood that the outcome will not materialize. By the same token, the experience of such uncertainty about a feared outcome should prove noxious because of the relatively high perceived likelihood that the feared event will occur. In short, uncertainty at high levels is unlikely to be hedonically neutral or even positive. It tends to produce decidedly noxious states (cf. Berlyne, 1960).

The fact that suspense has been conceived of as *pleasant* excitement, among other things, would indicate that uncertainty may have been assigned an entirely secondary role in suspense. Apparently, pleasant excitement can result only from the anticipation of desired outcomes when this anticipation is not tempered by a substantial likelihood of alternative undesirable, even dreaded outcomes. In other words, uncertainty about favorable happenings is likely to be pleasantly experienced only when it is negligible. Uncertainty, then, at least high levels of uncertainty, may not be as essential to suspense as has been commonly thought.

Suspense in Drama

Considering drama, the meaning of suspense is far more specific than indicated by these qualifications. First of all, the respondent is a *witness* to dramatic events involving *others* and is thus neither directly threatened nor directly benefited by the events. Whatever the mechanism mediating any affective reaction in the respondent may be, suspense can manifest itself only through the onlooker's perceived-likelihood of outcomes that either endanger or benefit others (i.e., the protagonists and other members of the cast) and/or through their reactions to the events producing these outcomes. But the

experience of suspense in drama is subject to further unique and seemingly universal restrictions: (1) the preoccupation with feared outcomes; (2) the selection of liked protagonists as targets for feared outcomes; and (3) the creation of high degrees of subjective certainty for the feared outcomes that threaten liked protagonists. We will briefly discuss these conditions.

Focus on Negative Outcomes. It is generally accepted that *conflict,* especially human conflict, constitutes the very essence of drama (cf. Marx, 1940; Smiley, 1971). The clash of two or more antagonistic, potentially hostile forces is viewed as a basic and necessary condition for drama. Any and every dramatic situation is said to arise from such conflict, and it is explicated or clearly implied that drama cannot exist without the display of conflicts and crises in one form or another. Suspense in drama, in turn, is viewed as the experience of apprehensions about the resolution of conflicts and crises. More specifically, suspense is conceived of as the experience of uncertainty regarding the outcome of a potentially hostile confrontation. This experience of uncertainty can derive, in principle, from (1) the fear that a favored outcome may not be forthcoming, (2) the fear that a deplorable outcome may be forthcoming, (3) the hope that a favored outcome will be forthcoming, (4) the hope that a deplorable outcome will not be forthcoming, and (5) any possible combination of these hopes and fears. It has been shown that the fears and hopes in question are largely a function of the onlooker's affective dispositions toward the antagonistic parties (Zillmann, Bryant, & Sapolsky, 1979; Zillmann & Cantor, 1976). Disposition–theoretical considerations lead to the expectation that:

1. the respondent will hope for outcomes that are (a) favorable to liked and deserving protagonists and (b) deplorable for disliked and undeserving ones; and that:
2. the respondent will fear outcomes which are (a) deplorable for liked and deserving protagonists and (b) favorable to disliked and undeserving ones.

With hopes and fears thus confounded, the question arises as to whether suspenseful drama thrives on hopes or on fears.

The issue can be construed in two ways. First, favorable and deplorable outcomes can be conceived of in relative terms. A sympathetic protagonist may be up against a hostile environment, for example, and the viewer is placed in suspense by watching him or her face a thousand dangers as he or she struggles through savage swamps toward safety. The respondent's affective reactions under these circumstances could be regarded as being mediated by the fear that the protagonist will be injured or killed; but they could equally well be considered to result from the hope for the protagonist's

welfare. If the respondent did not have the latter hope, it could be argued, he or she would not have the fear that presumably produces the gripping experience of suspense. Such reasoning suggests that hopes and fears are inseparably intertwined in the apprehensions that produce suspense. In fact, the conceptual separation of hopes and fears may appear to be pointless, because the two concepts seem to constitute two alternative ways of describing the same phenomenon of apprehension about an outcome.

Second, and in contrast, outcomes can be conceived of in somewhat more absolute terms. The experiential properties of potential outcomes can be classified according to *hedonic* criteria: Outcomes can be either noxious or pleasant to the protagonist, and they can assume the one or the other hedonic valence to different degrees. Death, mutilation, torture, injury, and social debasement can be categorized as negative outcomes, whereas gain of money, glory, and privileges can be classified as positive ones. Essentially, then, we can distinguish between outcomes that constitute *annoyances* and outcomes that constitute *incentives*.

If outcomes are thus conceived of, it becomes clear that suspense in drama is created predominantly through the suggestion of negative outcomes. As in the man–vs–swamp cliché, for example, protagonists often fight for dear life. Although there often is some glory attached to sheer survival and the avoidance of injury, the provision of incentives is obviously not a necessary condition for suspense to take. It appears that in suspenseful drama, generally speaking, the attainment of incentives is secondary to the creation of apprehensions about deplorable and dreadful outcomes. Suspenseful drama features such events as bombs about to explode, dams about to burst, ceilings about to cave in, fires about to rage, ocean liners about to sink, and earthquakes about to rampage. It features people about to be jumped and stabbed, about to walk into an ambush and get shot, and about to be bitten by snakes, tarantulas, and mad dogs. The common denominator in all of this is the likely *suffering* of the protagonists. It is impending disaster, manifest in anticipated agony, pain, injury, and death. Suspenseful drama, then, appears to thrive on uneasiness and distress about anticipated negative outcomes. In short, it thrives on fear.

This is not to say that suspense cannot be built on the anticipation of good fortunes. As many popular game shows on television attest, people can be thrilled with the uncertainty about grand prizes hidden behind curtains and in chests. This "treasure-hunt" type of suspense appears to derive to a large extent from the expectation of amassing great rewards. The contestants in such games are obviously not in any way placed at risk; the only "misfortune" that can befall them is the lack of good fortune. In relative terms, however, it may well be this possibility of losing in the sense of not winning that produces the experience of suspense in the viewer. Be this as it may, a close look at suspenseful drama should convince anyone that suspense is characteristically generated through the creation of apprehensions about bad fortunes rather

than good ones. Drama based on the competition for incentives requires more than not attaining the incentives; something more than not winning must be at stake.

The recent controversy in professional tennis, a case of "the drama of sports," bears on this point. Both the winner and the loser of a match received substantial amounts of money. In terms of cash, the loser had nothing to lose, but much to gain. The public uproar about such arrangements shows that the thrills of watching a sports contest are better served when the audience believes that what they are witnessing is a winner-take-all battle (cf. Zillmann et al., 1979). Under the latter condition, the loser would indeed gain nothing that could compensate for the negative experience of defeat per se. Suspenseful drama in fiction functions analogously, of course. A car race, for example, devoid of threats and dangers, with prizes and glory for all, would be most uncharacteristic of suspenseful drama—not to mention that it would presumably fail to induce suspense reactions of an appreciable magnitude. Apparently, the successful creation of the gripping experience of suspense depends on the display of credible endangerments. The audience must think it likely, for example, that the racing car will skid on the oil slick, that the driver will lose control, that a wheel will come off, or that the motor will catch on fire.

In sum, suspenseful drama relies heavily on the exhibition of threats and dangers to protagonists. It is designed, primarily, to evoke apprehensions about decidedly noxious experiences which the protagonists are about to undergo. Although suspense can be generated through the anticipation of favorable, pleasing outcomes, this technique of suspense induction is uncharacteristic, even alien to suspenseful drama as such. It should be recognized, however, that in suspenseful drama the primary technique of suspense induction, namely the creation of apprehensions about deplorable outcomes, is often confounded with the creation of the anticipation of favorable outcomes as a secondary technique.

Endangered Characters. It has been stated earlier that the audience's hopes and fears regarding likely events that would affect the protagonist's welfare are dispositionally mediated. Research evidence (e.g., Zillmann & Cantor, 1977) indicates that a positive outcome is enjoyed when the protagonist whom it benefits is liked, or at least in no way disliked. In sharp contrast, a positive outcome that benefits a disliked protagonist is deplored. The inverse applies to negative outcomes: A negative outcome is deplored when the protagonist whom it victimizes is liked, or at least in no way disliked. A negative outcome which victimizes a disliked protagonist, again in sharp contrast, is enjoyed. If it is assumed that these affective reactions are precipitated by hopes for and fears about certain outcomes, it follows that the hopes and fears regarding the same events will be totally different for liked

and disliked protagonists. Whereas liked protagonists are considered deserving of positive outcomes, the very possibility of a disliked protagonist's benefaction becomes deplorable and distressing. Even more important to suspenseful drama, whereas liked protagonists are regarded as undeserving of any negative outcome, the likely victimization of a disliked protagonist is usually not only not deplored but very much enjoyed. After all, the disliked protagonist, typically the obnoxious, mean, and evil character who demeans and torments others, is merely getting his just deserts (Zillmann & Bryant, 1975).

Obvious as the dispositional mediation of suspense may seem, it is not generally recognized. Smiley (1971), for example, feels that "suspense *automatically* occurs during all crises [p. 68, emphasis added]." Expressed in the dramaturgical nomenclature he employed, he proposed that any "hint" that (1) two identified, opposing forces will fight and (2) the one or the other party will win produces the experience of suspense in the "wait" (i.e., the period of time in which the fighting is about to erupt or is in progress) for the "climax" that comes with the resolution of the conflict.

The proposed automatic reaction of suspense is not only at variance with what is known about the dispositional mediation of affective reactions but is noncompelling intuitively. In the case where two intensely disliked parties are about to kill each other off, for example, the onlooker would seem to be quite indifferent about, rather than fearful of, the particular outcome. And in the case where a resented agent is about to walk into an ambush set by liked protagonists, the only source of suspense appears to be the possibility that something could go wrong with the hoped-for destruction of the villain and the "good guys" would suddenly be in danger. It would appear, then, that suspense in drama is characteristically created by the projection of negative and feared outcomes for liked protagonists—and not in such projections for just any member of the cast.

Subjective Certainty About Outcomes. Given this delineation of the characteristic and presumably most effective conditions for the creation of suspense in drama, it becomes clear that maximal uncertainty associated with a feared outcome does not necessarily constitute the point of maximal suspense. In fact, it seems quite unlikely that degree of uncertainty and intensity of suspense vary more or less proportionally. One would assume, for example, that witnessing the endangerment of an intensely liked protagonist produces less fearful apprehensions, and thus less suspense, when the odds for his or her safety are perceived to be 50:50 rather than, say, 25:75. Generally speaking, it appears that suspense will be more intensely experienced the greater the subjective certainty of the onlooker that the liked protagonist will succumb—this time—to the destructive forces against which he or she is struggling. However, although even odds may indeed constitute a condition of

rather moderate endangerment, total subjective certainty about the liked protagonist's forthcoming victimization does not, in all likelihood, produce maximal suspense. It may be argued that as soon as the onlooker is confident that a feared outcome is indeed forthcoming, he or she is no longer in suspense. The respondent may, at this point, start to experience disappointment and sadness. In fact, there is reason to believe that the onlooker's certainty about a forthcoming deplorable event will serve a preparatory appraisal function which protects him or her against overly intense noxious arousal in response to the depiction of the event once it materializes (cf. Lazarus, 1966; Leventhal, 1974; Zillmann, 1978). Subjective certainty about a deplorable outcome, then, not only seems to terminate the experience of suspense, but also to minimize the emotional impact of tragic happenings. According to these considerations in which uncertainty is treated as a necessary condition of suspense, the experience of suspense will be more intense the greater the onlooker's subjective certainty that a deplorable outcome will indeed befall a liked protagonist. However, as extreme levels of certainty are reached and the outcome is no longer in doubt, the experience of suspense vanishes and gives way to more definite dysphoric reactions.[1]

If this reasoning is applied to the other extreme of the uncertainty scale (i.e., to total certainty that the liked protagonist will not succumb to the forces that threaten and endanger him or her), it appears that one would have to project near-zero suspense levels for most dramatic fare. In television drama series, with recurrent characters and formats, it is clear from the outset that the main protagonists will survive whatever conflicts they become involved in. The situation in the movies is not all that different. There are usually sufficient cues to permit the viewer to infer with considerable certainty who the ultimate victor of any combat will be. Fearful apprehensions about deplorable outcomes thus seem to have no basis.

Considering the *ultimate* resolution of dramatic presentations, the above assessment appears to be quite compelling. The macrostructure of drama, the overall plot or "theme" (cf. Marx, 1940), may indeed contribute little if anything to suspense. But the experience of suspense can be produced repeatedly during the course of a play. In the microstructure of drama, specific plots can show the liked protagonists credibly endangered. Although loss of life may not be a viable threat, loss of limb may have considerable credibility, and the possibility of being beaten, stabbed, shot, or otherwise subjected to painful, agonizing, and humiliating treatment certainly does have great credibility. The viewer need not fear for the heroine's life in "Police

---

[1]Our expectations regarding subjective certainty in suspense were recently confirmed in an experimental investigation (Comisky, P. W. *Degree of outcome-uncertainty and degree of positive disposition toward the protagonist as factors affecting the appreciation of suspenseful dramatic presentations.* Unpublished doctoral dissertation, University of Massachusetts, 1978).

Woman," for example, but there is ample cause to worry about her being hit, raped, strangled, or severely injured.

Clearly, drama that has comparatively unpredictable themes (e.g., "Police Story") lends itself more than predictable fare to the creation of high levels of suspense. Yet, unpredictable plots that potentially generate heightened suspense do not necessarily produce superior appreciation. The enjoyment of suspenseful drama apparently depends on the respondent's sanction of ultimate outcomes (Zillmann & Bryant, 1975; Zillmann, Hay, & Bryant, 1975) and presumably also on the degree to which he or she tolerates affective disturbances—transitory and comparatively moderate as they may be. It is conceivable that drama which produces extremely high levels of suspense is too disturbing to be enjoyable (Berlyne, 1973), and that drama with a rather predictable macrostructure or theme and numerous unpredictable plots of suspenseful action constitutes an optimal condition for enjoyment.

This latter formula is obvious in children's fare. Liked protagonists are often nearly omnipotent (e.g., "Superman," "The Six-Million-Dollar Man"). They handle any predicament they find themselves in with ease, and involved, empathetic distress on the viewer's part seems a misplaced sentiment. This formula may also have given rise to popular melodramatic plays in which the good and the evil forces in conflict are sharply contrasted and outcomes, at least in the macrostructure, are never in doubt. These comments should make it clear that high levels of suspense cannot be directly equated with high enjoyment of drama, certainly not with great drama.

In accordance with the criteria put forth in the preceding discussion of the phenomenon of suspense, we now propose that the experience of suspense in response to dramatic presentations derives characteristically from *the respondent's acute, fearful apprehension about deplorable events that threaten liked protagonists,* this apprehension being conceived of as high but not complete subjective certainty about the occurrence of the anticipated deplorable events. In somewhat more dramatic language, drama is viewed as suspenseful whenever it features sympathetic protagonists in peril.

THE EMPATHY PARADOX IN THE ENJOYMENT OF SUSPENSEFUL DRAMA

It is a widely held belief that those exposed to drama featuring sympathetic, liked protagonists tend to "identify" with these protagonists and to "vicariously experience" whatever these protagonists experience. In fact, this view is commonly treated as a secure and unquestionable key element of our understanding of the enlightenment that drama provides. However, only bewilderment can result from any attempt to explain the enjoyment of

suspenseful drama primarily on the basis of some form of empathetic coexperience.

If, as suggested earlier, suspenseful drama does indeed thrive on the projection of deplorable rather than favorable happenings, those exposed to such drama, as they witness sympathetic characters in danger and in fear, should frequently find themselves in a state of empathetic distress. In suspenseful drama, distressing scenes are presumably not only more frequent, but also take up a longer period of time than scenes depicting the benefaction and happiness of liked protagonists. The opportunity provided for shared misery is thus far greater than that for shared happiness, and the respondent should accordingly experience more empathetic dysphoria than empathetic euphoria.

This apparent dominance of empathetic distress over positively toned empathetic reactions is obviously difficult to reconcile with the explanation of the enjoyment of suspenseful drama on the basis of vicarious affect and "experiential sharing." If vicarious responses were a crucial mediator of enjoyment, drama should be the more enjoyable the less distress-inducing happenings were involved and the more emphasis were given to the depiction of good fortunes and the liked protagonists' tranquility and joy. The assumption of vicarious affective responding ultimately leads to the proposal that the enjoyment of suspenseful drama can best be accomplished and furthered by the removal of its suspenseful parts. Obviously, only masochists would care to put themselves through the agony of the vicarious distress associated with suspenseful events. For nonmasochists, presumably the great majority of drama enthusiasts, the enjoyment of suspense is not readily explained by any reference to the respondent's vicarious involvement.

This assessment is not appreciably altered even when empathetic distress is not conceived of as a vicarious reaction. Suspense-induced empathetic distress may be viewed as "feeling *for* someone" rather than as "feeling *with* someone" (i.e., "feeling *instead of* someone," which means "vicariously"). In recent theoretical treatments of the empathetic process (e.g., Berger, 1962; Stotland, 1969), empathy is defined as an affective reaction to the witnessed display of emotion by another person, or to the anticipation of such a display. At times, the notion of empathy is restricted to instances of affective concordance (between the emotion witnessed or anticipated in another and that in response to it). But, on occasion, *any* affective reaction to the stipulated stimulus conditions (discordant as well as concordant) is viewed as an empathetic response. No matter which particular definition one might accept, it should be clear that the conception of empathy under consideration is broad enough to encompass both the notion that affective reactions are in response *with* or in response *to* the observed or anticipated expression of emotion in another person. The issue is actually further complicated by the

fact that, characteristically, an observer is cognizant of the conditions that induce emotional reactions in others, and that his or her affective behavior may, at least in part, be a response to the environmental cues that manifest these conditions (cf. Zillmann & Cantor, 1977).

The discussed ambiguities regarding the concept of empathy can readily be illustrated by the "trapped hero" suspense cliché. Imagine some youngsters watching their Wild West idol ride right into an ambush in Dodge City, with all the bad guys hiding on the roofs, their rifles ready for action. Such an exhibition of impending disaster may well cause distress in the onlookers. But is it because they "identify" with the endangered protagonist? Is it because they feel *with* him? Or could it be that they are disturbed because they feel *for* him, concerned about his welfare simply because they like him? Could it be that the children also respond to the signs of danger, regardless of the protagonist's coping with (and suffering from) his endangerment?

The characteristic reaction of small children to such suspenseful situations is a common observation and quite revealing. Children tend to talk to their heroes, shouting out warnings of the dangers their heroes face (dangers about which the heroes, because of the very nature of suspense, are ignorant). This kind of reaction—the overt components of which most more-mature drama enthusiasts seem to have learned to inhibit—casts doubt on the popular view that viewers, especially children, identify with liked protagonists. If a child did indeed identify with the hero witnessed in the described predicament— that is, if the child's affective reaction were determined by some sort of ego confusion with the hero—the child's affective behavior should be controlled by the hero's expression of calmness and self-confidence. The consideration of vicarious reactivity thus not only fails to explain distress in response to most scenes of entrapment and peril, but actually projects an absence of distress unless (or until) the hero is seen in fear and agony.

On the basis of common observation it would appear that the occurrence of emphathetic distress is not that severely restricted, however. As indicated earlier, suspense can be built and enhanced by a liked protagonist's apparent unawareness of acute danger, a condition that renders him or her especially vulnerable. It seems that the onlooker, regardless of the protagonists's potentially limited comprehension of the particular circumstances of the endangerment, utilizes all the information available, makes an appraisal, and responds in accord with this appraisal. If a protagonist is liked and deemed undeserving of a particular deplorable treatment, the imminence of that treatment should prove disturbing (Hitchcock, 1959). The onlooker could even be motivated to intervene and prevent the deplorable outcome he or she is unable to sanction (Zillmann & Bryant, 1975). Again, the mature drama enthusiast has learned to inhibit any attempt at intervention. Little children, in contrast, can become so engulfed in the dramatic happenings that they lose sight of the fact that intervention is pointless and yell their warnings anyway.

If such behavior entails an illusion, it is not identity confusion with the esteemed protagonist, nor is it an experience "instead of" the protagonist. Rather, the illusion lies in the fact that the respondent behaves as if he or she were there—as a *witness to real happenings*. Such behavior suggests that suspense-induced empathetic distress, in children and adults alike, can be dealt with as the affective reaction of a concerned "third party" who vehemently deplores impending outcomes. Assumptions about vicarious activities are not necessary and may in fact be counterproductive.

Although it appears that "feeling for" rather than "feeling with" is the likely mechanism of empathetic distress, the issue still lacks a final resolution. Fortunately in the consideration of suspense, the specific origination of empathetic distress is immaterial. It must be recognized, however, that empathetic distress—*in and of itself* and especially when it is frequently induced, of long duration, and of great intensity—cannot directly contribute to, let alone explain, the enjoyment of suspenseful drama.

THE AROUSAL-JAG RESOLUTION
OF THE PARADOX

Given that much suspenseful drama produces considerable empathetic distress (i.e., decidedly negative affective reactions), and given that such drama is nonetheless capable of generating great enjoyment, two principal related issues present themselves. First, it is to be determined exactly what within suspenseful drama fosters enjoyment. (It is stipulated, of course, that the stimuli which induce empathetic distress, at least for the period of time during which they have this effect, do not per se constitute enjoyment-evoking stimuli.) Second, it is to be determined how, if at all, the experience of distress can enhance enjoyment.

The first issue is readily clarified. Generally speaking, it is the benefaction of good and liked protagonists and the just, punitive treatment of their transgressive and resented opponents that evoke joyful reactions (Zillmann & Bryant, 1975; Zillmann & Cantor, 1976, 1977). But it is conceivable that the mere reduction or termination of the experience of empathetic distress, brought on by the *resolution* of the episode that produces distress in the observer, is a sufficient condition for enjoyment. As a sympathetic protagonist averts or eludes acute danger, the onlooker can "breathe a sigh of relief," and this experience of relief, one might surmise, constitutes a minimal condition for joyful reactivity.

The consideration of *relief* brings us to the second issue. If relief from distress is pleasantly experienced, and if relief is provided with any effective resolution of suspense (i.e., in principle, with the removal of the basis for apprehensions about deplorable happenings), a peculiar connection between

distress and relief becomes apparent: The intensity of empathetic distress seems to determine the intensity of the "euphoric" reaction to its resolution. The intensity of joy seems to vary proportionally with that of the antecedent state of dysphoria. According to this view, little suspense creates little distress, and in turn, little distress creates little relief and not much enjoyment. Great suspense, in contrast, produces severe distress, which in turn produces great relief and great enjoyment. It would appear possible, then, provided that suspense is resolved as stipulated, that suspense-induced empathetic distress can be converted into enjoyment.

The proposal that the mere reduction or termination of an aversive state, empathetic distress being a case in point, is a sufficient condition for the experience of positive affect has been advanced by Berlyne (1960) in his well-known arousal-jag model. This model concentrates on the physiological concomitants of aversion and relief rather than on the particular stimuli that induce these experiences, and the nomenclature employed is that of drive-reduction and reinforcement theory. But such emphasis and terminology notwithstanding, the model directly applies to the distress-relief connection discussed earlier.

Berlyne's principal contention in the arousal-jag model is that the reduction or termination of an aversion is rewarding. Aversion is conceived of as a noxious drive state, and any reduction of this state is viewed as reinforcing. Positive affect, or enjoyment for our purposes, enters the rationale as the experiential concomitant of reward. The rewarding experience of relief from aversion should not only be enjoyable but also make the aversion less aversive. Ultimately, it should make the aversion attractive and motivate the individual to seek out rather than to avoid further "aversion" of the kind in question. Berlyne (1960) illustrated this motivational aspect of the model in his discussion of thrilling fears: "One has only to visit the nearest fairground to appreciate the economic value of being tossed and flung through the air, and posters advertising the latest horror film will graphically depict the allurements of being scared out of one's wits [p. 198]." The conversion of fear into joy, in Berlyne's (1960) view, is restricted only by two conditions: "(1) that the drive is aroused to a moderate extent, and (2) that the arousal is promptly followed by relief [p. 198]." The arousal-jag model, then, projects that, with the exception of severe aversions, the greater the aversion and the speedier the recovery from it, the more intense the rewarding relief. As for suspense, the higher its level (i.e., the greater the empathetic distress) and the prompter its resolution, the greater the enjoyment. These projections are further explicated in Fig. 6.1.

At first glance, at least, Berlyne's proposal does appear to unravel the mystery of the enjoyment of suspense-induced distress. But how does the arousal-jag model fare vis-à-vis experimental evidence and under more rigorous theoretical scrutiny?

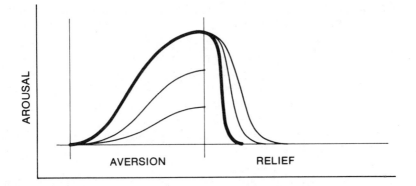

FIG. 6.1. The arousal-jag model applied to suspense and its resolution. Suspense translates into aversion, and its resolution into relief. The heavy line indicates optimal conditions for the enjoyment of suspenseful drama. Enjoyment is expected to be intense when the arousal reaction is pronounced and promptly followed by fast recovery.

Berlyne (1967, 1973) himself, after masterfully reviewing more recent pertinent research findings, expressed "grave doubts" about the mechanism he had proposed. New evidence makes it clear that a reduction in arousal is not a necessary condition for reward. Both decreases and increases in arousal have been found to constitute reward, a circumstance that motivated Berlyne (1967) to incorporate both types of change in the jag model: "I would modify the notion of the arousal jag. Data from many different sources now compel us to entertain the hypothesis that reinforcement, and in particular reward, can result in some circumstances from an increase in arousal regardless of whether it is soon followed by a decrease [p. 30]." This extension clearly does away with the stipulation that, regarding suspense, distress be promptly followed by relief. The model now predicts that suspense will be enjoyed if the distress induced is reduced *or boosted,* provided that the boost does not push arousal up to extreme and, in Berlyne's view, necessarily noxious levels.

In the consideration of the enjoyment of suspense, the latter prediction is highly counterintuitive and confusing. People simply are not known to rejoice as they watch the protagonists they like and care for "go from the frying pan into the fire." But even if the boost extension is disregarded, a close examination of assumptions and implications of the jag model leads to considerable confusion. Starting with the basic aversion-relief relationship, it would seem most parsimonious to assume that the experiential intensity of relief is equal to, if not less than, that of the antecedent aversion. With relief, the distressed individual "gets back to normal." In this return to a basal experiential level, there seems little cause for euphoria. Yet, in the arousal-jag

model it has been assumed all along that the experiential intensity of relief outdoes that of its antecedent aversion. Hedonically speaking, aversion and relief are not viewed as cancelling each other out; instead, a surplus of euphoria is expected. Berlyne (1967) explicates this formidable assumption as follows: "When the aversion system is inactivated, the reward system becomes active. This may be simply because it is disinhibited, but it is likely to be subject to *additional activation through a rebound mechanism* [p. 85, emphasis added]." Following the termination of aversion, then, the reward system is expected to overshoot on the rebound, making aversions rewarding indeed. Notwithstanding the fact that this view enjoys only scanty research support (e.g., Grastyán, Szabo, Molnar, & Kolta, 1968), it generates a considerable conceptual dilemma. Taking this view to its logical extension, the mere fact that an aversion comes to an end (and sooner or later every aversion has to come to an end) gives that aversion reward value and makes it enjoyable. Similarly, since the aversion-reward relationship is assumed symmetrical and reversible, the very fact that rewarding conditions are discontinued makes reward punishing. Needless to say, such reasoning transforms punishment into reward and reward into punishment—a most precarious situation even if one could conjure up some examples of the avoidance of a thoroughly good thing for fear that it would not last forever.

In light of the complications discussed, it is difficult to accept the arousal-jag model as a plausible and compelling resolution to the empathy paradox in the enjoyment of suspense. By the same token, and counter to much popular conviction regarding the subject, the notion of relief, even when relief is conceptualized in purely cognitive terms or in all conceivable psycho-physiological manifestations, cannot provide a fully satisfactory resolution to the paradox. Any model that bases its predictions of the enjoyment of suspense solely on the consideration of relief from aversion is bound to be unconvincing when truly euphoric reactions are to be explained. It would seem that the enjoyment of suspenseful drama derives its affective intensity from something more than the mere reduction of an annoyance.

THE EXCITATION-TRANSFER EXPLANATION OF THE ENJOYMENT OF SUSPENSEFUL DRAMA

We will now develop a rationale in which suspense-induced excitatory reactions, the physiological concomitants of empathetic distress, are also of central significance in accounting for the enjoyment of suspenseful drama. Unlike in the arousal-jag model, however, it is not a drop or a boost of arousal, but the level of sympathetic activity as such that is crucial. In addition, the hedonic valence of a particular reaction is not considered to be determined by the change in the level of excitation that may accompany it,

nor by a range into which the prevailing level of excitation may happen to fall, but is instead viewed to be mainly the result of cognitive operations. More specifically, the hedonic valence of the experiential state is seen to be determined by the individual's appraisal of the environmental stimulus conditions to which he or she is responding.

The reasoning we bring to bear in explanation of suspense derives from the excitation-transfer paradigm. This paradigm has been presented in detail elsewhere (Zillmann, 1971, 1978). In addition, its general implications for the effects of and on exposure to communication have been discussed previously (e.g., Tannenbaum & Zillmann, 1975). Suffice it here to present only those features and implications of the paradigm that are essential to the explanation of the enjoyment of suspenseful drama.

It is proposed that the individual who anticipates or witnesses the victimization of agents toward which he or she is favorably disposed: (1) experiences an elevation of sympathetic excitation; and (2) appraises his or her reaction as dysphoric. The intensity of the individual's feelings of dysphoria—feelings which we will refer to as "empathetic distress"—is determined by the prevailing level of sympathetic activity. (The dispositional part of this proposition derives from disposition theory [Zillmann, Bryant, & Sapolsky, 1979; Zillmann & Cantor, 1976, 1977]. The part regarding the function of appraisal accords with Schachter's [1964] two-factor theory of emotion.)

It is further proposed that, mainly because of the humoral mediation of the excitatory reaction, elevated sympathetic activity decays comparatively slowly. Portions of it may persist for some time after the termination of the arousing stimulus condition. Such residual excitation tends to go unrecognized, mainly because of poor interoception, and then to combine with the excitatory activity that is produced by subsequent stimuli.

Finally, it is proposed that the experiential status of any subsequent affective reaction is determined by the respondent's appraisal of the environmental circumstances that produce this reaction. (Obviously, the reaction's hedonic valence is part of the experiential status.) The intensity of the affective reaction, however, is determined by the union of (1) excitation specifically produced by the subsequent stimulus condition and (2) residual excitation from preceding stimulation.

Generally speaking, then, the experiential status of any affective reaction is viewed as being cognitively determined. The intensity of affect, in contrast, is viewed as being determined by the prevailing level of sympathetic activity. To the extent that an affective reaction is associated with sympathetic activity that derives in part from earlier stimulation, the intensity of affect will be higher than it should be on the basis of present stimuli alone.

This latter prediction of an affective "overreaction" to subsequent stimuli is the key element in our approach to suspense. We may conceive of suspense

and its resolution as a sequence of affective reactions in which residues of excitation from the antecedent condition intensify the reaction to the subsequent condition. The experience of empathetic distress during the suspense period may well be acutely negative, hedonically speaking. Regarding the excitatory residues from distress that may enter the resolution period, the consideration of hedonic valence is not relevant, however. Residues from negative states are expected to intensify positive or negative subsequent states just as much as residues from positive states. The residues are thus "unbiased" toward the kind of experience they come to intensify.

At this point, it becomes clear that the transfer paradigm projects the intensification of euphoria after empathetic distress only if euphoria is cognitively achieved. Only if there is a "happy turn of events" in the resolution of suspense can this be expected. The mere removal of the threat that produced empathetic distress in the first place may be considered a minimal stimulus condition for the cognitive switch from dysphoria to euphoria. But as we have indicated earlier, "happy endings" usually provide more than relief alone. They tend to confound relief with a wealth of gratifications that await the protagonist who had been endangered and that make the outcome satisfying to the onlooker (cf. Zillmann, Johnson, & Hanrahan, 1973). Characteristically, there is ample cause for the cognitive adjustment to positively toned affect.

Once the resolution of suspense accomplishes the discussed adjustment, the resultant feelings of euphoria should be enhanced by any residual excitation from the distress response to suspense. In fact, it is to be expected that the euphoric reaction to a satisfying, "happy" resolution of suspense will be more intensely experienced the greater the excitatory residues from the precipitating suspense-induced distress. To the extent that the cognitive reaction to the resolution of suspense in the macro- and microstructure of suspenseful drama produces enjoyment, the more such drama initially distresses the respondent, the more it is ultimately enjoyed. The better a suspense treatment takes effect—that is, the greater the empathetic distress it activates—the more enjoyment a satisfying resolution will liberate. And by the same token, it seems that the provision of the same satisfying resolutions, when not precipitated by arousing events, can only produce flat drama— drama incapable of generating a high intensity of euphoric feelings in the respondent.

It should be recognized that the predictions for the "enjoyment" of tragic events are quite different. Clearly, in response to a sad and "unhappy" turn of events, dysphoric feelings are to be expected. Analogous to our proposal regarding satisfying resolutions, it is to be expected that the dysphoric reaction to a dissatisfying, "sad" resolution of suspense will be more intensely experienced the greater the excitatory residues from the preceding suspense-induced distress. Ultimately, the more empathetic distress is activated by the

events preceding the resolution, the sadder the tragic resolution will appear (Zillmann, Mody, & Cantor, 1974). It seems, then, that if the creation of intense, deep feelings of sadness is accepted as the objective of tragedy, suspense-induced distress may serve well toward that end.

It was suggested earlier that the principal forms of a satisfying resolution (not just a relieving resolution) are the benefaction of good and liked protagonists and the just, punitive treatment of their transgressive and resented opponents. The contribution of these "gratifiers" to the enjoyment of drama—at the cognitive rather than at the gut level—should not be underestimated. Nonetheless, it must also be acknowledged that the display of gratifying happenings may occasion excitatory reactions of a nontrivial magnitude. Excitatory reactions are certainly not restricted to aversions and may well accompany joyous responses to hoped-for outcomes.

Such an acknowledgment would seem troublesome for the arousal-jag model in that the termination of aversion, which is assumed to trigger a drop in arousal, coincides with the onset of joy, which might boost arousal. Drop and boost may be expected to cancel each other out and lead to a nonappreciable change, a condition from which the jag model cannot predict anything. The situation for the application of the transfer paradigm is very different. In contrast to the jag model which favors steep gradients for the arousal drop (or boost), the transfer paradigm favors flat decay gradients, and it readily accommodates any increase in excitation due to the subsequent stimulation itself (i.e., during and after resolution). This principal difference between the models is clear from a comparison of Figs. 6.1 and 6.2. Expressed in terms of the enjoyment of suspenseful drama, the excitation-transfer

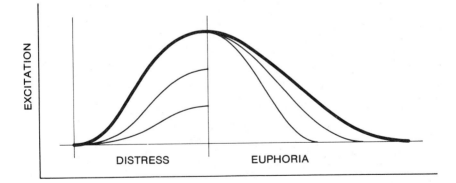

FIG. 6.2. The excitation-transfer paradigm applied to suspense and its resolution. Suspense is assumed to produce distress, and its resolution euphoria. The heavy line indicates optimal conditions for the enjoyment of suspenseful drama. Enjoyment is expected to be intense when the excitatory reaction is pronounced and long-lasting.

paradigm thus leads to the expectation that, other things being equal, such drama will be more enjoyed: (1) the more residual excitation from a suspense treatment persists during the satisfying resolution of this treatment; (2) the longer excitatory residues persist; and (3) the more excitation the resolution itself contributes. The third condition, in fact, may prove crucial in the creation of high intensities of euphoric feelings (i.e., intensities high enough to subdue and overpower any great impression that preceding reactions of distress might have made).

THE RESEARCH EVIDENCE
ON SUSPENSE AND ENJOYMENT

The implications of the level of suspense for the enjoyment of drama were first explored in an investigation by Zillmann, Hay, and Bryant (1975). Different versions of an audiovisual adventure story were created for child audiences. The style of the show followed that of the then-popular television program "Johnny Quest." Two boys were shown on an African safari with their fathers who sent them out on their first lion hunt without adult supervision. The depicted hunt was manipulated to accomplish a factorial variation of: (1) the level of suspense (low, intermediate, high); and (2) the resolution of suspense (resolved, unresolved). The variation in level of suspense was achieved by presenting the lion as differently dangerous. He was described as just a wild lion under "low," as a rather vicious one under "intermediate," and as a most ferocious beast that had killed men before under "high." The audiovisual depiction differed analogously: showing the lion at a distance, close by, or in close-ups that featured enormous roars and displays of the lion's teeth. Several "close calls" were shown as the boys stalked the lion. The boys' anxiety reactions to these happenings were also manipulated, with the least fear shown under "low" and the most under "high." The variation in resolution was achieved by the boys' successful completion of their mission (i.e., they killed the lion) under "resolved" and by their being unsuccessful under "unresolved." In the latter condition, the boys managed only to wound the lion, which escaped and could be heard roaring nearby as the boys made it safely back to camp. Suspense thus was made to linger on to the very end of the story, and the "resolution" was expected to be rather nonsatisfying.

Subjects were shown one of the six versions on a television monitor. While they were watching, physiological measures were taken (heart rate, vasoconstriction), and their facial reactions were secretly filmed. After exposure, they were interviewed about the show, the interview again being secretly recorded. Finally, the subjects rated their enjoyment of the show on a scale devised for children.

Both the video- and the audiotapes were coded by judges who were naive about the experimental conditions. These judges assessed the facial and verbal expressions of fear and enjoyment, among other things. The analysis of the expressions of fear leaves no doubt about the fact that the respondents' reaction to a suspense treatment is one of distress. As expected, the experience of empathetic distress was found to increase in intensity with the level of suspense. Sympathetic excitation was also found to increase—along with the perception of the protagonists' endangerment and the expression of distress—with the level of suspense.

The various measures of enjoyment employed produced rather redundant findings. The pattern of enjoyment that emerged with considerable consistency is displayed in Table 6.1. As can be seen, the enjoyment of drama increased with the level of suspense. As predicted, the more intense the induced empathetic distress, the greater was the enjoyment of drama which provided a satisfying resolution. (It should be remembered that the satisfying turn of events was identical in the compared conditions.) But the finding that under conditions of lingering suspense enjoyment also tended to increase with level of suspense comes somewhat as a surprise. The latter finding can be accounted for, however, if the resolution is considered to be mildly satisfying. The boys, after all, did make it safely back to camp and thus terminated their endangerment. The attempted "nonresolution" appears to have served as a "minimally satisfying resolution." Thus viewed, all the findings accord with the predictions from the excitation-transfer paradigm.

It is of interest to note that the analysis of changes in excitatory activity showed relief reactions only for the very satisfactory resolution. Counter to the arousal-jag model's projection of steep relief gradients, however, *slow* decay of sympathetic excitation was in evidence. Despite the absence of a drop in arousal, the removal of suspense (i.e., the death of the lion) prompted facial expressions of relief more or less instantaneously. If arousal, then, is

TABLE 6.1
Enjoyment of Suspenseful Drama as a Function of the Magnitude
and the Resolution of Threat

Resolution of Threat	*Magnitude of Threat*		
	Low	*Intermediate*	*High*
Very satisfying	1.9[a]	2.8[b]	3.6[c]
Minimally satisfying	1.5[a]	2.5[b]	2.6[b]

Note. Enjoyment was assessed on a scale ranging from 1 to 4. Means having different superscripts differ significantly. (Adapted from Zillmann, Hay, & Bryant, 1975.)

operationalized in peripheral manifestations of sympathetic activity, the proposal that the experience of relief results from a sudden arousal drop is not supported. It is also of interest to note that the minimally satisfactory resolution failed to produce a reduction of excitation for a considerable period of time. The fact that the stronger distress-induced excitatory reactions fostered nevertheless greater enjoyment than the weaker reactions—in the apparent absence of relief from arousal—further challenges the jag model.

It should be mentioned in this connection that additional and rather compelling evidence against the drive-reduction explanation of the conversion of fear into joy comes from research on parachuting. Klausner (1967), in particular, has observed that sports parachutists, as they prepare for a jump, become substantially aroused and experience considerable fear. The state of elevated excitation was found to be surprisingly stable during exit, after exit, and at the opening of the parachute. Just before and upon landing, excitation was still elevated, but the onset of recovery was in evidence. Although there was no arousal-jagging, the parachutists fluctuated between fear and joy. This fluctuation is apparently cognitively determined. According to Klausner, the parachutists experience a decline in fear and a corresponding increase in enthusiasm right after exiting. A moment of apprehension before the opening of the parachute converts enthusiasm back to fear, but after the opening, joy again becomes dominant. Klausner (1968) describes and explains this chain of events as follows:

> At any given time during the jump phase, fear and enthusiasm are negatively related. The peak of fear, which is experienced at the inception of the jump run, is positively correlated with the level of enthusiasm at subsequent points. The more frightened the skydivers are at the start of the jump run, the more enthusiastic they become later. Since the level of arousal is fairly constant throughout, it is the jumper's appraisal of the situation and of the task remaining before him that changes from point to point. Under one set of conditions the organisms's excitement is experienced as fear, and under other conditions this same energy, arousal, or excitement is experienced as enthusiasm—this is a "transformation" of fear into enthusiasm [p. 153].

This account is damaging to a jag interpretation, but accords perfectly with our explanation of the enjoyment of suspenseful drama.

Other research on parachuting is equally revealing. It has been found, for example, that novice parachutists, especially just prior to landing, experience a much higher level of excitation than experienced jumpers do (Epstein, 1967; Fenz & Epstein, 1967). Emotional habituation (cf. Janis, Mahl, Kagan, & Holt, 1969) to the fear-inducing stimuli involved in parachuting is in evidence, and this habituation may be expected to reduce the intensity of joy together with the intensity of fear. The findings thus suggest that the fascination with a

distress-based entertaining activity will vanish along with the fear involved. As the distress goes, so goes the joy; and what was initially exciting and fascinating becomes routine and dull. This syndrome relates directly to suspense: It shows that intense distress is the price to be paid for the high-intensity enjoyment of drama.

Returning to research on suspense as such, several recent investigations have further corroborated the validity of the excitation-transfer explanation of the enjoyment of suspenseful drama. These investigations have extended the earlier observations on children to adult audiences. But more importantly, they have examined the implications of additional principal variables of drama.

Bryant (1978a) explored the effect of a wide range of levels of suspense and of particular suspense-resolving agents on the enjoyment of drama. He took the rather stock plot of a Western hero in peril and created successively lower levels of suspense by successively removing the various elements of suspense involved. The story featured a pony-express rider who lost his horse to a hostile environment, was injured, and tried to fight his way to the next outpost through barren territory populated only by rattlesnakes and outlaws. In the condition of extreme suspense, the hero was severely wounded, outnumbered and cornered by outlaws, unable to move, and acutely endangered by a snake. These elements of threat and danger were then modified to the point where, in the condition of minimal suspense, the hero was only slightly injured and the rattlesnakes kept a good distance. The hero finally escaped his predicament either through his own actions or through the intervention of the cavalry.

The findings regarding the effect of the various levels of suspense are displayed in Table 6.2. Although the story as such fostered only very modest reactions of enjoyment, the tendency for enjoyment to increase with the level of suspense is clearly evident. The data also show a good correspondence between the magnitude of the excitatory reaction associated with empathetic distress and the later enjoyment of the resolution of the drama. Compared to

TABLE 6.2
Level of Suspense, Excitatory Reactions, and Enjoyment of Drama

	Level of Suspense				
Measure	Very Low	Low	Intermediate	High	Very High
Δ Heart rate	1.2[a]	1.9[a]	3.2[b]	4.8[c]	6.0[d]
Enjoyment	14[a]	19[a]	28[b]	40[c]	39[c]

Note. Δ Heart rate reports the observed increase in heart rate from the beginning to the end of the distress-inducing events featured. Enjoyment was assessed on a scale ranging from 0 to 100. Means having different superscripts differ significantly (horizontal comparison only). (Adapted from Bryant, 1978a, with permission.)

the resolution of suspense by outside intervention, the story was enjoyed to a greater degree when the protagonist resolved his dilemma through his own actions. This latter effect was independent of level of suspense.

In the two investigations of suspense discussed, the level of suspense was manipulated by varying the magnitude of the dangers that confront the protagonist. The severity of endangerment, however, is only partly determined with the magnitude of a particular threat per se. In the sense of "destructive power," a ferocious gorilla, for example, constitutes a certain degree of danger. But the endangerment of a protagonist produced by the confrontation with this danger would seem to depend greatly on the protagonist's ability to avoid or avert this danger. The confrontation with the gorilla should constitute an enormous endangerment for a meek, weak, and unarmed protagonist. For an experienced hunter, equipped with an elephant gun and ready to blast away, in contrast, it should prove minimally endangering. In the suspense movie "Wait until dark," the heroine is blind and so defenseless that even a small child could have created the endangerment that was accomplished by her confrontation with malicious characters of great physical strength. It should be clear from the preceding that high levels of suspense can be built with (1) great dangers; (2) a low capability to cope with them; or (3) the combination of these two elements. Characteristically, the endangerment of a protagonist, and for that matter, the level of suspense, is a joint function of the degree of danger and the protagonist's relative inability to protect himself against it. In suspenseful drama, the helplessness of a potential victim seems as important as the brute force of the perpetrators of evil.

The possibility of enhancing the enjoyment of drama through high levels of suspense built solely on the defenselessness of the endangered protagonist has been explored in an investigation by Bergman (1978; Master's thesis research under the author's supervision). Different versions of a miniature drama were especially written and produced for television. The drama featured a sympathetic female protagonist, a student, who lives with her boyfriend, also a student, in a university apartment. Both are putting themselves through college. Her income comes from tutoring students with math problems. While working at home with one of her students who is certain that they will be alone for some time, she finds herself threatened with rape. The threat of rape, manifest in the power the potential rapist could exert to force his victim to comply with his demands, was kept constant in all experimental conditions.

The condition of great endangerment was created by making the female appear weak and fragile, an appearance created in the initial interaction scenes with her boyfriend. In the conditions of minimal endangerment, these same interactions reveal that she is a karate expert. She asserts herself with ease and playfully dominates her boyfriend. When the rape threat materializes, the helpless protagonist panics and expresses great fear. In

contrast, the protagonist who is depicted as capable of defending herself confronts her assailant with little fear and in a self-confident manner. In both versions, the female ultimately gets hold of a pair of scissors and uses them as a weapon to scare off her assailant. A struggle ensues which results in a fatal injury of one of the parties involved. Obviously, the version in which the female is stabbed constitutes a disturbing, unsatisfying resolution of suspense. The ending featuring the female's victory over her assailant, although not exactly a happy ending, manifests a more satisfying resolution.

The endangerment of a liked protagonist appearing to be utterly incapable of coping with the situation proved to be very effective for creating a high level of suspense. As measured in changes of heart rate, of systolic and diastolic blood pressure, and of vasoconstriction, excitatory reactions in the high-endangerment conditions were substantially more pronounced than in the low-suspense conditions. Both males and females interpreted their reactions as distress, with female respondents predictably reporting the highest degree of disturbance.

The effect of this intensity of empathetic distress on the enjoyment of the drama as a whole is displayed in Table 6.3. As predicted, a high level of suspense enhanced the enjoyment of drama with a satisfying resolution. Also as predicted, the enjoyment of drama with a dissatisfying resolution tended to be impaired by great antecedent distress. The only puzzling finding is that under conditions of "low endangerment" the different resolutions failed to affect enjoyment. This lack of an anticipated difference may be due to the likely disappointment resulting from thwarted expectations. Respondents had reason to expect that the threatened but self-confident female, in a display of her karate expertise, would readily dispose of her assailant without injuring him severely. Instead, they find her struggling and resorting to the use of a deadly weapon. Her actions exhibit a certain degree of clumsiness, and the recognition of that may well have spoiled the enjoyment of her "victory."

Bryant (1978b) conducted another investigation that not only further corroborates the excitation-transfer prediction of increased enjoyment on the

TABLE 6.3

Enjoyment of Suspenseful Drama as a Function of the Protagonist's Ability to Cope with Endangerment and of the Resolution of Endangerment

Resolution of Endangerment	Degree of Endangerment	
	Low	High
Satisfying	32[a]	56[b]
Unsatisfying	32[a]	16[a]

Note. Enjoyment was assessed on a scale ranging from 0 to 100. Means having different superscripts differ significantly.

basis of residual excitation from distress, but also documents the dispositional mediation of empathetic distress proposed earlier. Various versions of a minidrama were again written and produced for the experiment. The story featured a female protagonist who was depicted either as a very obnoxious person, as a most sympathetic one, or as one to be met with feelings of indifference on the part of the audience. The variation in these affective dispositions toward the protagonist was accomplished by various interactions with other characters in the initial part of the plot (cf. Zillmann & Cantor, 1977). After the protagonist's character was thus developed, a rather standard suspense treatment was employed: The female was shown shopping at a late hour in a grocery store and being watched by a male who follows her to her car. Frightened, she seeks refuge in a nearby tenement building but is assaulted as she reaches it. The ensuing struggle terminates as one party is pushed down a flight of stairs and severely injured by the fall.

Level of suspense (low vs. high) was manipulated through the variation of both the apparent threat posed by the assailant and by the fear reactions displayed by the victim. In the condition of high suspense, the assailant was portrayed as an extremely sinister person and his victim was shown in extreme fear. The threat and the fear in response to it were presented in lavish detail by numerous close-ups. Threat and fear were simply de-emphasized in the condition of low suspense, mainly by omitting the detailed display of pertinent expressions. The resolution of the suspense was accomplished either with the protagonist's victory over her assailant (satisfying) or with her becoming the unfortunate victim of the assault (unsatisfying or dissatisfying ending).

In accord with the dispositional considerations outlined earlier, it was found that empathetic distress manifests itself only when the affective disposition toward the endangered protagonist is positive. Excitatory reactions proved to be minimal when the protagonist in peril was disliked or met with indifference. Whether the level of suspense was low or high, and regardless of the particular resolution, enjoyment was low and not appreciably different under conditions of negative affective disposition. As can be seen from Table 6.4 (in which levels of suspense are collapsed), the satisfying resolution prompted increased enjoyment under conditions of affective indifference. However, under conditions of positive affect, the enjoyment of suspense that is resolved in a satisfying manner reached substantially higher levels.

The suspense variation affected enjoyment only in the condition of positive affective disposition. This effect, which is displayed in Table 6.5, is redundant with that obtained in earlier investigations. Excitatory residues from more pronounced distress in the conditions of high suspense were found to enhance enjoyment only when a satisfying resolution was provided. Following the rather dissatisfying resolution, these same residues tended to lower enjoyment

TABLE 6.4

Enjoyment of Suspenseful Drama as a Function of the Affective
Disposition Toward the Protagonist and the Resolution of the
Endangerment

Resolution of Endangerment	Affective Disposition		
	Negative	Neutral	Positive
Satisfying	14^a	26^b	51^c
Unsatisfying	15^a	19^a	15^a

Note. Enjoyment was assessed on a scale ranging from 0 to 100. Means
having different superscripts differ significantly. (Adapted from Bryant,
1978b, with permission.)

TABLE 6.5

Enjoyment of Suspenseful Drama as a Function of the
Magnitude and the Resolution of Threat

Resolution of Threat	Magnitude of Threat	
	Low	High
Satisfying	39^b	63^c
Unsatisfying	17^a	13^a

Note. Enjoyment was assessed on a scale ranging from 0 to
100. Means having different superscripts differ significantly.
(Adapted from Bryant, 1978b, with permission.)

(or more correctly, further reactions of disappointment and sadness). Clearly,
these findings accord well with predictions from the excitation-transfer
paradigm; and taken together with the findings of the earlier investigations
discussed, they lend strong support to the transfer explanation of the
enjoyment of suspenseful drama.

A NOTE ON SUSPENSE SEEKING

It should be clear from the preceding discussion that the effect of suspense-
induced distress on the enjoyment of drama depends greatly on the resolution
of suspense. Without consideration of the particular ways in which
sympathetic protagonists in peril cope with and overcome their plight,
predictions of enjoyment, if meaningful at all, cannot be very accurate.
Similarly, it seems rather pointless, it not futile, to consider only the one or the
other element of the suspense-resolution sequence in the projection of the
enormous appeal of suspenseful drama. The resolution of suspense is an

integral part of suspenseful drama. Suspense and its resolution form a meaningful entity that must be kept intact for the explanation of the popularity of suspenseful drama.

If one were to isolate suspense conceptually and to disregard its resolution, the appeal of suspenseful drama might appear to be simply a case of stress- or distress-seeking (Klausner, 1968). Zuckerman (1974, 1976) recently proposed that people differ considerably with regard to their eagerness to confront stressful situations, and he suggested that the behavior of those who seek out intense sensations is governed by a "biological need" for high stimulation. It could thus be argued that the "thriller" enthusiast seeks out intense sensations, regardless of their hedonic valence, in order to satisfy a biological urge. According to this view, extremely disturbing tragedy should be enormously attractive. Given the far greater popularity of drama that features favorable outcomes, however, it would appear that the induction of intense but negative sensations does not, in and of itself, constitute a winning formula for drama. It seems that what is being sought is not simply intense stimulation but, ultimately, *pleasant* intense stimulation. In drama, according to our proposal, intense positive sensations are accessible mainly through initial distress. It may be assumed that the enthusiast has learned to expect this distress. But more importantly, he or she should also have learned to expect that this distress is generally followed by a favorable turn of events that triggers euphoric reactions. The enthusiast may thus have come to accept and *tolerate* a certain degree of aversion as an antecedent of pleasure.

If the suspense–resolution unity is left intact, it becomes clear that what may appear to be distress seeking is more likely distress toleration in the context of pleasure seeking. Distress is accepted not because it produces need-satisfying sensations, but because it is instrumental in achieving intense, euphoric reactions; and the drama enthusiast is willing to live through some initial discomfort because he or she has learned to anticipate the benefits that derive from it. The appeal of suspenseful drama is thus explained on the basis of a fundamental behavioral tendency (i.e., the maximization of pleasure), and assumptions about new motivational forces such as the sensation-seeking motive are not necessary. This view does not deny the possibility of potentially great individual variation in the willingness to endure empathetic distress, even when it is anticipated that the negative sensations will be superseded by pleasurable ones.

The recognition that suspense and its resolution constitute a functional unit is important not only in the consideration of the enjoyment of drama, but proves equally critical in the projection of the possible consequences of *continued* exposure to suspenseful drama. In contemporary society, the foremost forum of drama is, without a doubt, television. Suspenseful drama abounds in this medium of entertainment, and conflict, crises, threat, danger, crime, and violence, in turn, seem ever present because of it. This

circumstance has not gone unnoticed: The television industry has come under continuing attack because of the heavy diet of violence and mayhem it feeds to enormous audiences, a diet feared to produce a variety of ill effects (cf. Tannenbaum & Zillmann, 1975).

One of these potential ill effects is the possible creation of apprehensions about personal safety in the viewer. It is possible that continued exposure to muggings, stabbings, and shootings, to threats of rape and mutilation, to extortion, destruction of property, and, not least, murder, could make the respondent feel uneasy. The viewer could come to overestimate the dangers that confront him or her in daily life, and to fear for his or her welfare more than the circumstances warrant. Television, then, chiefly because of the high occurrence of transgressive behavior in the context of suspenseful drama, can be viewed as creating uncalled-for and maladaptive anxieties.

The above rationale has been expounded mainly by Gerbner and Gross (1976). These investigators have also furnished data which indicate that "heavy television viewers" (four or more hours a day) are more concerned about their safety than "light viewers" (two or less hours a day). Heavy viewers reported less trust in others than did light viewers. Additionally, the heavy viewers estimated the likelihood of their direct involvement in violence to be comparatively high—higher than the estimate that light viewers reported.

Although apparently aware of the tentative correlational nature of their data, Gerbner and Gross interpreted these findings as supporting the proposal that heavy exposure to suspenseful drama *causes* apprehensions and fear. Such an interpretation not only lacks validity in a technical sense, but it also seems to be at variance with basic psychological considerations. If exposure to transgression-laden suspenseful drama produces acute anxieties, the viewer should shun such dramatic fare. He or she should avoid repeating the aversive experience, and this avoidance should convert the heavy viewer into a light viewer. In short, it is difficult to see why the heavy viewer would keep up his or her heavy consumption of anxiety-generating fare.

It appears that the findings reported by Gerbner and Gross are equally (if not more) consistent with the alternative causal possibility: Anxiety may foster heavy viewing of programs that feature suspenseful drama. Unlike the Gerbner-Gross proposal, such an expectation is not based on the consideration of fear-inducing stimuli alone, but on the suspense-resolution unity instead.

Even a cursory look at television drama makes it quite clear that suspenseful drama does not merely present the victimization of liked protagonists and innocent bystanders by hordes of wrongdoers who plague society as they please. Although the display of transgression is undoubtedly an essential part of suspenseful drama, it should not be overlooked that such

drama almost always features the triumph of justice (cf. Zillmann & Bryant, 1975). Wrongdoers are caught and duly punished; justice is brought to the situation; society is freed from dangerous elements; rapists, murderers, and kidnappers are "put away." Even a hostile environment (e.g., an earthquake, an epidemic) is ultimately brought under control. If anything, suspenseful drama on television distorts reality more toward security than toward danger: It projects too just, and maybe too safe, a world. In real life, bank robbers, rapists, and killers are less frequently and less promptly brought to justice than in the world of television. To the extent that such portrayal of "crime and punishment" affects the viewer's perception of reality, one should expect the troubled and anxiety-ridden citizen to find comfort and seek refuge in drama that features the cleanup operations of law enforcers, "private eyes," and vigilantes. In fact, it may be argued that it is the very projection of a just and safe world that attracts those who are acutely worried more than it attracts those who experience little apprehension.

It is conceivable, then, that anxious people resort to watching much suspenseful drama because it reduces their anxieties. This possible chain of events is not only predictable from the consideration of the predominant theme of suspenseful drama on television—good forces weeding out the evil—but also accords with expectations that can be derived from behavior-modification theory (Bandura, 1969). It can be argued that those who are acutely fearful, presumably because of threatening events in their environment, respond intensely to the distressing parts of suspenseful drama. Analogous to the extinction of fear in a phobic person, which is, in its initial stages, accomplished by repeated exposure to a communication-mediated (and thus harmless) fear-inducing stimulus, the transgression-phobic person's distress reaction should undergo habituation. As a person who is fearful of snakes, for example, comes to tolerate them in word and photograph, in movies, and finally in live encounters, the troubled person, it would seem, can cure his or her own anxieties by heavy exposure to the very events and characters that make him or her tremble. The anxious person's heavy consumption of suspenseful drama thus could be viewed as a self-administered behavior-modification program.

Fenichel (1939, 1945) has entertained a very similar view. He suggested that the anxious person develops a "counterphobic attitude" that motivates him or her to confront—under safe conditions, to be sure—the fear-inducing stimuli. The continued experience of "mastery" of the situation, an experience Fenichel thought would provide a "functional pleasure," would ultimately reduce the individual's anxieties and prepare him or her for the confrontation with the actual fear-inducing event under normal conditions.

There is some research evidence that relates to these proposals. Boyanowsky, Newtson, and Walster (1974) have reported data that suggest that scared people develop an appetite for "scary drama." After the much

publicized brutal murder of a freshman woman at the University of Wisconsin, attendance at a movie shown locally that featured psychopathic killings greatly increased (relative to a control condition). Although the film must have reinstated salient anxieties, people apparently did not shun it. But did they seek it out, as Fenichel might have surmised, to learn "how much distress they could take?" Did they go there to reduce their anxiety, or to learn ways of coping with the threat? The data at hand do not give us the answers. They also do not tell us what effect, independent of the moviegoers' intentions, exposure to the movie may have had. It may well have reduced their anxieties, but it may equally well have exacerbated them. We simply do not know yet.

The main purpose of this discussion is, in fact, to caution against the uncritical acceptance of hasty and unwarranted interpretations of scanty research findings. At this stage, it has not been demonstrated that heavy exposure to transgression-laden suspenseful drama creates maladaptive anxieties. Nor has it been demonstrated that it helps to cope with anxieties. There are theoretical reasons for expecting ill effects. But there are equally, if not more compelling, theoretical reasons for expecting beneficial effects. In addition, a case could be made for the absence of side effects. It could be argued that the drama enthusiasts readily discriminate between fact and fiction, and that the viewers' consumption of suspenseful drama does thus not affect their perception of and their response to the real world. Obviously, the controversy can be settled only as more decisive research evidence becomes available.

Finally, it should be noted that, regardless of whatever side effect exposure to transgression-laden drama may or may not have, suspenseful drama that features a satisfying resolution is likely to be more intensely enjoyed by initially fearful persons than by people without apprehensions. The fearful person should experience more empathetic distress than the person without fear (Sapolsky & Zillmann, 1978), and the greater excitatory residues from this more intense distress reaction should intensify the enjoyment of the resolution to a greater degree. Should, for whatever reason, a person's anxiety dissipate, the intensity of distress from dramatic events should also decline, and along with that decline, enjoyment of the final dramatic happenings should also wane. These likely dependencies exhibit once again the seemingly paradoxical relationship between suspense and enjoyment: no stress, no joy! Put more affirmatively, the more initial distress, the more subsequent joy.

ACKNOWLEDGMENT

The author's research discussed in this chapter has been supported in full or in part by Grants GS-35165 and SOC-7513431 from the National Science Foundation.

REFERENCES

Bandura, A. *Principles of behavior modification.* New York: Holt, Rinehart & Winston, 1969.

Berger, S. M. Conditioning through vicarious instigation. *Psychological Review,* 1962, *29,* 450–466.

Bergman, S. *Vulnerability of the protagonist and suspense in drama.* Incomplete, unpublished master's thesis, Indiana University, 1978.

Berlyne, D. E. *Conflict, arousal, and curiosity.* New York: McGraw-Hill, 1960.

Berlyne, D. E. Arousal and reinforcement. In D. Levine (Ed.), *Nebraska Symposium on Motivation* (Vol. XV). Lincoln: University of Nebraska Press, 1967.

Berlyne, D. E. The vicissitudes of aplopathematic and thelematoscopic pneumatology (or the hydrography of hedonism). In D. E. Berlyne & K. B. Madsen (Eds.), *Pleasure, reward, preference: Their nature, determinants, and role in behavior.* New York: Academic Press, 1973.

Boyanowsky, E. O., Newtson, D., & Walster, E. Film preferences following a murder. *Communication Research,* 1974, *1,* 32–43.

Bryant, J. *The effect of different levels of suspense and of the source of the resolution of suspense on the appreciation of dramatic presentations.* Unpublished manuscript, University of Massachusetts, 1978. (a)

Bryant, J. *The effect of disposition toward a protagonist and of sex of viewer on the appreciation of dramatic presentations with variations in degree of suspense and ultimate outcome for the protagonist.* Unpublished manuscript, University of Massachusetts, 1978. (b)

Epstein, S. Toward a unified theory of anxiety. In B. A. Maher (Ed.), *Progress in experimental personality research* (Vol. 4). New York: Academic Press, 1967.

Fenichel, O. The counterphobic attitude. *International Journal of Psychoanalysis,* 1939, *20,* 263–274.

Fenichel, O. *The psychoanalytic theory of neurosis.* New York: Norton, 1945.

Fenz, W. D., & Epstein, S. Gradients of physiological arousal in parachutists as a function of an approaching jump. *Psychosomatic Medicine,* 1967, *24,* 33–51.

Gerbner, G., & Gross, L. Living with television: The violence profile. *Journal of Communication,* 1976, *26*(2), 173–199.

Grastyán, E., Szabo, I., Molnar, P., & Kolta, P. Rebound, reinforcement and self-stimulation. *Communications in Behavioral Biology,* 1968, *2,* 235–266.

Hitchcock, A. Interview by H. Brean. *Life,* July 13, 1959, p. 72.

Janis, I. L., Mahl, G. F., Kagan, J., & Holt, R. R. *Personality: Dynamics, development, and assessment.* New York: Harcourt Brace Jovanovich, 1969.

Klausner, S. Z. Sport parachuting. In R. Slovenko & J. A. Knight (Eds.), *Motivations in play, games and sports.* Springfield, Ill.: Charles C Thomas, 1967.

Klausner, S. Z. (Ed.). *Why man takes chances: Studies in stress-seeking.* Garden City, N.Y.: Anchor Books, 1968.

Lazarus, R. S. *Psychological stress and the coping process.* New York: McGraw-Hill, 1966.

Leventhal, H. Emotions: A basic problem for social psychology. In C. Nemeth (Ed.), *Social psychology: Classic and contemporary integrations.* Chicago: Rand McNally, 1974.

Marx, M. *The enjoyment of drama.* New York: F. S. Crofts, 1940.

Sapolsky, B. S., & Zillmann, D. Experience and empathy: Affective reactions to witnessing childbirth. *Journal of Social Psychology,* 1978, *105,* 131–144.

Schachter, S. The interaction of cognitive and physiological determinants of emotional state. In L. Berkowitz (Ed.), *Advances in experimental social psychology* (Vol. 1). New York: Academic Press, 1964.

Smiley, S. *Playwriting: The structure of action.* Englewood Cliffs, N.J.: Prentice-Hall, 1971.

Stotland, E. Exploratory investigations of empathy. In L. Berkowitz (Ed.), *Advances in experimental social psychology* (Vol. 4). New York: Academic Press, 1969.

Tannenbaum, P. H., & Zillmann, D. Emotional arousal in the facilitation of aggression through communication. In L. Berkowitz (Ed.), *Advances in experimental social psychology* (Vol. 8). New York: Academic Press, 1975.

Zillmann, D. Excitation transfer in communication-mediated aggressive behavior. *Journal of Experimental Social Psychology,* 1971, *7,* 419–434.

Zillmann, D. Attribution and misattribution of excitatory reactions. In J. H. Harvey, W. J. Ickes, & R. F. Kidd (Eds.), *New directions in attribution research* (Vol. 2). Hillsdale, N.J.: Lawrence Erlbaum Associates, 1978.

Zillmann, D., & Bryant, J. Viewer's moral sanction of retribution in the appreciation of dramatic presentations. *Journal of Experimental Social Psychology,* 1975, *11,* 572–582.

Zillmann, D., Bryant, J., & Sapolsky, B. S. The enjoyment of watching sport contests. In J. H. Goldstein (Ed.), *Sports, games and play.* Hillsdale, N.J.: Lawrence Erlbaum Associates, 1979.

Zillmann, D., & Cantor, J. R. A disposition theory of humor and mirth. In A. T. Chapman & H. C. Foot (Eds.), *Humor and laughter: Theory, research, and applications.* London: Wiley, 1976.

Zillmann, D., & Cantor, J. R. Affective responses to the emotions of a protagonist. *Journal of Experimental Social Psychology,* 1977, *13,* 155–165.

Zillmann, D., Hay, T. A., & Bryant, J. The effect of suspense and its resolution on the appreciation of dramatic presentations. *Journal of Research in Personality,* 1975, *9,* 307–323.

Zillmann, D., Johnson, R. C., & Hanrahan, J. Pacifying effect of happy ending of communications involving aggression. *Psychological Reports,* 1973, *32,* 967–970.

Zillmann, D., Mody, B., & Cantor, J. R. Empathetic perception of emotional displays in films as a function of hedonic and excitatory state prior to exposure. *Journal of Research in Personality,* 1974, *8,* 335–349.

Zuckerman, M. The sensation seeking motive. In B. A. Maher (Ed.), *Progress in experimental personality research* (Vol. 7). New York: Academic Press, 1974.

Zuckerman, M. Sensation-seeking and anxiety traits and states as determinants of behavior in novel situations. In I. Sarason & C. D. Spielberger (Eds.), *Stress and anxiety* (Vol. 3). New York: Halsted Press, 1976.

7 Humor and Catharsis: The Effect of Comedy on Audiences

Thomas J. Scheff
Stephen C. Scheele
University of California, Santa Barbara

This chapter concerns the problem of the effect of humor: Is laughter good medicine? In lay opinion, the answer is almost a truism: Laughter is widely thought to reduce tension, clear the air, and probably be beneficial in many other ways. Norman Cousin's (1976) article in the *New England Journal of Medicine* provides a dramatic representation of popular belief—he describes how he cured himself of what might have been an otherwise fatal illness, by taking a laughing cure. After 2 weeks in a hospital, with his malady still undiagnosed and getting worse, Cousins stopped taking all drugs and checked into a hotel. He started his own treatment of vitamin C and laughter:

> He sent out for Marx Brothers movies. A projector was set up in the room. "I watched *a Night at the Opera* twice. It's still funny. I watched *Animal Crackers*. I sent out for segments of old *Candid Camera* shows...." "And every day I watched the Marx Brothers and segments of *Candid Camera,* and the hours that were pain-free got longer and longer, and the more I laughed, the better I got." (Smith, 1975, pp. 13–14).

According to his own account, laughter was a central component in Cousins's cure. However, in theoretical discussion and in research, there is a difference of opinion. Among the proponents of laughter, Freud (1905) believed that certain kinds of laughter were tension-reducing, as did Berlyne (1971). In an earlier paper by one of the authors (Scheff, 1977), a theory of catharsis is described which posits laughter as one form of emotional discharge. Nichols and Zax (1977, p. 8) also list laughter as one of the cathartic processes, and other recent proponents include Fry (1963), Greenwald (1975), Mendel (1970), and Mindess (1971).

On the other hand, there are many approaches that question the value of laughter. In studies of humor in experimental social psychology there is a tradition of skepticism about the effects of catharsis, created in part by Berkowitz's (1962) work on aggression catharsis. Among psychoanalysts, laughter is often considered to be a defensive maneuver or a covert form of hostility (Kubie, 1970). Finally, there is a tradition in medical science of considering laughter only in connection with disease (e.g., epilepsy) or psychopathology (as in the case of hebephrenia) (Stearns, 1972).

The disagreement over the effects of laughter is one aspect of a more general controversy concerning catharsis. To understand the significance of the study of laughter in the following report, it is first necessary to place it in the context of the longstanding arguments for and against catharsis.

THE CATHARSIS THEORY

The theory of catharsis has been the subject of intensely heated debate for more than 2000 years. Responding to Plato's condemnation of drama for arousing the passions, and thereby undermining the state, Aristotle contended that drama produced catharsis by purging the audience of pity and terror (Wimsatt & Brooks, 1957). Judging from the deluge of commentary, Aristotle's statement on the nature and function of catharsis may be the most controversial sentence ever written (Lain Entralgo, 1970, pp. 183–239).

The debate over catharsis, in several forms, has continued to the present day. The argument between the advocates of catharsis, on the one hand, and the advocates of insight, on the other, has been a central issue almost from the beginning of psychotherapy. Freud at first advanced a cathartic theory (Freud & Breuer, 1895/1966). In his later work, Freud abandoned cathartic techniques to develop psychoanalysis—emphasis is placed on conscious insight. In contemporary psychotherapy the controversy continues, with some types of therapy (such as Gestalt, Bioenergetics, and Primal Therapy) emphasizing catharsis, and others, such as psychoanalysis and Behavior Modification, suggesting that it has little if any benefit.

In their analyses of the social functions of ritual, anthropologists have long been involved in a similar dispute. Malinowski (1948), representing the positive orientation toward catharsis, argues that ritual serves an important function in that it alleviates the anxieties of the participants in areas of uncertainty. Other anthropologists, however, deny the cathartic function of ritual. Radcliffe-Brown (1952), for example, answered that it is just as reasonable to assume that ritual creates emotional distress, as it is to assume that it alleviates it. Other anthropologists, such as Evans-Pritchard (1965), concurred. In recent years the theory of catharsis has lost its central position among students of ritual. In contemporary anthropology the emphasis has

shifted away from catharsis to a concern for cognitive and symbolic functions (Douglas, 1970; Levi-Strauss, 1969; Turner, 1967). A similar movement has occurred in psychotherapy and psychology. Once of central importance, the theory of catharsis is now considered passé by many researchers in all these fields.

In this chapter we argue that the closing of the debate over catharsis has been premature. The theory of catharsis has never been adequately tested in order to determine whether it should be retained or discarded, either because of a lack of careful definition of what constitutes catharsis or because of a lack of systematic data to evaluate the theory. The absence of an adequate test of the theory can be shown in each of the various debates.

In psychotherapy, the majority of psychoanalysts uncritically accepted Freud's (1910; 1949) criticisms of catharsis, even though they are brief and casual compared to the careful documentation of the effectiveness of catharsis in *Studies on Hysteria* (Freud & Breuer, 1895/1966). Neither Freud nor any other psychotherapist provided any systematic evidence showing that catharsis was invalid. One systematic study suggests the opposite, that catharsis is by far the most frequent cause of success in psychotherapy (Symonds, 1954). In recent years, the success of a cathartic technique for treating pathological bereavement, called "re-grief therapy," provides clinical evidence for the validity of the theory (Volkan & Josephthal, 1979).

As in psychotherapy, the dispute over the function of ritual has proceeded without systematic evidence. Radcliff-Brown and Evans-Pritchard pointed out that Malinowski had no real evidence to support his hypothesis that ritual alleviated anxiety, which was true. However, it was equally true that Radcliff-Brown and Evans-Pritchard also had no data themselves to contradict the hypothesis. Like the argument between Plato and Aristotle over drama, and early Freud and late Freud over psychotherapy, the argument over the functions of ritual was in the nature of a theoretical disputation.

Aggression and Catharsis

The same cannot be said about the debate over "aggression catharsis" that is going on in experimental social psychology. Berkowitz (1962) and Feshbach and Singer (1971) and many, many others have produced a large body of systematic research about the effects of aggression and vicarious aggression on subsequent levels of hostility. Although the problem with these studies is certainly not the lack of systematic data; there is a lack of conceptual definition regarding what constitutes catharsis. Berkowitz (1962) and others have tested the hypothesis that catharsis occurs through aggressive *behavior*. In a typical study, Berkowitz has shown that active retaliation against an aggressor not only does not lower the level of hostility of the person who is retaliating, but may actually raise it. Although this seems to be an important

finding, its relevance to the theory of catharsis is virtually nil since neither Aristotle's doctrine nor Freud and Breuer's technique proposes catharsis in terms of behavior. Nichols and Zax (1977, pp. 187–188) make similar criticisms of the studies of aggression catharsis. Both dramatic and psychotherapeutic theories involve the reexperiencing of past emotional crises in a context of complete security: in the safety of the theatre or therapy, somewhat as in Wordsworth's definition of poetry—strong emotion recollected in tranquility. (In the following discussion, we use the concept of distancing in discussing the balance between involvement in, and detachment from, strong emotions.) The extension of catharsis to include aggressive retaliation seems unwarranted.

The studies of vicarious aggression appear to be more relevant to the theory of catharsis, especially the studies of the effects of viewing television violence, since the contexts studied are similar to dramatic or psychotherapeutic settings envisioned by theorists of catharsis. Even with these studies, however, there is a serious conceptual problem. The treatment variable in the studies of the effects of television is the *viewing* of dramatic violence. However, it is probably a mistake to equate the process of catharsis with the stimuli which may cause it to occur. Presumably catharsis involves a particular type of emotional response within the individual. The viewing of dramatic violence may or may not give rise to this response, depending on the characteristics of the stimuli, the viewers, and other conditions.

Feshbach and Singer (1971) were able to show that high school students who viewed violent TV fare committed fewer aggressive acts than those students who did not view it, a phenomena presumably demonstrating the effect of catharsis. The correlation they found, however, was weak. According to our theory, if the researchers had had some way of separating the viewers of violent fare into those who experienced a cathartic emotional response from those who did not, the data would have shown still stronger support for the theory of catharsis. Among the viewers of violent fare who experienced catharsis, the drop in aggressive behavior would have been greater than the amount reported in the study, and among the viewers of violent fare who did not experience a cathartic response, there would have been no reduction of aggressive behavior at all, thus isolating the causative process: the occurrence of a cathartic response in the context of viewing violent TV fare. The theory of catharsis would be more amenable to testing if catharsis were defined independently of the arousing stimuli.

An operational definition of catharsis that is applicable to the Feshback–Singer study, and similar studies, can be found in a theory of catharsis that has been outlined elsewhere (Scheff, 1979). The theory states that two conditions are necessary for catharsis: first, stimuli which give rise to distressful emotion, such as grief, fear, anger, or embarrassment, and second, adequate distancing. We would argue that all of the violent programming in

the media probably meets the first criterion, in that it gives rise to emotions of fear and/or anger in the viewers. Only some of the violent programming, however, meets the second criterion: adequate distancing. Realistic violence is apt to be underdistanced for most viewers: too much like real life violence and therefore too overwhelming to feel and discharge. At the other extreme, some violent programming may be overdistanced: so stylized or abstract that no fear or anger is aroused in the viewers. Cartoons may be an example of adequately distanced violence: the cartoon animals are sufficiently like human beings so that the viewers identify with them, and therefore feel some vicarious fear and anger, but so obviously harm-proof (the characters feel no pain and shed no blood) the viewers can be simultaneously detached. I have defined the balanced combination of identification and detachment as the optimal distance for vicarious emotions—the distance, therefore, at which catharsis is most likely to occur.

Catharsis and Humor

Spontaneous laughter is defined as the visible, external sign that catharsis, an internal process, is occurring. This discussion suggests, therefore, that studies of the effects of violent programming, as in violent cartoons, should distinguish viewers who laugh and those who do not. According to this theory, maximum catharsis of anger would occur in those subjects in which the greatest amounts of laughter occur.

Laughter is the signal not only for the catharsis of anger, but also of embarrassment. Humorous programming which does not contain violence is mostly about characters making mistakes in public, which gives rise to vicarious embarrassment in viewers. Many comedic forms contain both anger and embarrassment elements. Slapstick comedy, for example, usually provides many episodes of both public mistakes and distanced violence or aggression.

The present study of laughter and humor seeks to test one particular aspect of the theory of catharsis: whether or not catharsis, in this case represented by laughter or humor, reduces tension. Mirroring the theoretical disagreement about whether or not catharsis has beneficial effects, earlier studies of the effects of humor report contradictory findings. The studies which have used a subjective measure of effect, a mood adjective check list (MACL), have inidcated that exposure to a humorous stimulus has a relaxing effect. There have been three such studies: Berkowitz (1970), Dworkin and Efran (1967), and Singer (1968). However, there are studies using objective, physiological measures that have indicated the opposite effect, or no effect: humor or laughter is arousing, or at least not relaxing. This finding has been most clearly established with heart rate (HR) as the measure of effect. There have been six studies of humor and HR: Averill (1969), Fry (1969), Godkewitsch

(1976), Jones and Harris (1971), Langevin and Day (1972), and Martin (1905). These findings have been interpreted by Godkewitsch (1976, p. 135) as contradicting Freud's idea that humor may be tension reducing, and Arnheim's (1971) "cosmic principle" that tension reduction is the source of all reward and pleasure.

How can the difference between the subjective and objective findings be explained? One possibility is that the adjective check list score and HR are not tapping the same phenomenon. HR may not be a valid measure of tension. The position that Lacey and Lacey (1974) take can be interpreted in this way. They argue that the evidence on the relationship between HR and somatic or behavioral processes is quite mixed: some studies report constant relationships, others an absence of relationship, and still others, unexplained reversals. In response, Obrist and his collaborators (1974) suggest that under certain conditions, such as at low levels of arousal or sympathetic influence, there are invariant relationships. Since these conditions obtain in the study of humor and laughter, we will seek the explanation elsewhere.

Another possible explanation concerns the difference in methods used in two sets of studies. It is clear in the MACL studies that the check lists were administered before and after the exposure to the entire set of humorous stimuli. The effect measured would therefore be the net change of subjective tension level caused by the whole period of exposure. Not so with the HR studies. Although each study used a slightly different method, it is immediately apparent that they did not measure the net change in HR. Martin (1905) measured HR only during a short period (approximately 10–15 seconds) following exposure to each humorous stimulus. Langevin and Day (1972) obtained a mean change in HR, but only during the 15 seconds of exposure to each cartoon. Godkewitsch (1976) used a procedure identical to Langevin and Day. Jones and Harris measured HR for only four seconds after the stimulus. Although all of the studies used a series of humorous stimuli, none examined the cumulative or net effect of the series. Fry made no measurements at all; he simply showed a chart which seemed to indicate HR elevation was associated with laughter in two cases.

At first sight, Averill's (1969) study would seem to use a before-and-after design similar to that used in the adjective check list studies. Averill's study also had assumed importance in that it is the only one of the nine studies which used both subjective and objective measures of effect. However, a close inspection shows that his study did not measure net change either. His before measurement is appropriate since it is the mean rate for 6 minutes before exposure to the comic film. But instead of taking his after measurement during the corresponding 6 minutes after the film was over, it was taken during the film's last 6 minutes. Since he states that 78% of the subjects included one or more scenes from the last 6 minutes among the funniest in the film, it is quite likely that laughter occurred during the after-measurement

period. Averill's procedure thus seems to have confounded HR change during laughter with the net change resulting from exposure to the whole film.

Given the difference between the two sets of methods, it can be seen that the HR and MACL findings could both be correct: during or after laughter or exposure to the humorous stimulus, tension increases, as indicated by elevated heartrates but the net effect of a period of laughter or exposure is relaxation, as indicated by the MACL studies. How is it possible HR could be elevated by each laugh but the net effect of a number of laughs would be to decrease HR? Perhaps after each laugh ends, HR not only returns to baseline but overshoots, leading to a decrease in HR for a period of time. If a small amount of this decrement cumulated with each succeeding laugh, a gradual decrease in HR over the entire period of laughter would occur, resulting in the net decrease reported earlier.

The pattern of momentary elevation follwed by a decrease is congruent with Berlyne's (1972) "arousal-jag" hypothesis: an event which initially raises arousal may be pleasurable if it is followed by a prompt arousal reduction. It is also congruent with Gellhorn and Loofbourrow's (1963) model of the "tuning" of the autonomic nervous system: at optimum levels of activation, the firing of the sympathetic nervous system (SNS) is followed immediately by rebound firing of the parasympathetic system, which in turn is followed by a rebound of the SNS, and so on in sequence until the autonomic nervous system is exactly in balance. Finally, this pattern also would support Scheff's (1977) model of the discharge of emotional distress at optimal distance. This model proposes that catharsis takes place when there is an exact balance between emotional distress, on the one hand, and a feeling of complete security, on the other.

In this earlier paper, it was argued that the exact balance between distress and safety may appear to the individual as the simultaneous experience of participation in, and observation of, the individual's own distress, but that the seeming simultaneity of these two disparate experiences is probably only apparent. Rather, as in Gellhorn's model, the balance between distress and discharge would be a product of an alternation between the two states that is so rapid that the two states would be experienced as fused into one.

We would therefore hypothesize the net effect of a period of laughter to be a decrease in heartrate, as well as subjective feelings of tension. In order to test this hypothesis we designed the present study to be different from the earlier studies, in that it is concerned with the net effect of a period of laughter on both mood scores and heart rate.

Humor and Laughter

A second difference between the present study and earlier studies concerns the difference between the effects of laughter, as such, and the effects of exposure to a humorous stimulus. All of the earlier studies in this area that were

available to us have involved the effects of exposure to stimuli, such as cartoons, jokes, or comedic films.

The practice of using exposure to humorous stimuli as the independent variable gives rise to two issues which require discussion. The first, and more troublesome, issue is that it is difficult without monitoring laughter to be sure that the stimuli are actually humorous to the subjects. Let us return to the major study in this area (Averill, 1969) once more. As already indicated, the results of this study are difficult to interpret because of the confounding of momentary and net effects. But even if these effects had been measured correctly, there would be another ambiguity in his findings.

Is the lack of any significant change in HR in the comedy condition (as compared with the control condition) due to the fact that humor does not effect HR, or is it because the subjects did not find the comic film humorous? One must raise this question here because Averill reports, in passing, that only 11 of the 18 subjects in the comedy condition laughed. He does not report how much they laughed. Averill sought to resolve this issue by having the subjects rate the humor of the film they viewed. On a 4-point scale, with a higher rating being judged funnier, the humor film was rated 1.3, as against a rating of .5 for the control group film, a travelogue. If one accepts humor ratings as valid, these data at least suggest that the comedy film was perceived by the subjects as slightly funnier than the travelogue.

It seems necessary at this point to raise the question of the validity of humor or funniness ratings. Humor is probably partly an emotional response, as well as a cognitive one. It seems possible that funniness ratings may overemphasize the cognitive component of humor, at the expense of the emotional component. Ordinarily, there would seem to be something missing when the response of a person to jokes is to say "That's very funny," rather than laughing.

The available data that can be interpreted as bearing on the validity of funniness ratings report the relationship between funniness ratings and laughter is not reassuring. Singer (1968) found an intercorrelation of .74 between humor ratings and laughter. Pollio, Mers, and Lucchesi (1972, p. 227) found different levels of association for four different comedy routines: 0.01, 0.36, 0.57, and 0.78. The only study to center an experiment solely on this question (Branch, Fine, & Jones, 1973) found that for the tapes of seven different comedians, the correlations between the number of laughs and funniness ratings were: 0.05, 0.30, 0.34, 0.51, 0.52, 0.68, and 0.69.

These findings suggest that although ratings are not independent of laughter, they are also not a reliable index. Of 12 correlations, only 2 are large enough to account for more than half of the variance, while 7 correlations are so small that they account for less than a third of the variance. It would appear that funniness ratings usually tap aspects of humor other than its laughter potential. In addition to the question of immediate and net effects discussed

earlier, there is a second ambiguity in Averill's findings: it is possible that the lack of significant HR changes he found is due to the fact that the subjects in his study did not find the comic film they saw funny.

A second issue that the use of exposure to a humorous stimulus raises concerns the interpretation of causal processes. Even in those studies which show that humor reduces tension, there is no indication of the process through which this effect occurs. Humor is a rather abstract concept; it might include several processes, such as the perception of, and cognition about, humor, as well as mirth (defined by Zigler, Levine, & Gould, 1967, as laughter or smiling). Mirth is more specific but still does not differentiate between the effects of laughing and the effects of smiling. For this reason it would be useful to have a study that made some attempt to differentiate between the effects of the different processes that occur as a result of exposure to a humorous stimulus—perception, cognition, smiling, or laughter.

In an earlier paper (Scheff, 1977) it was proposed that spontaneous laughter (especially that occurring in response to a comedic stimulus) usually has a reflex character, standing in relationship to the tension of embarrassment (or other distressful emotion) as orgasm stands to sexual tension. Spontaneous laughter, therfore, is seen as signaling the extremely rapid resolution of tension which otherwise may have continued unabated. This tension need not be conscious or current; it could be a delayed reaction from earlier situations.

Given this approach to catharsis, it would be desirable to choose laughter, rather than exposure to a humorous stimulus, as the causal agent in a research design. Such a choice would allay the feeling of uncertainty about the humorousness of the stimulus to the subjects, and it would also facilitate interpreting the causal processes involved. Tests of the catharsis hypothesis that use exposure to a humorous stimulus as the causal agent seem to us to confound the external trigger, which may give rise to catharsis, with catharsis itself, an internal process that may or may not occur.

However, for the very reason that laughter is unpredictable, it is difficult to use it as the treatment variable in an experimental design. With a sufficiently large treatment group, one might subdivide, after the fact, into groups in which there were varying amounts of laughter, say high, medium, low, and none. In this way one could differentiate between the effects of laughter and the effects of exposure to a humorous stimulus. Because of limitations in the size of the treatment group that was available, the design of the present study is a compromise: we first conducted a field study in which laughter was the independent variable, and then an experiment in which exposure to a humorous stimulus was the treatment. The field study tested the hypothesis (in two different audiences) that reduction of tension (for individuals in a film comedy audience, as measured by HR and by mood scores [MACL]) is positively correlated with the number of laughs reported by those individuals.

In the experiment, the hypothesis is that exposure to a comedy tape will result in reduction of tension, again as measured by HR and MACL scores, as compared with a group which listens to a nonhumorous lecture. Number of laughs for each subject, as recorded by observers, and funniness ratings by the subjects were also obtained for subsequent analysis.

FIELD STUDY

A brief before-and-after questionnaire was given to two different audiences. From some 300 persons who viewed the film *Harold and Maude,* 243 usable questionnaires were obtained. From some 150 persons who viewed *Everything You Always Wanted to Know about Sex,* 125 usable questionnaires were obtained. Both films had similar running times of approximately 90 minutes.

Measurements

The before questionnaire contained two sections. The first concerned pulse rate. The experimenter instructed the audience how to find and count their pulse. He then asked the audience to count their pulse for the 30-second interval that he timed. On the *Harold and Maude* showing, the pulse was counted only once. For *Everything You Always Wanted* it was taken twice, and the mean of the two was used as the measure of heart rate.

The second section of the questionnaire was an adjective check list, which assessed subjective feelings of tension and relaxation. (Studies establishing the reliability of mood adjective check lists are reported by Nowlis in Tomkins and Izard, 1965, pp. 367–369.) It contained the following adjectives indicative of tension: sad, tense, withdrawn, confused, jittery, fearful, grouchy, annoyed, angry, drowsy; and the following adjectives, indicative of relaxation: attentive, happy, energetic, carefree, lively, pleased, relaxed, refreshed, clear, alert. In the questionnaire the relaxation and tension adjectives were listed alternatively. After each adjective, the respondents were asked to check "Yes," "Some," or "No."

The after-questionnaire contained the same pulse and check list sections, plus a third section on the amount of laughter. Here the question was: "About how much do you think you laughed during the movie?"

1. A lot—over thirty times
2. Pretty much—between 15–30 times
3. Some—between 5–15 times
4. Hardly at all

Change scores, based on the difference between before and after measures, were calculated for each subject. The change score for the pulse rate involving subtracting the after-pulse from the before-pulse, with a positive-change score indicating a decrease in tension. Change scores for the adjective check list were calculated by scoring a "Yes" for the relaxation adjectives as +2, "Some" as +1, and "No" as zero, and a "Yes" for the tension adjectives as –2, "Some" as –1, and "No" as zero. The overall change scores involved subtracting the total of the before-scores from the total after-scores. The larger the total change score, the more relaxed the subject had become.

Results

To test the hypothesis that the more laughter, the more relaxation, the joint distributions of laughter and pulse change, and laughter and mood score change were calculated for the two audiences. The number of laughs were divided into these ranks: a lot, pretty much, and some or none. Mood change was ranked as low, medium, or high.

All four of the distributions are correlated in the direction predicted by the hypothesis: the more the laughter, the more the decrease in pulse, and the more decrease in subjective tension, as reflected by the adjective check list. Three of the four correlations (tau = 0.17, 0.19, 0.23) are statistically significant, one is not. (The correlation between the decrease in pulse rate and the amount of laughter for the *Harold and Maude* audience [tau = 0.05] is not significant at the 0.01 level. A possible source of error in this correlation, as compared to the other showing, is the pulse count which was only taken once, instead of twice as in the other showing.) Although the correlations between amount of laughter and tension reduction support the hypothesis, the support is weak because the correlations are low. Also, the direction of causation is not clear because the design concerns a naturally occurring situation, rather than a controlled experiment. We therefore designed an experiment to investigate in a more controlled manner the relationship between humor and tension.

EXPERIMENTAL STUDY

Subjects in groups of three were exposed to either experimental or control stimuli (comedy or noncomedy tapes) in a small-group laboratory setting. Subjects were seated so that they could be observed through a one-way mirror. They were randomly assigned to either the treatment (comedy) or control (lecture) condition. Before and after measures were MACL and HR. An after-measure was taken of funniness ratings of the tape. The laughter of each subject was coded and rated by independent raters.

The 60 subjects were volunteers from undergraduate sociology classes. Groups of three were tested in a random sequence across treatment and control conditions to avoid time or maturation effects.

Materials

The comedy tape was 14 minutes in length, containing material from 2 sources. The first part consisted of four minutes by Cheech and Chong, "Let's Make a Dope Deal"; the second part, a series of sketches from the Richard Pryor album, "That Nigger's Crazy." These routines were chosen after pretesting several different tapes. The control tape, also 14 minutes in length; was the introductory portion of an anthropology lecture, "Biculturalism," delivered at a Midwestern college. This tape was also pretested. No occurrence of laughter was recorded.

Independent Measures

The number of laughs was recorded for each subject by raters through a one-way mirror, one rater for each three subjects. The rating was "blind" in the sense that raters had no information regarding the experiment except for instructions as to how to code laughter. An interrater reliability check was made by randomly assigning raters to count the number of laughs by a single random subject, six times. It was found that interrater reliability was 0.98.

A laugh was defined as beginning when a subject showed any chest or head movement indicative of the muscle contractions associated with laughter and the accompanying vocalization. The laugh was defined as ending when any pause in such movement and vocalization could be noticed. A funniness rating was taken after subjects listened to the tape. The rating consisted of a scale from one ("not funny at all") to nine ("extremely funny").

Effect Measures

The subjective measure of tension was the same mood adjective check list used in the field study, with the exception that each adjective was given a score from one ("not at all") to nine ("completely") by the subjects. The scores for the tension and relaxation adjectives were then added for both before and after, and the difference was computed to determine the change score. A positive score indicates relaxation; a negative one, and increase in tension.

The objective measure of tension was the HR change, accomplished by having the subjects count and record their pulse rate 4 times successively for 15 seconds each, before and after listening to the tape. Southard and Katahn (1967) found that when the subjects took their own pulse for 4 15-second checks, the correlation between the self-report and that recorded by a Grass

Polygraph was 0.98, which demonstrates the accuracy of the self-reported rates.

Procedures

Subjects in groups of three were seated in a waiting room eight minutes in order to record accurate baseline heart rate when the experiment began. They were seated in the laboratory near the tape recorder, facing the one-way mirror. Subjects first determined their pulse, then filled out the first adjective check list. The experimenter explained that they were to hear a tape, during which the experimenter would leave the room. Afterwards, the experimenter returned and the subjects again recorded the 4 pulse rates and completed the MACL within 30 seconds of the end of the tape. Following this, they completed the funniness ratings, concluding the procedures. Raters recorded the laughter identically for both groups.

Results

As can be seen in Table 7.1, the treatment tape resulted in considerable laughter, the mean number of laughs being 42.1 (with a range from 7 to 140), and the control tape, less than one. The requirement that the treatment stimulus be perceived as much more humorous than the control stimulus is thus fulfilled.

In the treatment condition, the mean change in HR of –2.9 beats per minute is somewhat but not significantly greater than that in the control condition

TABLE 7.1
Experimental and Control Comparisons

	Experimental	Control	t Value
Mean HR before	73.7	70.7	
Mean HR after	70.7	70.4	
Mean HR change	–2.9	–0.3	–1.6
Mean MACL before[a]	1.2	1.7	
Mean MACL after[a]	1.9	1.4	
Mean MACL change[b]	+0.6	–0.2	3.6[c]
Mean funniness rating	6.0	1.6	13.3[c]
Mean number of laughs	42.1	0.3	8.5[c]

[a]Figures indicate mean unit distance from mean of scale (4.5).

[b]Figures indicate mean change toward either relaxation (+) or tension (–), expressed in units on a scale of 1 to 9.

[c]$p < .001$.

(–0.3). For the MACL score, the treatment condition showed relaxation (+0.62 units on a 9-point scale), a significant change ($p < 0.01$) from a baseline of 1.3, while the control condition showed an increase in tension, –0.2 units. The treatment condition thus shows a relatively greater decrease in tension on both measures (although not significantly so in HR), as predicted by the theory.

However, it should be noted that the before-measure indicates a higher level of tension in the treatment condition than in the control, even though assignment of subjects was random; mean HR in the treatment condition is three beats per minute higher than in the control and the mean MACL score is 0.4 units lower (more tense). For this reason, an analysis of covariance was performed across the treatment and control conditions with the prestimulus measures of HR and MACL score, the covariates (see Table 7.2). We assume that the MACL ratings form an equal interval scale, so that the analysis will be the same for MACL scores and HR. For HR change, neither the treatment nor the prestimulus score was related at the 0.01 level of probability. For MACL change, both treatment and the prestimulus score were significant at the 0.01 level.

To determine the relationship of the number of laughs and funniness ratings to changes in tension, the rank correlation between the three measures was calculated across treatment and control conditions. As indicated in Table 7.3, the funniness rating is more highly correlated with MACL change ($r_s = 0.60$) than with laughter ($r_s = 0.31$). This result might have been expected, since both MACL score and funniness rating are cognitive tasks. Surprisingly, however, number of laughs and funniness ratings correlates HR change equally well ($r_s = 0.36$). One might expect the number of laughs, to the extent that it reflects an emotional reaction, would predict HR change better than the funniness rating. This finding raises some questions about the use of number of laughs as an index of emotional response. Perhaps amount, rather

TABLE 7.2
Analysis of Covariance

	Sum of Squares	DF	F	P
Prestimulus HR	181	1	5.0	.03
Treatment	68.8	1	1.9	.18
Explained	250			
Residual	2082			
Prestimulus MACL	6022	1	24.4	.001
Treatment	2588	1	10.5	.002
Explained	8610			
Residual	14060			

TABLE 7.3

Rank Correlations of Number of Laughs and Funniness Ratings With HR
and MACL Score Changes, Across Treatment and Control Conditions

	Number of Laughs	Funniness Rating
Number of Laughs		.59
HR change	−.36	.31
MACL change	−.36	.60

than number, of laughs would make for a better emotional measure. This could be indexed by observers' ratings of number, duration, and intensity of laughs. By intensity of laughter we mean the extent and strength of bodily involvement, ranging from the slight involvement of a giggle to the complete and strong involvement of a belly laugh. It is possible that funniness ratings are more sensitive to the amount of emotional response than the number of laughs, which is only a mechanical count that does not discriminate between a short giggle and a lengthy belly laugh.[1]

Finally, in the debriefing of subjects following the experiment, less than 10% of the subjects reported being aware of being observed during the discussion. None of the subjects were aware of the hypothesis of the study.

Discussion

The results of this study with respect to effects of humor on mood are quite clear. In all three tests (the two audiences in the field study and the experiment) the findings support the hypothesis that humor lowers tension. These findings further confirm the results of the three earlier studies of the effect of humor on mood. In addition to this confirmation, the present study also suggests that laughter, perhaps in addition to the other processes resulting from exposure to a humorous stimulus, leads to tension reduction because of the positive correlation between the number of laughs and relaxation on the MACL.

With respect to HR change, the findings are less clear. On the one hand the relationship between HR and humor is in the direction predicted by the hypotheses in all three tests. However, in two of these three tests the relationship is not statistically significant. A cautious interpretation of these findings would be that the initial hypothesis that humor results in a decrease in HR was not supported. By the same token, and exercising the same level of caution, one must also state that the hypothesis that humor results in an increase in HR, as suggested by five earlier studies in this area, also fails to

---

[1]For a completely different approach to the relationship between laughter and funniness ratings, see G. C. Cupchik and H. Leventhal (1974).

find support. From this viewpoint, the present findings do not demonstrate than any change in HR occurred.

In our judgment, such an interpretation would be excessively cautious. Since the initial theory was stated in terms of tension levels, rather than in terms of the two indices of tension (HR and MACL scores), the results should be interpreted in terms of the overall success of the theory. By this standard, the data support the theory, since the results were in the direction predicted in all six of the tests, an outcome exceedingly unlikely to occur by chance.

However, given the modest size of the correlations and the potential importance of some of the issues that have been raised, further research seems to be required before any definitive statement can be made about the relationship between humor and tension. One fruitful line of investigation would be to assess both the moment-to-moment and the net effects of laughter on HR. This procedure would allow one to assess the goodness of fit of the various models of catharsis described above (i.e., those of Berlyne, Gellhorn, and Scheff) as well as to test the theory of catharsis itself. Perhaps if observations of the amount of laughter were made (that is, of the number, duration, and intensity of laughs), the process, as well as the fact, of catharsis, could be elucidated.

There is one further refinement that should be included in a subsequent study. Neither the present study, nor any of the earlier studies cited, investigated the duration of the net effects of humor. If humor causes net decreases in tension but these decreases are short-lived (as the elevations reported in the earlier studies seem to be), these findings would still be of considerable theoretical significance, in that they would increase our understanding of the relationships between emotional processes like laughter and mental and physical states, like mood and HR. However they would have little practical significance. If, on the other hand, the mental and physical changes caused by laughter were relatively long lasting, they might have some immediate implications for practical matters of health, as well as theory. Two hypotheses that might be tested are: first, the momentary increase in HR caused by a laugh would be proportional to the duration and intensity of the laugh. Second, the duration of the net decrease in HR caused by a series of laughs would be related to the number, duration, and intensity of the laughs. To the extent that these two hypotheses were confirmed, the results would be of considerable theoretical and practical importance.

REFERENCES

Arnheim, R. *Entropy and art.* Berkeley: University of California Press, 1971.

Averill, J. R. Autonomic response patterns during sadness and mirth. *Psychophysiology,* 1969, 5, 399–414.

Berkowitz, L. *Aggression: A social psychological analysis.* New York: McGraw-Hill, 1962.

Berkowitz, L. Aggressive humor as a stimulus to aggressive responses. *Journal of Personality and Social Psychology,* 1970, *16,* 710–717.

Berlyne, D. E. *Aesthetics and psychobiology.* New York: Appleton-Century-Crofts, 1971.

Berlyne, D. E. Humor and its kin. In J. H. Goldstein & P. E. McGhee (Eds.), *The psychology of humor.* New York: Academic Press, 1972.

Branch, A. Y., Fine, G. A., & Jones, J. M. *Laughter, smiling and rating scales: An analysis of responses to tape recorded humor.* Reprinted from the Proceedings of the 81st Annual Convention of the American Psychological Association, Washington, D.C., September 1973.

Cousins, N. The anatomy of an illness (as perceived by the patient). *New England Journal of Medicine,* 1976, *295,* 1548–1563.

Cupchik, G. C., & Leventhal, H. Consistency between expressive behavior and the evaluation of humorous stimuli: The role of sex and self-observation. *Journal of Personality and Social Psychology,* 1974, *30,* 429–442.

Douglas, M. *Natural symbols.* London: Barrie and Jenkins, 1970.

Dworkin, E. S., & Efran, J. S. The angered: Their susceptibility to varieties of humor. *Journal of Personality and Social Psychology,* 1967, *6,* 233–236.

Evans-Pritchard, E. E. *Theories of primitive religion.* Oxford, England: Claredon Press, 1965.

Feshbach, S., & Singer, J. Television and Aggression. San Francisco: Jossey-Bass, 1971.

Freud, S. *Jokes and their relationship to the unconscious.* New York: W. W. Norton, 1960. (Originally published, 1905.)

Freud, S. *Five lectures on psychoanalysis.* London: Hogarth, 1910.

Freud, S. *A general introduction of psychoanalysis.* New York: Perma Giants, 1949.

Freud, S., & Breuer, J. *Studies on hysteria.* New York: Avon Books, 1966. (Originally published, 1895.)

Fry, W. F. *Sweet madness: A study of humor.* Palo Alto, Calif.: Pacific Books, 1963.

Fry, W. F. Humor in a physiological vein. In *News of Physiological Instrumentation.* Palo Alto, Calif.: Beckman Laboratory, 1969.

Gellhorn, R., & Loofbourrow, G. N. Emotions and emotional disorders: A neurophysiological study. New York: Hoeber, 1963.

Godkewitsch, M. Physiological and verbal indices of arousal in rated humor. In A. J. Chapman & H. C. Foot (Eds.), *Humor and laughter: Theory research and applications.* London: Wiley, 1976.

Greenwald, H. Humor in psychotherapy. *Journal of Contemporary Psychology,* 1975, *7,* 113–116.

Jones, J. M., & Harris, P. E. *Psychophysiological correlates of cartoon appreciation.* Proceedings of the Annual Convention of the American Psychological Association, 1971, *6,* 381–382.

Kubie, L. S. The destructive potential of humor in psychotherapy. In W. Mendel (Ed.), *A celebration of laughter.* Los Angeles: Mara Books, 1970.

Lacey, B. C., & Lacey, J. I. Studies of heart rate and other bodily processes in sensorimotor behavior. In P. A. Obrist, A. H. Black, J. Brener, & L. V. DiCara (Eds.), *Cardiovascular psychophysiology.* Chicago: Aldine, 1974.

Lain Entralgo, P. *The therapy of the word in classical antiquity.* New Haven, Conn.: Yale University Press, 1970.

Langevin, R., & Day, H. I. Physiological correlates of humor. In J. H. Goldstein & P. E. McGhee (Eds.), *The psychology of humor.* New York: Academic Press, 1972.

Levi-Strauss, C. *The raw and the cooked.* New York: Harper and Row, 1969.

Malinowski, B. *Magic, science, and religion.* New York: Anchor, 1948.

Martin, L. Psychology of esthetics: Experimental prospecting in the field of the comic. *American Journal of Psychology,* 1905, *16,* 35–116.

Mendel, W. *A celebration of laughter.* Los Angeles: Mara Books, 1970.

Mindess, H. *Laughter and liberation.* Los Angeles: Nash, 1971.

Nichols, M., & Zax, M. *Catharsis in psychotherapy.* New York: Gardner Press, 1977.

Nowlis, V. Research with the mood adjective check list. In S. S. Tomkins & C. Izard (Eds.), *Affect, cognition, and personality.* New York: Springer, 1965.

Obrist, P. A., Howard, L. L., Lawler, J. E., Galosy, R. A., Meyers, K. A., & Gaebelein, C. J. The cardiac-somatic interaction. In P. A. Obrist, A. H. Black, J. Brener, & L. V. DiCara (Eds.), *Cardiovascular psychophysiology,* Chicago: Aldine, 1974.

Pollio, H. R., Mers, R., & Lucchesi, W. Humor, laughter, and smiling: Some preliminary observations of funny behavior. In J. H. Goldstein & P. E. McGhee (Eds.), *The Psychology of Humor.* New York: Academic Press, 1972.

Radcliffe-Brown, A. R. *Structure and function in primitive society.* Glencoe, Ill.: Free Press, 1952.

Scheff, T. J. The distancing of emotion in ritual. *Current Anthropology,* 1977, *18,* 483–505.

Scheff, T. J. *Catharsis in healing, ritual, and drama.* Berkeley: University of California Press, 1979.

Singer, D. L. Aggression arousal, hostile humor, catharsis. *Journal of Personality and Social Psychology,* 1968, Monograph Supplement 8, 1–14.

Smith, A. *Powers of the mind.* New York: Random House, 1975.

Southard, L. D., & Katahn, M. The correlation between self-reported and mechnically recorded pulse rates. *Psychonomic Science,* 1967, *8,* 343–344.

Stearns, F. R. *Laughing: Physiology, pathophysiology, psychology, pathopsychology and development.* Springfield, Ill.: Charles C. Thomas, 1972.

Symonds, P. A comprehension theory of psychotherapy. *American Journal of Orthopsychiatry,* 1954, *24,* 193–207.

Turner, V. *The forest of symbols.* Ithaca: Cornell University Press, 1967.

Volkan, V. D., & Josephthal, D. Brief psychotherapy in pathological grief: Re-grief therapy. In T. B. Karasu & L. Bellak (Eds.), *Specialized techniques in psychotherapy.* New York: Brenner/ Mazel, 1979.

Wimsatt, W. K., Jr., & Brooks, C. *Literary criticism,* New York: Random House, 1957.

Zigler, E., Levine, J., & Gould, L. Cognitive challenge as a factor in children's humor appreciation. *Journal of Personality and Social Psychology,* 1967, *6,* 332–336.

8 Toward the Integration of Entertainment and Educational Functions of Television: The Role of Humor

Paul E. McGhee
Texas Tech University

The original impetus for the preparation of this volume came from the assumption that most people watch television because they want to be entertained, not because they are seeking intellectual stimulation or other forms of personal enrichment. When given a choice between educationally oriented programs and light entertainment programs, Americans generally prefer the latter. Documentaries or other "specials" occasionally do draw large viewing audiences, but it is likely to be the entertaining style of presentation that is responsible for this. Thus the program "Roots" would have enjoyed considerably less success if it had followed a more typical educational format instead of a dramatic format.

The television industry claims to be giving the viewing public what it wants, using the old formula of adding new shows similar to those that received the highest ratings during the pervious year. But we have all heard rumblings of dissatisfaction about available programs for the past 20 years. The key question is whether these rumblings occur only among more educated viewers, or among the population generally. Steiner (1963) documented the widespread nature of this dissatisfaction in his finding that over half of a sample of 2400 viewers felt that there were not enough educational programs available. At first glance this finding is puzzling, since these same viewers do not watch educational programs even when they are available. Undoubtedly some of these individuals registered this complaint simply because they felt that one *should* watch more educational programs, that is, give a socially desirable response. If this is the case, there may be no pressing need to modify existing programming practices.

It is possible, however, that Steiner's (1963) respondents were being honest in their complaint. They may be interested in watching programs with more substance to them, while being unable to get interested in the formal or abstract presentations of typical educational programs. It is frequently argued that specials, documentaries, programs on educational channels, and other programs whose main function is to impart information are dry and uninteresting in format and presentation, though the subject matter covered is interesting. It may be, then, that we simply have not yet discovered the right "formula" to make informative programming interesting and popular to the mass of television viewers. If humor, drama, music, etc. were used to present information to viewers in a more entertaining fashion, would the popularity of educationally oriented programs increase? These forms of entertainment do not seem to play an important role in determining whether a small minority of viewers watch programs mainly designed to inform. However, it may be that for the large numbers of viewers whose enjoyment level is determined mainly by the entertainment value of a program, some effort must be made to integrate entertainment segments with the more serious material presented.

There has been some conviction within the television industry that television should perform the dual function of both informing and entertaining the public. The informational role has been filled mainly in the form of daily news broadcasts, some discussion shows, and periodic special news programs. Considering the extent of the knowledge explosion in the past few decades, however, it is questionable whether present efforts meet the public's need to regularly add to existing knowledge. There seems to be little doubt that educational programs in the traditional sense will not satisfy this need, since relatively small numbers of people view them. Even if an attempt is made to remedy this situation by making such programs more entertaining the programs may still be categorized in many viewers' minds as being "educational," and this labeling may serve to reduce any prior interest in viewing the program for a substantial number of viewers.

An alternative approach would be to increase the informational potential of programs now conceptualized by most viewers to be in the "light entertainment" category. A striking example of the potential of this approach may be seen in the success enjoyed in the 1970s by the program "All in the Family." This program affords an opportunity for the viewer to learn about basic issues in racial or other aspects of social relations while being entertained within a basic situation-comedy format. Since most viewers already view this type of program very positively, the integration of entertainment and educational content might meet with a more favorable reaction if it were accomplished by increased emphasis on educational contributions of primarily entertaining shows. This chapter examines issues related to how this integration might be most effectively achieved.

To this point, the greatest success in integrating entertainment and educational functions of television has been enjoyed in the area of children's television. The outcome of efforts by the Children's Television Workshop (see Gibbon, Palmer, & Fowles, 1975; Lesser, 1972, 1974) in the development of "Sesame Street" and "The Electric Company" suggests that it might be possible to develop comparable programs for adults. Personal discussions with representatives of the Public Broadcasting System indicated that there is already active speculation about the feasability of such programs for adults. Their primary concern for the immediate future seems to be the establishment of means of increasing the entertainment level of the majority of their programs without sacrificing the capacity of programs to stimulate, enrich, or inform the viewing audience. The achievement of this goal could increase the competitiveness of their programs with those of commercial television and might even serve to stimulate the producers of commercial programs to attempt to elevate the informational level of some of their "pure entertainment" fare. One previous attempt at extending the "Sesame Street" formula to adult programming was "Feeling Good," developed in an effort to provide basic health information in an entertaining fashion. The poor reception of this program may have made the television industry wary about initiating comparable programs in the future. It remains unclear at this point, however, whether the failure of this effort was due to the manner in which this particular program was produced, or whether the failure stemmed from the fact that the majority of viewers simply do not want much educational content with their entertainment. This experience does suggest that the best approach to develop more informative types of programming may be to extend the educational contribution of programs which are already watched because of their entertainment qualities.

Regardless of which of these two approaches is adopted, there would appear to be many production techniques that might be utilized to achieve the optimal balance between opportunities for entertainment and some form of personal enrichment in a program. This chapter considers the potential contribution of humor to the achievement of such a balance. There are several lines of support for the view that humor might be a good candidate for this task. Most important, of course, is the fact that comedy programs have been popular since the beginning of television. Also, Lesser (1972, 1974) concluded after an examination of various approaches adopted by the Children's Television Workshop that there is "no more important single ingredient in children's television than humor." Since humor is very effective in sustaining children's attention to nonhumorous aspects of a program as well, it may prove similarly effective with adults.

Lundgren (1972) argued that any good instructional television program must have an element of humor in order to maintain a high level of motivation in large numbers of people to watch the program. We discuss later in this

chapter the fact that humor does a good job of increasing the interest value of otherwise boring speeches and lectures; thus it might have a similar effect on viewers' reactions to educational materials that are otherwise considered boring. An overly serious manner of presentation is often cited as the reason for dissatisfaction with programs (Snow, 1974), so if the inclusion of humor can help minimize the extent to which a program is perceived as being serious in intent, it should increase enjoyment of the program.

The proposal that humor or other entertaining devices should be used more frequently by producers of educational or public service programs is not a new one. Seldes (1962) argued over 15 years ago that such "razzle-dazzle" devices may be necessary to get and hold the viewer's attention in many primarily informational programs. He noted that most educationally oriented program personnel feel that such devices are irrelevant to the content of the program and serve to lower its integrity. Although this loss of integrity may lead some viewers to stop viewing, it may also serve to draw even larger numbers of viewers to the program who normally do not view programs intended mainly to educate.

The importance of avoiding the classification of a program as educational may be seen in Steiner's (1963) finding that most Americans report watching television in order to relax and "take it easy." Programs were most frequently selected because they were relaxing at the same time as they were interesting and entertaining. The importance of a program's ability to foster relaxation seems to be due to the fact that most adults watch television primarily in the evening, after a hard day's work. Given the state of mental or physical fatigue the viewer is likely to be in at this time, educationally oriented programs may simply require more mental effort than most are willing to put out. The inclusion of humor, however, may create a set of conditions in which the exertion of higher levels of effort are more rewarding. Also, if humor does serve to make a program more entertaining, viewers may become less conscious of the mental effort required to process other aspects of the program material.

The relatively greater importance of relaxation than information seeking as the underlying basis for program selection is evident in a recent study by Robinson (1972). Only 10% of his sample indicated information seeking or some other form of personal enrichment to be their primary basis for choice of programs to view. This small percentage of viewers may also form the bulk of viewers of educational TV. New opportunities for learning seem to play a central role in determining the entertainment level of a program for these viewers. The enjoyment of more challenging levels of mental involvement by viewers of educational channels is not surprising, in light of the fact that they: (1) are better educated; (2) are more achievement-oriented; (3) attach higher value to self-improvement (as opposed to relaxation); and (4) are more likely to be seekers of information in a general sense (Schramm, Lyle, & deSola

Pool, 1963). Viewers of educational programs are more likely to thrive on opportunities for knowledge expansion and intellectual stimulation and to consider a diet of light programs on the commercial stations to be a waste of time. Viewers who watch light entertainment programs almost exclusively, on the other hand, are not interested in using television "to get educated." Most informational programs on both commercial and educational channels seem to be geared primarily to the former group of viewers. This group is most likely to be entertained by such programs even if no extensive efforts are made to present the substance of the program in an entertaining fashion. Thus they should not be considered to be the target group of any efforts to integrate the educational and entertainment aspects of programs. These efforts should be directed toward the great numbers of viewers who do not normally seek out more informative types of programs.

Viewing patterns during the early years of British television suggest that considerable difficulty may be expected in getting a sizeable majority of viewers to respond positively to an opportunity to be both better informed and entertained at the same time. Himmelweit (1963) found that the extent to which individuals seek out and enjoy more informational programs depends on both the nature and the number of available alternatives. When only one BBC channel was operating in the early 1950s, documentaries and other educational types of programs were commonly listed by adolescents as favorite programs, along with various fictional categories, game shows, etc. As light entertainment shows proliferated with the establishment of a second channel, such educational programs were watched less and less frequently. Given the presence of at least three or four channels in most areas of the United States, these findings suggest that most viewers will not watch educational material on television unless it is in some way integrated into entertainment programs. Humor would appear to provide an ideal vehicle for accomplishing this integration.

THEORETICAL CONSIDERATIONS

Arguments drawn from existing theoretical views can be advanced both in favor of and against the position that expanded informational segments can be added successfully to light entertainment programs. In order to be considered successful, such efforts must result not only in interest maintained throughout the program, but in expansion of personal experience and knowledge as well. Although there is little doubt about the contribution humor makes to the enjoyment of a program, there is some reason to question humor's ability to foster learning or cognitive change. Views suggesting both a facilitating and inhibiting effect are reviewed in the following subsection.

Arousal Changes Associated With Humor

Berlyne (1960, 1972) has convincingly argued that humor is associated with characteristic forms of arousal change. The experience of humor may be accompanied by either moderate increases in arousal or by a more extreme increase in arousal that is suddenly reduced. Presumably, arousal increases when an attempt is made to understand a cartoon or joke, but then decreases when the insight required to get the joke is suddenly achieved. Empirical support for this position was provided by Goldstein, Harman, McGhee, and Karasik (1975). Berlyne (1967) reviewed existing anatomical, physiological, and psychological data along these lines and concluded that each of these forms of arousal fluctuation is typically experienced as pleasurable. Humor is an example of only one type of pleasure associated with such changes. Given the reward value of humor, it should prove capable of increasing the enjoyment derived from informational components of a program that might otherwise be judged uninteresting. The associational link between humor and educational material should lead to both more effective learning and better retention of material.

When humor is added to the kind of abstract and highly intellectualized programs typical (in the eyes of many viewers) of educational programs, it may also serve to keep arousal within the moderate bounds generally considered to be optimal for learning and retention. If the viewer is beginning to "tune out" for any reason, humor might provide a kind of emotional "slap in the face," drawing attention and interest back to the program. Humor could play a similar role in light entertainment programs, of course, but it would only be one of several production devices having this effect in such programs. Regardless of whether emotional arousal is analyzed from a physiological or psychological perspective, Berlyne's position suggests that humor would function well in the role of combining basic learning processes with the enjoyment of entertaining programs.

Stress Reduction and Coping Functions

Psychoanalytic theorists (e.g., Freud, 1960; Grotjahn, 1957) have argued for decades that humor provides a very effective means of reducing stress and tension. The mechanism by which this occurs has not been fully clarified, but humor does seem to be able to take an individual out of a negative frame of mind and substitute a more positive and relaxed one in its place. This may be one of the reasons comedy programs are consistently popular during weekday evenings. Assuming that a sizeable portion of the adult working population comes home in the evening in some sort of condition of fatigue or mild stress, they are not likely to be in a frame of mind conducive to a desire for enrichment and learning. Even if a generalized desire for personal growth

through television viewing did exist in such individuals, their motivational state at the time would interfere with effective learning from the programs watched. Humor may play the important role, then, of providing therapy to millions of viewers. By enabling us to forget about sources of tension and stress during the day, it should help produce a mental state in which informational material is well received. From this perspective also, then, humor would appear to be an excellent vehicle for executing the integration of the entertainment and educational functions of television.

Distraction and Interference Effects

Schramm (1973) emphasized the need for caution in using humor as a learning aid in television programs. The problem with humor, in his view, is that it tends to distract the viewer from attending to the more serious informational aspects of a program. The contrast between the educational and entertaining segments may be so great that the viewer becomes dissatisfied with the former, giving it less than full attention. Or, thought about the funny segments may continue while the nonhumorous segments are being presented. In either case, this would seem to be a less than optimal circumstance for fostering cognitive growth and enrichment. In Schramm's view, distraction effects due to humor are so difficult to overcome that its use should be minimized in any program concerned with the imparting of information. Lesser (1972, 1974) has outlined a format for using humor in children's programs which should reduce such distraction effects. He concluded that humor should facilitate learning as long as it is directly and meaningfully integrated into the material to be learned. Rather than distracting the viewer, this kind of integration should help draw the viewer's attention toward distinctive and salient features of the information presented. If this integration is not successfully achieved, the intended effect may backfire so that thought processes related to the humor actually compete with thought related to the educational material presented.

If the presence of humor does interfere with the retention or learning of accompanying material, it may be the result of a disruption of basic rehearsal processes. Typically, we spend some amount of time reflecting about communications as they are directed toward us. This kind of active thinking may play an important role in producing permanent cognitive change (long-term learning), especially in connection with many of the complex social issues confronting today's society. If the individual is especially responsive to the joking material presented, this activity is likely to be disrupted, with the predictable negative effect on learning.

Smith, Ascough, Ettinger, and Nelson (1971) obtained evidence in support of this distraction effect of humor, although considerable individual differences in distraction were noted. In a test-taking situation among college

students, humor facilitated recall among those with high anxiety, but interfered with recall among those with moderate levels of anxiety. The latter group complained that the humorous material in the test distracted them and made it difficult to concentrate. Of course, one's own living room is a considerably more relaxed environment than a college classroom in a test-taking situation, so these findings may have limited relevance to long-term learning from television. Also, the fact that television viewers are usually not held accountable for remembering the material presented should minimize any possible effects of anxiety on the production of cognitive change. These findings are valuable, though, in that they suggest that personality or other individual-difference variables may have an important influence on the extent of benefits derived from attempts to combine humor with opportunities for learning. The relative balance of humorous and nonhumorous material presented may be especially important in this respect. Each viewer may have an individualized "threshold" which separates facilitative from inhibitive effects. Whereas the inclusion of humor up to the point of this threshold may enhance attentional and other processes important for learning and retention, too much humor may distract to the point of seriously interfering with these processes.

Induction of a Playful Set

Researchers studying humor have argued that humor tends to put people in a playful frame of mind (Berlyne, 1969, 1972; Eastman, 1921; Flugel, 1954; Fry, 1963; Lieberman, 1977; McGhee, 1971, 1972, 1977, 1979). Since it is difficult to take communications seriously when in this state, a playful set may actually interfere with the kinds of cognitive change required for new learning and enrichment. McGhee has emphasized that an individual must be in a more serious frame of mind for permanent cognitive change to occur. The "stretching" of existing concepts to incorporate discrepant or novel incoming information does not occur in this type of state. Thus, if a program like "All in the Family" is adopted as a means of informing viewers about racial and ethnic attitudes and stereotypes, some consideration must be given to factors influencing whether viewers take the information to reflect the actual conditions of our society. Again, an important factor along these lines may be the amount of humor included in a program. It may be only after some threshold is reached that we stop taking any aspect of what is presented seriously. Clearly, research needs to be initiated on the extent to which individuals fluctuate between more serious and playful modes of processing information in a program containing both serious and humorous communications. More importantly, we need to determine the degree to which such fluctuation facilitates or inhibits basic learning processes in connection with informational segments of the program.

THE COMMUNICATIVE IMPACT OF HUMOR: PREVIOUS RESEARCH

Research on the communicative functions and influences of humor has been surprisingly meager. Moreover, the work that has been completed has been restricted to situations in which the primary goal was to impart specific types of information. That is, given a primary concern about teaching new information or changing attitudes, these studies have explored the effect of inserting different amounts and qualities of humor. No attempt has yet been made to study the effect of adding varying kinds and amounts of more substantive information to communications or programs that are primarily humorous or playful in nature. The inconsistent findings reported in the following with respect to the former approach suggest that the latter may provide a more effective means of achieving combined entertainment and educational goals.

"Lessons" from Children's Programming

To this point, it is only in the area of children's television that any systematic attempt has been made to make primarily educational programming highly entertaining as well. The Children's Television Workshop has taken the lead in trying to discover new ways to make entertainment instrumental to children's learning (Lesser, 1972, 1974). Numerous production techniques have been utilized in efforts to reach this goal. Some are designed to catch the child's attention initially (e.g., music, sound effects, repetition, etc.), whereas others are designed to direct attention to key features of the material to be learned (e.g., action, animation, surprise, and incongruity). Lesser notes that surprising incongruities have proven especially effective in directing attention, since children show strong motivation to resolve incongruities as early as the first year of life (Piaget, 1952). In effect, the incongruity provides the child with a puzzle or problem to be solved, and the child continues to think about it (up to a point, at least) until some resolution has been achieved. Since adults also show this reaction to incongruous events, it may prove fruitful to extend these production techniques to adult programming.

The Children's Television Workshop appears to be operating under the assumption that humorous and nonhumorous forms of incongruity are equally effective in promoting learning and cognitive change (Gibbon, Palmer, & Fowles, 1975). Lesser (1972, 1974) concluded that once action, animation, surprise, incongruity, etc. have captured the child's attention and directed it toward the desired audiovisual elements, humor provides one of the most effective means of sustaining directed attention. In this sense, he feels that humor is more important than any other ingredient in children's television. But, Lesser (1974) further acknowledges that:

> We know virtually nothing about how to make humor instrumental to learning. Forms of learning that rely upon the captivity of its students perhaps can continue to survive without such knowledge, but the televised teaching of children is so completely dependent on the effective use of humor that some beginning understanding of it is demanded [p. 145].

In the case of "Sesame Street," the types of humor that have been most effective in sustaining attention include: (1) farcical or absurd visual incongruities; (2) slapstick (exaggerated physical action); (3) turning the tables on someone else's trickery; (4) demonstrations of adult errors and incompetence; and (5) alliteration, rhyming, or other simple alterations of the sounds of words. Puns and other forms of jokes requiring an understanding of double meanings are generally not understood by preschool children (McGhee, 1974; Shultz, 1974; Shultz & Horibe, 1974; Shultz & Pilon, 1973).

"The Electric Company" is designed to improve school-aged children's reading skills. This program does take advantage of its viewers' presumed capacity to understand double meanings by creating humorous inconsistencies in relation to particular words (Gibbon et al., 1975). For example, after reading instructions from a recipe with the directions "beat well," a woman begins to flog her bread dough with a riding crop. Other examples place relatively less emphasis on action components as part of the humor: (1) "What has four wheels and flies?" "A garbage truck." (2) A cow reads "I know I am a cow," mixing up the two "ow" sounds; a farmer then reads it correctly for the cow, and she responds "You're not a cow!" Fowles and Glanz (1976) studied children's comprehension of humor segments on "The Electric Comnpany" and concluded, in agreement with Lesser (1972, 1974), that to be an effective teaching device verbal humor must focus attention on (or in some way be centrally linked to) the material to be learned, rather than competing with attention to that material. They found that, especially in the case of poor readers, a visual counterpart in the humor episode may interfere with comprehension of verbal components of the humorous event. If visual forms of humor are used simultaneously with verbal ones, they should be clearly related to one another.

Unfortunately, the Children's Television Workshop has not yet made any attempt to demonstrate empirically its assumption that humor does facilitate learning. It has been demonstrated, of course, that considerable learning of basic concepts does occur as a result of viewing "Sesame Street" (Ball & Bogatz, 1970, 1972; Bogatz & Ball, 1971). There has been no demonstration, however, of the part that humor plays in this learning. There seems to be little doubt that humor makes the program more enjoyable to most children, and that it is very effective in sustaining their attention for long periods of time. It does not automatically follow, though, that this increased attention and enjoyment will improve learning and retention of the material presented. It is

also unclear to what extent such techniques will prove to be effective with adult viewers.

Humor and Classroom Learning

Teachers from the elementary school grades through college frequently argue that one must know how and when to insert humor into the teaching situation in order to be an effective teacher. Yet virtually no attempt has been made to study humor's capacity for promoting learning in the classroom. Kaplan and Pascoe (1977) found that the use of humorous examples in a college lecture did improve long-term (six weeks) retention of material which was meaningfully related to the humorous examples. Without this meaningful connection, humor had no facilitating effect. Studies using children have failed to show either a positive or negative impact of humor on learning (Curran, 1972; Neumann, 1972). In one puzzling finding, Hauck and Thomas (1972) found that children's incidental learning is facilitated by humor although intentional learning is not.

Factor analytic studies of college students' ratings of teacher effectiveness have consistently indicated that both the amount of humor and degree of enthusiasm exhibited in the classroom contribute significantly to students' perceptions of the value of the course (Feather, 1972; Field, Simpkins, Brown, & Rich, 1971; Frey, 1973; McKeachie, Lin, & Mann, 1971). Ware and Williams (1974) also found that these teacher qualities were especially effective in stimulating in students a desire to learn more about the subject matter. This finding held apart from the level of factual content represented in the lecture. If these findings can be extended to reactions to television programs, they support the view that humor might be an especially effective tool to be used in integrating the medium's entertainment and educational functions.

Humor as a Means of Persuasion and Attitude Change

The greatest amount of research dealing with the effect of inserting humor into otherwise "serious" communications has been completed within the context of studies of persuasion and attitude change. Markiewicz (1974) reviewed this research and concluded that the use of humor in persuasive speech neither increases nor reduces the extent of attitude change, relative to a serious version of the same communication. Ten out of thirteen studies failed to show any significant effect at all, and the remaining three yielded inconsistent findings. In a more recent review, Gruner (1976) reached a similar conclusion with respect to both humor and satire.

Interestingness of the Communication.   Humor does appear to make speeches and other forms of communication more interesting (Gruner, 1976; Markiewicz, 1974), even though it has no influence on persuasion. However, Gruner (1970) found this effect only for speeches initially judged to be dull.

Message Retention.   Studies of attitude change and persuasion have yielded no evidence in support of the view that humor enhances retention of the content of a message. The majority of studies suggest that humor neither facilitates nor inhibits retention (e.g., Gruner, 1965, 1967, 1970; Kennedy, 1972; Markiewicz, 1972a; Taylor, 1964), although three studies point toward an interference effect (Markiewicz, 1972b, 1973; Taylor, 1972).

Humor in Advertising.   For most Americans, one of the most frequently encountered forms of persuasive communication occurs in television commercials. A recent content analysis of over 2000 commercials indicated that about 15% use humor in some way (Kelley and Solomon, 1975). However, few published studies have attempted to determine the effectiveness of humor in leading to improved retention of the name and qualities of products advertised. (It should be noted that a considerable amount of such research appears to have been completed by advertising agencies and other private organizations but has not been published.) The limited data which are available suggest that humor sometimes increases sales (Phillips, 1968; Weingarten, 1967) and sometimes reduces them (Weingarten, 1967).

Implications of Research Findings

These findings provide mixed support for the view that humor might be effectively used to obtain more of a balance between the entertainment and educational functions of television. Whereas some studies suggest that humor can facilitate processes associated with learning and retention, others suggest either a negative effect or no effect. This inconsistency is surprising to many teachers and advertisement writers who use humor daily. Several investigators have commented on the importance of having the to-be-remembered messages integrally and meaningfully linked to the humor used. This may account for some of the inconsistency, since meaningfulness was not controlled for in many of the studies.

Although there is little doubt about the capacity of programs such as "Sesame Street" and "The Electric Company" to promote new learning in young children, the extent to which humor contributes to the gains in concept development and the development of reading and other intellectual skills is not clearly established. Available research seems to point consistently to the fact that humor makes surrounding events and communications more interesting and enjoyable to watch and listen to, but this has no direct

implications for its role in facilitating learning as such. In spite of this inconclusiveness regarding humor's role in the process of learning and cognitive change, these findings do suggest that comparable efforts directed at adults might be successful. However, the process of application may be more difficult with adults than with young children since the latter have not yet developed differential conceptions of being educated and being entertained. Children enjoy the process of learning in its own right, and any incidental entertaining accompaniments are merely "icing on the cake." Adults, on the other hand, may approach television viewing with an established concept of what is entertaining and what is educational. The fact that most viewers avoid programs they consider to be educational in intent and seek out those heavy on entertainment content suggests that any attempt to develop a "Sesame Street"-type program for adults must be careful to avoid being perceived as primarily informational in intent.

At present, most television programs can be easily identified as having exclusively entertainment or educational goals. Most programs with educational goals occur in the form of documentaries or specials, or appear on one of the specialized public channels. In order to avoid instilling a negative educational set toward a new program with combined educational and entertainment goals, it would be desirable to develop the program in a manner more consistent with traditional entertainment formats. There appear to be at least two different ways of using humor to accomplish this end. One would entail essentially copying the approach of the Children's Television Workshop with humorous segments alternating with information on topical issues of interest and concern to most people. Considerable research would be required in order to determine the most effective way of integrating humorous with more serious forms of communication (see following section). It might also prove fruitful to combine humor with other forms of entertainment (such as music and drama) in order to achieve the most satisfactory balance between entertaining and informative segments of the program. Of course, viewers would quickly become aware of the educational slant to this kind of program, so the entertaining segments must be of sufficient quantity and quality to maintain interest throughout the entire program.

A second approach to providing informative material within an entertaining format would involve the addition of such material to an already established program without modifying its basic format (such as "All in the Family"). This program and at least one of its spin-offs, "Maude," have been used to demonstrate the nature of racial and ethnic prejudice, traditional sex role behavior and expectations, and have provided commentary on other social issues. Although this type of program is enjoyed and watched regularly ("All in the Family" was frequently in the top 10, and usually in the top 20 in the Nielsen ratings through the mid 1970s), the extent to which such regular

viewing is associated with a greater or deeper understanding of racial, sexual, and ethnic attitudes has not been fully determined. (A book summarizing research which has been done on "All in the Family" was due to be published some time after the publication of this volume.) Research in other areas suggests that such social attitudes are not altered appreciably through humor, although regular viewing should make many viewers more aware of them as social issues. Any such increased awareness and breadth of understanding are valuable educational accomplishments for a program that is perceived to be strictly light entertainment. The extension of this approach to other controversial issues within a situation comedy format might prove to be equally broadening to viewers.

A comedy program may also be more effective than a straightforward dramatic presentation at providing a platform for opposing sides of a controversial, complex issue. Since the issues themselves are likely to be of a serious nature, it would be difficult for a straight dramatic program to present both (or several) sides without taking on the air of a drama/documentary. As this occurs, the perceived entertainment level is likely to go down for most viewers. The regular occurrence of joking material in a situation comedy maintains the high entertainment level, while giving ample opportunity for representing different sides of an issue in the ongoing dialogue.

CONSIDERATIONS FOR FUTURE RESEARCH AND PROGRAM DEVELOPMENT

Future research aimed at determining the effectiveness of humor as a means of integrating the educational and entertainment functions of television should proceed along several different lines. Basic research needs to be completed, both within and outside of a television context, on the question of whether humor facilitates or interferes with basic processes associated with learning and retention. Several modifying variables also need to be studied in connection with these processes. Assuming that humor eventually proves to support learning and cognitive change, additional studies need to be completed in order to determine how to most effectively utilize humor in the context of a particular program. This kind of research would have to be undertaken separately for purposely informational programs like "Sesame Street" and entertainment programs like "All in the Family."

Basic Research Issues

Ideally, programs of the type discussed here would provide intellectual stimulation and challenge at the same time as they are entertaining viewers. Although it is difficult to determine the degree to which such stimulation

actually occurs, it is possible to determine whether such programs increase one's breadth or depth of knowledge about a given issue or content area. It is probably safe to assume that any program that provides a diversity of ideas to viewers is intellectually enriching, but in order to determine humor's effectiveness in promoting such enrichment as it entertains, comparison programs lacking in humor must also be developed. Care must be taken to isolate the influence of humor from other factors that might be related to the extent to which new knowledge is acquired. Given the large amounts of money required to produce a single television program of any type, it might be of value to carry out initial studies in a traditional laboratory setting. Again, the basic consideration in all of this research is whether humor promotes or interferes with expansion of existing knowledge.

Amount of Humor: Achieving the Best Balance. The frequency and duration of humorous segments in a program are among the more obvious factors in need of investigation. It was suggested earlier in this chapter that as humor increases beyond some threshold, mood changes may be expected to occur such that the viewer's frame of mind becomes incompatible with learning and cognitive change. A limited amount of humor might be very effective in maintaining interest in a program, and this amount should be more effective in promoting learning of the information conveyed than would long and frequent humor segments. Experimental studies of humor's effect on learning should systematically vary both the frequency and duration of humor episodes in order to determine the point at which this threshold occurs. Since widespread individual differences are likely to occur in connection with the point at which increasing humor stops facilitating learning and begins to interfere with it, an attempt should be made to determine this threshold separately for different subgroups of viewers.

If the influence of humor on learning is conceptualized along a continuum, a curvilinear relationship should occur; that is, an increasing positive relationship should occur up to a point. Past that point, the curve might either gradually level off or drop quickly. It may be that an optimal amount of humor (for learning) occurs at a point considerably lower than the point at which humor begins to have a negative impact on learning. It is this optimal point which needs to be incorporated into television programs aimed at teaching as they entertain.

Funniness of Humor Segments. Assuming that some control can be exercised over the funniness of the joke material presented in an entertaining educational program or an educational entertaining program, what level of funniness is optimal for learning? To answer this question, pretesting must be completed in order to obtain data on the funniness of jokes to be used. Once several distinctive levels of funniness of humor material have been achieved,

this dimension should be experimentally manipulated while holding informational components of the program constant. Again, this research may be completed within the context of a television program or through the use of speeches, lectures, or other forms of communication in a nontelevision setting. Increased face validity makes the former approach more desirable, but cost factors suggest that these basic research questions regarding humor's effect on learning might best be undertaken in other experimental contexts first. There would appear to be no a priori grounds for predicting a differential outcome in these different settings. As was suggested with respect to the amount of humor associated with an informational message, extremely funny segments may serve to create a mood incompatible with effective learning, or otherwise distract the viewer from attending to the information presented. Milder forms of humor may serve to maintain interest and enthusiasm for the program, while maximizing the probability of drawing fuller attention to all aspects of the program.

Relevance of Humor to Informational Content. Regardless of whether humor is used to promote learning in an instructionally oriented program or in a typical situation-comedy format, the extent to which the humor used is meaningfully connected to the information presented may turn out to have a strong impact on what is learned and remembered from a program. The Children's Television Workshop studies concluded that, in order to be an effective aid to learning, humor must be meaningfully related to the material to be learned (Gibbon et al., 1975; Lesser, 1972, 1974). In Lesser's words, the humor should "coincide perfectly with the critical learning opportunity." Although these conclusions were drawn from work in children's television, they should hold for adult programs as well. When humor is meaningfully related to other information presented, it should provide an additional associational link to that information making it easier to both learn and retain. Unlike a joke that is simply "tacked on" at the appropriate time, a joke that is meaningfully integrated into a broader informational presentation should become part of the conceptual structures formed by that information. If certain features of the joke(s) make it easier to remember than the surrounding information, and this information is stored in close connection with the joke, the individual may have an inroad to memories that would otherwise be less available.

Explaining the Link Between Jokes and the Intended Message. If a joke or other form of humorous event does have a meaningful connection with the more serious informational component of a program, should the nature of that link be outlined for viewers? If humor is better able to promote learning and retention when it is relevant in some way to the material to be learned,

explaining how the humor relates to that material should maximize the probability of viewers actively formulating the link.

Television is frequently criticized for being a "passive" medium; that is, the viewer has no control over the rate and manner in which information is presented. The program goes on in a predetermined fashion regardless of the perceptions or reactions of the viewing audience. The viewer is easily lulled into taking in events as they occur without actively thinking about what is presented. If television viewing is conducive to this type of mental sluggishness, it may prove advantageous to have attention drawn to key concepts and ideas by characters in the program. This approach is commonly adopted following many important news events, such as a televised speech by an important political figure. News analysts promptly summarize the key points of the speech and discuss the implications of these points for various other key issues. Although some viewers are offended by this policy, arguing that they can think for themselves and draw their own conclusions, most respond relatively favorably to a skilled analyst performing this function for them. The extent to which such integrative explanations are useful in connection with joking material must be studied experimentally if informative and humorous program segments are to be effectively integrated.

A hazard in attempting this kind of approach in connection with humor lies in the popular belief that humor loses its appeal when explained. When the point of a joke is carefully analyzed and verbalized, it often becomes stale and loses its "punch," a point which has been experimentally demonstrated by Rothbart (1976) with children. If viewers react negatively to any form of explanation of humor, this should interfere with attentional and other cognitive processes important for learning. However, this negative effect might be avoided if explanatory links were offered in the context of ongoing dialogue between characters in the program. In "All in the Family," for example, Archie Bunker makes frequent jokes at the expense of other races or ethnic groups. If Michael (Archie's son-in-law) were to explain how these jokes indicate prejudice toward blacks, Poles, Jews, etc., viewers might obtain a better understanding of the nature and origins of prejudice. Since the explanatory link in this situation is offered in the context of ongoing entertaining dialogue, the viewer is likely to perceive it as simply part of the entertainment rather than an attempt to educate viewers about prejudice. Caution should be exercised, then, in attempting to extrapolate nontelevision laboratory studies along these lines to situation comedies or other programs in which analyses of the humor used are carefully integrated into ongoing entertaining segments.

Timing. Every comedian knows that timing in the delivery of a punchline is one of the most important factors in determining an audience's reaction to a

joke. A joke can fall flat simply because the punchline comes too early or too late.

The timing of humor in relation to informational segments of a program may prove to be equally important. Joking material might be presented at varying amounts of time before or after the information "to be learned." If the humor is presented first, there is the risk that the viewer may still be laughing or thinking about the joke when the more substantive information is presented. If it is presented after the material to be learned, attentional involvement with the joke may disrupt rehearsal or other cognitive processes which aid in the transfer of information to long-term memory storage. Each set of circumstances, then, should interfere with the desired goal of achieving effective learning while being entertained. Experimental studies could manipulate this timing dimension in order to determine its combined effects on appreciation of the humorous materials and retention of accompanying nonhumorous communications. Since the meaningfulness of the notion of one form of communication being first is reduced in an ongoing program characterized by alternation between joking and informative material, the important issue here may turn out to be simply the amount of time separating humorous and nonhumorous segments.

Type of Humor.   Humor researchers have typically distinguished between "tendentious" (aggressive, sexual, and other themes that are emotionally salient) and nonsense or incongruity humor since Freud's (1960) initial distinction between these categories. The distinction is an important one because of the greater amount of laughter typically associated with tendentious forms of humor. Even casual attention to "The Tonight Show" is sufficient to reveal that the best way to assure a big laugh at a joke is to include elements of aggression or sex in it. A recent content analysis of humor in prime-time television (Stocking, Sapolsky, & Zillmann, 1977) indicated that aggressive humor is by far the most common (69%). The limited frequency of sexual humor (11%) appears to be due to the censorship of sexual themes during family-viewing times.

Before automatically extending this pattern of predominantly aggressive humor to programs designed to coordinate the achievement of entertainment and educational goals, research needs to be completed on the relationship between the thematic content of jokes and their effect on the learning of accompanying information. In the case of aggressive humor, the target or butt of the joke may be a particular person or a social, political, racial, or other group. Previous research has suggested that appreciation of hostile humor is determined by the nature of one's identification (LaFave, 1972; LaFave, Haddad, & Maesen, 1976) or disposition (Zillmann & Cantor, 1976) toward both the aggressor and victim in the joke. We find jokes funnier when we have a positive attitude toward the aggressor and a negative attitude

toward the victim than when the reverse is true. Thus, blacks find antiwhite jokes funnier than antiblack jokes, whereas whites hold the reverse preferences. The same pattern holds for political jokes, ethnic jokes, and other forms of humor centering around distinctive social groups. The critical issue, given the concerns of the present chapter, is whether comparable findings will be obtained with respect to learning material presented in connection with jokes that disparage different groups. If Archie Bunker tells a joke putting down Poles at the same time that information is being provided on the nature and function of water softeners, is this going to facilitate or interfere with the learning of this information by Poles and non-Poles? If one's positive identification with the individual or group put down in a joke creates some form of negative reaction in the viewer, this is likely to disrupt attention to the accompanying information about water softeners, so that an interference effect should occur.

Because of the large viewing audience during prime-time viewing hours, humor perceived as putting down particular groups will always risk being seen as insulting by large numbers of viewers. Accordingly, it may prove most fruitful (for learning) to seek out butts of jokes which nearly all viewers can respond favorably to. Consideration should also be given, however, to the proportions of incongruity-based humor added to hostile and sexual forms of humor. If hostile forms of humor are eventually shown to disrupt learning and memory processes (even though the joke itself is well remembered), emotionally neutral incongruity humor might be alternated with hostile humor. Audiences would probably become bored with incongruity humor quickly in the absence of sexual or aggressive content, but they might respond favorably to it when it is provided to achieve a balance of different forms of humor. The key informational segments might then be presented in connection with incongruity-based jokes that provide a more favorable frame of mind for receiving and processing nonjoke information.

Canned Laughter. One of the most conspicuous characteristics of television comedy programs is the addition of canned laughter. This practice is based on the assumption that laughter is contagious, and that if artificial laughter can increase laughter in home viewers, it should also lead to increased enjoyment of the program. Experimental studies of the effects of adding canned laughter have shown that increased laughter does occur (Chapman, 1973; Cupchik & Leventhal, 1974; Leventhal & Mace, 1970; Smyth & Fuller, 1972), although the viewing audience does not consistently increase its intellectual evaluation of the funniness of the film or program.

Although canned laughter does facilitate audience laughter, there is limited evidence that it may interfere with the learning of informational messages. Zillmann (1977) cited data obtained by Keith Mielke at Indiana University regarding the program "Feeling Good," a recent unsuccessful attempt to

teach health-related information in an entertaining fashion. In the development of this program, the issue of whether to include canned laughter came up. To test the impact of canned laughter on both appreciation of the humor presented and comprehension of the information accompanying it, two versions of the same show were produced. These shows differed only in terms of the presence or absence of canned laughter. Although the audience that received the laugh track evaluated the show to be funnier and more enjoyable, comprehension of the health message was poorer than that of the audience that did not hear a laugh track. Additional research along these lines should be completed before production decisions are made about the inclusion of canned laughter in programs designed to both inform and entertain the viewing audience.

Subject Samples.   In many cases, the principal investigators in television research projects are members of the university community rather than the television industry. If research along the lines proposed here is completed in a college setting, investigators must be careful not to restrict their subject sample to college students. A college sample should not only have stronger motivation to learn more substantive forms of information from a television program, but should possess better skills for learning as well. Care should be taken to assure that the samples used for research purposes closely approximates the sample of television viewers in general or of the program under consideration in particular.

The Role of Mental Effort and Intellectual Challenge

Entertainment is conceptualized in several different ways in this volume. Some views emphasize the role of relaxation or diversion from sources of stress and conflict, whereas others focus on the role of drama, emotional arousal, amusement, humor, etc. One characteristic of entertaining events, though, seems to override all others. Any event perceived to be entertaining engages our attention in an enjoyable fashion. Thus, we might point to different stimulus events that produce this enjoyment (such as drama, music, humor, and so forth), psychological or social functions fulfilled by these events (including relaxation, tension reduction, distraction from conflict, strengthening friendships, and others), or physiological changes associated with them as being the most important properties of the experience of entertainment. Extension of our investigation of entertainment into these directions is essential to achieving an overall understanding of entertaining events, but we must avoid equating entertainment with any of these more limited conceptualizations.

There is now evidence in support of the view that the most primitive (that is, occurring in early infancy) form of entertainment occurs in the context of

simply exercising one's mental capacities in an attempt to understand objects and events around us. Piaget (1952, 1962) suggested this some time ago, but it is only in the past decade or so that experimental research has confirmed this view. Piaget noted that infants and young children are most likely to attend to events that are familiar in some respects and yet novel in others. McCall and McGhee (1977) reviewed research on infant attention and concluded that attention occurs as an inverted-U function of the amount of discrepancy between the new event and a well-familiarized standard. More importantly, smiling is most likely to occur at moderate levels of discrepancy between the event and existing schemas. Kagan (1967, 1971) argued that the amount of effort required for successful assimilation of a novel or discrepant event is the major determinant of whether smiling occurs, with moderate levels of effort being most pleasurable. McGhee (1979) has argued similarly: it is built into the organism to enjoy processing information which requires some optimal moderate amount of effort for meaningful comprehension. Smiling (and sometimes laughter) is the overt manifestation of pleasure resulting from the successful meeting of mild intellectual challenges to comprehension. Harter (1974) and Kagan (1971) found that older children also derive maximal enjoyment from solving moderately challenging problems. Finally, it has been shown that moderately challenging jokes are also funnier than either very simple or complex jokes (providing low or high amounts of challenge) (McGhee, 1976; Zigler, Levine, & Gould, 1967).

If these findings are extended to adults and their television-viewing habits, it would appear that the optimal level of challenge for most viewers is a relatively low one. We noted earlier that the most popular programs consistently provide little in terms of intellectual stimulation and the opportunity for expansion of knowledge. This same trend appears to hold for humor preferences. Zillmann (1977) reported unpublished data based on an analysis of the amount of joke work involved in humorous incidents in prime-time comedy shows (variety shows and situation comedies). Simple or blunt humor constituted 58% of the total shown, whereas only 42% was at a more sophisticated level. Thus more obvious forms of humor are included more often that subtle and refined forms. Consistent with these findings, Cantor (1977) found that programs with large viewing audiences are composed mainly of tendentious humor, whereas programs with smaller viewing audiences rely less on this form of humor. The popularity of tendentious humor among producers undoubtedly stems from the fact that aggressive and sexual jokes do not have to be very clever in order to produce hearty laughter.

Zillmann (1977) reported additional unpublished data showing that the intake of alcohol serves to increase appreciation of blunt humor and decrease appreciation of more sophisticated humor. In his view, this effect is due to the fact that alcohol intake impairs the smooth functioning of basic cognitive skills. In terms of the arguments advanced earlier in this section, the optimal

level of intellectual challenge in humor appears to drop because even simple jokes become more challenging under the influence of alcohol.

If this effect holds for alcohol, it may also hold for any set of conditions that reduces the efficiency of intellectual functioning. Thus, if most viewers watch television in the evening following a mentally or physically fatiguing day's work, this would be expected to produce a preference for less challenging forms of entertainment. The fact that most viewers want the programs they watch to be relaxing (Steiner, 1963) supports the view that they are not interested in exerting high amounts of mental effort while they are being entertained. In the only study to investigate the effect of extended mental effort on humor preferences, Reutner and Kazak (1976) found that more complex forms of humor were less funny after cognitively demanding tasks. However, appreciation of simple forms of humor did not change as a result of such activities.

These studies suggest a promising avenue to follow in future investigations of entertainment. Since the majority of adults' television watching occurs in the evening, investigators should examine the relationship between extent of both mental and physical fatigue and the enjoyment of programs providing varying levels of intellectual challenge. Individuals might be asked to engage in either physical or mental tasks requiring varying degrees of exertion in order to produce different levels of fatigue. They might then be asked to rate different programs along different entertainment-related dimensions, or to choose from among different programs those which they would prefer to view. In addition to increasing our understanding of the general nature of entertainment, this kind of research should be helpful in planning the level of sophistication to be provided in both informative and pure entertainment segments of a program.

For programs attempting to combine educational and entertainment goals, research should also be undertaken to determine the effect of humor on the sophistication or complexity of material enjoyed. At any given point, each of us must have a range of program sophistication that we find most entertaining and enjoyable. Below this range boredom sets in; above it, disinterest is likely because it is difficult to follow what is going on in the program without the exertion of considerable mental effort. At some point as the amount of effort required to understand a program increases, the task becomes more effort than the reward, and we either change stations or find ourselves increasingly distracted by other events. If humor is added to the program, does this make the exertion of mental effort to follow the program more worthwhile? If humor adds enjoyment for the viewer, this may provide the incentive needed to continue attending more informative segments of the program. If other aspects of the program begin to become too mentally taxing, humor might provide a period of rest before returning one's attention to the more substantive content of the program.

REFERENCES

Ball, S., & Bogatz, G. A. *The first year of "Sesame Street": An evaluation.* Princeton, N.J.: Educational Testing Service, 1970.

Ball, S., & Bogatz, G. A. *Reading with television: An evaluation of "The Electric Company."* Princeton, N.J.: Educational Testing Service, 1972.

Berlyne, D. E. *Conflict, arousal, and curiosity.* New York: McGraw-Hill, 1960.

Berlyne, D. E. Arousal and reinforcement. In D. Levine (Ed.), *Nebraska Symposium on Motivation* (Vol. 15). Lincoln: University of Nebraska Press, 1967.

Berlyne, D. E. Laughter, humor and play. In G. Lindzey & E. Aronson (Eds.), *Handbook of social psychology* (2nd ed., Vol. 3). Reading Mass.: Addison-Wesley, 1969.

Berlyne, D. E. Humor and its kin. In J. H. Goldstein & P. E. McGhee (Eds.), *The psychology of humor: Theoretical perspectives and empirical issues.* New York: Academic Press, 1972.

Bogatz, G. A., & Ball, S. *The second year of "Sesame Street": A continuing evaluation.* Princeton, N.J.: Educational Testing Service, 1971.

Cantor, J. R. Tendentious humor in the mass media. In A. J. Chapman & H. C. Foot (Eds.), *Its a funny thing, humour.* Oxford, England: Pergamon Press, 1977.

Chapman, A. J. Funniness of jokes, canned laughter and recall performance. *Sociometry,* 1973, *36,* 569–578.

Cupchik, G. C., & Leventhal, H. Consistency between expressive behavior and the evluation of humorous stimuli: The role of sex and self-observation. *Journal of Personality and Social Psychology,* 1974, *30,* 429–442.

Curran, F. W. *A developmental study of cartoon humor appreciation and its use in facilitating learning.* Unpublished doctoral dissertation, Catholic University of America, 1972.

Eastman, M. *The sense of humor.* New York: Scribners, 1921.

Feather, N. T. Teaching effectiveness and student evaluation. *Australian Psychologist,* 1972, *7,* 180–187.

Field, T. W., Simpkins, W. S., Brown, R. K., & Rich, P. Identifying patterns of teacher behavior from student evaluations. *Journal of Applied Psychology,* 1971, *55,* 466–469.

Flugel, J. C. Humor and laughter. In G. Lindzey (Ed.), *Handbook of social psychology. Vol. 2: Special fields and applicatons.* Reading, Mass.: Addison-Wesley, 1954.

Fowles, B. R., & Glanz, M. *The use of visual humor in televised reading instruction: A media design problem.* Unpublished manuscript, 1976.

Freud, S. *Jokes and their relation to the unconscious.* New York: Norton, 1960.

Frey, P. W. Student ratings of teaching: Validity of several rating factors. *Science,* 1973, *182,* 83–85.

Fry, W. F. *Sweet madness: A study of humor.* Palo Alto, Calif.: Pacific Books, 1963.

Gibbon, S. Y., Palmer, E. L., & Fowles, B. R. "Sesame Street," "The Electric Company," and reading. In J. B. Carroll & J. S. Chall (Eds.), *Toward a literate society: A report from the National Academy of Education.* New York: McGraw-Hill, 1975.

Goldstein, J. H., Harman, J., McGhee, P. E., & Karasik, R. Test of an information-processing model of humor: Physiological response changes during problem- and riddle-solving. *Journal of General Psychology,* 1975, *92,* 59–68.

Grotjahn, M. *Beyond laughter.* New York: McGraw-Hill, 1957.

Gruner, C. R. An experimental study of satire as persuasion. *Speech Monographs,* 1965, *32,* 149–153.

Gruner, C. R. Effect of humor on speaker ethos and audience information gain. *Journal of Communication,* 1967, *17,* 228–233.

Gruner, C. R. The effect of humor in dull and interesting informative speeches. *Central States Speech Journal,* 1970, *21,* 160–166.

Gruner, C. R. Wit and humor in mass communication. In A. J. Chapman & H. C. Foot (Eds.), *Humour and laughter: Theory, research and applications.* New York: Wiley, 1976.

Harter, S. Pleasure derived from cognitive challenge and mastery. *Child Development,* 1974, *45,* 661–669.

Hauck, W. E., & Thomas, J. W. The relationship of humor to intelligence, creativity, and intentional and incidental learning. *Journal of Experimental Education,* 1972, *40,* 52–55.

Himmelweit, H. T. An experimental study of taste development in children. In L. Aron & M. May (Eds.), *Television and human behavior.* New York: Appleton-Century-Crofts, 1963.

Kagan, J. On the need for relativism. *American Psychologist,* 1967, *22,* 131–143.

Kagan, J. *Change and continuity in infancy.* New York: Wiley, 1971.

Kaplan, R. M., & Pascoe, G. C. Humorous lectures and humorous examples: Some effects upon comprehension and retention. *Journal of Educational Psychology,* 1977, *69,* 61–65.

Kelley, J. P., & Solomon, P. J. Humor in television advertising. *Journal of Advertising,* 1975, *4,* 31–35.

Kennedy, A. J. *An experimental study of the effect of humorous message content upon ethos and persuasion.* Unpublished doctoral dissertation, University of Michigan, 1972.

LaFave, L. Humor judgments as a function of reference group and identification class. In J. H. Goldstein & P. E. McGhee (Eds.), *The psychology of humor: Theoretical perspectives and empirical issues.* New York: Academic Press, 1972.

LaFave, L., Haddad, J., & Maesen, W. A. Superiority, enhanced self-esteem, and perceived incongruity humour theory. In A. J. Chapman & H. C. Foot (Eds.), *Humour and laughter: Theory, research and applications.* London: Wiley, 1976.

Lesser, G. Assumptions behind the production and writing methods in "Sesame Street." In W. Schramm (Ed.), *Quality instructional television.* Honolulu: University of Hawaii Press, 1972.

Lesser, G. *Children and television: Lessons from Sesame Street.* New York: Random House, 1974.

Leventhal, H., & Mace, W. The effects of laughter on evaluation of a slapstick movie. *Journal of Personality,* 1970, *38,* 16–30.

Lieberman, J. N. *Playfulness: Its relationship to imagination and creativity.* New York: Academic Press, 1977.

Lundgren, R. What is a good instructional program? In W. Schramm (Ed.), *Quality instructional television.* Honolulu: University of Hawaii Press, 1972.

Markiewicz, D. *Can humor increase persuasion, or is it all a joke?* Paper presented at the meeting of the Speech Communication Association, Chicago, December 1972. (a)

Markiewicz, D. *The effects of humor on persuasion.* Unpublished doctoral dissertation, Ohio State University, 1972. (b)

Markiewicz, D. *Persuasion as a function of humorous vs. serious message or contexts.* Unpublished manuscript Northern Illinois University, 1973.

Markiewicz, D. Effects of humor on persuasion. *Sociometry,* 1974, *37,* 407–422.

McCall, R. B., & McGhee, P. E. The discrepancy hypothesis of attention and affect in infants. In I. C. Uzgiris & F. Weizman (Eds.), *The structuring of experience.* New York: Plenum, 1977.

McGhee, P. E. Development of the humor response: A review of the literature. *Psychological Bulletin,* 1971, *76,* 328–348.

McGhee, P. E. On the cognitive origins of incongruity humor: Fantasy assimilation versus reality assimilation. In J. H. Goldstein & P. E. McGhee (Eds.), *The psychology of humor: Theoretical perspectives and empirical issues.* New York: Academic Press, 1972.

McGhee, P. E. Development of children's ability to create the joking relationship. *Child Development,* 1974, *45,* 552–556.

McGhee, P. E. Children's appreciation of humor: A test of the cognitive congruency principle. *Child Development,* 1976, *47,* 420–426.

McGhee, P. E. A model of the origins and early development of incongruity-based humor. In A. J. Chapman & H. C. Foot (Eds.), *It's a funny thing, humour.* Oxford, England: Pergamon Press, 1977.

McGhee, P. E. *Humor: Its origin and development.* San Francisco: Freeman, 1979.

McKeachie, W. J., Lin, Y. G., & Mann, W. Student ratings of teacher effectiveness: Validity studies. *American Educational Research Journal,* 1971, *8,* 435–445.

Neumann, L. E. *Humor in classroom instruction: A comparative study of cartoon humor in high school biology instruction.* Unpublished doctoral dissertation, St. Louis University, 1972.

Phillips, K. When a funny commercial is good, its great! *Broadcasting,* May 13, 1968, p. 26.

Piaget, J. *The origins of intelligence in children.* New York: International Universities Press, 1952.

Piaget, J. *Play, dreams, and imitation in childhood.* New York: Norton, 1962.

Reutner, D. B., & Kazak, A. E. The effect of cognitive task difficulty on humor ratings of captioned cartoons. *Bulletin of the Psychonomic Society,* 1976, *7,* 275–276.

Robinson, J. P. Toward defining the functions of television. In E. A. Rubinstein, G. A. Comstock & J. P. Murray (Eds.), *Television and social behavior. Vol. 4: Television in day-to-day life: Patterns of use.* Washington, D.C.: U.S. Government Printing Office, 1972.

Rothbart, M. K. Incongruity, problem-solving, and laughter. In A. J. Chapman & H. C. Foot (Eds.), *Humour and laughter: Theory, research and applications.* London: Wiley, 1976.

Schramm, W. *Men, messages, and media: A look at human communication.* New York: Harper & Row, 1973.

Schramm, W., Lyle, J., & deSola Pool, I. *The people look at educational television.* Stanford, Calif.: Stanford University Press, 1963.

Seldes, G. *Educational television: The next ten years.* Stanford, Calif.: Institution for Communication Research, 1962.

Shultz, T. R. Development of the appreciation of riddles. *Child Development,* 1974, *45,* 100–105.

Shultz, T. R., & Horibe, F. Development of the appreciation of verbal jokes. *Developmental Psychology,* 1974, *10,* 13–20.

Shultz, T. R., & Pilon, R. Development of the ability to detect linguistic ambiguity. *Child Development,* 1973, *44,* 728–733.

Smith, R. E., Ascough, J. C., Ettinger, R. F., & Nelson, D. A. Humor, anxiety, and task performance. *Journal of Personality and Social Psychology,*1971, *19,* 243–246.

Smyth, M. M., & Fuller, R. G. C. Effects of group laughter on responses to humorous material. *Psychological Reports,* 1972, *30,* 132–134.

Snow, R. P. How children interpret TV violence in play context. *Journalism Quarterly,* 1974, *51,* 13–21.

Steiner, G. A. *The people look at television.* New York: Knopf, 1963.

Stocking, S. H., Sapolsky, B., & Zillmann, D. Sex discrimination in prime time humor. *Journal of Broadcasting,* 1977, *21,* 447–457.

Taylor, P. M. The effectiveness of humor in informative speeches. *Central States Speech Journal,* 1964, *5,* 295–296.

Taylor, P. M. *The relationship between humor and retention.* Paper presented at the meeting of the Speech Communication Association, Chicago, December 1972.

Ware, J., & Williams, R. Studies on the effects of content and manner of lecture presentations. *Behavior Today,* 1974, *5,* 120.

Weingarten, J. Is far out advertising entertaining the public more but selling it less? *Dunn's Review,* July 1967, pp. 27–28.

Zigler, E., Levine, J., & Gould, L. Cognitive challenge as a factor in children's humor appreciation. *Journal of Personality and Social Psychology,* 1967, *6,* 332–336.

Zillmann, D. Humour and communication: Introduction to symposium. In A. J. Chapman & H. C. Foot (Eds.), *Its a funny thing, humour.* Oxford, England: Pergamon Press, 1977.

Zillmann, D., & Cantor, J. R. A disposition theory of humour and mirth. In A. J. Chapman & H. C. Foot (Eds.), *Humour and laughter: Theory, research, and applications.* London: Wiley, 1976.

9 Television News as Entertainment

Leo Bogart
Newspaper Advertising Bureau

The mass media are a mirror of reality to the degree that they depict what is merely out of range of our senses but acceptable as an extension of them. They provide us with reference points to which we can anchor ourselves in a world that extends beyond the experiences we know firsthand. But the media also change the world we know.

The *form* in which we perceive reality has been transformed by the evolution of communications technology, of which television is the most recent example, and further important changes are on the way. Although it is generally believed that the new technology has steadily increased our understanding of what is "really" going on around us, I would argue that the barrier between the real and the illusory is actually harder than ever to define.

The audience turns to television primarily for entertainment, that is to say, for diversion from the cares and pace of everyday life experience (Bower, 1973; Steiner, 1963). And television programming deals primarily with the world of make-believe. Of all network programs in the 1976–1977 broadcast season, 86% were devoted to fictional drama of one kind or another, and another 6% represented variety or musical entertainment. News, public affairs, and sports made up 5% of the programs. (The remaining 3% were "miscellaneous.")

Yet news (which reports changes in the *real* world) has become an increasingly important component of American television. Although people are more likely to get news from a newspaper on any given day than to get it from TV (Bogart, 1977), by an increasing margin they say they depend on TV as their main source of news of what is going on in the world (Roper Organization, 1974). This incongruity between actual media exposure and

subjective judgment seems to reflect a feeling that TV provides a sense of reality that is more complete, more intense, and more valid than what can be conveyed through print. If faced with a discrepancy, they say they would give more credence to a television news report than to a newspaper article (Roper Organization, 1974).

TV's coverage of news and public affairs encompasses a number of different elements:

1. There is direct television broadcasting of live events, including sports events. In the past dozen years, satellite transmission has made this possible on a worldwide basis.

2. Television creates news by interviewing news makers on programs like "Meet the Press" and by broadcasting panel discussions on public issues.

3. Television documentaries encapsulate and interpret ongoing news stories and sometimes provide a vehicle for significant investigative reporting (perhaps most notably in the case of Edward R. Murrow's landmark exposé of Senator Joseph McCarthy in the early 1950s).

4. Television news programs now are broadcast for an average of three hours a day on the average U.S. station (usually an hour fed from the network and two hours produced locally).

It is the latter type of programs that people generally have in mind when they are asked about TV news (Bogart, 1975) and that accounts for the great bulk of TV-news viewing time. A nationwide survey in 1977 found that 62% of the population over 18 years old watch at least one newscast on an average weekday. Twenty percent watch both network and local news, 12% only network news, and 30% only local news (Bogart, 1977).

Although it is now generally agreed that news on television has (perhaps inevitably) taken on certain properties of TV's entertainment format and style, most of the evidence on this subject is anecdotal in character and perhaps unacceptable to the tradition of empirical social research. The observations in this chapter are therefore to be regarded as tentative, and the reader seeking suggestions for future research might read them as a series of hypotheses awaiting testing. At the core of this analysis are the following propositions:

1. Functioning adults are able to distinguish between what is real and what is not.

2. Whereas viewers recognize most television programming as fiction, they accept televised news as real.

3. TV news gives the impression of providing direct first-hand sensory exposure to events. Actually, TV reconstructs reality no less than print journalism does and perhaps more.

4. TV's portrayal of reality is limited by the entertainment context in which news programs are set and by commercial pressures to enhance audience size. These factors have led to an emphasis on the newscaster rather than the news and have encouraged the selection and presentation of items by criteria that derive from the world of entertainment rather than from journalism.

5. There are serious political consequences to the transformation of news by television. There is also a change in the public's perception of what constitutes news, and a growing confusion between what is taken to be real and what is contrived to be entertaining within the TV-news programming format.

This chapter begins by discussing the nature of news and the dimension of "human interest" that captures the involvement of the audience. How does the attraction of news compare to that of fictional entertainment? Since television news must be entertaining for commercial reasons, we consider how this affects its content. Content is also shaped by the format of television news. We describe the long-standing difficulty of reporting news objectively and discuss the peculiar distortions introduced by TV technology. TV news, we conclude, has changed our perceptions of the real world and may have dulled our willingness to cope with its real problems.

NEWS AND THE TV EXPERIENCE

Activity and Symbolic Meaning

To what extent are the viewers of TV news seeking information and to what extent are they merely passing time? Our contact with mass media always has two simultaneous aspects: activity[1] experience and symbolic experience. The activity experience carries its own measure of satisfaction without regard for the meaning of the message, unless this is actually objectionable. (We go to the movies to get out of the house. We tune in to radio for companionship.)

The symbolic experience involves the *meanings* of what the media communicate. Our response to those meanings determines how we spend time or money within the framework of a particular media activity. We pick one movie or program or newspaper over another, or we may decide not to engage in the activity at all.

There are powerful indications that the *activity* experience accounts for a good deal more of audience behavior than the symbolic content. Mass media

---

[1]"Activity" is used here in a behavioral sense and without regard to the fact that some media experiences such as reading involve more cognitive participation than the comparatively passive task of watching television.

are associated with particular parts of the day's routine or with particular recreational needs. Television viewing, for example, takes place at any given time of day in relation to the cycle of work and sleep, quite apart from the number of stations or the character of the programming choices before the viewer.

News and Audience Flow

Similar to every other kind of TV programming, news attracts audiences in proportion to the amount of time it is given on the air. Except on extraordinary occasions, the size of the broadcast news audience is unrelated to the importance of the particular day's events. The reader can zip through his newspaper rapidly on a dull news day and toss it aside, or he can study and linger over it when big news has happened. The TV viewer generally stays with the news to the end, as he would with any other kind of program, and for much the same reasons: It flows in time, he is filling his time, and there is another show coming on right afterward.

Just as a news program derives a substantial part of its audience from viewers already tuned to the particular station, so it passes on a large part of its audience to the program that follows. For the networks, which begin the evening "feed" to their affilitates with their newscasts, these programs are vital to the never-ending competitive struggle to capture a larger share of the prime-time audience. TV-news programs, both for networks and stations, have been commercially profitable, and they have a desirable stability of format and audience size.

News has served as a device by which the networks and individual stations have established a distinctive identity, which their entertainment programming singularly lacks.

Elmer Lower, then president of ABC News, told a National Association of Broadcasters' Convention in March 1974: "If a station's local news has a high degree of acceptance or credibility, viewers will hold that station in high regard, and this is directly reflected in ratings not just for news but for other kinds of programming as well."

In fact, an examination by ABC's Seymour Amlen of November 1973 ratings for the network affiliated stations in the 100 largest markets found that of 98 stations that rated highest in their early evening newscasts, 52 ranked first in prime-time program ratings and 33 were second. Of the 80 stations whose news programs ranked third, most also ranked lowest in prime time, and only 9 ranked first.

The interrelationship between television news and entertainment is best demonstrated by the fact that those people (especially older ones) who watch a large amount of television in general are also above average in the time they spend with television news. But TV news also attracts an above-average

proportion of people (especially better-educated ones) who are oriented to news from all sources.

It is hard to place any precise weight on the value that the TV-news audience ascribes to the news itself, apart from the ritual aspect of welcoming the familiar personalities who appear on the tube at a regular hour. San Francisco viewers remembered only 1.2 items out of 19.8 on a half-hour network newscast viewed earlier on the same evening; one-half could not recall even one item spontaneously (Newman, 1976). This suggests that for many it is the experience of viewing, rather than the content of the news, that represents the major attraction (Levy, 1977). No doubt readers of a newspaper are similarly forgetful of much that they have read soon after they have read it, and similarly comforted and reassured merely by the ritual of attending to the customary pages at the customary time of day. But the reader's personal relationship with the reporters and editors who produce his paper can not have the same intensity as his relationship with TV newscasters whose faces and voices appear in his living room day after day.

News printed in the newspaper has a tangible reality that puts it on the record. Even when the reader discards the paper, he knows that the news still uncomfortably exists, visible to other eyes. By contrast, television news occurs as part of the movement of broadcast programming. One can literally turn it off; the bad news can be made to vanish: It can be exorcised.

Managing the News Format

The format of TV news is readily amenable to the same kind of manipulation that is now taken for granted with any entertainment product. Format and substance can not be dissociated. The same criteria of responsible news reporting generally apply in broadcast news as in print. Still, the viewers' total impression of what is happening in the world around them must be shaped by show business principles that determine the length of stories, the use of film clips, the selection of items to meet dramatic criteria or to make use of existing film footage.

Because news shows are paced, balanced, orchestrated, and packaged according to the rules of show business, they fit smoothly into TV's fantasy world. Audience ratings are the prevailing criteria of their accomplishment, and program doctors are called in by local stations to provide advice on how to boost ratings by featuring more "good news" and by bringing in newscasters with the right combination of cheerful smiles and sex appeal. Wilbur Mills's stripteaser friend, Fanne Fox, was hired in 1976 to do the weather report for a satirical newscast called "Metronews, Metronews" on KTTV in Los Angeles. (One item dealt with a man who leaps out of cakes nude.)

This was an aberration, but not too far from the standards being set by more eminent and powerful practitioners. Earlier, William Sheehan, another former president of ABC News, had ordered his staff:

> I want more stories dealing with the "pop people." The fashionable people. The new fads. Bright ideas. Changing mores and moralities.... The back of our show must be different from the competition's. Provocative. Funny. Interesting because we're getting to the subjects that people are interested in, and people are interested in many things that are not intrinsically important (Powers, 1977, p. 92).

Local newscasts have become increasingly dominated by young announcers with colorful, identical blazers going through their paces on expensive stage sets and sharing private jokes between news items.

Frank Magid, a prominent consultant on television news programs, has been a proponent of the "action news" format, characterized, according to the *New York Times* of December 25, 1975, "by lengthy menus of short, snappy news items cheerfully served up to the viewer by 'teams' of newscasters chosen for their winning personalities and sprightly ad libs." Magid believes:

> that the viewing public is not interested in the routine "political palaver" of candidates and not especially interested either in political campaigns, even as a spectator sport.... If indeed nothing of significance is said, what reason is there to waste the time? That time is very valuable. You cannot use it indiscriminately.... Most people exercise selective perception. Most people don't cast informed votes. Maybe only two per cent cast informed votes.

In a client report, Magid advised: "Ratings rise when the broadcaster is successful in exposing the listener to what he *wants* to hear, in the very personal way he wants to hear it. In terms of news, this means ratings are improved not when listeners are told what they *should* know, but what they want to hear" (Powers, 1977, p. 78).

Thus the style of newscasting may come to dominate the substance of what is communicated. The reality of the news, with its diversity and confusion, is subordinated to the orderliness of the format: 18 bulletins read by the talking head, punctuated by 9 intervals of videotape (selected to provide contrast rather than necessarily to illustrate the latest or most important stories, and reflecting camera crew assignments rather than unexpected new developments). The commercials that interrupt this presentation represent the true reality that reminds the viewer that he is still safely in the main line of U.S. TV prime-time entertainment and not adrift in that turbulent sea of disasters, rivalries, and hassles that constitutes the news.

THE NATURE OF NEWS

Defining News

News undergoes redefinition with every succeeding generation, and in the era of televised news this reassessment has taken place rapidly but without general awareness. If a man bites a dog, it is generally known today that that is not news. It would be considered a contrived act of publicity, a "media event," of which it would be infra dig to take notice.

What type of information do we call "news"? Is it a report of events that are literally new? "No," answered Ecclesiastes, "there is nothing new under the sun." That statement holds in the sense that familiar human foibles, emotions, and interactions resurface in every society and in every epoch. But the perennial dramas are reenacted in different disguises and contexts, so that the news is something more than the repetition of those ancient universal myths that tell of the common human experience.

Does the freshness, novelty, or immediacy of the event itself make it news? No, what matters is not the timing of the event, but the word of it. The report of the American Declaration of Independence was big news in England when it arrived there by slow boat many weeks after July 4, 1776. The Pentagon Papers made big news when the *New York Times* published them years after they had been written.

Does this mean that news reports something noteworthy that the public had previously not known? What is true of the public at large is not necessarily true of any individual. We may say, "It's news to me," when we learn of something long after it has already appeared in the press and if we have happened to overlook it. Yet the news can hardly be defined as something of significance previously unknown to a given individual because this might cover most of human knowledge.

Most people are probably unfamiliar with the exact details of the occurrences that led up to the Whiskey Rebellion. We would hardly consider them news if they were reported in tomorrow's newspaper. On the other hand, if documents should be discovered tomorrow that cast fresh light on this relatively obscure subject, that would be news. Public ignorance rather than individual ignorance determines what is news and what is not, and news media periodically run stories that are already familiar to "insiders" but strike others as news.

Nor is the news simply "what happened," a report of events. It may be a new explanation or interpretation of already familiar events or a concatenation of known but isolated events into a single narrative that shows previously unknown relationships.

Robert Park (1940) observed that, "History is often quite as interesting as news. But the events history records have ceased to be important because there is nothing one can do about them. On the other hand, when there is nothing to be done about the events recorded in the newspapers, they have ceased to be news [p. xvii]."

This seems in retrospect to be a questionable criterion. Much of the daily flow of news encompasses unique and nonrecurring stories about which no one can do anything, and almost all of it reports events over which the overwhelming majority of the audience feels no sense of control or influence whatsoever. Could not precisely this feeling of remoteness from what is reported account for the public's massive ignorance of happenings, places, and personalities that are the subject of news reports to which it is repeatedly exposed?

The news encompasses useful current information that is not necessarily *generally* important but is of considerable importance for some people. Stock and commodity quotations, baseball scores, movie timetables, and the prices of merchandise offered for sale might not be considered news in the traditional sense, but they represent information that for at least some members of the news audience is both fresh and meaningful. Unlike newspapers, television news cannot report such useful minutiae, which are tedious to anyone not seeking them out.

News and Human Interest

News encompasses not only those stories that are inherently important because of their implications for the general welfare, but those of "human interest," which are dramatic and involving, either because they deal in the universals of human experiences and passions or because of their bizarre and curious character.

Park points out that real-life human interest stories reported in the news are hardly distinguishable from fictional stories in which a writer's imagination recreates and reorders reality to mobilize the reader's attention and enrich his understanding of the human condition. For Park:

Time and place are the essence of news, and this is precisely the difference—to use the language of the newsroom—between a news story and a fiction story. Another way of stating the matter is this: news has to do with events in a real world and gets whatever importance it has from that fact. Fiction and art, generally, are symbolic in character and concerned with incidents in an ideal world beyond time and space. For that reason, fiction and art have no importance in the sense in which that term applies to the news.... Events, if they are to have for the reader the character of news, must be not merely interesting but important. Importance seems, however, to be a quality like hot and cold; that is, relative to time and space [p. xvii].

But time and space are subject to constant redefinition as a result of new technology in communications and transportation. Thus editors and news producers worry about the newsworthiness of items already reported a few hours earlier through other media. The traditional parochialism of judgments regarding newsworthiness is diminishing because of increased population mobility and the corresponding growth in the public's exposure to national rather than local news media (i.e., to TV network news and the news magazines in contrast to local newscasts and newspapers). Thus what is of human interest in the news is likely to touch universal concerns rather than to be a matter of geographic propinquity.

News as the Unexpected

It is the unexpected that makes news most exciting and dramatic, just as it may be the unexpected that captures our attention in fiction. The news that is being made today that will most fascinate us when we read or hear it is the news that we could not possibly anticipate. This by no means suggests that such events are unplanned (Pearl Harbor, after all, took quite a bit of planning), but it implies that their timing and character must have been kept secret not only from the public but from the news media as well.

Events that are both unanticipated and important occur infrequently, however. The bulk of the hard news that comes our way occurs either on a fixed schedule (election days, press conferences, ground-breaking ceremonies, and the like) or in relation to an established reportorial "beat" (the police blotter, the United Nations, the motion picture industry) in which personalities and situations are covered as a matter of course. There is always a certain amount of uncertainty in the handling of such conventional assignments, but there is also much that is predictable, and the real surprises are rare. Much hard news, in fact, follows continuing stories that merely inch along from day to day but that must be followed because of their inherent significance. The public regarded news of the Vietnam war as important but also considered it tedious because of the absence of major military engagements.

The flow of news as it emerges through the 24 hours of the day from a wire service ticker is very different from the news in its packaged form as we read it in the paper or hear it on the air. Much of what comes over the wire consists of updates, amplifications, and corrections of what has come before, so that there is an almost imperceptible sense of change through time as the same bulletins are endlessly repeated. Anyone who follows a 24-hour-a-day radio station for a period of hours can quickly develop the illusion that nothing new ever happens at all. But characteristically, the news audience takes bites of the news only at occasional intervals and in distinctive and familiar formats. And news value, it is generally understood, reflects not merely what is new and what is pertinent, but what arouses the attention of the audience.

THE NEWS FORMAT

The Newscasters

Every news organization works within a functional framework that gives order and priority to the events it reports. The authenticity of real-time, live coverage of news in the making is carried over to enhance the believability of the newscast, which reports brief episodes after the fact, in a sequence and a juxtaposition devised for dramatic effect.

The fact that the news is packaged in a familiar and predictable format creates the comfortable feeling that confident forces are in control; it reduces anxiety about its content.

The network anchorman may be thought of as an all-seeing father who watches over his flock and makes everything come out all right merely by his reassuring "good night" sign-off and the knowledge that he will be back tomorrow. More often than not, he presides over the special broadcasts—political conventions, Senate hearings, moon landings—that show the news as it happens and that provide TV with most of its more memorable moments. Even the sassier figures on local news programs become as familiar as members of the family and can be welcomed back as companions day after day.

The personalities who present the news are "stars" whose glamor, attractiveness, and self-assurance invest them with the same magical aura that surrounds others in show business who are universally known to be universally known. Their personal appeal accounts for much of the variation in audience size between competing programs and makes it possible for them to command large salaries (of which Barbara Walters's million-dollar-a-year contract with ABC in 1976 was merely a dramatic illustration).

Some viewers endow TV newsmen with the power to manipulate the events they report on. During the Watergate hearings, CBS Newsman Daniel Schorr received phone calls from viewers asking him to get rid of boring witnesses and to bring back "that nice John Dean" (Schorr, 1976).

The newscaster's personality is the main reason for the choice of a particular news program, apart from the fact that the viewer was already tuned in to the channel. Newscaster's personality is mentioned far more often than the professionalism of the news organization (Bogart, 1977).

But the interposition of the newscaster inevitably changes the relationship of the audience to the independent reality of the news. Seeing Walter Cronkite announce the death of President Kennedy represented a different kind of experience than reading about the assassination of President Lincoln from a newspaper headline because Cronkite himself was part of the event.

The Limits of Time

There is yet another type of distortion that arises from the constraints of the TV-news format, on which Cronkite himself has commented: "the inadvertent and perhaps inevitable distortion that results through the hypercompression we all are forced to exert to fit one-hundred-pound sacks of news into the one-pound sack that we are given to fill each night."

Consumers of news routinely make allowances for the exigencies of format. The newspapers that reported the assassination of Lincoln had headlines of identical size over advertisements in the adjacent front page columns. And even the newspapers of our own day reported with equal prominence the news of a tornado and news of a space ship landing on Mars.

Television news conventionally strings together brief pellets of information in what is assumed to be their order of importance rather than in terms of their functional relationship. A balance must be struck between film clips that entertain the audience and the newscaster's "talking head," reciting the bulletins on which no film is available.

The public expects that the content of a newscast will not be uniformly informative and that some of it will be informative in a way that has nothing to do with its novelty or newsworthiness. The varying amounts of hard news that are worth reporting can always be extended and interlarded with "soft" background or feature material to fill the available time.

On dull days, the news media must convert non-news into news to meet an allotment of space or time, because the advertisers who support the media expect their own messages to be balanced by content of more general interest. For newspapers and newscasts to develop regular audiences they must satisfy the public's demand for something to pass the time, quite apart from the meaning of what has happened in any given day. Adherence to the format of publication or programming is necessary to sustain the audience's reading or viewing habits, on which the commercial prosperity of a medium depends. But the resulting uniformity in the volume of output can easily add to the difficulties that face public and newsmen alike in determining which items reported as news are real contributions to the chronicle of current history and which ones are merly incidental accompaniments to the main show.

Time Limits and Human Interest

The tremendous time limitations and the episodic character of the television-newscast format typically reduces the presentation of each item to its skeletal essence. Serious issues are normally dealt with at adequate length in panel discussions and documentaries, but these are likely to come on the air at off-hours and do not command the large audiences of the regular evening news.

The result has been criticism of TV's ability to go beyond the surface and convey the meaning of events.

For example, Thomas E. Patterson and Robert D. McClure (1976) conclude harshly:

> The nightly network newscasts of ABC, CBS, and NBC present a distorted picture of a presidential election campaign... play only limited attention to major election issues... almost entirely avoid discussion of the candidates' qualifications for the presidency... devote most of their election coverage to the trivia of political campaigning that make for flashy pictures... Consequently, steady viewers of the nightly network newscasts learn almost nothing of importance about a presidential election [pp. 21–22].

Explanation of the news consumes expensive time and may bore those already familiar with the background. Hence, moments of conflict or confrontation are routinely reported as though they had no historical antecedents. Or individual incidents are reported without any attempt to probe into their setting, origins, and implications. But the necessary clarifications that go beyond the most skeletal recitation of occurrences inevitably demand the intrusion of subjective interpretations, with the attendant problems already discussed.

Time limitations also delimit TV's ability to arouse that sense of empathy and involvement that Park describes as the essence of "human interest" in the news. The human interest story defies summary; it must be permitted to run its natural course. This can be done superbly in "Sixty Minutes" but rarely in two.

Anecdotes of human interest are more likely to be introduced into the news when more important things are not happening. Every news organization works with a "budget" or calendar from which reporters can be assigned to cover anticipated events or stories. But many news items are the product of accident rather than of deliberate planning, and on television it is their accidental recording on camera that can give them extraordinary impact.

Relative News Values

The positioning and prominence of a news story, the extent to which it is covered in depth, are in any medium not merely a reflection of its inherent importance but also a function of what other stories are breaking that day. The same story that may be the lead new item on one day may be crowded into the back of the newspaper on another and may not even make it into the evening newscast if other matters of compelling urgency intervene. Individual local-TV news programs make widely different uses of the network "feed" of news film and their pick-up of network news documentaries. (Such a major

event as CBS's interview with Soviet Premier Khrushchev in 1965 was carried by only 105 stations in the network, whereas 220 carried the Ed Sullivan show the same night.)

The formal structure and style of news media imposes a sense of order and priority that is inevitably converted by the public into attributions of importance or unimportance for different items. Feature, background, and staff-generated stories that may have been sitting around for days or weeks may be perceived by the public as fresh and important news when they are positioned appropriately. This positioning is in part determined by the competition for time or space in the news budget of a particular day; in part it is determined by the recency of a story's delivery, even though it may be timeless in content. News people working under pressure tend to select from the top of the pile in the in-box.

A real news story occurs at a pace that rarely conforms to the deadlines reporters must meet. It commonly involves participants and locations that may be widely separated geographically. A reporter must bring these separated people and events together to a single focal point. This is easily enough done when the story is merely being recited or written down. When the story is constructed from live signals, tape, or film, recorded by a number of different cameras, it involves no less a selection than the transcriptions from a reporter's notebook. Still it is less likely to be perceived as a partial summary and more likely to be regarded as the literal record, simply because the viewer faces the familiar moving images and "sees for himself" what is happening.

The Importance of Video

Visual coverage of the news is generally understood to have more audience appeal than a mere recitation of copy by the newscaster. The effect of this is to shift the proportions of news items covered and of the air time they get.

One-third of the items in the average half-hour network-TV newscast are illustrated with film clips showing the actual events (Bogart, 1975). However, the actual air time for items illustrated by film is longer than for bulletins merely read. An analysis by Richard Townley (1971) shows that 55% of the evening news time on New York's 6 commercial television stations in 4 days of January 1971 was devoted to film clips, most of which were follow-ups to ongoing stories also covered by other media. Of this time, 24% was given to nonvisual material, mostly rewritten wire service stories; 15% went to regular features like weather, sports, and reviews; and only 6% could be classified as original reporting. (Of 430 news segments reported, 85% had already appeared in newspapers or wire-service reports before air time.)

When TV news viewers are asked to recall specific stories, they remember a purely visual image in half of the cases and something they had heard in one

story out of five (Patterson & McClure, 1976). Items with video accompaniment are much better remembered than those simply read by the newscaster. Surprisingly, moving pictures do not make news more memorable than still illustrations. Interviews are recalled best, because they typically take more time on the air than other items (Katz, Adoni, & Parness, 1977).

In editing film, the timing of sequences can be transposed, and a sound track from one sequence can be used to accompany video from another (Altheide, 1976). Another distortion in the presentation of news on television arises from the sheer expense of sending out a news team to cover a story. A newspaper reporter can return from an assignment and tell the editor that there was no news that warranted a line of copy. A TV news producer who has sent out a camera crew has made an investment from which the producer is ordinarily inclined to want a return. Especially on local news shows produced with limited manpower resources, there is an economic pressure to use the available film footage.

News that is unanticipated can be covered only in retrospect and the camera is a far less valuable instrument than when it is set up in advance. News is made behind closed doors, on battlefields forbidden to the press, and in innumerable secret hiding places from which it must be ferreted. And all such news must be presented on television after the fact, with video imagery that may be old or irrelevant when stock or old film is used to illustrate the location where action took place.

FACT, FICTION, AND OPINION
IN THE NEWS

The Doctrine of Objectivity

Media mediate. They interpose filters between the audience and the events on which they report. The notion that their respresentation of reality should be taken as the literal truth is of fairly recent origin. In preliterate societies, reports of contemporary happenings are almost indistinguishable from recollections of the past and from myth and legend. The Old Testament might be taken as an illustration of how current events, oral history, and tales of the supernatural can be woven together into a document that is accepted by many people as having monochromatic meaning.

Written history has always incorporated a certain amount of public-relations puffery for the rulers and potentates of the day. But it has generally distinguished between the reports of the historian's own epoch and the undocumented sagas passed on by earlier generations. In the oral tradition, stories of current events repeated and transmitted in the telling acquire the

patina of mythology. The chronicles of the real Norse kings emerge imperceptibly from the fantasies of Valhalla.

It is no wonder, then, that from its beginnings, the news-reporting profession has been regarded by cynics as a subspecialty of fiction writing. In Samuel Johnson's words:

> To write news in its perfection requires such a combination of qualities that a man completely fitted for the task is not always to be found. In Sir Henry Wooton's jocular definition, an embassador is a man of virtue sent abroad to tell lies for the advantage of his country; a newswriter is a man without virtue who writes lies at home for his own profit. To these compositions is required neither genius nor knowledge, neither industry nor sprightliness; but contempt of shame and indifference to truth are absolutely necessary. He who by long familiarity with infamy has obtained these qualities may confidently tell today what he intends to contradict tomorrow; he may affirm fearlessly what he knows that he shall be obliged to recant, and may write letters from Amsterdam or Dresden to himself.

Early newspapers carried dispatches, often arriving long after the event, that announced specific occurrences, usually in the most cursory bulletins. Reports of shipwrecks, royal successions, battles, treaties, and the like were often summarized in a single sentence or paragraph. But there were occasional articles of political commentary or geographical travelogue that could not literally be tied down to individual events.

Because eighteenth-century journalism necessarily relied on reports that were fragmentary or self-serving, it was commonly understood that they had to be taken with a grain of salt. It was the reader's privilege and responsibility to make his own judgment of the accuracy and merits of what he read. As James Madison suggested, "Could it be arranged that every newspaper, when printed on one side, should be handed over to the press of an adversary, to be printed on the other, thus presenting to every reader both sides of every question, truth would always have a fair chance."

In the nineteenth century, the burden was transferred from the consumer to the purveyor of news. The descriptive or narrative news dispatch became common along with the telegraph, cheap newsprint, and the rotary press, which made possible the "penny newspaper" and its vast readership.

Although newspapers and magazines commonly carried serialized novels as well as straightforward news reports and expository articles, the reader was expected to distinguish fiction from fact. Later, a distinction developed between news reports and interpretation, political commentary, and editorial comment.

The doctrine of "objective" reporting was rooted in the idea that there was a "true" view of events, independent of opinion or bias, to which the journalist had to come as close as possible. But as competing news organizations

constantly demonstrate, the same reality is still commonly seen from different angles and reported with different meanings.

The ordinary and expected biases in news reporting that reflect differences in national or social-class political interests take on a new dimension as a result of official state policies of deliberate falsification and contrivance. The news media of antagonistic countries customarily provide disparate accounts of the same happenings, but those accounts that are made up out of whole cloth are presented with every bit as much authority and substance as those that are uninhibited and objective. For the consumer of news, the fantasies of the propagandist are generally indistinguishable from the realities observed by honest reporters.

Dictatorships rewrite current history as a matter of routine, just as they revise the past. The press in most countries deals in a world of illusion, ideological or ethnocentric in character, and the illusions it purveys are largely uncontested.

In a democracy, the relationship of the press to government hinges on popular acceptance of its truthfulness, as Spiro Agnew was well aware. (If the public did not believe in the honesty of the *Washington Post* and of CBS News, there would have been no need for the Nixon Administration to seek to bring them to heel.) Those who direct mass media in the United States are preoccupied with the question of their credibility. They agonize over whether the public accepts what they report as true and the way they report it as accurate.

The public's judgment as to the truth of news reports involves not only their content but also the significance attributed to them. We may know the correct facts about trivia, but if we are told that they are more important than they really are, we are left with a false view of reality. Thus in considering the unique properties of TV news, we must be concerned not merely with its distortions, but with its proportions.

Radio and Film: Live Coverage and Montage

Unlike print, the twentieth-century media are experienced in time at a pace determined by the producers. This carries implications both for the kinds of feelings they can generate in the audience and for the sense of reality they project. Whereas reporters and editors mediated between the event and the audience, in radio the event could be captured as it happened, with the audience following it directly in *real* time.

Instead of reading about the World Series in the evening paper in a report prepared by someone who already knew the outcome and imposed this perspective on what was written, the listener could hear a play-by-play description as the game took place, delivered by an announcer whose anticipations were no different than the listener's own. For the first time in

history, a national leader could reach out and address vast multitudes over the radio, the unseen audience taking precedence over those actually within earshot. The listener to Roosevelt's fireside chats or to the speeches of Hitler and Churchill could draw his own conclusions about their character and credibility. In the very fact that a mass audience had been assembled to hear it, the broadcast itself becomes a news event. A fireside chat was important not merely because of what the president said, but because of the numbers who heard it.

The movie newsreel did not give its spectators radio's sense of participating in events *as* they were actually happening, but it did give them the illusion of seeing those events the *way* they actually happened. Since "the camera could not lie," audiences could form their own judgments of those in the news. They could see for themselves the exotic places that were only datelines in newspaper dispatches. They could observe the grisly aftermath of disasters, the triumph of athletes, the tumult and agony of battle. With the advent of sound film, the vicarious sensory experience was almost complete. And through the art of montage, the juxtaposition of incongruous images for dramatic effect, the newsreel producer could reassemble the ingredients of the reality he reported in such a way as to express what he saw as their true essence. This tradition, transferred to the making of television news, has profoundly shaped contemporary experience.

The Radio and Film Documentary: Remaking Reality

In both radio and film, fact and fiction were sharply demarcated by conventional designations. From the start, radio newscasts and the motion picture newsreel presented clearly labeled introductions ("This is the News") that broke the ensuing reports away from the surrounding entertainment. However, in both media during the 1930s and early 1940s, a new form, the documentary, evolved. This was a selective depiction and analysis of a subject not linked to a particular news story.

Instead of providing a brief episodic report of a specific news event, the documentary showed the evolution of a news story at length. It brought together specific facts that in the original news accounts had been spread over days, weeks, months, or even years, but which now were concatenated, clarified, and reinterpreted. In this respect, the radio- and film-documentary format merely followed what had long been customary in the "background" type of magazine or newspaper article. But something significantly new was also added.

The radio documentary, as exemplified by "The March of Time," used dramatic recreations of original events, with actors and a prepared script. Fictionalized episodes were interwoven with actual recordings of the voices of real personalities making the news. This was, in effect, a new form of

depicting "truth." It translated into the time-bound broadcast medium the peculiar capacity of a reporter to bring together, into a continuous narrative, sequences of events that had actually occurred at different times, in different places, and with different participants.

In resorting to fictional devices, the radio documentary producer's objective was not to falsify reality, but to convey it in a more compelling and believable way. The public's familiarity with this genre, and the acceptance of it as an accurate depiction of reality, was most vividly illustrated in the panic reaction of many people to Orson Welles's "War of the Worlds" broadcast, which used documentary techniques to dramatize a science fiction story. The line between reality and fantasy had been blurred.

TV: THE ALL-SEEING EYE?

TV's "Unique Perspective"

As Kurt and Gladys Lang (1953) observed early in its history, TV produces an edited version of reality. Occasionally it offers a concocted or rehearsed version. At the same time, it maintains the audience's illusion of seeing and being part of the real thing. The mere fact that a story is covered at all may be considered to give importance to it and to place it on the agenda of public discussion.

Televised reportage has an immediacy and authenticity that the filmed newsreel never achieved. It can add to the illusory verisimilitude of film an additional touch of illusion: that of simultaneity. Not only do we have the sense of seeing things as they are, we have a sense of seeing them as they happen. In the words of Edward R. Murrow and Fred Friendly, we "Are There."

Attention and emotion are mobilized by the immediate in ways that differ from response to accounts of things past. This is a condition that never existed on a nationwide scale prior to broadcasting, because rumor moved slowly. In times past, an event was reported after it was over. Today's radio listener or TV viewer learns of it as something going on *now;* he can be an eyewitness and may be tempted to become a participant if he has a sense of ongoing mass action (as has happened at times of racial disturbances). And yet the viewer's impression that he is at the scene is belied by the technical necessities of broadcasting.

It is the tradition of journalism to describe individual happenings. This fragmented reportage contrasts with the exposition of evolving stories that unfold continuously and that are therefore inherently undramatic. An event is "new" each time it is reported and must be explained afresh each day, even though it may be part of an evolving series of developments and may have a

long history behind it. The result may be boredom on the part of the audience, which feels that the news is always the same.

Packaging

To enhance its entertainment appeal, TV news must be "packaged" in a form that heightens its dramatic or stylistic qualities.

Walter Lippmann (1969) comments: "Broadcast journalism has not only a terribly simplifying effect, but a distorting effect, I think, because it makes everything more dramatic than it should be, more interesting, more amusing. And the world of life isn't that. It's prosaic [p. 7].

The serious practitioners of TV journalism are well aware of the medium's dangerous capacity to pass off surface manifestations as though they were the essential facts. NBC's former board chairman, Walter Scott, observes that: "Because television is a visual medium, it may scant the background and significance of events to focus on the outward appearance—the comings and goings of statesmen instead of the issue that confronts them."

NBC News's Reuven Frank wrote in a staff memorandum about TV interviews:

> Most people are dull, that is, they communicate ineptly. If they are dull, their description of interesting events will be dull. Sometimes they are interesting, but for the wrong reasons. They suffer from speech defects, tics, or strabismus, and what may make them interesting is precisely what interferes with their contribution to communication. Those who communicate eptly—politicians, actors, and the like—tend to be self-serving. It takes a professional journalist to know what sentence in a speech or in his own interview should be pulled to the top, set in large type, quoted in the headline and the banner line. In our business we cannot pull that sentence out and up. The audience must pick its own sentence and set its own front page around it and do it before we have passed that story and gone on to the next.

Frank seems to be suggesting that the television-news audience has considerable latitude to interpret what is truly newsworthy about what it sees and hears, to use its own judgment of the character of those in the news and of the meaning of events, rather than to accept anyone else's definition. Actually, the audience's judgment is inevitably constrained by what it is shown and how, although it may be quite unconscious of this constraint on its freedom of observation.

Alternate Perspectives

Kurt and Gladys Lang (1968) describe the "refraction" of "actuality" that occurs as television producers "weave together many visual elements into a

coherent news story to bring an event into focus *while* it is happening [p. 154]."

Any observer of an event that is subsequently defined as news and reported in the media is inevitably distressed by the disparity between what was experienced and what the media made of it. The observer must then reconcile the reality that has been lived through with the "reality" as it has been reported and as it is then generally understood by others.

For both electronic and print journalists there are always alternative ways of making sense of the same raw material. Harry Ashmore (1970), a Pulitzer Prize-winning editor, observes that:

> The journalist who attempts to do no more than simply record what he and others saw and heard at the site of the news will not only have an unreadable report but a hopelessly incomplete one; selecting and ordering the available facts and placing them in context is a subjective process, and if he is dealing with any human event that really matters his own values will color his judgment [p. 17].

In television, the same interpretive elements are involved, as Edward Jay Epstein (1973) describes in his study of television news:

> Despite the frequent public defense of news as a "mirror of society," in private discussions most [TV news] executives seemed to regard news stories as problematic discussions. Indeed, they more or less operated on the assumption that a news story could be shot, edited, and narrated in a number of different ways, and that the producer was responsible for reconstructing it along lines that met the standards and policies of the network [p. 230].

Only events of rare importance warrant the effort and expense of providing multiple reportage to the same audience. If the news is generally reported from only one of a large number of possible perspectives, this may well be in the nature of the beast. In a democratic society, the public has an almost infinite tolerance for this kind of subjectivity as long as it is randomly distributed. When the subjectivity is both predictable and unchallenged and also recognized as such, the agencies that present the news are inevitably suspect.

Covering the Conventions

The limited length and episodic character of newscasts makes it difficult to achieve dramatic impact with any individual news item. But live-television coverage of an event with an uncertain outcome can be dramatic indeed. This is illustrated by the periodic spectacle of the political party conventions. Being reported at length, they very clearly demonstrate the power of TV-news

producers to select and organize, from among many possible alternative perspectives, a presentation that clarifies the prevailing confusion and that keeps the viewers interested and entertained.

It is no longer possible to think of the presidential election process in the United States without regarding the party conventions as projected by television as a pivotal event. It is well understood that what the TV viewers see is something totally distinct from the "real" experience they would have if they were there, the experience which newspaper and wire service reporters seek to report and which represents the public's sole perception of the political realities of party conventions in the prebroadcast era.

At the 1976 Democratic Convention, many delegates and guests in Madison Square Garden brought portable TV sets on which they viewed and heard the proceedings with far greater ease and clarity than if they tried to make sense of the great buzzing, booming confusion around them. The booths of the three networks physically dominated the convention hall. What was happening was what was on TV, not what the eyes and ears of those present could take in.

An NBC news executive, surveying the Republican Convention scene in 1964, remarked, "I have the feeilng this is the lull before the lull. But if it gets deadly we are prepared to make our own show." This has continued to be true of TV's convention coverage, in which the newsmen have been the most prominent personalities and in which delegates have been given printed instructions as to how to behave on camera. Nowhere else do the makers of television news wield such political power as in their choice of whom to interview and what to show.

The producer for each TV network faces a battery of monitor screens depicting all the varied images being picked up at the very moment by the network's camera crews. What the producer chooses to show for how long and in what sequence determines the viewer's impression of events. It becomes the "truth" of what has happened.

Edwin Newman (1976) recalls that during the 1964 Democratic convention:

> As President Johnson spoke about freedom and liberty, a black woman in the Freedom Party group began to cry. I told the NBC producer in charge of our coverage. Should he cut away from the President? If he did, why to this one person out of thousands in the hall? Again, if he did, what did it show—that she was weeping for what she knew about the United States, or the President, or the Democratic Party, or Mississippi? Or was she simply overwhelmed by being where she was [p. 36]?

Arthur Miller (1968) describes TV's multiplicity of faces, as seen at the 1968 Democratic Convention in Chicago:

In the main CBS workroom behind the auditorium, I watched a row of five TV sets. NBC was showing the attack by the club-swinging police, the swarming squads of helmeted cops, and one heard the appalling screaming. Next to it, CBS was showing the platform speaker inside the auditorium and the applauding delegates. Next to CBS was ABC with closeups of bleeding demonstrators being bandaged. Then a local station showing a commercial; Mr. Clean having his mustache rubbed off. The last was another station whose screen showed some sort of ballet.

Dr. Edgar Berman, Hubert Humphrey's physician and a member of his campaign staff, charged that TV's rules of propriety prevented viewers from getting an accurate picture of the events in Chicago. Television showed episodes of police brutality but did not transmit:

the chants of "up against the wall, mother fucker" or "LBJ eats shit," which were reverberated through bullhorns all night long by these polite young people in the park. Yes, America saw "its own rebellious children" as the camera was directed, but the TV watchers didn't see the neat young middle class ladies, their Levis down, squatting to fill plastic bags to be thrown at police or just squashed in hotel lobbies. Nor did they see their male counterparts lined up to fill bags with urine for the same purpose. I saw this—but not on TV (Efron, 1971, p. 165).

Congressman Lionel Van Deerlin (in an address to the Radio and Television News Directors Association, Los Angeles, November 23, 1968) alleged that film footage showing demonstrators provoking the police was suppressed by the networks, but he acknowledged that "any time you have four hours that have to be reduced to one hour you are going to have somebody charging that you left out the most important part."

From the viewpoint of the authorites, the TV crews were themselves indistinguishable from the demonstrators. At the end of the convention week, Mayor Richard Daley said that the newsmen "never identify themselves. They're in the crowd and many of them are hippies themselves in television and radio and everything else. They are a part of the movement and some of them are revolutionaries and they want these things to happen."

There was a striking dramatic irony in TV's juxtaposition of the rowdy demonstration scenes with its shots of Hubert Humphrey's nomination in the convention hall miles away. The disturbing imagery thus created placed Humphrey at a disadvantage which may well have resulted in Richard Nixon's subsequent narrow victory.

War and the Accidents of Human Interest

It has been suggested that the unpopularity of the Vietnam war was due to the scenes of battle that television projected into the nation's living rooms. Whether or not this is so, scenes of human suffering on television are vivid and

memorable in a way that transcends mere verbal reports of the facts. Thus the cold-blooded execution of a prisoner, in close-up, and the agonized flight of a napalmed child become almost universally held images of what was happening in Vietnam. But these dramatic episodes become symbolic because of the chance presence of the TV cameramen.

The audience can sustain the illusion of knowing what war is like, on the basis of highly selected and concentrated representations. In Vietnam, TV crews were under orders to "shoot bloody" for maximum dramatic effect. However, extensive televised footage showing the dead and dismembered casualties was invariably censored by the producers as unfit for showing to a family audience at dinner time.

Robert MacNeil (1968) writes:

> By cutting out what is most unbearable, it may be that television has built up a tolerance for the frightful, a feeling that war really is bearable. The grisly truth has been shown in the screening rooms of the network news departments. There would be closeup footage with the sound of the young soldier whose leg had been shot away a moment before, screaming obscenities at the medics, pleading with them in desperation to stop his agony [p. 66].

This footage was not shown on the air. But of course print accounts of battles also do not generally dwell at length on descriptions of the wounds received or the physical condition of the dead.

The reports of a war are generally reports of objectives taken or positions lost, interspersed with the statistics of battle losses. Rarely, and often only by chance, are the stories infused with the human touch. Incidents of human interest are commonplace in wartime, but they enter reportage in the mass media only in the occasional story that a reporter happens to hear about or observe and happens to get published on a day when there is not more important news of strategic changes in the battlefield to report.

The accidental experiences of journalists often become the only source, or at least principal source, of the public's perceptions of major news stories. Television makes idiosyncratic reporting appear authoritative. Consider the following critique (McLaughlin, 1969) of the coverage of a Vietcong rocket attack on Saigon:

> Reporter David Culhane of CBS described the early morning rocket attack as "sounding like the whole world was coming apart," and CBS cameras graphically recorded the strewn glass, bricks, metal, and sections of galvanized tin roofing blown off the Parliament building. Tony Sargent of CBS reported on a Japanese correspondent who was killed by flying shrapnel. The cameras drained from the scene all its living (and dying) color, relentlessly fixing on the correspondent's oozing blood, a neighbor's curious face, a woman overcome with grief, the doctor massaging the newsman's chest, and mercifully the arrival of the Jeep ambulance.

Sargent's accompanying prose was a vivid and at the same time an overheated journalese. What Sargent did not stress was that the rocket that killed the newsman miraculously spent its fury on an eight-story garage next to the Oscar [Hotel], that only one person was killed, and that there were none seriously injured.

What Culhane did not stress was that the damage done to the Parliament Building was not nearly as serious as his edited footage suggested. In fact, the building was used routinely the same day. Both reports left one with the impression that Saigon was paralyzed by the VC assault. In plain fact, however, life and business in Saigon went on that day almost exactly as usual.... I do not wish to minimize the horror of the shellings. My point is that they must be seen in perspective.... What the CBS correspondents failed to do is relate these events in any meaningful way to the larger context of the War. This could have been done had they simply stood before the camera and read the report of their own Bureau chief [pp. 66–67].

Had the correspondents done this, of course, they would not have provided the kind of pictorial coverage which producers regard as the essence of TV news.

The reproductions of reality to which the mass media have accustomed us redefined our reactions to the genuine experience. Daniel Boorstin (1962, pp. 126–127) observes that "at the Gauguin show at the Chicago Art Institute in 1959, visitors complained that the original paintings were less brilliant than the familiar reproductions." And the music critic, Harold C. Schonberg, writes in the *New York Times* of September 22, 1968:

Most recordings, ever since the introduction of magnetic tape, are dishonest in that the majority are collages... the result of many takes. Wrong notes and phrases are corrected and spliced in. Voices are boosted to the point where a pipsqueak soprano can sound like Nilsson. Pianists can repeat a passage until their fingerwork on the disk is as impeccable as Rachmaninoff's.... The medium itself becomes the real thing. The real thing becomes an imitation.

Similarly our view of what goes on in the world is now inseparable from the conventional montage of its televised representation. Robert Thompson (1969), the South East Asia specialist, cites the case of a British Broadcasting Corporation (BBC) correspondent in Vietnam whose normal practice was to:

visit trouble spots in a fairly relaxed manner, to interview knowledgeable people on the spot and then to have a quiet look round himself. At the end of this he would record a short five-minute objective summary of the situation as he saw it. At the time of the Tet offensive... he complained that he was just being dragged around by the cameraman and would probably get shot. He could only comment on the pictures which the camera could take and had little idea what was going on anyway. When he got to Hue and saw American aircraft

divebombing the citadel still held by the Vietcong, all he could think of saying into the microphone was: "My God! It's just like watching television!" [p. 9].

TV RECONSTRUCTION OF REALITY

Self-Consciousness on Camera

Television, more than other news media, stands open to the charge that it changes events by the mere fact that it reports them. The perfection of lightweight light-sensitive portable cameras has vastly expanded the mobility of TV-news crews and reduced their intrusiveness into the events they are reporting. Still, TV's cameras, bright lights, sound equipment, and hordes of technicians introduce a new dimension of visibility into news coverage. They evoke a far different response than the unobtrusive newspaper reporter armed only with pencil and notebook, and in many ways become direct intruders into the news they ostensibly are merely recording.

An anthropologist, Edmund Carpenter (1973), describes a visit to a Papuan village that had been visited a few months earlier by a Lowell Thomas film crew:

> The instant they saw cameras they rushed about for props, then sat in front of the cameras, one chopping with a stone axe, another finger-painting on bark, a third starting a fire with bamboo—Santa's workshop. They were all Equity actors (quoted in review by Hugh Kenner, *New York Times Book Review,* July 29, 1973, p. 7).

Not dissimilarly, R. W. Apple, Jr., in the *New York Times,* commented on the behavior of the House Impeachment Committee in the final stages of the Watergate drama:

> The presence of the cameras held the members to a reasonable standard of relevance and decorum and guaranteed that all would be in their seats. It also gave those who feared that they were voting against the grain of their constituents a better chance to explain themselves than could a whole year of speeches, newsletters and news conferences (Barrett, 1975, pp. 62–63).

In the words of *Broadcasting* magazine, "Never has a committee been more conscious of its deportment. Suits were pressed, linen was fresh, hair was combed, and members stayed awake. The last, by itself, would justify the continued presence of live cameras in the Congress."

President Kennedy's fatal journey past the Texas Schoolbook Depository was made necessary because the luncheon group he was to address had been moved from its original site to the roomier Trade Mart, to make things easier

for the television crews. An F.B.I. agent, testifying before the Warren Commission compared the conditions at Dallas Police Headquarters during the interrogation of Lee Oswald to "Grand Central Station at rush hour, maybe like the Yankee Stadium during the World Series games." The commission's report notes that "in the lobby of the third floor, television cameramen set up two large cameras and floodlights in strategic positions that gave them a sweep of the corridor in either direction. Technicians stretched their television cables into and out of offices, running some of them out of the windows. (U.S. Warren Commission, 1964, p. 202)."

On the occasion of Khrushchev's visit to the United States, CBS alone had 375 cameramen and technicians covering the story. The three networks spent over $2,000,000 in production costs. Harry Skornia (1968) comments:

> Instead of seeing Khrushchev greeted by restrained, polite, small crowds, as he traveled about America, television audiences saw him constantly surrounded by hundreds of individuals, milling about excitedly. The fact that these individuals were principally television personnel was difficult for viewers, or foreign observers, to know. For they clearly saw "eager throngs," supporting Moscow propaganda claims that "thousands" turned out to greet Khrushchev wherever he went [p. 24].

Faking the Real Thing

The television newsman carries a burden unknown to the print journalist; he is under pressure to go beyond the mere description of events and to *show* them. He can easily stumble into the documentarist's familiar device of reenacting what has really happened in order to make the visual or aural record *seem* complete.

During the Little Rock disturbances of September 1957, CBS News crews got anti-integration demonstrators to stage actions which had actually taken place spontaneously beforehand but had not been observed by the cameraman (Mickelson, 1972). In 1966, CBS helped finance an armed invasion of Haiti in exchange for the exclusive news coverage rights. (The expedition was aborted by the U.S. Customs Bureau). The CBS-owned station WBBM-TV in Chicago broadcast a program ("Pot Party at a University") in November 1967 that a congressional committee later found to have been produced as the result of a specially staged marijuana party at Northestwestern University. The committee's report said that the station "contrived and staged the filming of pot parties so as to enhance its news ratings for the time periods involved and thereby increase its advertising revenues."

Testimony before a subcommittee of the House Commerce Committee cited a number of episodes of faking by TV newsmen: A young man was hired to buy dynamite and photographed to show how easily it could be done. A

police cruiser on an "emergency run" was actually being raced for a film crew. "Gamblers" at Las Vegas were actually actors. "Dead sea life" photographed on a California beach were actually preserved specimens placed there to illustrate a feature on water pollution.

A CBS evening-news item on October 9, 1967 showed an American soldier cutting the ear off a dead Vietcong soldier as a battle trophy. At his subsequent court-martial, it turned out that he had acted on a dare after being offered a knife by the CBS cameraman (Lewy, 1978).

Distorted and falsified reporting is not unknown in the contemporary annals of American print journalism. What is interesting about the occasional derelictions of TV-news crews is that they deal in visual misrepresentations that carry the mark of authenticity. And they generally seem to arise from an effort to make an invisible truth visible, dramatic, and entertaining.

The Contrived Image

TV news' appetite for striking visual imagery makes it inevitable that suitable material should be manufactured for it by those with an appetite for publicity. Harold Wilensky (1969) calls the results "Crisis Journalism":

> This is a world where most of the "events" reported with an air of breathless urgency do not happen at all in any spontaneous or natural sense... [but are] made to happen by journalists in order to satisfy the demand for sensational inside dope, by public relations men, in order to build up their clients or knock down their enemies, or by government officials in order to sell or justify policy [p. 149].

News organizations routinely provide reports on what Daniel Boorstin calls "pseudo-events" contrived to fit some purpose. Ben Bagdikian (1971), the press critic, notes that "every press conference is a pseudo-event. We live in a system of great centralized networks of communication and not in primary communities where we talk face-to-face or depend on word of mouth. So what has come to be called a pseudo-event is, in fact, the usual way of entering the news net."

One pertinent conclusion from this is that the viewing public draws no distinction between those elements especially created for the purpose and other items in the news. And if pseudo-events are not really fictional, they may come remarkably close.

Putting Drama into the News

The audience expects drama and excitement from the news. Yellow journalism, with its screaming headlines, created mystery and horror on demand from the daily grist of police reports. Critics of the news media have

long complained that they overemphasize disaster and that the traditional reporters' beats—police headquarters and the criminal courts—convey a misleading picture of the peaceful and positive aspects of society. A properly written news lead, it has been suggested, might begin, "While 4,000 students of Central High School went diligently about their studies today, one of their number assassinated the principal." On television news it is even more difficult to maintain perspective. The very size of the television screen dictates an emphasis on individual news personalities, on people who are colorful, dramatic, controversial, and entertaining to watch.

Television's stock in trade is the human face in closeup. Public figures, who appear on the news repeatedly, acquire "images" that may be critical to their political fortunes. Politicians who in an earlier era would have been thought of as remote and impersonal figures now take on the aura of intimates. They may be judged less for their ideas than for the personality roles they project on camera. (This attribute of TV was used with great skill by Egyptian president Anwar Sadat when he visited the United States in early 1978.)

It is widely recognized that TV has transformed American politics, but conventional political candidates or officeholders, defending conventional viewpoints, rarely generate entertaining news items.

Confrontation Politics and TV

Journalism has always been most responsive to the views of the articulate and impassioned. The newspaper headline, the radio bulletin, the 1-minute film clip on TV, present a shortened, heightened, focused—and therefore distorted—version of a much more complex and dull reality.

An obscure figure in conflict with the law can become a powerful political force because of the attention devoted to him by the media. It was not word of mouth but the media, including those who expressed editorial disapproval, who elevated Lester Maddox from the role of a racist restaurateur to the governorship of his state, and it was the media, not word of mouth, that established spokesmen of the radical minority as nationally known black leaders. (Long before the point was echoed by Spiro Agnew, Whitney Young of the Urban League had observed that Stokely Carmichael's following consisted of a handful of Negroes and 500 white reporters.)

The Black Panthers first achieved national prominence when a group of them, armed with shotguns, paraded into the vistors' gallery of the California legislature. If, as Bobby Seale, chairman of the group, later acknowledged, the object of the demonstration was to get on national-TV news programs, the maneuver was highly successful (Seale, 1970). Similar tactics have been used by the handful of eccentrics who make up the American Nazi Party.

In reporting extensively the dramatic words and actions of Nazis, black revolutionaries, and Yippies, the news media simply followed their long-

standing practice of giving play to what is unusual or dramatic or exciting. It is impossible for good newsmen to ignore a confrontation, even though it is self-evidently a planned provocation staged for their benefit. The resulting problems are not unique to television. But television has been most easily manipulated by the skillful practitioners of confrontation politics. In Yippie Jerry Rubin's words, "TV packs all the action into two minutes—a commercial for the Revolution."

The essence of revolutionary strategy is the expectation of mass response to isolated acts of terror. For the revolutionary movement to catch on, objective conditions must call forth expressions of support and sympathy. In the rebellious period that closed the 1960s, there were attacks on police cars, the ransacking of schools and welfare offices, the occupation of university buildings, and the bombing of offices. All of these may have represented spontaneous expressions of grievance, to a degree, just as, to a degree, they represented deliberate planning by self-styled revolutionary groups. But to be successful, such actions must also encourage imitative behavior; they must become fads.

As individual acts of civil disorder occurred and were dramatically reported, they inevitably encouraged acts of emulation. The further reporting of these acts produced the impression of a snowballing effect; we now might have a "trend," a "movement." A solitary act of assault, looting, or arson does not constitute a riot, but a solitary act reported by the news media with an air of concern and excitement can be the seed of a riot. (In New Iberia, Louisiana, a false radio news report of critical injuries to two white high school students led to serious racial disturbances in August 1969.)

Eric Sevareid observes, "If television puts a lot of protestors on, I don't think it's necessarily because a lot of editors and producers are all for the protestors, in their private political hearts. Some may be. I think some are. It's a matter of ingrained reflexes on what is news and what isn't."

NEWS, REALITY, AND FICTION

Information and Entertainment

News represents information about the real world. To the degree that TV has repositioned the news as entertainment, this represents a crucial change in the way it is gathered, presented, and perceived by the public.

Clearly, information and entertainment are not mutually exclusive. What is informative for one person may be merely entertaining for another, and vice versa. There is information in any entertainment, even those like dance and music, which use symbols of gesture and sound rather than of language. Conversely, the process of acquiring information has an entertainment aspect

to it and is not wholly utilitarian. People "enjoy" looking at stock tables and batting averages, just as they "learn" something when they hear a popular song for the fiftieth time.

Entertainment is a way of passing time and must be savored in time. Information can be taken as an end in itself rather than as a tool for the pleasure of learning, though there are aesthetic and social satisfactions in acquiring it. (It would be marvelous, though, to go to sleep with a set of electrodes on one's forehead and awake in the morning with a full knowledge of Chinese, without the need for study and practice!)

Whereas information deals with reality and represents a means of contending with reality, entertainment may be regarded as an evasion of reality, either through reduction of cognitive activity (as in watching dance or listening to music) or through a reconstruction of reality in the form of fantasy.

Television entertainment may be considered to appeal to viewers because it facilitates such evasion, because it lulls and diverts them with visions of a life lived by beautiful or intriguing characters engaged in a series of perilous confrontations or comic escapades. The viewers know, of course, that the news is "real" although the preceding movie is not, just as they may have changed their mind set from an earlier quiz show to the movie. But what does the prevailing pattern of entertainment mean for their perception of the news?

The Role of Fantasy

As with any other medium of fiction, TV's capacity to entertain arises from its ability to transport viewers into an imaginary world.

It is commonplace to note that we retreat into fantasy to escape from our real troubles. In their study of the unemployed of Marienthal, Paul Lazarsfeld, Marie Jahoda, and Hans Zeisel (1933) found that the newspaper that emphasized political and economic subjects lost 60% of its circulation, although it lowered its price, whereas the paper that stressed entertainment and sports lost only 27% of its readers, even though its price remained constant.

Fiction evokes the uniquely human ability to imagine things other than as they are. Since fantasy represents a reconstruction of reality, it can run the gamut from idle, wishful thinking through the daydreams of Walter Mitty, to the wild, waking dreams of paranoia.

Fantasy may be considered to have both a functional and a nonfunctional aspect. To the extent that it represents an evasion or distortion of reality, or an inhibition of the will to cope with a real situation or environment, fantasy weakens the individual's ability to handle the world around him successfully. In this sense it is nonfunctional.

But fantasy also serves the functional purposes of diversion and relaxation; it is a device for handling and controlling tedium, for explaining the mysterious and inexplicable. It is a way to explore and test alternative courses of action, and its probes can lead to insights that help solve real problems.

Fantasies permit an individual to reorganize what he knows of reality into an imaginary form that is more satisfying to his needs. Personal fantasy becomes powerful to the degree that we can project ourselves or our surrogates into this reassemblage of experience. This is the secret of involvement in any narrative of real or fancied events. And involvement is what makes the difference between mass-media communication that is ignored and communication that is compelling.

Distinguishing What Is Real

Do adult viewers generally distinguish the imaginary character of TV's fictional content from the reality of their everyday-life experience? We may assume that they do, for an important part of the socialization process is the development of the distinction between real and not real. The evolution of the child's sense of reality is inseparable from the imposition of order on all the dimensions of sensory experience. Jean Piaget's observations on this subject have been summarized as follows:

> The child is confronted at every turn with apparent alterations which mask an underlying permanence. Such masks prevail on both the physical and social planes of reality. Whether the child is looking at a spoon that appears bent in water or is listening to a hostess pleading for him to stay when she really wishes him to go, he must distinguish between how things look and how they really are if he is to effectively adapt to his world (Elkind, 1974, p. 4).

Children of 3 are already sufficiently responsive to perceptual cues that they show awareness of the transition from a TV program to a commercial (Wartella & Ettema, 1974). But by the age of 5, half of them still believe that commercials always tell the truth (Ward, Wackman, & Wartella, 1976).

Hawkins (1977) breaks down the child's perception of TV's reality into two aspects: "Magic Window reality" which is acceptable as depicting "ongoing life or drama," and "Social Expectations" of the real world, with which television characters and events may be compared. Acceptance of TV's literal reality decreases as children grow older. But at least up to the age of 12, there is no decrease in the degree to which TV characters and events are considered *similar* to those of the real world.

In the psychological laboratory, experiments show that films of aggressive behavior presented as "real" get more of a reaction than the same material

understood to be "staged" (Berkowitz & Alioto, 1973; Feshbach, 1972). Disadvantaged children, with the greatest fantasy needs, retain the greatest illusions regarding TV's reality (Atkin, 1976; Greenberg, 1974; Greenberg & Reeves, 1974; Hawkins, 1977). TV's most intense and violent programming has its greatest appeal to poor black children. Among adults the same pattern is maintained: the heaviest viewers are found among the deprived. Poor people also have least interest in the news.

Fantasy and Fiction

Fiction is by definition something made up, fancied, though it may represent the heart of truth in a deeper sense. Fiction is created by the fantasy or the imagination of a writer and is successful insofar as it evokes fantasy and imagination by way of response. What is the difference in the response when we remind ourselves as we read or watch, "It is only a story," and when we think, "My God, could this actually have happened?"

Something that actually happened is usually more unsettling to us. The events that occurred are immutable, whether or not we like how they have turned out. The satisfaction in fiction is inseparable from its superficial untruth, from the fact that the audience can remake the ending of the story.

A television cartoon show (or for that matter, a newspaper comic strip) is presented in a format that is readily distinguishable as unreal, at least by an adult. But photographed fiction is uncomfortably close to real events, and since fiction dominates television the viewer's way of looking at it may carry over to the real documentation of news programming. This is probably particularly true of those unusual moments in which we are shown actions and passions that we normally associate with TV drama—a killing or a confrontation, even a scene of grief.

Fiction Read and Fiction Portrayed

The relationship between news and fiction, so central to Park's (1940) discussion of the "human interest story," is also critical to the understanding of how TV-news programming is designed to attract audiences in an entertainment environment.

There is one basic psychological difference between the workings of fiction in literature and fiction in the theater and its derivatives in the performing arts (including television). Written fiction, being wholly symbolic in character, is accepted by the audience as something that must be interpreted and recreated by them. The reader fills in. No novelist can possibly describe (or would want to) every feature of the appearance of every one of his characters, every furnishing of every room, or every act and every gesture that accompanies the conversation presented. The reader is expected to cover the gaps, to embellish

the outline with details. Similarly, it is understood that the author must be highly selective in what he tells us.

The fact that the reader determines the color of the hero's eyes and hair, the shade of the draperies in his bedroom; that the reader furnishes the backgrounds from imagination and past experience—all this is what makes the art of fiction compelling. Literature is intended to be evocative. The reader's attention is expected to wander, so that he often catches himself at the end of a paragraph, realizing that his mind has not followed what his eyes have just read, because his imagination was racing off in amplification of what the writer had said earlier.

By contrast, theatrical fiction pulls the audience along with it; it cannot stop in midcourse while the playgoers collect their thoughts. Drama presents an interplay of personalities embodied in specific actors, wearing perfectly visible costumes, and usually performing against sets that leave little to the imagination. This very specificity imposes restraints on our fantasy, and thus on identification. Because a good play is a concentrated experience, it holds the audience together and attentive. It mobilizes empathy but does not necessarily create a direct sense of identity with any of the characters. More often than not, a protagonist in a novel is someone whom we see or understand from the inside, and whom we therefore imbue with our own values. The protagonist of a play exists outside ourselves because he is there in someone else's human flesh. The observer can feel himself with the protagonist without regarding him as a direct extension of his own ego.

Word Images and Visual Images

We accept word images in print as a selective or distorted refraction of reality. This same sense of disengagement is latent when we watch live actors in a theater perform within the restricted limits of the stage, because those limits are never beyond the threshold of our awareness. But in film, the boundaries disappear because the screen is an optical frame rather than a purely psychological one similar to that separating live actors from the audience. Thus with film the illusion of reality can be maintained whether we are seeing documentary photographs of the world as it is or the enactments of fantasy, because the direct evidence of our eyes and ears is so compelling. Motion pictures watched in the dark, and larger than life, are the most intense mass-media experience. They have the greatest capacity to envelop us, to turn on our emotions, to give us dreams or nightmares, and to prompt us to relive our original exposure in the imagination. More than any other form of communication, motion pictures bridge the gap between real and dream worlds.

Television borrows some of these attributes but, with its small screen and its continual interruptions, television normally cannot mobilize the same

concentration of attention and emotion. However, television can arouse a high pitch of audience involvement when it reports the news live. And viewers may turn even to the ordinary newscast with extraordinary anticipation when they realize that something exciting is afoot.

The fragmented, episodic nature of the TV-newscast format makes it difficult to sustain the level of attention and arousal that can be mobilized in a televised play. Yet TV-news producers must use the devices of fictional drama in order to attract and hold the viewers they need to be successful.

News as Drama

As with an ongoing fictional drama, a continuing news story, being incomplete, is more likely to arouse our propensity for role-playing, our imagination and our emotions than a news report of a completed event. The story whose outcome is in doubt is the one that impels us to seize the latest word; once our interest is engaged, we cannot get enough of the news through every source that might add, however little, to what we already know. Watergate had some of this flavor and so does an occasional important trial. Battles and wars have this character when our futures depend on them, and our concern is higher when the enemy is at the gates than when he is 10,000 miles away.

But much of the news deals with nonrecurring events and not with those that are still happening. To create audience identification, a news story must be on a human scale; it must deal with individuals. Casualty figures arouse few emotions when they appear as statistics without names and faces. A report of 9,000 dead in an earthquake in West Irian, Indonesia, was given 5 inches in the *New York Times*. A dispatch from the scene would get more public attention and more space from editors or producers if it came from an eyewitness observer who reported specific instances of heroism as well as suffering.

Park's (1940) insistence that news must be both interesting and important sets a standard that can be met by comparatively few events on any given day. However, those stories that combine these attributes are the most compelling and memorable; they can not only arouse the public's emotions but change its mind. For this to happen may require a conviction that what is being learned—good news or bad—has a direct bearing on the individual, that it relates to his own life. There is a threat to one's own personal security in any local crime report where the setting is more familiar and the victim a subject of empathy. The more we are told, if the telling is skillful, the more familiar the setting will appear to be and the better we will seem to know the characters involved. How better can we seem to know them than by seeing their faces and hearing their voices within our own homes—even on television?

NEWS AND INVOLVEMENT

The news reporting process, as I have described it in this chapter, inevitably distorts the reality it represents by funneling it through the prism of a particular observation point and fitting it into a format dictated by technology and economics. The transmutation of reality by television news may be regarded as an inevitable consequence of technological and economic imperatives. It occurs in spite of a continuing strong professional urge, on the part of the TV-news organizations and their practitioners, to tell the truth.

Print journalism similarly provides an account of current events that is inevitably parochial and selective and often biased. But the reader of newspapers is never unaware that he is getting the news secondhand, whereas the TV viewer has the impression that he is seeing what actually happened.

TV "humanizes" the news. It makes its people and places familiar in a way they never were before. Does this enhance the public's interest in the news by dealing with events in terms of specific individuals who can be seen and identified with? Or might this very sense of familiarity *reduce* involvement by making people in the news only a part of TV's unending parade of faces?

What makes something in the news seem meaningful and important to us, what gives it its "human interest"? Is it not its ability to make us reflect on it, to inject ourselves into it—in short, to fantasize on it?

A bare summary reduced to headline or bulletin form is generally too weak a stimulus to evoke fantasy. Vicarious participation in an event through television sets the same limitations on fantasy as actual participation does. If one has the feeling of having been there, of having seen it for oneself, there is less effort of imagination required to recreate it than would be true in following a verbal report. Involvement in the news arises from an understanding of one's own self-interest in relationship to what is reported. There is nothing more boring than reading about somebody else's tax rates or plumbing problems. The level of interest rises sharply when these matters suddenly impinge upon the way one spends one's own money and time.

In an interdependent and complex world, the events that are objectively important are also less and less likely to be interesting to great masses of people. Political interest and participation depend on the conviction that what is in the news is *really* happening and that an individual who knows what is happening thereby wins some control over what is going to happen next.

What is real and what is not real is less pertinent than what the public perceives as real and unreal. By selectively rejecting awareness of the unpleasant news, by failing to assimilate and learn what is repeatedly spread before it, the public denies its reality. Terrifying news on a massive scale (of massacres or concentration camps) is considered "too fantastic" to have happened.

Saul Bellow (1976) writes: "On television the other night, people in Beirut were murdered before my eyes. Palestinians under siege shot down two of their own comrades, prisoners who had been sent by their Christian captors to ask for a truce. And these are not fictions that we see on the box but frightful realities—'historical events,' instantaneous history [p. 72]."

Yet when fictional horrors are commonplace, real horrors may also acquire the aura of fiction. After Watergate, many people simply found it impossible to believe that the events about which they were hearing and reading could actually have happened. They were "incredulous" at what the media were showing them, rather than mistrustful of the media's "credibility" (Edelstein, 1974).

The greatest news of our time is, of course, not newsworthy. It lies in the evolving story of discrepancies between the collective human interest and individuals' perceptions of their self-interests. Occasionally, aspects of this anomaly surface in the spot news of the day, and we are reminded of food shortages, energy crises, population bombs, environmental pollution, nuclear terrorism, and other disagreeable subjects. They are in fact so disagreeable, so overwhelming, so remote from our capacity to control that we prefer to think of them as beyond control and therefore as unreal.

If the media were to return to these big important stories day after day, they would be abandoning the tradition of reporting on current events objectively. They would also rapidly lose audiences accustomed to avoiding thinking about the unthinkable. Yet, to the degree that the media tell us of what is transitory, and hence more likely to be entertaining, they immerse us in the illusion that the news they report represents the reality that mankind confronts.

NEXT STEPS IN RESEARCH

Empirical studies of television news have included content analyses, studies of news producers, demographic descriptions of the audience, surveys of viewer reaction to particular newscasters, comparison of audience attitudes with those toward other media, and assessments of political influence.

It is not unlikely that some of the most needed research on television news and its audience has already been done but remains unpublished because of its proprietary nature. This includes the substantial amount of qualitative research prepared by TV consultants for individual stations gauging audience reactions to individual newscasters and news programs. Also unpublished are the analyses routinely prepared for stations and networks by the ratings services analyzing "audience flow" from program to program (or even, with meter data, within a program from minute to minute), the accumulation of audiences for a given news program from one day to the next, and differences

in the news-viewing pattern for different demographic groups. Perhaps $10,000,000 a year is being spent for such studies. The publication of these data, or their replication under noncommercial auspices, would provide valuable amplification of existing knowledge of the audience for TV news.

Newscasters and Their Publics

It would be especially useful to gain a better understanding of those audience characteristics that are associated with the habitual choice of a particular newscast. Are there perceived status differences among the leading TV-news personalities, and how are these reflected in the attributes of their audiences? Do viewers gravitate toward newscasters with whom they identify as being either like themselves or like authority figures in their personal experience? Or do they choose newscasters who impress them as being most competent as journalists? To what extent is any significant part of the public's choice determined by reactions to members of the on-air reporting team, apart from the anchorman? Does the newscaster's importance as a reason for choice increase with the total amount of news viewing or with the regularity of viewing the particular broadcast? What characterizes the people who view newscasts more or less randomly without a clearly defined preference? What is the reaction of viewers when an established and familiar news personality is replaced? How do different kinds of viewers respond to the personal interplay or banter between the anchorman and his associates or to the introduction of personal asides intended to "humanize" them?

We have noted that most viewers tend to view the local and network early-evening news on the same channel. This suggests that special attention should be paid to those who deliberately switch channels but whose total news-viewing activity is otherwise identical with those who are ruled by inertia.

Content Analysis

Any deeper analysis of how the audience reacts to different types of news items or to different formats of news presentation must begin with a more thorough examination of news-programming content itself. For network news, a comprehensive archive of videotapes and transcripts maintained for a number of years at Vanderbilt University provides a definitive but underexploited resource. Unfortunately there is no counterpart for local newscasts, but in major cities the existing videotaping facilities of Broadcast Advertisers' Reports and of other commercial services could be used to assemble an appropriate sample of programs. Broadcasts have been analyzed in terms of the number and length of items, their distribution by broad categories of subject matter, and the incidence of items illustrated by still photographs or videotapes. But to date, such analysis has merely scratched

the surface. What subtle cues are transmitted through the juxtaposition of news items, the choice of imagery in film clips, the display of public figures, the portrayal of violence or its aftermath, the vocabulary and tone of accompanying commentary and interpretation? To what extent is the news made up of self-contained story units and to what extent does it consist of updates on developing or continuing stories? What proportion of leading news items, on how many days, represents fresh or "breaking" stories that no one could anticipate?

At least one highly controversial major content analysis (Efron, 1971) has examined the issue of alleged political bias in the networks' news coverage. Examination of both network- and local-TV news treatment of a variety of politically charged subjects would be useful both to identify one-sidedness and to determine the degree of consensus or variability in the practice of different news organizations. The role of television in modifying public attitudes on issues like abortion, minority rights, or energy conservation can not be understood without an initial examination of its actual content.

Audience Motivation and Response

Serious public issues may at first glance appear to be remote from our primary focus on television entertainment, but the heart of our concern is with the question of how information is conveyed and responded to in an entertainment setting. The analysis of content must go together with more intensive study of audience reactions. Broad-scale survey research in this area quickly seems to reach a point of diminishing returns. People may be able to report with reasonable accuracy on their news-viewing habits and preferences and even to express their levels of interest in various news subjects. But, as has been noted, memories of particular news broadcasts fade very quickly, and the residual generalizations may be of only marginal interest.

This suggests that the most useful methods for intensive new research on the TV-news audience must be "artificial" in character. These might include:

1. use of observers to record the natural home-viewing behavior of other household members, relating item-by-item indications of interest, detachment or distraction, conversation, commentary, etc., beginning a half-hour before the evening's first (early-evening) newscast and continuing for a half-hour after the last one (it is unlikely that this technique can be used surreptitiously);

2. self-administered questionnaires in which a panel of cooperating news viewers record their ratings of the interest, importance, or entertainment value of each broadcast news item;

3. a laboratory approach, in which groups of viewers record a metered like/dislike response and are subsequently interviewed in group discussions to find out why they liked or disliked particular items.

The last method lends itself to comparisons of news programs using different philosophies or formats and to experimental manipulation of the program ingredients (for example, using the same news item with a talking head or a film clip or using the same script with different newscasters).

Verbal association and recall tests might be used to compare audience reactions to: (1) different types of news items; (2) identical news items presented by the announcer and with still and film illustrations; and (3) filmed material presented as current news, as documentation several years old, and as dramatic reenactment.

Personality and News-Viewing Patterns

Techniques like these can generate bodies of data linking individual responses to individual elements of TV-news content. With clinical testing of the same individuals, it would be possible to relate their personality attributes to their patterns of news viewing in order to begin an assessment of some of the propositions advanced in this chapter. Do individuals with strong dependency needs turn to newscasters who are authoritative and paternal in style? Do those who are dissatisfied with their lot in life respond with exceptional affect to news of crimes and disasters? Do people with strong self-esteem tend to be more oriented to the facts of the news reports and less to the manner or style of presentation? Such questions must be raised less for their own sake than for the light they might shed on the larger issue of motivation for news viewing, the acceptance of TV news, in substance and format, as a report on reality, and the derivation of comfort from the knowledge that the newscasters and their newscasts remain as the captains and the kings depart.

REFERENCES

Altheide, D. L. *Creating reality: How TV news distorts events.* Beverly Hills: Sage, 1976.

Ashmore, H. S. Uncertain oracles. *Center Magazine,* November/December 1970, *3,* 17.

Atkin, C. *Effects of realistic vs. fictional television violence on aggression.* Paper presented at the meeting of the Assocation for Education in Journalism, Madison, August 1976.

Bagdikian, B. *The information machines.* New York: Harper & Row, 1971.

Barrett, M. (Ed.). *Moments of truth?* The fifth Alfred I. Dupont–Columbia University survey of broadcast journalism. New York: Thomas Y. Crowell, 1975.

Bellow, S. Reflections. *The New Yorker,* July 12, 1976.

Berkowitz, L., & Alioto, J. T. The meaning of an observed event as a determinant of its aggressive consequences. *Journal of Personality and Social Psychology,* 1973, *28,* 206–217.

Bogart, L. How the challenge of television news affects the prosperity of daily newspapers. *Journalism Quarterly,* 1975, *52,* 403–410.

Bogart, L. *How the public gets its news.* Speech presented to the Associated Press Managing Editors, New Orleans, October 27, 1977.

Boorstin, D. *The image; or what happened to the American dream?* New York: Atheneum, 1962.

Bower, R. T. *Television and the public.* New York: Holt, Rinehart & Winston, 1973.

Carpenter, E. *Oh, what a blow that phantom gave me.* New York: Holt, Rinehart & Winston, 1973.

Edelstein, A. S. Media credibility and the believability of Watergate. ANPA News Research Center Study. *News Research Bulletin,* January 10, 1974.

Efron, E. *The news twisters.* Los Angeles: Nash, 1971.

Elkind, D. *Children and adolescents: Interpretive essays on Jean Piaget.* New York: Oxford University Press, 1974.

Epstein, E. J. *News from nowhere.* New York: Random House, 1973.

Feshbach, S. Reality and fantasy in filmed violence. In J. P. Murray, E. A. Rubinstein, & G. A. Comstock (Eds.), *Television and social behavior. Vol. II: Television and social learning.* Washington, D. C.: U.S. Government Printing Office, 1972.

Greenberg, B. S. Gratifications of television viewing and their correlates for British children. In J. Blumler & E. Katz (Eds.), *Annual review of communication research, 3.* Beverly Hills: Sage, 1974.

Greenberg, B. S., & Reeves, B. *Children and the perceived reality of television.* Paper presented at the meeting of the International Communication Association, 1974.

Hawkins, R. P. The dimensional structure of children's perceptions of television reality. *Communications Review,* July 1977.

Katz, E., Adoni, H. & Parness, P. Remembering the news: What the picture adds to recall. *Journalism Quarterly,* Summer 1977, *54,* 231–239.

Lang, K., & Lang, G. E. The unique perspective of television and its effects: A pilot study. *American Sociological Review,* 1953, *18,* 3–12.

Lang, K., & Lang, G. E. *Politics & television,* Chicago: Quadrangle, 1968.

Lazarsfeld, P., Jahoda, M., & Zeisel, H. *Die Arbeitslosen von Marienthal.* Leipzig: Hirzel, 1933.

Levy, M. R. *The uses and gratifications of television news.* Unpublished doctoral dissertation, Columbia University, 1977.

Lewy, G. Vietnam: New light on the question of American guilt. *Commentary,* February 1978, *65,* 29–49.

Lippmann, W. On understanding society. *Columbia Journalism Review,* Fall 1969, *8,* 5–9.

MacNeil, R. *The people machine: The influence of television on American politics.* New York: Harper & Row, 1968.

McLaughlin, J. Making the war worse than it is. OPC *Dateline,* April 1969.

Mickelson, S. *The electric mirror; politics in an age of television.* New York: Dodd, Mead & Co., 1972.

Miller, A. The battle of Chicago: From the delegates's side. *New York Times Magazine,* September 15, 1968.

Newman, E. A world in your ear. *Television Quarterly,* Fall 1976, *13,* 35–40.

Park, R. E. Introduction. In H. MacG. Hughes, *News and the human interest story.* Chicago: University of Chicago Press, 1940. (Westport, Conn.: Greenwood Press, 1968.)

Patterson, T. E., & McClure, R. D. *The unseeing eye; the myth of television power in national politics.* New York: Putnam, 1976.

Powers, R. *The newscasters.* New York: St. Martin's Press, 1977.

Roper Organization, Inc. *Trends in public attitudes toward television and other mass media, 1959–1974.* Television Information Office, 1974.

Schorr, D. "Network" news. *Rolling Stone,* December 16, 1976.

Seale, B. *Seize the time.* New York: Random House, 1970.

Skornia, H. J. *Television and the news—A critical appraisal.* Palo Alto, Calif.: Pacific Books, 1968.

Steiner, G. *The people look at television.* New York: Knopf, 1963.

Thompson, R. *No exit from Vietnam.* New York: David McKay Co., 1969.

Townley, R. Television journalism—an inside story. *TV Guide,* May 15, 1971, 6–15.

Ward, S., Wackman, D., & Wartella, E. *Children learning to buy: The development of consumer information processing skills.* Cambridge, Mass. Marketing Science Institute, 1976.

Wartella, E., & Ettema, J. S. A cognitive developmental study of children's attention to television commercials. *Communication Research,* 1974, *i,* 44–69.

Wilensky, H. *Organizational intelligence: Knowledge & policy in government & industry.* New York: Basic Books, 1969.

Author Index

Italics denote pages with complete bibliographic information.

Subject Index

ABOUT THE AUTHORS

WENDY RUE is the founder of the National Association for Female Executives (NAFE), America's most prestigious women's organization whose membership totals more than a quarter of a million career women and entrepreneurs. A self-made entrepreneur at 17, as a teenager in L.A. she launched a highly profitable string of teen boutiques—a retail industry first. She then moved east to create a highly successful recruiting business in the fashion industry. Often called a "visionary," Rue brings an intensely personal business philosophy to her ventures. Now independently wealthy, her track record for building highly successful businesses has won her national recognition.

KARIN ABARBANEL is the founding editor of NAFE's award-winning magazine, *Executive Female*. An expert on women's career trends, and a frequent guest on TV and radio, she is the author of several business books, including *How to Succeed on Your Own* and *The Woman's Work Book*.